WINNERS

WINNERS

A Who's Who of
Motor Racing Champions

Edited by
Brian Laban

Orbis Publishing
London

© 1981 by Orbis Publishing Limited
First published in Great Britain by
Orbis Publishing Limited, London 1981

Printed by Morrison and Gibb, Edinburgh
ISBN 0–85613–042–7

INTRODUCTION

The history of motor racing now spans almost a full century. In that time the sport has changed immeasurably. City to city marathons gave way to racing on closed circuits, brute force has stepped aside for technology and the role of the major manufacturer has waxed and waned in the face of commercialism. Yet motor racing has remained the most glamorous, dangerous and spectacular of sports and central to its mystique have always been the personalities around whom the sport grew. *Winners* tells the stories of 123 of the drivers who have shaped the history of motor racing.

The heroes were once the men who built the cars, later the rich, adventurous sons of the aristocracy. Between the wars some were tools of nationalism and in recent years they have become highly paid professional sportsmen. This book, written by a number of prominent motor sport journalists, encompasses the pioneers and the modern world champions. They are extroverts, introverts, aristocrats and peasants, rich and not so rich. They come from all over the world, for motor racing is a truly international sport, and they reflect the different eras in which they lived.

No book, of course, can be a complete record of every driver who has ever stood on the winner's rostrum and *Winners* does not claim to be so. Part of the attraction of any sport is the scope for argument over who were its 'greats'. Motor racing is no exception and many people's personal heroes may not appear here. That is more a reflection on the limitations of space than on any shortage of claimants for inclusion; perhaps the hardest part of compiling such a book is in deciding who will *not* be included. In the end the list is inevitably a personal choice by the editors and the authors, although it is based in this case around all the Grand Prix winners from the beginning of the World Championships; it also includes the great sports car drivers, American heroes, the truly significant pioneers and the charismatic figures who have always enlivened the sport, and acknowledges too some drivers to whom the record books do scant justice.

As well as mere results, this book aims to reveal something of the characters of its subjects – the single-minded determination of the Fangios, Laudas and Nuvolaris, the more relaxed approach of the Irelands, Hawthorns and Regazzonis, even the forgivable reticence of some ladies to reveal their birth dates! Through these 123 drivers *Winners* covers the whole history of motor racing, much more than a single era or branch of the sport, because their stories *are* the story of motor sport itself.

AUTHORS

The following is a list of the authors who have contributed biographies to this book and who are identified by their initials at the end of each entry:

Andy Anderson (AA)
Nick Brittan (NB)
David Burgess Wise (DBW)
Laurie J. Caddell (LJC)
Peter G. Hull (PGH)
Mike Kettlewell (MK)
Brian Laban (BL)
Cyril Posthumus (CP)
L.J.K. Setright (LJKS)
Mike Twite (MT)
Mike Winfield (MW)

ACKNOWLEDGMENTS

Photographs were supplied by the following:
Mirco Decet – nos. 7, 10, 15, 16, 17, 19, 20, 22, 23, 25, 26, 30
Ford Motor Company – no. 6
LAT – nos. 1, 2, 4, 5, 8, 9, 11, 12, 13, 24, 27, 28.

MARIO ANDRETTI (b.1940)
USA

Not every American enthusiast would grant Mario Andretti the accolade of being America's greatest racing driver, but few would dispute his outstanding versatility. The Italian-born, naturalised American, who they affectionately dub 'SuperWop', is one of a rare breed of driver who has not only tried many diverse forms of motor sport, but has the even rarer distinction of having been successful in all of them. Andretti has scored victories in almost every branch of the sport, from saloon racing to Indianapolis and from sports cars to Formula One. He races anything and everything – 'because I don't know how to do anything in life apart from race cars'.

By any standards, Andretti's career has been spectacular. During the long haul towards winning the World Championship in 1978, he has been three-times United States Automobile Club champion and, in 1969, he realised the great American dream, winning at Indianapolis.

For all the prestige that the Indy win brought, perhaps the most personal tribute came from the people of his home town, Nazareth, Pennsylvania. The street in which Andretti lives is now called Victory Lane.

The great Andretti trademark is determination, for the road to the top has not been easy. Mario Gabriele Andretti is one of twin brothers born on 28 February 1940 to a farming family in Montona, Italy. His early life was hard: German troops occupied his homeland and, with thousands of compatriots, the Andrettis were herded into a camp for displaced persons. With the end of the war, the family moved south to Lucca and there, like all good Italian boys, the Andretti twins developed a passion for motor racing.

Their early teenage years were spent learning to drive, parking cars for a local garage owner. The same garage owner sowed the seeds of addiction to motor racing by taking the brothers to see the Mille Miglia. By the time they were fifteen, they had convinced a wealthy local businessman that they should drive his Formula Junior car; before their father announced his decision to emigrate to America, Mario and brother, Aldo, had scored over twenty victories in local races. It was difficult for the boys' father to realise that he was upsetting his sons' plans for stardom as they had omitted to mention their racing to him.

The Andrettis moved to Nazareth in 1955, and the brothers immediately set out to rebuild their racing careers. They earned their living in their uncle's garage, mainly so that they could be near to cars. Their first competitive outings were at Nazareth Speedway in 1959 with an eleven-year-old Hudson saloon. Aldo won on the first outing and Mario took the honours the following week.

It took Mario until 1963 to become really established as a racing driver. In the intervening years, Aldo had faded from the scene after surviving a huge accident at Hatfield, Pa. The accident fractured his skull and finally revealed the boys' secret racing to their parents.

Mario, however, worked his way through the ranks, scoring strings of victories in sprint and midget races. He drove anything available, to gain experience and to pay the bills. That experience, when he often had to turn an uncompetitive car into a winner simply to pay his expenses, was the foundation for much of his future success.

In 1964, Mario broke into big-time racing with his first regular drive on the USAC championship trail. To most Americans, motor racing means something very different from the European style of racing on 'road' circuits. The American way is much more flamboyant and, with the exception of the two annual US Grande Prix and a handful of domestic road races, American races are held exclusively in purpose-built stadia on simple oval, or tri-oval, courses. Two main bodies sanction the races, the United States Automobile Club – whose championship is for single-seater racing cars to a strictly governed formula – and the National Association for Stock Car Auto Racing, which governs racing for highly modified production, or 'stock' saloons. These two organisations provide some of the most spectacular motor sport in the world, with cars battling wheel to wheel, at average speeds approaching 200 mph, for huge prize funds.

Mario's first USAC drive came after Chuck Hulse, regular driver for the Dean Van Lines team, was injured at New Bremen, Ohio. Andretti scored thirteenth place at Terra Haute, Indiana, and a week later he raced again to fourteenth position. For 1964, he made his biggest break, driving for sponsor Al Dean in the USAC championship. Dean's faith reaped its reward the following year when 'SuperWop' carried off the first of his three USAC championships – albeit with only a single victory and a string of second and third places.In the same year, Andretti made his debut at the American 'Holy of Holies', Indianapolis. In Dean's car and under the watchful eye of veteran mechanic Clint Brawner, Andretti drove the team's Brabham-based Hawk to third place and the 'Rookie of the Year' title.

Also in 1965, Andretti had a meeting which changed the whole pattern of his future racing. Connecticut Ferrari dealer, and ex-racing driver, Luigi Chinetti invited Andretti to drive one of his North American Racing Team Ferraris in a World Championship sports-car race at Bridgehampton. Although Mario was completely new to this type of car and racing, he improved his lap times by 27 seconds before the clutch failed.

In 1966, he again won the USAC championship, capturing pole position at Indy but not finishing the race. He finished first in eight races out of fifteen in that year. More significantly, he began to develop his enormous talents in the direction of road racing: with the late Pedro Rodriguez, he took fourth place for Ford at the 1966 Daytona 24-hour race and from then on he was set on becoming the all-round racer.

1967 saw his first major road-racing victory with the late Bruce McLaren at Sebring. He also raced for the first time at Le Mans, but was injured in the infamous accident which eliminated all but one of the Ford team's cars. Underlining his versatility, he won the Daytona 500 – most famous of all the NASCAR classics – and a victory which, he admits, gave him great personal satisfaction.

In 1968, Dean died and Andretti and Brawner took over the team. Although without major successes, Andretti was again second in the USAC standings. Perhaps the most important race of his 1968 programme was one in which he did not even finish. For that year's US Grand Prix at Watkins Glen, he was drafted into the Lotus Formula One team and astounded the establishment by snatching pole position at his first attempt.

The end of 1968 saw the start of a major phase in Andretti's career, when STP chief Andy Granatelli bought the whole of the Andretti racing operation. Mario rewarded them in 1969 with his third USAC crown and the biggest prize of all – victory at Indy. In his four years with Brawner, he had matured from Rookie to winner. He scored 27 championship victories and earned over $750,000 in prize money, but his ambitions lay in Europe.

1970 should have seen his big break into Formula One, with his STP sponsors buying Mario a seat in the embryonic March Grand Prix team. He soon found the impracticability of trying to combine racing on opposite sides of the Atlantic and both projects foundered.

For 1971, he realised a dream when he signed to drive Formula One and sports cars for Scuderia Ferrari. His first race for the Maranello team was a sensation, as he won the South African Grand Prix to lead the World Championship. The rest of the season, unfortunately, was all downhill and, again, split schedules effectively ruined his chances. He scored fourth place in Germany and thirteenth in Canada to finish in eighth place in the championship. His USAC record was even worse and his best result was a second place. To finish what had started as a most promising season he finally ended his long-time association with the STP Corporation.

As occasionally happens, a phoenix rose from the ashes and Andretti joined former USAC champions Al Unser and Joe Leonard in the Vels-Parnelli Jones USAC team. The contract left him free to race for Ferrari when time permitted. Again his conflicting schedules caused both programmes to suffer; his best Grand Prix results were fourth in South Africa, sixth in the United States and seventh in Italy. He won with the all-conquering Ferrari sports car at Brands Hatch and Watkins Glen, co-driving with Jackie Ickx, but his major achievement of the season was in committing the Vels-Parnelli team to a future in Grand Prix racing.

While the team spent 1973 designing and building the car for their attack on the World Championship, Mario gained valuable road-racing experience in the American Formula 5000 championship. Despite winning several races, he was beaten into second place in the series by Englishman Brian Redman.

For the final two races of 1974 the first of the Parnelli Formula One cars appeared. Andretti managed a promising seventh place in Canada, but retired from his home Grand Prix.

'Every winter I weigh out the situation and see which way to go,' said Mario before the 1975 season. 'I've always wanted to drive the Grand Prix circuit full time and I'm glad my chance finally came with an American team.' With those words, Andretti embarked on a full season of Grand Prix racing with Vel Miletich's ambitious organisation, giving himself three years for a full-scale attack on the World Championship.

Unfortunately, the team suffered teething troubles and Andretti had another frustrating year. After retiring from the Argentine Grand Prix and finishing seventh in Brazil, Andretti put the new Parnelli into the lead of a Grand Prix for the first time in Barcelona. His moment of glory lasted for only nine laps before he crashed. He managed nine more laps in Monaco before retiring with his engine in flames. He missed the Belgian Grand Prix to take part at Indy and the Dutch to race in the Pocono 500, which he won. His best result of the year came in Sweden, where he just beat fellow American Mark Donohue to fourth place. The rivalry between Parnelli and Donohue's First National City Bank-Penske team was a feature of the season, but sadly it ended in Austria, when Donohue crashed heavily during practice and died soon afterwards. Andretti scored a fifth place in France, a stirring drive from fifteenth place on the grid, and that was his last championship point of the season, giving him a total of five points and fourteenth place in the drivers' list.

1976 will be remembered as the year when Andretti really became a consistent front runner on the Grand Prix trail. At the beginning of the year, the wheel had turned full circle and Andretti was back, for one race, the Brazilian Grand Prix, in a Lotus – the marque in which he had made his debut. It was a brief return, which lasted only as far as the second lap, when he collided with his team-mate Ronnie Peterson; however, he was happy with the team and they with him. After two last abortive efforts in South Africa, where they scored a single championship point, and in the US Grand Prix, West, the under-financed Parnelli team finally quit. Andretti did one non-championship race for Frank Williams's team at Silverstone and then, in a blaze of publicity, rejoined Lotus. After that he began to show exactly why he is so respected by the Grand Prix circus, taking what was essentially a very difficult car and, by concentrated testing, making it behave well enough to lead the Swedish Grand Prix for 45 laps before retiring. He scored his first points for Lotus with a fifth place in France, but otherwise his performances up to the German Grand Prix were more promising than rewarding, and mostly ended in retirements. He added fifth in Austria and third places in both Holland and the USA, ending with a first in Japan.

Many people thought Andretti was robbed of the 1977 title only because the points scoring system did not place enough emphasis on winning races. He won more Grands Prix – four, in Long Beach, Spain, France and Italy – than any other driver, his USAC-style repertoire of setting-up techniques further flattering the already sensational Lotus 78. Yet while Niki Lauda backed his three wins with a host of minor placings, Mario suffered five major engine blow-ups, three other mechanical failures and two controversial accidents.

Nevertheless, few were surprised when in 1978 Andretti added the World Championship to his list of accomplishments. He won the season opener in Argentina and won in Belgium, France, Germany and Holland. He took second place in Long Beach, fourth in Brazil and sixth in Italy, where his title was confirmed under the saddest of circumstances. At the start of the race Andretti's team-mate, Ronnie Peterson, who had dutifully maintained his 'number two' status throughout the year, was critically injured in a multiple accident and died from his injuries the next morning. Mario won the restarted race – believing at the time that Peterson would recover – but was penalised for a jumped start and relegated to sixth place.

The sadness, confusion and acrimony of Monza could not alter the fact that Andretti was World Champion and now undeniably the most complete all-rounder the sport had ever known, underlining his versatility by winning the Trenton 150 USAC race during his busy Grand Prix season.

For 1979 Mario stayed with Lotus, alongside Carlos Reutemann, vowing to forego even Indy in his quest to prove once again that he was the best in the world, but it was to be the beginning of a dismal period for Andretti. The results just would not come; from a position of dominance, Lotus became also-rans. The reigning champion could manage only tenth place in the 1979 championship, with third place in Spain, fourth in South Africa and Long Beach and fifth in Argentina and Italy. All except the last of these results were scored before Lotus ditched the radical new Lotus 80 for the older 79. In spite of a dismal mechanical record (with nine retirements), less than cordial relations with Reutemann and many offers from other teams, Mario stayed with Lotus for 1980, now joined by young Italian, Elio de Angelis, and with sponsorship from Essex. Fortunes did not improve much, however, and Andretti again suffered retirement after retirement, often with gearbox problems and twice from first lap shunts (in Brazil and at Long Beach). There were glimmers of hope, Mario running in the points several times before being side-lined – including a memorable dice for fourth place in Holland with Reutemann's Williams, before first the oil pressure and then the fuel ran out.

The smile came back just a little at the end of the year when Mario won a CART championship race for Penske at Michigan Speedway, and scored his only World Championship point of the season for sixth place at Watkins Glen.

Determined to go out of Grand Prix racing on more of a high note, Andretti resisted the temptation to forego Europe and return to a programme based in the United States; for 1981, he joined the rapidly improving Alfa Romeo team, looking for the chance to show that he could still be the world's greatest all-rounder.   BL

RENÉ ARNOUX (b.1948)
France
In the late 1970s, France underwent a truly remarkable revival in its Grand Prix fortunes, with a sudden emergence of new drivers and a return of French marques to the front of the grids. In becoming a race winner in a French car, René Arnoux put himself firmly on the road to even greater success.

René Alexandre Arnoux was born at Pont-charrat, near Grenoble, on 4 July 1948. He studied mechanical engineering in Grenoble and, like so many successful drivers, he made his competition debut racing karts, starting at the age of twelve and racing for six invaluable years. When he ended his education he forged a further link with motor sport, working in a garage preparing rally cars. After a brief interlude for his military service he joined Conrero at Moncalieri in Italy.

In 1972, his appetite whetted by his kart-racing successes, René arrived at the famous racing drivers' school at Magny Cours, from which point his progress was rapid, if somewhat erratic.

In 1973, against the background of the French racing revival, Arnoux began to make a name for himself by winning the national Formule Renault title – narrowly beating another future French Grand Prix driver, Patrick Tambay. Rather than follow the standard French route to the top by progressing to Super Renault, René effectively wasted much of 1974 in campaigning a sadly uncompetitive McLaren M19, entered by Ted Kitchener and backed by ShellSport, in the European Formula 5000 Championship. By mid-season, sadly disillusioned, he had fallen out with the struggling team and he finished the year with his first, tentative taste of Formula Two, campaigning his Elf-backed Martini against the likes of fellow countrymen Patrick Depailler (who won the championship), Tambay, Jacques Laffite (all future Grand Prix stars) and the man who would eventually be his own Formula One team-mate, Jean-Pierre Jabouille.

In spite of his unsuccessful season, Arnoux was at least being noticed, even to the extent of signing a testing contract with Lotus, although he never actually drove one of their cars.

For 1975, he moved back to Super Renault, winning the championship and a seat in the Martini-Renault Formula Two team for 1976. He was a revelation in the rapid French cars, winning three races – at Pau, Enna and Estoril – and being denied the title by just a single point at the final round, at Hockenheim, where Jabouille and his team-mate Michel Léclere engineered a superb technical and tactical result to clinch the title for Jabouille's Elf. But for an engine failure in the previous round, Arnoux might have been champion himself.

In any case, he only had to wait until the following year to redress the balance, winning the title with relative ease. Having won the opening round, at Silverstone, he was challenged but never headed. He won two more races – at Pau and Nogaro – and scored three second places on his way to the championship.

In 1978 Arnoux's Formula Two mentor Tico Martini ventured into Grand Prix racing with the straightforward, Cosworth-powered Martini MK23. René's Formula One debut was not auspicious; he failed to qualify in South Africa. He raced the Martini in Belgium, France, Austria and Holland (finishing ninth in Belgium and Austria), but the project was already doomed through lack of finance.

When Martini pulled out of the fray after the European races, Arnoux had two very impressive outings for the Surtees team, in Canada and at Watkins Glen. Sadly, Surtees too was forced to pull out of Grand Prix racing at the end of the season but Renault team manager Gerard Larrousse was one of several who had followed René's progress and in November 1978 Arnoux signed to drive in the ever improving Renault team, alongside Jabouille.

The turbocharged Renaults were sometimes fast but invariably fragile. Although 1979 was somewhat frustrating, Arnoux underlined his ability with pole positions in Austria and Holland, second places in Britain and at Watkins Glen, and third – after a sensational, no-holds-barred, last lap fight with Gilles Villeneuve – in France, where Jabouille scored the first win for the turbo Renault.

It was not long before Arnoux's obvious potential was fulfilled; in 1980, having crashed in Argentina, he stormed away to two successive wins in Brazil and South Africa, raising real hopes for the championship. Thereafter, however, Renault suffered endless mechanical misfortunes and problems with their Michelin tyres, and René did well to get into the points in Belgium and France. At the end of the season he had 29 points and sixth place in the championship to show for some exceptional performances. For 1981, undaunted and always smiling, Arnoux was to stay with Renault, in spite of the split between FISA and FOCA, the sport's governing body and the constructors' own organisation, which threatened to separate the non-Cosworth teams from the main stream.   BL

ALBERTO ASCARI (1918-1955)
Italy

When Antonio Ascari won the 1924 Italian GP at Monza his six-year-old son Alberto posed with him and the P2 for the photographers. Also present were Enzo Ferrari and Antonio's nephew Giovanni Minozzi – a keen admirer of his uncle – who after Antonio's death frequently recounted his racing feats to young Alberto. Minozzi himself was attached to Alfa Romeo on the racing side, so the young Ascari grew up in a fervent atmosphere of racing.

Like many Italians, he began his career on motor cycles, riding Sertum, Gilera and Bianchi machines in trials and races and scoring a dozen wins between 1936 and 1939. By then he badly wanted to race cars like his father, but 1940 was a year of uneasy peace in Italy and races were few.

However, a 'substitute' Mille Miglia sports car race was being held over nine laps of a long closed circuit between Brescia, Cremona and Mantua, and the eager Alberto visited Enzo Ferrari – former team-mate of his father and later chief of the Scuderia Ferrari which raced the factory Alfa Romeos in the '30s. Ferrari had left Alfa Romeo in 1938 and built two Type 815 straight-eight, 1½-litre sports cars, one of which he entrusted to Alberto Ascari for the Mille Miglia, with his cousin Minozzi as co-driver. In this, his first car race, Alberto took the class lead, but he drove hard with little sympathy for the machinery, and quickly retired with a broken valve.

Then he bought a half-share in Piero Taruffi's 1938 1½-litre six-cylinder Maserati, being placed ninth in the Tripoli GP, but retiring in the 'substitute' Targa Florio over a short street course in Palermo. War came, and six years elapsed before young Ascari could resume this fascinating sport. By then he had developed the heavy build of his father and friends called him 'Ciccio', an Italian equivalent to 'Butch' meaning literally 'meat'. He returned to racing in 1947, in Egypt curiously enough, for a special race on Gezireh Island, outside Cairo, promoted for the new 1100 cc Cisitalia Monoposto cars, and this time he drove extremely well against many old racing hands to be placed second. Again with a Cisitalia, he retired in the Rome GP but came fifth at Albi in France.

Alberto now plunged deep into Grand Prix racing, driving a Scuderia Ambrosiana Maserati with Luigi Villoresi as his number one and willing teacher. The racing situation then was very different from that in his father's time, for whereas in the '20s a 'season' meant perhaps six races, in Alberto's day it totalled two dozen or more, with racing almost every weekend for him to keep in trim and perfect his driving. In 1947 he raced at Nice, daring to duel with the great Wimille, and came fourth.

Then came his first win, a lucky one in the Modena GP for sports cars. He was leading in a two-litre Maserati when the race was stopped halfway after another car crashed into the crowd.

Alberto Ascari's rise to professionalism thereafter was startling. In 1948 he drove the new low-chassis 4CLT/48 Maserati to its first victory in the San Remo GP, won the Pescara sports car GP, was fifth at Monaco and Berne, fourth in the Italian GP behind the dominant Alfas and second in the British GP at Silverstone. Alfa Romeo paid the son of their revered Antonio Ascari signal honour by offering him a place in their team for the French

GP, where he drove impeccably to third place behind Wimille and Sanesi.

In 1949 he and Villoresi left Maserati for Ferrari, and Ascari became Italian champion, with Grand Prix victories in the Swiss and European GPs, and others at Silverstone, Bari, Reims and in Argentina. His 1950 score was equally impressive, including the Penya Rhin, German, Reims, Rome, Luxembourg, Mons, Garda and Modena GPs, plus another Argentinian race, while in 1951 he rose to fullest might with the 4.5-litre GP Ferrari, defeating the all-conquering Alfa Romeos in his third German GP victory, and in the Italian GP, besides winning the San Remo GP and Formula Two events at Monza, Naples and Modena. He and Villoresi also showed their versatility by coming first in the Sestriere Rally with a Lancia Aurelia.

The following two seasons saw Ascari the complete maestro. He was now the 'famous son of a famous father', driving with the same dash and mastery, extremely fast through the corners and a formidable opponent to other masters such as Farina and Fangio. Like his father he preferred to seize an early lead and once ahead was extremely hard to catch. In 1952 Grand Prix racing switched to Formula Two, and 'Ciccio' with the two-litre, four-cylinder Ferrari won no less than twelve races, including the British, Dutch, French, German, Italian and European/Belgian GPs! His 1953 score was slightly less impressive with seven GP victories, but he also won the Nürburgring 1000 km race with Farina in a sports Ferrari.

Naturally Ascari became a very worthy World Champion, both in 1952 and 1953, but just when it seemed that nothing could check his headlong run of successes, he did it himself by leaving Ferrari and signing – with Villoresi – to drive the new GP Lancias when they were ready. They did not appear until late in 1954, so Alberto had a lean season, although he won the Mille Miglia – a race he hated – with a 3.3-litre V6 sports Lancia. In the Spanish GP, his only 1954 race with the GP Lancia, he led for ten laps, made fastest lap, then retired.

By 1955 the cars were raceworthy, and Ascari won two races in quick succession, at Turin and Naples. Then came the Monaco GP in which, following the retirement of Fangio and Moss in Mercedes, he took the lead. He covered only one more lap, however, when the tricky Lancia took charge, left the road and dived into the harbour. Ascari swam to safety but was taken to Monaco hospital in case of shock. He remained there, fretting to get back to Italy, for two days, then went to Monza on Wednesday, 26 May and took out Castellotti's three-litre sports Ferrari for a few laps.

It was expected that he could share the car in the Supercortemaggiore GP that coming Sunday but, lacking his crash helmet, he had no intentions of going very fast on this occasion. He completed four laps and started a fifth when suddenly the Ferrari went out of control on the sweeping Vialone left-hand curve and overturned, killing Alberto Ascari instantly. Two long skid marks preceded the scene of the crash, but the cause of his death remains unknown to this day.   CP

ANTONIO ASCARI (1888-1925)
Italy

It is very unusual for a father and son to follow the same path through life so closely as the Ascaris – Antonio and Alberto. Both were gripped by the excitement and joy of fast driving, both took up motor racing, both reached the peak of their profession, both died at the wheel at the age of 36 and by an even crueller coincidence, both left a widow and two children.

The thirty years that separated their respective careers showed living and motor racing in two very different phases of development. Antonio Ascari's early life was not easy. He was born in 1888 at Sorga in Verona, son of a corn merchant, and was apprenticed to a cycle repairer. A strong and conscientious worker, he loved machinery and driving and after a spell at maintaining agricultural machines he took a job in Milan as mechanic with the de Vecchi concern, builders of sound, conventional, four-cylinder cars in the Via Peschiera.

In 1909, Antonio and his brother Amedeo emigrated to Para, in Brazil, to work on cars, but his brother died from yellow fever and a saddened Antonio returned to Italy and to de Vecchi, where he became service manager. The firm's chief tester, Ugo Sivocci, arranged that Antonio should drive one of their touring cars in the 1911 six-day Criterium of Regularity based at Modena and he did well before having to retire. No further chance came to drive before World War I when he was busily engaged on aircraft repair work with a firm called Falco, but with the return of peace Ascari set up an Alfa Romeo agency in Milan.

An unexpected chance to go motor racing came in the very first post-war Italian event, the Parma Poggio di Berceto hill-climb in October 1919. This was a hectic 32.8-mile point-to-point dash over tortuous mountain roads – and when the Fiat company withdrew its entry shortly beforehand, Ascari bought one of the cars the Turin company intended to run. This was a 4.5-litre S57/14B built for the 1914 French GP, and in a resounding climb with his new acquisition Ascari broke the old record by nearly four minutes, being over 5½ minutes quicker than the second fastest.

Three weeks later he and the Fiat repeated the performance in the 9.9-mile Consuma Cup hill-climb near Florence, winning by over two minutes. With two starts and two wins, this new Italian driver found himself among the favourites in the 1919 Targa Florio race on 23 November. Before the race, however, it rained, hailed and snowed, and Ascari, after making a tremendous getaway, suffered a locked front brake on the first lap of the snow-covered mountain road, beyond Polizzi. A tremendous skid landed the Fiat and its crew at the bottom of a deep crevasse, Ascari breaking a thigh while his mechanic had broken ribs and spinal damage.

Ascari spent seven weeks in Palermo hospital, then returned home to recuperate, devoting most of his time to his now thriving business. He sold the Fiat to Count Masetti and, as befitted an Alfa Romeo agent, drove cars of that make thereafter. He joined the factory team alongside his old friend from de Vecchi days, Ugo Sivocci, as well as Campari and Ferrari and 1920 brought him a win at Garda, but little else. In 1921 he scored a class win in the Parma Poggio di Berceto hill-climb, though only fourth fastest overall this time, while in the Targa Florio a broken camshaft prevented him from even starting.

The Sicilian classic became something of a pet enemy to Ascari. In 1922 he made the distance, won his class and was fourth overall. In 1923 he was leading with a lap to go when a tyre punctured and he spun; the wheel was changed but his engine would not restart immediately, Sivocci passed to win and Antonio was a furious second, though still a class winner. In 1924 he again had the lead on the final lap when, only fifty yards from the finish, his Alfa spun and stalled. Mechanic and driver strove frantically to restart the engine but to no avail and by the time they had pushed it over the line two others cars had passed.

That was Ascari's last Targa Florio, but fortune was kinder elsewhere. In 1923 the four members of the Alfa team each won an Italian race; Ascari's was the Circuit of Cremona, where he averaged 83.37 mph, while he also scored a class win and third overall at Mugello. 1924 brought the famous two-litre, eight-cylinder Alfa Romeo P2 Grand Prix car and at short notice the company decided to make the Circuit of Cremona a test race before the all-important French GP at Lyons. As 1923 Cremona winner, Ascari was selected to drive the new car and his performance was sensational – the P2 was timed at 121.164 mph through a 10 km stretch, setting a world record for the distance, and Ascari averaged 98.3 mph, winning the 199-mile race by almost an hour from the second car.

He next shared an RLS sports Alfa Romeo with Marinoni in the Monza 24-hour race; they finished second, unexpectedly beaten by a three-litre NAG from Germany. Then came the French GP, in which Ascari seemed to have things all his own way, leading until three laps from the end of the 500-mile race. Then his engine went sick and Campari passed to win, while Ascari stopped at the pits, where he and his mechanic repeated their Targa Florio act, attempting in vain to restart. A cylinder had cracked and they failed to finish.

In the Italian GP at Monza five weeks later, Ascari led from the start and was quite unassailable this time. He won the 497-mile race at 98.6 mph, heading a glorious Alfa Romeo 1-2-3-4 victory by sixteen minutes and setting fastest lap at 104.24 mph. He put on a similar performance in the 1925 Grand Prix of Europe at Spa, in Belgium. He and team-mate Campari were the sole finishers, twenty-two minutes apart, Ascari's winning average of 74.46 mph including a leisurely stop for a meal during the race!

Came the 621-mile French GP, held at Montlhéry on 26 July 1925, and yet again the dashing Ascari rocketed ahead. He led by an ever-increasing gap until the twenty-third lap, when drizzle made parts of the course unexpectedly slippery. On a 115 mph left-hand curve his P2 slid an inch or so too close to the wooden paling fence, a hubcap entangled, the car ripped down a hundred yards of the fence in a mighty convulsion then overturned into a ditch. Antonio Ascari, who had made strong objections to the organisers about this dangerous type of fencing before the race, died on his way to hospital. Today that part of the

Montlhéry circuit is called Ascari Curve and is marked by a monument to the great Italian driver.   CP

LORENZO BANDINI (1936-1967)
Italy

The fanatical Italian motor racing enthusiast expects much of his home born heroes, for nothing less than victory will satisfy these most demanding of supporters. In return, a successful driver will receive the sort of adulation reserved for footballers and film stars in other countries. The Italian enthusiast cares little for mechanical matters and is not interested in the fact that some foreign cars might be faster than his beloved Ferraris and Alfa Romeos.

Enzo Ferrari tends to pair a very fast foreign driver with an Italian driver in his Formula One team, with the result that the Italian driver often drives too fast for his ability. In the past, drivers like Luigi Musso, Eugenio Castellotti and Lodovicco Scarfiotti have lived and died in the shadows of team mates like Juan Manuel Fangio, Mike Hawthorn, and Chris Amon, while Bandini invariably had to play second fiddle to Phil Hill and John Surtees in the Ferrari team.

Despite this emotional and psychological handicap, Lorenzo Bandini captured the imagination of the Italian public as well as the press, for he was darkly handsome in the. typical Latin manner and behaved the way Italians felt their motor racing heroes should behave.

Bandini was born in Cyrenaica, North Africa to Italian parents in 1936, but in 1939 the family returned to Italy and he spent the war years in Florence. When Bandini's father died, at an early age, Lorenzo was obliged to take a job as a motor mechanic in Milan, but he was fortunate in his choice of employer, for Goliardo Freddi was a racing enthusiast who helped the young Bandini by loaning him saloon cars for local events. His racing career began in 1957 and he soon graduated from cars like the Fiat 1100 to the more potent Fiat V8 sports car.

In 1958, Freddi loaned Bandini a Lancia Appia Zagato with which he won his class in the Mille Miglia. Bandini knew, however, that to get anywhere in motor racing he had to take part in single-seater racing. When the new Formula Junior was announced he rapidly acquired first a Volpini and then a

Stanguellini. Although these front-engined Italian cars were no match for the mid-engined British types, which were setting drivers like Jim Clark, John Surtees, Peter Arundell and Trevor Taylor on their way to the top, Bandini gained some good victories in Italian events during 1959 and 1960, bringing his name to the notice of Ferrari who considered him for a place in his team in 1961. In the end Bandini, however, was passed over in favour of Giancarlo Baghetti.

Despite this setback, Bandini did drive in Formula One during 1961, as the Italian private entrant, Guglielmo Dei, provided him with a Cooper-Maserati. This was not a very competitive car, but the young Bandini placed it third in his first Formula One race at Pau in France behind Jim Clark and Jo Bonnier. He followed up with a third place in the Naples Grand Prix which gained him a drive in the Ferrari sports car team. At the end of the season he won the Pescara Four-hour sports car race, co-driving with Giorgio Scarlatti. He also found time to win the Coppa Junior at Monza with his Formula Junior Stanguellini and, in the winter of 1961/62, he toured New Zealand with a Cooper-Maserati.

For 1962 he was signed by the Ferrari factory for both Formula One and sports car racing but, with drivers such as Phil Hill, Ricardo Rodriguez, Willy Mairesse and Giancarlo Baghetti in the team, he did not get many drives. However, he finished a brilliant third in the Monaco GP and, with Baghetti, co-drove a Ferrari to second place in the Targa Florio. He also beat Baghetti to win the Mediterranean GP at Pergusa, Sicily at the end of this short but promising season.

Ferrari allowed Bandini to go in 1963 so Mimmo Dei of the Scuderia Centro-Sud offered him a 1½-litre V8 BRM, painted in Italian red, for Formula One races. The BRM had good handling, having given Graham Hill the World Championship the previous year, and Bandini enjoyed the English car, picking up his idiomatic English from the BRM mechanics who looked after it. Later in the 1963 season, Ferrari realised his mistake and signed Bandini as number two to Surtees. In the 1½-litre Ferrari he finished third in the Rand GP, fifth in both the South African and United States GPs and won the Le Mans 24-hour race, co-driving a Ferrari with Scarfiotti.

Bandini remained faithful to Ferrari for the rest of his career. In 1964 he finished second in the Syracuse GP and third in the Italian, German and Mexican GPs, as well as obtaining several good sports car placings. His team leader, John Surtees, won the World Championship in 1964.

Bandini's first Formula One victory came in 1965 on the rough Zeltweg airfield course where the Austrian Grand Prix was first held. He finished second in the Monaco GP, third at Syracuse and fourth in the Italian and United States GPs. He also co-drove the winning Ferrari in the 1965 Targa Florio, with Nino Vaccarella.

John Surtees remained with Ferrari in 1966 and Bandini was becoming fretful at having to stay in the shadow of a foreign driver, but he drove the new Ferrari to second place at Monaco and Syracuse and third place at Spa. Then Surtees had a much publicised row with the Ferrari team manager at Le Mans and abruptly left, elevating Bandini to the position of number one in the team. However, success did not come, for his best places subsequently in 1966 were a couple of sixth places in the Dutch and German GPs. The 3-litre Ferrari was much bigger and heavier than the fleet little Brabham which was doing most of the winning in 1966.

Bandini was now a prosperous garage owner and married to Margherita Freddi, the daughter of his first benefactor. He started the 1967 season as Ferrari team leader, very conscious of his position in Italian eyes. Victories in the sports car races at Daytona and Monza early on augured well for the season, as did a good second place in Britain's Race of Champions at Brands Hatch. Then in the Monaco GP he was running second to Denny Hulme's Brabham when his Ferrari touched the barriers at the chicane; the car flew across the road, mounted the straw bales, overturned and caught fire. The primitive fire-fighting equipment was unable to cope with the blaze and every time the flames appeared to be under control it would flare up again. None of the fire crew had protective clothing and could not approach the blaze. It was several minutes before the fire was finally quenched and the terribly injured Bandini was taken across Monaco harbour to hospital. By some miracle, he survived until the following Wednesday, but he finally succumbed to his injuries. He was 31.

Bandini's death came as a great shock to the members of the Grand Prix 'circus' and his death gave the first impetus to the great drive for safety in motor racing which is still being pursued energetically by so many people.   MT

WOOLF BARNATO (1895-1948)
Great Britain
Of all the larger than life team of racing drivers known as the Bentley Boys, the most outrageously extrovert was Woolf Barnato, whose vast personal fortune helped the Bentley company survive its mid-1920s financial crises; yet the Barnato millions dated back only one generation to the 'Babe's' father Barney, son of an East End of London shopkeeper called Isaac Isaacs.

Young Barnett Isaacs, armed with little more than his wit, changed his surname to Barnato, emigrated to South Africa and made a vast fortune in the diamond fields. When he vanished overboard on a boat sailing home from Cape Town, in the 1890s, his money went mostly to his two-year-old son, Woolf, born in 1895.

Woolf grew up to be a keen sportsman, with a consuming desire to excel at whatever he did. He was a big man who liked big cars and his first venture into motor racing was with a 48 hp 8-litre Locomobile he had brought back from a visit to the United States. He entered this for the Brooklands Automobile Racing Club's Easter 1921 meeting, coming third in the 100-mile Long Handicap.

By the Whitsun meeting, he had transferred his allegiance to a bilious yellow Calthorpe, replaced for the next season by Malcolm Campbell's old 2.6-litre Talbot and an Ansaldo.

For 1923, Barnato changed to a Wolseley Moth, which he also ran at Brooklands in 1924, the same year that he set up Class H (7784-13,929 cc) records up to 300 miles at the wheel of his touring 8-litre Hispano-Suiza. In 1925 he bought his first Bentley, the prototype short-chassis, 100 mph 3-litre, which he had fitted with a pretty, boat-tailed, two-seat body by Jarvis of Wimbledon. With this car, which still survives, Barnato won several major Brooklands races and, partnered by John Duff, set a new world 3-litre 24-hour record of 95.03 mph in September 1925.

It was around this time W. O. Bentley persuaded Babe Barnato to back Bentley Motors; Barnato, a natural gambler, sank nearly £100,000 in the venture, as a calculated risk investment – which failed to pay off. Though Barnato was prepared to risk money on this scale, and spent around £1000 a week on his lavish social life, he was parsimonious in small things, and expected full value for his investment.

So one condition of Barnato's backing Bentley was that he had his pick of the firm's products for his own use – he always had a brace of 6½-litres, one open, one closed – another was a place in the works team, which was revived on his orders.

But Barnato was no rich dilettante – on the contrary, W.O. Bentley regarded him as the best driver of the period, and one who never made a mistake and always obeyed orders. 'I think the danger of motor racing is greatly over-rated,' commented Barnato, who didn't believe in life insurance. 'It is not as dangerous as it seems.'

In 1928, Barnato shared a 4½-litre Bentley with Bernard Rubin in the Le Mans 24-hour race. As both were in their first Le Mans, theirs was the slowest of the three team cars, but the other two cars, driven by Birkin and Benjafield, were put out of the running by a wheel failure and a broken oil feed respectively, leaving the team honour in Barnato's hands.

The Babe managed to overhaul his principal rival, Brisson's Stutz, which eventually dropped back with stripped gearing, but at the expense of a cracked frame, which caused the engine to lose all its water 40 miles from the finish. Somehow Barnato managed to nurse the sagging car to the finish – and win. He repeated the victory the following year in easier style, driving a 6½-litre Bentley. The team took the first four places in the event and the victory was celebrated with a particularly wild party at Barnato's huge country house, Ardenrun, near Lingfield, Surrey.

In 1930, Barnato pulled off the unique feat of three Le Mans wins in a row, after a spirited battle with Rudolf Caracciola's Mercedes; it was also his last Le Mans for the team, and the Bentley team's last race.

By 1931, Bentley's finances had become so strained that Barnato's advisers recommended that he put no more money into the company which passed into the hands of Rolls-Royce.

Ironically, Barnato had bought a large holding in Rolls-Royce, not long before Bentley Motors was liquidated, and by 1934, he was on the board of Bentley Motors (1931) Ltd.

In 1934, Barnato decided to sponsor a Brooklands track-racing car; his mechanic, Wally Hassan, converted Barnato's 6½-litre Bentley tourer into an offset single-seater, with the chassis underslung at the rear. On its first outing, it lapped Brooklands at 115 mph – and burst. Hassan replaced the damaged engine with an 8-litre unit with raised compression, running on alcohol. In 1935 Oliver Bertram took the All-comers Brooklands lap record in the Barnato-Hassan at 142.6 mph; the car was further modified in 1936, but was not fast enough to beat the Brooklands handicappers, though Bertram managed to lap at over 143 mph in an attempt to regain the track record from John Cobb.

Woolf Barnato died in 1948 and, despite his seat on the new Bentley board, it was one of the 'old school' Bentleys which drove to his graveside to pay its last respects.   MT

JEAN BEHRA (1921-1959)
France
Jean Behra fitted, only too well, the popular conception of a racing driver of the 1950s. He was short, stocky, muscular, completely fearless and covered with the scars from the numerous crashes which he miraculously survived – all except the last.

Behra, born in Nice in 1921, soon fell for the lure of speed on wheels: first he took up cycling, then motor cycling, his prowess on two wheels earning him the French motor-cycle-racing championship, three years in succession. Like so many motor-cycle racers before and since (including Tazio Nuvolari, Piero Taruffi, Jean-Pierre Beltoise, John Surtees and Mike Hailwood), Behra hankered after four-wheel racing and, as soon as organised motor racing began in Europe, following World War II, he was at the wheel of a Talbot which he drove to sixth place in the Coupe du Salon meeting at Montlhéry, near Paris in 1949.

In the following year he drove a Simca 1100 in the Monte Carlo Rally, showing his versatility by finishing third overall; he drove another Simca in the Le Mans 24-hour race, but was forced to retire. Later on in 1950 he won his class at the Mont Ventoux hill-climb, in a Maserati, and his exploits brought him to the notice of Amédée Gordini, known as 'Le Sorcier', because of his supposed wizardry with racing engines. He was the only man seriously to attempt to uphold French prestige in single-seater racing and he gave Behra a seat in his Formula Two team for 1951. He finished third in his first race with the Gordini, but the firm was perpetually short of finance and the cars seldom had the power to become competitive. All the same, Behra managed the occasional win, including a memorable victory over the Ferrari works team at Reims.

Despite a very bad crash at the Pau circuit in southern France during 1953, when he suffered severe back injuries, he was soon back in racing and continued with Gordini until 1954. This was his best year with the French marque with wins at Montlhéry, Pau and Cadours.

For 1955, he was signed by the Maserati factory team for Formula One and sports-car racing and was immediately successful, winning the Formula One Pau and Bordeaux GPs, as well as several sports car races, with the Maserati 300S. He suffered another crash while driving on the dangerous Dundrod TT circuit in 1955 and he lost an ear when the lens of his spare goggles cut it off. He was given a plastic substitute and he would often horrify the ladies by removing it at opportune moments. He stayed with Maserati in 1956, but had no success in Formula One, although he shared the winning sports car in the Nürburgring and Paris 1000 km races.

Although he again drove for Maserati in 1957, he was always driving in the shadow of men like Moss and Fangio, and early in 1957 he approached Raymond Mays of BRM to ask if BRM would provide him with a car for the Caen Grand Prix in western France. Mays jumped at the chance, for the team was short of drivers. Two cars were taken, one for Behra and one for the Franco-American Harry Schell. Despite a lack of practice, Behra won the race with ease, admittedly against modest opposition. Behra followed this up by leading a BRM 1-2-3 victory in the International Trophy race at Silverstone, in front of a 100,000 crowd. Behra became the darling of the British enthusiasts and his enthusiasm for the car endeared him to everyone at the BRM works. Despite his almost total lack of English he spent countless hours pointing out ways to improve the car and did a great deal to restore some confidence in the BRM team. He was contracted to Maserati for the rest of 1957 and managed to win the Moroccan and Modena GPs as well as sharing victory in the Swedish GP and Sebring 12 hours, driving the monster 450S Maserati.

Behra signed for BRM in 1958, but in his first race for them at Goodwood, suffered a much publicised accident when the brakes failed and he collided with the notorious brick

chicane at speed. He was badly shaken by the crash and his confidence had hardly returned when he suffered another brake failure at Aintree, fortunately without hitting anything. He suffered other accidents, including smashed goggles at Silverstone and a hair-raising spin at Spa, and he never really got to grips with the BRM again, although he finished third in the Dutch GP. He fared better with the RSK Porsches in sports car races, notching up wins at the Nürburgring, Avus, Reims and Mont Ventoux.

Not surprisingly, Behra left BRM in 1959 and joined the Ferrari team. He won the Aintree 200 with the Dino 246 Ferrari, but, later in the season, he quarrelled with the Ferrari team manager Romolo Tavoni and left the team. By this time he had evolved his own Formula Two car, based on a Porsche sports car, and spent a great deal of time on this project; he also drove an RSK Porsche sports car, being one of the quickest drivers on the circuits.

He took the RSK to the German sports-car GP at the dangerous Avus track near Berlin and, in the race on a wet track, he passed Jack Brabham at high speed going into the enormous high banking at the end of the long, fast straight; instead of rounding the banking normally, the Porsche suddenly shot to the top, hitting the concrete barrier. Behra was flung from the car, striking a flagpole as he was thrown out. The plucky, and often unlucky, 38-year-old Frenchman died instantly.   MT

JEAN-PIERRE BELTOISE (b.1937)
France

One of the most determined racing drivers of all, Jean-Pierre Beltoise achieved the high spot of a patchy Formula One career by winning the rainsoaked 1972 Monaco Grand Prix at the wheel of a BRM. Born on 6 April 1937 and married to Jacqueline Cevert (sister of the late François), Beltoise had come up the hard way, with more than his fair share of tribulation and injury.

Beltoise won eleven French national motor cycling championships before turning to four wheels, in 1963, with a drive in a 1-litre Bonnet. He had a few inconsequential races for the team and took a class win at Le Mans before suffering a terrible crash in the Reims 12-hour race the following year. He still limps and has a weak left arm as a permanent legacy of this serious accident. By the time he recovered, he found that the French Matra missile firm had taken over the Bonnet organisation and built a Formula Three car. Thereafter he helped to mould the late-1960s renaissance of French motor racing.

Despite being only partially recovered, Beltoise won the French Formula Three championship, in 1965, and went on to triumph in the prestigious Monaco Formula Three race the following year. He was then invited to drive the Matra-Ford Formula Two car and campaigned in several Grand Prix races with this machine in 1967. The Matra had to be fitted with extra ballast to bring it up to the minimum weight limit but Beltoise still finished seventh in the United States and Mexican Grands Prix.

He was given his first real Formula One opportunity in the 1968 Spanish Grand Prix at Madrid, deputising for Jackie Stewart in Ken Tyrrell's new Matra-Ford V8, after the Scot had injured his wrist in a Formula Two incident. Beltoise led the race for several laps before an oil leak caused his retirement. For the remainder of the season he drove the Matra V12 for the factory team, scoring a very impressive second, in soaking wet conditions, at Zandvoort but the team decided to withdraw from racing for 1969 in an effort to get their motor performing reliably. Beltoise also became European Formula Two Champion in 1969, driving a Matra-Ford.

For 1970, Beltoise joined Ken Tyrrell's team and drove Matra-Ford V8s alongside Stewart. He took second place at Clermont-Ferrand and nearly won the Italian Grand Prix at Monza after spectacularly outbraking both Stewart and Rindt into the last corner, only to run wide coming onto the finishing straight. Driving one of the V12 Matra sports cars, he scored the team's first major success by winning the Paris 1000 kilometres race at Montlhéry and, when Matra returned to Grand Prix racing with their works cars in 1970, was invited back to lead the team.

He led the French Grand Prix at Clermont Ferrand for many laps before being delayed with an oil leak and puncture and the best placings of a rather disappointing year were thirds at the Belgian and Italian Grands Prix.

For 1971, he was joined in the team by Chris Amon. That year started on a low note with Beltoise being held responsible for the death of Italy's Ignazio Giunti, after Giunti's Ferrari prototype crashed into the Matra which Beltoise was pushing (contrary to regulations)

slowly towards the pits at Buenos Aires. He ran for much of the 1971 season with the threat of licence suspension and even criminal proceedings hanging over him, taking just a single sixth place in the Spanish Grand Prix at Barcelona.

Beltoise was dropped from the works Matra Formula One team at the end of 1971 when it was decided to field just a single car for Amon. A controversial move, this was quickly followed by Beltoise signing to lead the multination British BRM team, which had just received major sponsorship from the Philip Morris cigarette concern. He distinguished himself by leading the first wet Monaco Grand Prix for over thirty years from start to finish, out-pacing acknowledged wet weather maestro Jacky Ickx, who freely admitted that there was just no way he could catch the Frenchman.

The rest of the year was indifferent for Beltoise. The works BRMs lacked power and he did not feature in the victory circle again until the end of the year, when the unsuccessful BRM P180, which was subsequently abandoned, took a freak victory in the final Brands Hatch non-championship race.

He stayed with BRM in 1973, although the arrival of Clay Regazzoni and subsequently Niki Lauda demoted Beltoise to effective 'third string' status. It was a less than happy season, punctuated by accidents at Monaco and Silverstone, although he was actually running second in the controversial and confusing Canadian Grand Prix until two laps from the finish, when Emerson Fittipaldi and Jackie Oliver passed him and pushed him down to fourth. In Formula Two he was asked to join the works March-BMW team for several races, but many of these clashed with his Matra sports car commitments and, when he did race, the BMW engines did nothing but give him trouble. He drove a Matra MS670 with François Cevert at Le Mans but mechanical difficulties forced them to relinquish their lead and the car was subsequently retired.

Beltoise signed with BMW for 1974 but once again his talent was hardly matched by the car. He started the season well, scoring fifth place in Argentina, second – in the new P201 – at Kyalami and fifth in Belgium. They were his only points of the season and at the end of 1974 he left Formula One to concentrate on sports car racing.

He became involved with the French Ligier team, who were spending a further year in sports car competition until their Formula One project reached fruition. Again the arrangement was a failure as the cars were totally uncompetitive.

When the Ligier Grand Prix car appeared, for the 1976 season, Beltoise did the initial testing of the car but was soon usurped by his young countryman Jacques Laffite, and this time Jean-Pierre retired for good.   NB

B. BIRA (b.1914)
Thailand

Only a couple of generations after the redoubtable Mrs Anna Leonowens had turned the Siamese Court upside down (which inspired the musical, *The King and I*), the English influence was still strong. So it was natural that the King's nephews, the three young Siamese Princes, Abhas, Birabongse and Chirasakti, should come to England in the 1920s for their education. Birabongse, the second oldest (he was born in 1914), had been crazy about cars ever since, as a little boy, he had sat on the lap of a chauffeur and steered one of the royal cars.

He didn't get the chance to drive on the roads, however, until he was sixteen at Eton; his elder cousin and guardian, Chula, allowed Bira, as he was known, to drive his 1928, 12hp, sleeve-valve Voisin – 'a wonderful little machine'.

In 1932, Chula presented Bira with an MG Magna, soon replaced by a 4½-litre Super Sports Invicta, which itself was succeeded by a 3½-litre Rolls-Bentley in June 1934. The cousins were keen fans of motor racing, but Chula refused to let Bira compete in speed events. However, he bought him a Riley Imp for reliability trials; in 1935 Bira managed to get Chula's permission to turn the Imp into a racing car, and it was taken to Thomson & Taylor at Brooklands for tuning.

For their racing livery, the cousins used a light blue based on the colour of an evening frock belonging to a young Danish girl, Barbara Grut: this later became the Siamese national racing colour (yellow was added to it in 1939).

Birabongse decided to adopt the *nom de course* of 'B. Bira' and first appeared at Brooklands at the opening meeting of the 1935 season; the Imp proved too slow, and Bira looked around for a new car. Cecil Kimber of MG offered him the very last supercharged MG Magnette ever built, which had been specially prepared for the Mille Miglia but refused entry papers for Italy. The MG gave Bira much valuable racing experience, but its top speed of around 110 mph was not quite fast enough to put him in the prize money, though it enabled him to establish a reputation as a driver of consistent ability – and his distinctive Siamese pit signals caused a great deal of attention.

The new ERA cars were just beginning to enjoy their first international racing success, so Chula decided to buy a 1500 cc ERA as a present for Bira's birthday, which fell on 15 July 1935. Five days later, Bira took second place in the 1500 cc race at Dieppe, beating such polished drivers as Earl Howe (Delage), Raymond Mays, Dick Seaman and Humphrey Cook (ERA) and Veyron (Bugatti); only an oiled plug prevented him from taking first place.

This success inspired Bira to enter the 1500 cc Swiss Grand Prix at Berne; again he came second after a well driven race, this time beaten by Dick Seaman. However, a drive for Aston Martin in the Ulster TT ended in failure when an oil pipe broke on the second lap.

Nevertheless, a few days later, Bira set up a new Mountain -Circuit lap record at Brooklands with the ERA and then achieved fifth place in the Donington GP, the highest position taken by a 1½-litre car in this race. He wound up his first season by setting up fastest time at the Gatwick Speed Trials in the ERA, then, at the other end of the speed cycle, won a gold medal in the Veteran Car Run at the tiller of a 1903 Oldsmobile.

In 1936, Bira added to his stable, buying a 2.9-litre 8CM Maserati, with which he won the British Empire Trophy at Brooklands; two of the 1927 1½-litre Delages (which were still capable of winning races in the hands of Dick Seaman) were subsequent additions. They were fitted with ugly streamlined bodies and independent front suspension, but these modifications seemed to break the winning streak.

Bira drove a wide variety of cars, but he achieved his most notable victories with ERA – he eventually had three of them – *Romulus* and *Remus,* both B-types, and the C-type *Hanuman,* named after the Siamese monkey-god.

Most successful was his 21st birthday present, *Romulus,* which took ten first places, eight seconds, five thirds, one fourth and one fifth in the 1935 to 1939 seasons, only retiring five times.

Bira returned to racing in 1946 with *Romulus* and *Hanuman* (which had been rebuilt as a B-type after a crash in 1939) and won the Ulster TT. In the 1947 Pau Grand Prix, *Romulus's* engine disintegrated in full view of 20,000 spectators.

Bira had by now bought a new 4CL Maserati, but on its first outing, in the 1947 Junior Car Club race in Jersey, the engine seized solid and Bira returned to the pits on a borrowed bicycle. His old 2.9 Maserati failed him in practice for the 1947 Grand Prix des Frontières at Chimay, so he substituted the 1½-litre car and finished an easy winner, despite trouble with failing oil pressure.

Later in 1947, Bira had his first works drive for the Simca-Gordini team, winning the Coupe des Petites Cylindrées at Reims. He then had an easy victory in the Manx Cup Race, came second in the Prix de Lyons and, in the Prix de Leman at Lausanne, he narrowly beat his team-mate Sommer.

The 1948 season saw a third at Jersey and a win at Zandvoort, both in 1½-litre Maseratis (the latter victory in one of the new 4CLT/48 cars), and at the end of the year his partnership with Chula was dissolved.

In 1949, Bira continued racing his new Maserati, winning the Swedish GP, coming second in the Argentine Mar del Plata GP, the GP de Roussillon at Perpignan, the Albi GP and the GP of the Associated French Motor Clubs, and taking third places at Zandvoort and in the GPs of Europe and Italy.

In 1950, Bira had an unsuccessful season with the Maserati, gaining only a first and a fourth, and the transplant of a V 12, 4.5-litre OSCA engine into the Maserati brought little better fortune in 1951. Bira returned to Siam in 1952-3, but was back on the circuits in 1954 with a new 250F Maserati, gaining one first, two seconds and a fourth; the next year he won the New Zealand Grand Prix and came third in the Silverstone International Trophy, but decided to retire permanently from racing and sold the Maserati.

Bira returned to his native Thailand to run an airline.   DBW

TIM BIRKIN (1896-1933)
Great Britain

To a generation of motor-racing enthusiasts, Sir Henry R.S. (Tim) Birkin was the epitome of the glamour of motor racing, the fearless driver at the wheel of a great Bentley, blue-and-white spotted silk scarf a-flutter at his throat.

Yet he was small of stature, stuttered badly and his driving could mechanically wreck a car faster and more completely than any other top racing motorist of the late 1920s.

Birkin was born into a wealthy Nottingham family in 1896, and turned to motor racing in 1921 as a relief from the boredom of post-war office work. His first competition car was a DFP, which he raced at Brooklands, achieving no better than a second place in a minor event. After his first few races, business reasons compelled him to give up racing for several years and he did not appear in serious competition again until 1927, when he and his brother Archie – killed a month later practising for the motor-cycle TT – drove a 3-litre Bentley to third place in the Essex MC Six-hour race at Brooklands.

The next year, Tim Birkin's 4½-litre Bentley again came third in the Six-hour race and this made him decide, despite opposition from his father, to make motor racing his profession.

In the 1928 Le Mans, Birkin was partnered by the veteran Jean Chassagne. Their Bentley led for the first 20 laps until a rear tyre burst at 100 mph and the tyre canvas jammed itself steadfastly in the brake mechanism. As the Bentleys, to reduce weight, were not carrying jacks, Birkin had to try and free the wheel with 'a jack-knife, a file, a hammer and some pliers'.

After 90 minutes he had the remains of the tyre off the wheel, and began to drive back to the pits on the rim at 60 mph. At Arnage, three miles from the pits, the wheel disintegrated and the Bentley slid into the ditch. Birkin ran for help and when he arrived at the pits the 47-year-old Chassagne murmured, *'Mainte-nant, c'est à moi'* (now it's my turn), picked up a jack in each arm, ran back to the car, jacked it up and put the Bentley back in the running. On the last lap of all Birkin beat the lap record to run the car into fifth place. 'A pleasant little triumph,' he commented.

By now Birkin had become fascinated by supercharging, seeing it as the easiest way of increasing the power and speed of the 4½-litre Bentley: he had obtained backing from the Hon. Dorothy Paget and set up a factory at Welwyn, where the first supercharged conversion of the 4½-litre was built in 1928-9. However, it was with an unblown 6½-litre Bentley that Birkin achieved his most notable victory of the season – first place at Le Mans.

The first appearance of the 'Blower Bentley' was at the Essex Six-hour race at Brooklands on 29 June 1929. The car retired, but the supercharger was shown to have given 'an increase of 100 hp – 35 of which it required for itself – and a far swifter acceleration'. The top speed was also raised from 108 to 125 mph – 'more than worth the trouble', opined Birkin. W.O. Bentley, however, wasn't so sure: 'To supercharge a Bentley engine is to pervert its design and corrupt its performance.'

In the Irish Grand Prix in July, Birkin, in 'No. 1 Blower Bentley', hounded 'Scrap' Thistlethwayte's supercharged 6.8-litre Mercedes to such good effect that the German car retired with a blown gasket. Boris Ivanowsky's Alfa had too great a lead on handicap, however, and won, with Glen Kidston's Speed Six Bentley second and Birkin third.

No. 1 Blower was adapted, in 1929, for Brooklands work (even though Birkin hated the track, it being 'out-of-date, inadequate and dangerous') with a narrow fabric covered two-seater body, which caught fire when the flexible exhaust pipe broke in the 1929 500-mile race. This body was therefore replaced with a single-seat shell designed by Reid Railton. The engine had now been tuned to give more than twice the power of the standard 4½-litre unit.

Birkin had persuaded Bentley to produce a series of 50 blown cars to qualify the model for entry in the 1930 Le Mans 24 hours.

During the 1930 season, Birkin began a series of assaults on the Brooklands lap record, then held by Kaye Don's V12 Sunbeam Tiger. On his first attempt, Birkin lapped at 135.3 mph, beating the record, and then flew back to Le Touquet to claim the dinner Barnato had promised him if he exceeded Don's speed.

At Le Mans in June, Birkin led the harrying of Caracciola's Mercedes, a Bentley tactic which led to the German's withdrawal, although Birkin threw a tyre tread as he was overhauling Caracciola, running for several miles on the canvas at 125 mph. Birkin's car, having eventually fallen back to seventh place, retired after 20 hours when a con-rod broke and punched a hole in the crankcase.

The end of the Bentley company was now becoming increasingly apparent, and Dorothy Paget withdrew her support from the Blower team in October 1930, although she continued to back the single-seat No. 1 car. Birkin saw the season out in appropriate style by bringing a Blower 4½ into second place in the French

Grand Prix at Pau against the far lighter and more manoeuvrable Bugattis.

Tim Birkin tried his hand with a Bugatti at Brooklands, in the Gold Star Handicap, but was disqualified after he had apparently won. In 1931, he eventually settled on an Alfa Romeo for sports car events and a Maserati for Grands Prix. Partnered by Lord Howe, he won Le Mans in the Alfa, came fourth in the Belgian GP, with the Hon. Brian Lewis as co-driver, and crashed in the Ulster TT.

The 1932 season saw the single-seat Blower Bentley out at Easter, when Birkin at last managed to crack the Outer Circuit record again, with a speed that was to stand for two years, a remarkable 137.96 mph, only beaten by John Cobb's 24-litre Napier-Railton.

In June, Birkin drove a new 2.3 Alfa and won the second day of the Dublin, Phoenix Park, races. He retired at Le Mans, however, with a blown head gasket.

At the end of July, Birkin's Bentley and John Cobb's Delage had a famous challenge match at Brooklands, which Birkin won by 25 yards after a 137 mph lap. It was one of the most enjoyable races of Birkin's career.

In 1933, he took delivery of a new 8C 3000 Maserati, with which he came third in the Tripoli Grand Prix, behind Nuvolari and Varzi. During practice he burned his arm against the exhaust pipe while picking up his cigarette lighter. The wound turned septic, hastened by the effects of malaria which he had contracted in wartime while serving with the Royal Flying Corps in Palestine.

Early in June 1933, Birkin, his arm still bandaged after treatment, threw one of his customary parties at Ciro's Club, but the septicaemia spread and, on the 22nd of the same month, he died in the Countess Caernarvon Nursing Home in London. DBW

JOAKIM BONNIER (1930-1972)
Sweden

Joakim Bonnier, who was killed during the 1972 Le Mans 24-hour race, had a long and distinguished motor-racing career which reached its zenith in 1959 when he joined the BRM Formula One team and won the Dutch Grand Prix for them. Bonnier was one of the first Swedes to tackle motor racing seriously in the post-war years and led the way for other Swedish drivers like Ronnie Peterson and Gunnar Nilsson.

Bonnier was born in Stockholm in 1930, the

son of a professor who ensured that his son had an international education in Paris and Oxford before taking up employment with his uncle's publishing business. However, like so many young men born into a comfortable way of life, he forsook it and first of all spent three years in the Swedish Navy as a lieutenant, before taking up motor racing seriously. He had, in fact, been taking part in rallies since he was eighteen, specialising in the type of rough-road rallies at which the Scandinavians excel.

He also took part in ice racing using Citroën and Alfa Romeo cars and it was his success with Alfa Romeo that prompted the Italian company to ask him to distribute their cars in Sweden. This naturally gave him access to the best competition cars from the Italian firm and he used a 3½-litre Disco Volante Alfa Romeo to good effect, winning the 1955 Stockholm Grand Prix. He also made his debut in England that year, taking the Disco Volante to a fine victory at Oulton Park, and this victory did much to bring his name to the attention of the British racing teams.

In 1956, he became a full-time professional, running a privately owned 1½-litre Maserati in international events, albeit with little success. He was then taken into the Maserati sports-car team for 1957 and in 1958 had his first real taste of Formula One, driving a 2½-litre 250F. Unfortunately, this was the year that Britain's Vanwall team swept all before them and his only successes were in the Naples GP and the non-championship United States GP.

For 1959, Bonnier was invited to join the hitherto unsuccessful BRM team and promptly won for them the 1959 Dutch Grand Prix, a race which was also remarkable for the fact that every one of the starters finished the race and not a single pit stop was made. The Dutch victory was a flash in the pan for BRM, however: although Bonnier stayed with them in 1960, he never finished a race in a higher position than fifth. In sports-car racing he was driving for Porsche and, as well as enjoying several minor wins, he co-drove the winning Porsche with Hans Herrmann in the 1960 Targa Florio.

He raced the Porsche 1½-litre Formula One car in 1961 and 1962. Although the car was not fast he collected several third places.

By the early '60s, it had become evident that Bonnier did not have the qualities to become World Champion, for he lacked the sheer speed to win Formula One races; in sports-car racing, though, he was much in demand.

From 1963 to 1965, Bonnier drove for the Rob Walker private team in Formula One races, first with a Cooper and later with a Brabham. His best placings in either of these cars were fifth places at Monaco, Spa and Mexico. However, in sports-car racing he continued to excel, winning the 1963 Targa Florio and the 1964 Reims 12-hour race, with Graham Hill, for Ferrari. He was second at Le Mans in 1964, again with Graham Hill, in a 330P Ferrari, and won the Paris 1000-kilometre race at Montlhéry.

When Formula One changed to 3-litres in 1966, Bonnier was obliged to buy his own car to remain in top-class motor racing. He purchased a Cooper-Maserati, which was uncompetitive even in faster hands than Bonnier's, and his best placing in 1966 was sixth at Mexico. The following year he scored a fifth place in the German Grand Prix and sixth in the United States GP. His sports-car prowess remained, however, and he drove the American Chaparral in 1966, winning the Nürburgring 1000-km race, with Phil Hill as his co-driver.

For 1968, he tried a Formula One McLaren-BRM, but had little success during the year, apart from sixth place at the Italian GP. He was given a drive in the Honda V12 Formula One car at Mexico that year and finished sixth.

He purchased a Lotus 49 for the 1969 season and looked forward to a more successful year but crashed the car at Oulton Park and never raced it again. He switched to a McLaren M7C for Formula One but by 1970, at the age of 40, he was not at all competitive against younger men in newer machinery and he wisely retired from single-seater racing that year, making the grand gesture of hanging his McLaren on the sitting room wall of his home in Lausanne, Switzerland.

Like so many drivers before him, he could not forsake the wheel, so he switched to the new 2-litre European Sports Car Championship with a Lola, and on many occasions showed younger men that his skill had not gone, by notching up victories at several European tracks.

For 1972, he purchased two of the new 3-litre Lola T280 sports cars, with which he planned to tackle the World Sports Car Championship. The cars proved to be very fast but rather fragile and ill-maintained. He managed to win the mini-Le Mans four-hour race in 1972 and led in the early stages of the 24-hour race. He dropped to eighth in the early hours of Sunday morning but started to make up time rapidly, after a pit stop with brake problems. He was lapping a Ferrari Daytona when the two cars collided and the tiny Lola shot over the safety barrier into the trees lining the track at Indianapolis corner. Bonnier was killed instantly.

Bonnier's main claim to a place in the history of motor racing is not for his racing record, excellent though it was, but for his ability as an international diplomat, pleading the cause of motor racing safety and advancing the image of Grand Prix drivers from that of glorified playboys to international stars. He founded the Grand Prix Drivers' Association, in 1962, and was its chairman until he died, leading the fight for drivers' rights. With his fluent command of six languages and aristocratic bearing he added a lustre to the sport of motor racing. Joakim Bonnier lived and died for his sport; he will never be replaced.   NB

PIETRO BORDINO (1890-1928)
Italy

Pietro Bordino, probably the finest road-racing driver of his generation, was born in Italy in 1890. In 1904, he was acting as riding mechanic in Fiat racers, accompanying Felice Nazzaro, Vincente Lancia and Ralph de Palma. By 1908 he had become a competition driver himself, making his debut at the Château-Thierry hill-climb. In 1911, he went to England with the giant four-cylinder, 28-litre, 300 bhp Fiat racer, which made a number of high-speed runs at Brooklands. His career did not start in earnest, however, until 1921, when his twin-ohc Fiat took the lead at the start of the 1921 Brescia Grand Prix and kept it until the fourteenth lap; first tyre troubles and then a broken oil pipe caused his retirement. As it was his first appearance in an international event, Bordino's performance – which included a record lap speed of 96.3 mph – was doubly remarkable.

Already he had established a reputation as a driver whose methods were of a type likely to endear him to every enthusiast who met him, since he believed most firmly in getting the absolute maximum from his car whether it would last or not.

These were the characteristics which marked his performance in the 1922 French Grand Prix at Strasbourg: he left his two team-mates, the veteran Felice Nazzaro and his nephew Biagio,

far behind, leading from the second lap. Valve-stem trouble eliminated his principal rivals, the Sunbeams, and it looked as though the race would be a walkover for Bordino, when two laps from the end his back axle fractured. This was a fault common to all three team cars and had already cost the life, earlier in the race, of young Biagio Nazzaro, although Felice Nazzaro's car lasted the distance to win.

The opening of the new Monza Autodrome in September 1922, provided Bordino with two sensational victories, the first in the 373-mile Voiturette Grand Prix, in which he led a 1-2-3-4 Fiat victory at a speed of 83.25 mph, followed a week later by a clear-cut victory in the first European Grand Prix, his winning speed being 86.90 mph, with a fastest lap of 91.3 mph.

'No man could handle a racing machine better at high speed on really tricky corners,' said *Autocar*. On the twisting Tours circuit used for the 1923 French GP, Bordino justified that statement by setting up the fastest lap (85.6 mph) in practice, eclipsed this in a shattering burst of speed with an 87.18 mph opening lap and led for the first eight laps until the supercharger on his Fiat swallowed flying stones and choked.

The European GP at Monza brought deeper disappointment: a stub-axle broke in Bordino's car during practice, killing his passenger, Giaccone, and injuring Bordino to such an extent that his new mechanic had to shift gears for him during the race. Even so, he led for more than half the distance, until a violent skid, caused by the loss of a rear tyre tread, prompted him to retire.

He opened the 1924 season with fourth place in the Targa Florio, even though his little 1½-litre supercharged Fiat was quite the wrong car for the Madonie circuit. He fainted on the fourth lap and Nazzaro had to finish the race for him.

He soon went into the lead in the 1924 French Grand Prix at Lyon, and put up a magnificent performance until brake failure put his car out.

It was the high point of his career. He managed tenth place at Indianapolis in 1925, but the new 1926-7 1½-litre GP formula was not to his liking, and he made few appearances, although he won the 1927 GP of Milan at Monza with the new type 806 V12 Fiat. Soon after this, Fiat finally withdrew from racing.

Bordino changed to a Type 35 Bugatti, with

which he took seventh place in the three-litre class of the 1928 Mille Miglia, but shortly afterwards, while practising on the Targa Florio circuit in Italy, he collided with a large dog, which jammed the steering, causing him to crash fatally.

'Not only was he a fine driver, he was an exceedingly pleasant rival,' recalled his obituary in *Autocar*. Only a few days after Bordino's death the first Coppa Pietro Bordino race was run over the Allesandria circuit.

This turned out to be the first major victory for the driver who was to replace Bordino in the affection of Italian motor racing fans – Tazio Nuvolari.   DBW

JACK BRABHAM (b.1926)
Australia

John Arthur Brabham was the man who began the great invasion of Grand Prix racing by the men from 'Down Under'. Although Australians and New Zealanders had raced in Europe before, he was the man who put Australia on the international motor racing map and, by his example, encouraged drivers like Bruce McLaren and Denny Hulme and talented designers like Ron Tauranac and Ralph Bellamy to throw up their lives in the Antipodes for the risky profession of racing driver or mechanic in Europe.

Born in Sydney in 1926, Jack Brabham was the son of a greengrocer, whose father had emigrated to Australia from London's East End in 1885. Although there was no family background in engineering or competition motoring, the young Brabham soon became involved in cycling, motor cycling and cars. He did best at technical subjects in school and when he left school, at 15, he went into a garage to learn the trade. He was called up for the Australian Air Force towards the end of World War II and spent a couple of years repairing Beaufighters.

When he was demobbed from the RAAF, in 1946, he had a workshop built at his grandfather's house and began to service and maintain cars from the neighbourhood. He might still have been there but for the arrival in Hurstville of an American, Johnny Schonberg, who had married a local girl. Brabham and Schonberg became friendly and one day the American invited Brabham to join him on an expedition to Darwin to buy war surplus trucks. On the way there, they had to stop in Brisbane. Schonberg took Brabham to a speedway track where midget cars raced. Schonberg was quite a star driver at the Sydney track, but Brabham had never gone to watch. Interested by the spectacle of these tiny cars broadsiding their way round the cinder covered ¼-mile oval, Brabham soon became a regular spectator back at the Sydney track and before long, he decided that he could build a better car than the one Schonberg was racing. Using parts from a Morris Cowley, an Amilcar, and a Harley-Davidson motor cycle, Brabham built up a car powered by an 1100 cc JAP twin-cylinder engine. The engine proved unreliable so he built up a new 1350 cc engine, making most of the engine parts himself. This engine was very powerful and Schonberg went through a successful season before his wife began to complain about his dangerous hobby. Up to this time, Brabham had given little thought to the possibility of driving, as the engineering challenge was more interesting to him at that time. However, Schonberg offered him a drive in the car when he retired, and after a few lessons on some nearby mud flats Brabham was taken to the Paramatta Speedway and entered for his first race.

There was no storybook beginning to the Brabham career – he finished dead last in his first race, and the next, and the one after that. But after nights of eating the cinders thrown up by the other cars he was beginning to get the hang of driving the midget and when, on the third night, he was started from the front row of the grid, with the best drivers right at the back, he stayed in front to notch up his first victory. Once he had acquired the taste of winning he became almost unbeatable. He won the New South Wales championship in his first season and he carried on for six more years as a professional midget racer, until one night in Adelaide the venerable JAP engine blew itself to pieces and he decided he'd had enough of midget racing.

Brabham was almost lost to motor racing at that point: he nearly joined his father in the greengrocery business, but by then he had met Ron Tauranac, who was later to become the chief designer of Brabham cars. Tauranac was involved in hill-climbing, a strictly amateur sport, and Brabham became interested. He used the midget in a hill-climb and was far faster than most of the opposition, so he turned to the sport seriously, changing the midget for a Mk. IV Cooper 500 and then a Mk. V Cooper with a 1000 cc Vincent HRD engine. By this time, Brabham had married Betty, who was, fortunately, a great motor racing fan.

Brabham's first step on the road to fame in road racing came when a Cooper-Bristol was put up for sale in Australia. This front-engined car was considered quite a 'hot' machine in Australia and he was able to buy the new car at a good price when the original purchaser committed suicide before taking delivery. He had obtained sponsorship from Redex for the car, which was to be called the Redex Special, but Australia's ruling body, the Confederation of Australian Motor Sports, had ruled that advertising would not be permitted so the aggrieved Brabham took his car off to New Zealand in 1954 where he raced in the New Zealand Grand Prix and met some of the international stars for the first time. He finished sixth and his appetite was whetted.

Jack spent some time racing the Cooper-Bristol in Australia and New Zealand, winning at most of the major circuits and getting his name known. He took part in the 1955 New Zealand GP, finishing fourth, but more important he met Dean Delamont, the Competitions Director of the RAC. Delamont impressed the young Brabham with his stories of racing in Europe and suggested that Brabham come to England and try his hand at 'real' motor racing.

He agreed to give it a try for a season so he sold the Cooper-Bristol and bought a Cooper-Alta, which he thought would be more competitive. Unfortunately, the engine kept breaking down and he bought a Bristol engine to install. This went much better and he soon came to the notice of the public because of his tail-out cornering style, inherited from his days with the midget which seldom travelled in a straight line. He naturally met the builder of his car, John Cooper, and the two became firm friends. Cooper invited Brabham to work at the Cooper factory in Surbiton, Surrey, although he was paid no wage. In return for his help in the factory, Cooper allowed him to build up a rear-engined Cooper-Bristol which proved to be very fast. It did not manage to win against the top-class opposition available in Britain but he was able to mix it with the likes of Stirling Moss on wet tracks and he realised that, with a more competitive car, he could drive on equal terms with the Europeans. He took the Cooper-Bristol back to Australia, won the Australian GP with it and promptly sold the car before returning to England. With the proceeds of the sale he bought a 250F Maserati from the Owen

Organisation for the 1956 Formula One season, but this car was very troublesome and almost bankrupted him before it got into a race.

John Cooper came to his rescue and asked him to drive for the works team, using the little bobtailed Cooper-Climax 1100 in sports car races and the new 1½-litre Coventry-Climax engined single-seater in Formula Two.

The year 1957 was the first season that Brabham (who had become known as 'Black Jack', because of his permanent five o'clock shadow) fully realised he could mix it with the Grand Prix stars and hold his own. The little four-cylinder Coventry-Climax engine was stretched to 2.2 litres in time for the Monaco Grand Prix and Brabham got the car into third place with three laps to go, only to have the fuel pump fail; he pushed the car home to finish sixth. Brabham spent most of his time in Formula Two races where the little Cooper was very successful but none of the other manufacturers had the wit to copy the Cooper, sticking instead to their ungainly front-engined cars.

Brabham took the 2.2-litre Cooper to New Zealand in early 1958 and won the New Zealand GP – his first win in five attempts. The rest of the season wasn't so successful as there were several niggling faults with the Formula One car. The main problem was the gearbox, for Cooper was using an ordinary Citroën front-wheel-drive saloon car gearbox, but eventually it was completely stiffened and improved in other ways, and by 1959 the Cooper had its own gearbox.

Still no one had cottoned on to the potential of the Cooper in 1959, and with all the problems sorted out and the engine now at a full 2½ litres Brabham began to win races; he started off with a victory in the Daily Express Trophy and followed up with wins in the British and Monaco GPs as well as several other good placings, which gave him the World Championship for 1959. He became the first British driver in a British car to win the championship.

Brabham's shyness and dislike of publicity were put to the test in the celebrations of his victory and certainly he did not capitalise on the win in the way that Stirling Moss would have done. In 1960, the Cooper was even more successful and Brabham won the Grands Prix of Belgium, Holland, France, Britain and Portugal to clinch the championship comfortably.

For 1961 Formula One changed to 1½-litres

and Cooper's dominance ended, but it had paved the way for the rear-engined revolution that was to come. In 1961, Brabham shook up the Indianapolis establishment with his ninth place in the Formula One Cooper, but he had few real victories that year, for the Coopers were thoroughly outclassed.

In 1961, Brabham decided to build his own cars, an ambition which he had long nurtured because he only felt safe in a car which he had personally constructed or supervised. He was allowed to do this at Cooper, but when called upon to drive other cars such as the Aston Martin sports cars and a Formula One Lotus, which he drove briefly in 1962, he was never fully competitive because he did not know every part of the car intimately.

By now, he was a successful garage owner in Chessington, with a tuning business as well, and his friend, Phil Kerr, came over from Australia to manage it, while Ron Tauranac joined him to design the first Brabham car, which was originally called an MRD. The shy Brabham hated the thought of his name on a racing car, but he was eventually persuaded to name it a Brabham.

Brabham's first Formula One car appeared during 1962, using a Coventry-Climax V8 engine, and was first raced at the German Grand Prix where he retired. Later in the season he gained a second place at the Mexican Grand Prix. In 1963, he won the Australian, Solitude and Austrian Grands Prix and, in 1964, was third in the French Grand Prix at Rouen, a race which gave team-mate Dan Gurney his first championship Grand Prix victory and the first ever championship victory for a Brabham car. Brabham, in fact, had to wait until 1966 for a Grand Prix championship win in his own car.

By this time, the 3-litre engine capacity limit had been imposed on Grand Prix racing and the Australian Repco company developed a V8, 3-litre engine for use in the Brabham. Although not the most powerful motor on the circuit, it was extremely reliable and that year the nimble Brabham machines earned their maker victories in the French, British, Dutch and German Grands Prix. Thus, Jack Brabham gained not only his third World Championship title, but the manufacturers' championship as well, a feat that no other man in motor racing has achieved. For this, he was awarded the OBE.

In 1967, Brabhams were again all-conquering, but this time it was Brabham's number two, the burly New Zealander, Denny Hulme, who swept all before him.

In 1968, however, Jack's luck was out. The new 4-ohc Repco engine proved troublesome and, for 1969, Brabham turned to the Ford-Cosworth motor. He won the Silverstone International Trophy but during the season had several retirements due to unreliability. However, he had a better end to the year, finishing fourth in the US Grand Prix, third in the Mexican Grand Prix and second in the Canadian Grand Prix.

He started the 1970 season well, winning the South African Grand Prix in his new monocoque BT33 and seemed certain to win the Monaco and British Grands Prix, but in both races last-lap troubles (an error at Monaco, running out of fuel at Brands Hatch) held him down to second place. He later finished third in the French Grand Prix and eventually in fourth place in the 1970 drivers' championship. His last Formula One race was the 1970 Mexican GP, after which 44-year-old Brabham announced his retirement and returned to Australia, having sold the Brabham company to Bernie Ecclestone, who continued to race the cars using Brabham's name.

During Brabham's twenty-year career he took part in 127 World Championship races, of which he won 14, gaining three world titles. His successes in 1959 and 1960 pioneered the development of the rear-engined Grand Prix car which dominates racing today.

In the 1979 New Year's Honours List, Jack Brabham – at the suggestion of the Australian Prime Minister, Malcolm Fraser – became Sir Jack Brabham. It was a fitting tribute to a man who continued to devote his life to the sport which he had dominated both as a driver and as a constructor.   MT

VITTORIO BRAMBILLA (b.1937)
Italy

It is hard to imagine that Vittorio Brambilla could have been anything other than a racing driver. He was born right at the heart of Italian motor racing, in Monza, on 11 September 1937, into the family garage business. Like many racing drivers before and since, his first forays into the world of motorised competition came on two wheels; in 1960 he took the Italian national championship, riding a 175 cc Parilla. After a further two seasons of motor cycle racing, his career was halted for a while when he did his National Service.

His obligations to his country fulfilled, he returned to working in the family garage business, while gradually turning his mind more and more towards a career on four wheels. Again like so many successful drivers, his first tentative steps into four-wheeled racing came with karts; in 1963 he won the 200 cc World Championship.

At that stage in his life Vittorio was far from being a committed racer and once again he 'retired' to working in the garage. Motor racing was never far away from his mind of course; at that time his older brother Ernesto, or Tino, was making something of a name for himself in Formula Three and, later, in Formula Two racing. In 1968 Vittorio made the big step when he drove Tino's Formula Three Birel, an Italian copy of the successful Brabham, for the first time. He continued to drive the car sporadically through that first season and emerged at the end of it as runner-up in the Italian Formula Three championship. From there on, he lost most of his interest in bikes and launched himself on the path that took him to Formula One fame.

Infamy may be a better way to describe the swarthy Italian's public image; for a long time on the road to the top he had a reputation of being very hard on cars, and a marked propensity for falling off the road. In fact, to some extent, the reputation was unjustified and the rather unkind nickname of 'The Monza Gorilla' exaggerated things even more. He spent 1969 consolidating his position in Formula Three, this time winning the Italian championship with the Birel, and even venturing to race outside Italy.

For 1970 the brothers joined forces and resources to attack the European Formula Two Championship. While still competing and occasionally succeeding in Formula Three, Vittorio had his first dabble in the senior formula with an elderly Brabham BT23, while Tino drove a more youthful BT30. His first appearance was at Barcelona, where he impressed in quite exalted company before spinning out of contention. He had several more races with the BT23, retiring from most of them with wrecked engines, before his chance came to try a BT30. With that car he was more impressive. At Salzburg he lost out to Jacky Ickx, in the forerunner of the latterly invincible BMWs, by a mere 1.7 sec. Later in the season he was leading the Imola race when he wrote the car off. He finished the season by taking the rebuilt car to a fine second place in

Munich. Despite odd tastes of success, the season had been a frustrating one for Vittorio, his growing ambition being strangled by the team's continuous lack of proper finance. The following year found the Brambillas back in business with the BT30s but Vittorio made a disastrous start to the season by writing off his car in successive races at Pau and the Nürburgring. The Brabhams were eventually replaced by a trio of March 712Ms but once again the cash supply faded and with it the results.

1972 was just a season for marking time; Vittorio drove the March, the still-successful Birel and an Abarth sports car in Group 5 events but it was generally a very low-key year.

1973 was the turning point; Beta Tools is a large manufacturing company with factories close to Monza and for some time they had given help to the Brambillas in small ways. For 1973 they were to back Vittorio to the full.

For once, things could be done properly and, armed with a new March, the old Gorilla was tamed. He finished the season with two wins at Albi and the Salzburgring, where he soundly beat the hitherto untouchable works car of championship-winner Jean-Pierre Jarier. He furthered his ties with BMW during the year, driving the Schnitzer-prepared Coupé in saloon car races.

From Formula Two the only way to go was up and in 1974 Beta livery appeared on a Formula One March for Vittorio. He quickly settled into his new world. Having survived a huge accident in Spain, he came close to scoring his first championship points in Sweden, before the engine failed within sight of the finish. After a string of mid-order finishes he scored his first point with a strong drive into sixth place in Austria. Although it was his only point, in a year again punctuated by several accidents, he had earned new respect and many eyes were on his future.

The highlight of his racing career came in Austria one year after his first point was scored. This time he won his first Grand Prix – or rather his first half Grand Prix, for the race was stopped prematurely, due to torrential rain, and only half points were awarded. In the most appalling conditions, he had driven the race of his life for a thoroughly deserved victory. He celebrated by spinning and knocking the nose off the car only yards past the flag! The rest of the season brought only fifth place in Spain and sixth in Great Britain – both in shortened races. He had led the Belgian race and was placed on pole position in Sweden.

Brambilla and Beta both stayed with March for 1976 but, despite some stirring performances, his best result by the tail of the season was a sixth place in Holland. He also seemed to revert to his old driving style with several accidents, including four at the German Grand Prix alone, marring his record.

He crashed again in Austria, scored a point for sixth place in Holland and wound up the season with retirements at Watkins Glen and in Japan. He also maintained an interest in Formula Two, making sterling efforts to produce a competitive Lancia-based engine.

Brambilla joined the exodus from March and signed for Surtees for 1977. Although he was one of the few drivers to contest each of the season's eighteen Grands Prix he scored only six points – for fourth place in Belgium, fifth in Germany and sixth in Canada, where he crashed shortly before the finish. His record in sports cars was much better and, driving for Alfa Romeo in the World Championship for Sports Cars, he won four rounds, at Monza, Vallelunga, Imola and Salzburgring.

He stayed with Surtees for 1978 but was soon back to his old ways, having his first accident in practice in Argentina. His second came the same day, his third the following day! He finished eighteenth, plagued by suspension problems. In Brazil, Vittorio failed to qualify – a situation which he repeated in Monaco. His season was sadly uncompetitive and he scored his only point for sixth place in Austria. Then at Monza, Brambilla was involved in Ronnie Peterson's fatal accident and was critically injured when he was struck on the head by a flying wheel. Happily the damage proved not to be permanent and Vittorio made a full, if very slow, recovery.

During 1978 he had spent time developing Alfa Romeo's own Grand Prix car, Surtees dropping out of racing. Brambilla's comeback came at his native Monza, just a year after his near fatal accident. He finished a gallant twelfth in the older Alfa. A promising outing in Canada ended in retirement and he failed to qualify at Watkins Glen, but he stayed on the Alfa Romeo driving strength for 1980. He did some testing but had only two Grand Prix outings, in Holland and Italy, both of which ended with minor accidents. He also took in a couple of sports car races but towards the end of the season he announced that he would retire from racing to work on Alfa Romeo's new turbocharged Grand Prix contender. BL

TONY BROOKS (b.1932)
Great Britain

When Juan Manuel Fangio was planning his retirement from motor racing, he was asked who would succeed him as World Champion. He instantly named Tony Brooks – a prophecy that never came true because Brooks was up against such other talented British drivers as Stirling Moss, Mike Hawthorn and Australia's Jack Brabham.

Brooks was an unlikely looking candidate for a World Champion, or even a racing driver at all for that matter, as he was slightly built, studious and self-effacing – certainly not cast in the swashbuckling, tearaway mould of some of the other hard driving, hard drinking, womanisers of the racing world of the '50s.

Born in 1932, the young Brooks was weaned on sporting cars because his parents were keen drivers, although he seemed set on a career as a dentist until a family friend offered him the loan of a Healey Silverstone sports car for club races. He scored numerous wins with this car as well as with Frazer-Nash and DKW cars loaned by friends and admirers over the next three years. In 1955, he was offered a drive in a single seater Formula Two Connaught. In the race, at Crystal Palace, he finished fourth behind three Formula One cars driven by Mike Hawthorn, Harry Schell and Roy Salvadori. The young Brooks, still only 23, had arrived and he soon began to receive tempting offers which persuaded him to abandon temporarily his dental career.

His first works drive was with Aston Martin, who signed him on for their successful sports car team in 1955. He drove a DB3S to third place in the Goodwood Nine hours and, shortly afterwards, placed a Connaught sports car, loaned by the factory, into second place at Aintree behind the very rapid Colin Chapman in a Lotus. This performance prompted the Connaught directors, Mike Oliver and Rodney Clarke, to offer him a drive in their Formula One Connaught at the Syracuse Grand Prix in Sicily. This was asking a lot of any driver, especially as Brooks had never driven a Formula One car before, had never raced abroad and had never even met the top Continental drivers like Musso and Villoresi, who were racing the works Maseratis at Syracuse. As it was not a World Championship event, some of the top names were missing, but Brooks made third fastest time in practice and in the race he toyed with the opposition before going away to a comfortable victory, leaving the bewildered Italian stars way behind. He also set a new fastest lap for the Syracuse circuit. His cool and unruffled driving showed that he had that indefinable talent which all top drivers seem to possess.

Brooks's victory was doubly important because not only was it his first Grand Prix victory but it was also the first by a British driver in a British car since 1924. This was the first sign of the British domination of Grand Prix racing, which was to come in the near future.

For the 1956 season, BRM signed Brooks to partner Mike Hawthorn, but the BRM was a troublesome car and Brooks suffered an accident at Silverstone, when the car caught fire after overturning; Brooks was thrown out, but not seriously injured. He gained a few wins in Aston Martin and Cooper cars, but left the BRM team for Vanwall in 1957.

The Vanwall team, owned by G.A. Vandervell of Vandervell bearings, was just coming to the fore and Brooks finished second in the Monaco GP and shared the winning car at the British Grand Prix with Stirling Moss. Brooks had overturned his Aston Martin at Le Mans prior to the British GP and was suffering from badly burned legs so, when Moss's car broke at Aintree, Brooks handed over his car and Moss went on to victory. Brooks later won the Nürburgring 1000 kilometre race in an Aston Martin.

He stayed with Vanwall in 1958, the year Fangio predicted he would win the World Championship, but although he won the German, Belgian and Italian GPs, he did not gain the championship, largely because his team-mate Stirling Moss also won several races. The championship finally went to Mike Hawthorn.

For 1959, Brooks joined the Italian Ferrari team, but the big front-engined cars were now up against the little rear-engined Coopers and, although Brooks won the French and German GPs on the faster circuits, Jack Brabham's Cooper took the championship, with Brooks in second place.

1960 saw Brooks joining the privately owned Yeoman Credit Racing Team with a Cooper, but little success came his way and, after a poor 1961 season, driving the new 1½-litre BRM, he decided to retire from racing.

After his retirement, he set up a garage business, appropriately within sight of the famous banking at the old Brooklands track in Weybridge, Surrey.   MT

GIUSEPPE CAMPARI (1892-1933)
Italy

They called Giuseppe Campari *Il Negher* – 'Blackie' in the dialect of his Milanese birthplace – because of his swarthy, suntanned complexion. It's difficult to imagine anyone who looked less like a racing driver than this portly 16-stone lover of good food and grand opera, who was liable to burst into an aria from Rigoletto, in his fine baritone voice, whenever he felt elated. In fact Campari, born in 1892, was a natural. He joined Alfa as a test driver, making his first mark on motoring history by coming fourth in the 1914 Targa Florio. The Targa was his first post-war venture too, but, like his fellow competitor Enzo Ferrari, Campari was unplaced. In the first race on the tricky Mugello road circuit, however, Campari achieved his (and Alfa's) first victory, winning at 37.8 mph over a distance of 242 miles.

Campari won at Mugello again in 1921 and took third place in the Targa Florio. In the Gran Premio Gentleman at Brescia, his 1914 GP Alfa retired when leading, with a holed radiator, just a lap from the finish. With the same car, he came eleventh in the Targa Florio in 1922, but it was Vittorio Jano's new P2 Alfa Grand Prix car that really clinched Campari's claim to fame. The combination won the 1924 French GP at Lyon, the first major race in which the P2 had appeared. Appropriately, Campari won the special Hartford Shock Absorber trophy for this feat – a 12ft long, 10-stone sausage, garlanded with ribbons.

Campari led the 1925 French Grand Prix at Montlhéry until the halfway mark; then, learning of the death of his team-mate Ascari, he (and Count Brilli-Peri in the third Alfa) retired in mourning. The Monza GP, later that season, saw Brilli-Peri first and Campari second; he was second, too, in the 1927 Circuit of Milan.

The year 1928 witnessed the first of Campari's two successive victories in the Mille Miglia, inaugurated in 1927 over a course covering all types of road, from main highways to mountain passes. In 1928, Campari and his partner Giulio Ramponi averaged 51.9 mph; in 1929 their speed was 55.69 mph.

Their mount was an Alfa Romeo 1750 sports. Campari's performance with this model in the 1929 Targa Florio was not quite so impressive, for he came fourth; his team-mate Brilli-Peri was first, with Bugattis second and third. The Alfas were not invulnerable.

Other 1928/9 successes included first place in the Coppa Acerbo at Pescara in both years and second in the European Grand Prix at Monza in the P2 Alfa.

Of course, Campari was there for the 1930 Targa Florio; he and Nuvolari were driving the new 1750 Alfa sports, while the third member of the team, Achille Varzi, was driving his old, battle-scarred P2. Too dangerously powerful for the twisting Targa course, claimed the pundits but they were wrong and Varzi won, leaving Campari the poor consolation of fourth place and a new lap record. Three weeks later, in the Rome GP, Campari's Alfa was again fourth but the Ulster Tourist Trophy saw Campari take second place with his blown 1750 Alfa.

Spring 1931 saw the debut, in competition, of the new straight-eight Alfas: the 2.3 sports and the P3 racer. For the Mille Miglia, however, Campari stayed with the older six-cylinder model. It was a wise choice, for the fast 2.3 Alfas tore their tyres to shreds – Nuvolari had to change eighteen covers – and, although slowed a little by tyre trouble, Campari came second behind Caracciola's far more powerful Mercedes.

Campari drove one of the new P3s in the 1931 Italian Grand Prix. In practice, Arcangeli's twelve-cylinder Alfa left the track, killing the driver. The shocked Alfa team planned to withdraw, but Mussolini telegraphed; 'Start – and win!' – so they did their best.

Nuvolari drove the twelve-cylinder car for the first two hours, but the team manager brought him in and, for the next eight hours, Nuvolari and Campari took turns to drive the P3. They fulfilled Mussolini's command.

Campari shared his P3 with Borzacchini in the 1931 French GP, taking second place; he won the Coppa Acerbo in one of the Type A twin-twelve-cylinder-engined models, probably the ill-starred monster car's best performance.

IL Negher was Maserati-mounted for the French Grand Prix of 1933: he was lying only two seconds behind the leader, Etancelin (Alfa), when he had to make a pit stop. The car wouldn't restart, and it took two mechanics and a bystander to get it going. It was a breach of the rules, but Campari, who won, was only fined a nominal Fr1000 by the race committee.

It was Campari's last victory; after his next race, he announced, he would retire, devoting himself to opera. In the first heat of that race, the Monza GP, Count Trossi's Duesenberg voided its sump on a fast bend, the oil being casually covered with sand between heats.

Campari and Borzacchini came hurtling into the bend in the lead of the second heat. The two cars skidded and crashed; Campari was killed instantly, Borzacchini died later.   DBW

RUDOLF CARACCIOLA
(1901-1959)
Germany

Rudolf Caracciola was frequently called 'Der Regenmeister' (rain master) because of his unmatched skill at driving fast in heavy rain: although he came to epitomise all that was best in Grand Prix racing, Caracciola started his competition career in a very modest way.

Born in 1901, he made his track debut in 1922, driving a Fafnir light car, with which he won a class victory at the Berlin Avus track. The next year, he began racing in earnest, with a borrowed Ego, matched against makes of such stunning obscurity as the Omikron, the Coco and the Grade. Parts to bring the Ego up to racing trim had been provided by the car's makers on the firm understanding that, if Caracciola won, the parts were free, but if he lost he'd have to pay for them. As he had just blown his remaining cash on a square meal before the race, the threat was of little moment. He won all the same and, on the strength of this victory, he applied to the Mercédès racing team for a place.

'Patience, perhaps one day you will be a driver,' said Christian Werner, head of the Mercédès team, who then offered Caracciola a job selling cars in Dresden. Soon, young Rudi had his first works drive, at the wheel of a 1½-litre blown Mercédès, with which he won several speed trials and hill-climbs, including the Muennerstadt Hill-Climb, where he won four events, and the Teutoburgerwald Circuit which he won in 1924-5-6-7.

After a succession of such minor victories came Caracciola's first international win, in the original German Grand Prix, held over 20 laps of the Avus circuit. His mount was a 2-litre, straight-eight Mercédès, a model not renowned for good handling, and the asphalt surface of the Avus was slippery with rain: thus was the legend of *Der Regenmeister* born. Just to prove his versatility, Rudi also made fastest time at the Semmering hill-climb.

The secret of Caracciola's success was his unflappable calm, even in the most exciting of races. Commented George Monkhouse in

1936: 'He appears to have some uncanny premonition of what the car is likely to do before it does it, and makes the necessary correction on the steering wheel. Like a first class horseman, Caracciola has perfect hands.'

When the new Nürburgring circuit was inaugurated in 1926, Caracciola won the sports car race with the new 6.8-litre Mercédès S; he also recorded a number of sprint and hill-climb victories. At the Nürburgring again, he won the 1928 German Grand Prix; in 1929, he appeared at the first Monaco GP with a liberally-drilled SSKL Mercedes, a car so manifestly unsuitable for the twisting Monegasque circuit that his second place behind Williams's Bugatti was all the more remarkable.

It poured with rain during the 1929 Ulster TT: *Der Regenmeister* obliged with a faultless victory. In 1930, he raced in his first Mille Miglia, finishing sixth, partnered by his old mentor, Christian Werner.

Next year, Caracciola returned to Italy for the Mille Miglia and won, after one of the most epic drives in the history of motor racing, piloting his SSKL Mercedes the entire distance unaided and averaging 62.84 mph over the 1000 miles, including stops – a new record. Rain, at the start of the 1931 German Grand Prix, favoured Caracciola, who led from the start on this twisting and writhing circuit; though the sun came out for the last six laps, the others couldn't catch the flying Mercedes.

At the end of 1931, however, Mercedes-Benz withdrew from racing and Caracciola joined Alfa Romeo for 1932, winning the Eifel, Limburg, German and Monza Grands Prix.

In 1933, Rudi drove an Alfa Romeo under the auspices of Scuderia CC, run by him and Louis Chiron.

Practising for the Monaco GP, Caracciola braked too late and rammed a wall, breaking his thigh in several places, which left him with a permanent limp.

He was out of action for over a year, a tragic period in which his wife was killed in a ski-ing accident. Eventually, though, Mercedes persuaded him to carry out tests of their new GP car, designed, at the behest of Hitler, for the 1934 unlimited capacity, 750 kg formula.

In the 1934 Italian Grand Prix, Caracciola shared the winning car with Fagioli, his first victory since 1932.

His *annus mirabilis* was certainly 1935: he won the Grands Prix of Tripoli, Germany, France, Spain, Belgium, Switzerland, the Eifel and Penya Rhin to become European – and German – Champion. Two years later, he again took the double crown, with the introduction of the more powerful W125 Mercedes; a new formula for 1938 saw the W154, with which Caracciola won the Swiss GP and Coppa Acerbo. He also drove a streamlined record car at 267 mph to set up a new 5-8 litre class record. The year 1939 saw Caracciola's last victory, the German GP, his sixth victory in this race.

He tried a comeback in 1946 at Indianapolis, having spent the war in Switzerland, but crashed in practice, sustaining more serious injuries.

In 1952 he drove his last Mille Miglia, after a 20-year interval, and finished fourth in a Mercedes 300SL. Rudi's career ended, following the 1954 Prix de Berne, when his car locked a wheel and skidded into a tree. Caracciola broke a leg, this time the other one, and had to retire from racing. He died in 1959.   DBW

FRANÇOIS CEVERT (1944-1973)
France

French, charming and good looking, 29-year-old François Cevert had reached the very pinnacle of his career as a Grand Prix driver and looked to be possibly the first Frenchman with the ability to win a World Championship when he was killed in practice for the United States Grand Prix at Watkins Glen on 6 October 1973. Driving one of Ken Tyrrell's Ford-engined Grand Prix cars as number two to Jackie Stewart, Cevert had won the United States Grand Prix in 1971 and finished second in five championship races through the 1973 season. At the time of his death, he was holding third place in the points table behind Stewart and Emerson Fittipaldi.

Born in Paris on 25 February 1944, the son of a jeweller, Cevert encountered some parental opposition to his taking up motor racing, as his father wanted him to devote his time to becoming a concert pianist. But François decided to set about earning sufficient money to pay his way at a motor racing school. He won the Volant-Shell competition at Magny Cours at the end of 1966, earning a drive in an uncompetitive Alpine-Renault for 1967. Despite having just one decent fourth place to his credit, Alpine offered him a works Formula Three drive for the following year, but he declined and purchased an Italian Tecno. Running with some financial help from the Sicli fire extinguisher concern, Cevert triumphed in the French Formula Three championship.

Tecno were extremely impressed by his performances and invited him to drive one of their 1600 cc Formula Two cars in the works team, alongside Nanni Galli, in 1969. He distinguished himself by winning the last major international on the Reims road circuit in France. He was just a tenth of a second clear of a pack which included his future team-mate and World Champion Jackie Stewart.

He was also invited to drive in the Matra works sports-car team from time to time and stayed with Tecno for Formula Two into the 1970 season. Fellow Frenchman Johnny Servoz-Gavin decided to retire from motor racing, following the Monaco Grand Prix at the end of May, thus vacating a place alongside Jackie Stewart in Ken Tyrrell's Grand Prix team; Cevert was selected to fill the place. At that time, the Tyrrell team was sponsored by the French Elf petroleum concern.

Cevert's Grand Prix debut took place in the 1970 Dutch Grand Prix at Zandvoort, where he drove Tyrrell's second March 701, but failed to finish. He scored his first World Championship point with a sixth at Monza and then continued as regular number two to Stewart into 1971. The first Stewart-Cevert 1-2 finish came with the Frenchman following the Scot home in the French Grand Prix and was followed up with a repeat performance in the German race, where Cevert took the Formula One lap record. He finished third in the Italian Grand Prix and then crowned a successful first Grand Prix year with a superb victory in the United States Grand Prix.

Throughout 1971 he had also been busy taking in a full Formula Two programme, with Elf, who were now backing the works Tecno team. The season started on a high note with wins at Hockenheim and Nürburgring, giving Cevert an early lead in the European Championship series. The Tecno team was also developing a new motor in anticipation of the 2-litre Formula Two regulations for 1972 and a spate of mechanical fragility ruined the Frenchman's chances. He ended up fifth overall in the championship and wrecked the car in the penultimate round where he was scalded by hot water when the car's cooling system burst.

1972 provided many disappointments, the Tyrrell team were apparently beset by problems, developing a new car and contending with Stewart's unfortunate stomach ulcer, which kept him out of one Grand Prix.

Cevert didn't sparkle with the older car and actually crashed the new Tyrrell 005 in practice for the French Grand Prix. This was followed by another accident in the British Grand Prix with the older car and a couple of disappointing races in Germany and Austria. However, by the time the United States Grand Prix at Watkins Glen came round again, Cevert was back on form to finish second to Stewart once more and the team shot back to the top.

In 1973, Cevert really came into his own. He opened with a splendid second place in Argentina, only conceding the lead to World Champion Emerson Fittipaldi very near the end of the race, he took an excellent second in Spain and a fourth at Monaco after a pit stop. In the Belgian Grand Prix at Zolder he looked absolutely uncatchable before spinning, although managing to fight back to second place. His season was topped off with a couple of close second places behind Stewart at both the Dutch and German Grands Prix, while he retired in the Austrian after an early misunderstanding and resultant collision with Merzario's Ferrari.

The 1973 season saw a much more mature Cevert who would probably have achieved number one status had he been recruited to any other team. He drove a Formula Two Elf to victory in the round-the-houses race at Pau in south-west France earlier in 1973, thus achieving one of his greatest personal ambitions.

His consistency in the World Championship races earned him second place in the points table at one stage in his final season's racing but Emerson Fittipaldi's second place, behind Ronnie Peterson, in the Italian Grand Prix pushed François back to third. It was while practising for the American Grand Prix at Watkins Glen, his final chance to win a Grand Prix in 1973 after having to retire in the Canadian, that Cevert's Tyrrell cannoned out of control into the guard rail and killed its talented driver. It was a great loss to France, for Cevert was due to lead the Elf Team Tyrrell challenge in 1974, alongside South Africa's Jody Scheckter, when Jackie Stewart retired from racing. The Tyrrell team withdrew from the race as a mark of respect to Cevert and a distraught Jackie Stewart.

Tall and good looking, with film star features (he could number Brigitte Bardot as one of his girlfriends), Cevert was single at the time of his fatal accident.   NB

LOUIS CHIRON (1900-1979)
Monaco

The principality of Monaco is so postage-stamp tiny, it is remarkable that it should have produced one of the most outstanding Grand Prix pilots of all time – Louis Chiron, who in a career spanning more than 35 years won numerous Grands Prix, including the race in his native Monaco which he played a large part in devising and organising.

Chiron was born in 1900 and, like so many of his generation, gained his first experience of motoring during World War I. Even at that age he must have been an outstanding driver, for it is recorded that in 1919 he was chauffeur to the great Maréchal Foch himself. The young Monegasque spent his early career working in the Hotel de Paris in Monte Carlo, and his love for motor racing was nurtured in this sybaritic atmosphere. He first appeared in competition in 1923 at the wheel of a Brescia Bugatti. He enjoyed little success until 1927, when he bought the first supercharged 2.3-litre type 35B Bugatti to be produced. He made his Grand Prix debut in the Spanish GP, taking over Dubonnet's Bugatti in the latter half of the race to such good effect that he could have finished in second place had not a breakdown, five laps from the end, eliminated him. Later that year, Chiron finished fourth in the British Grand Prix at Brooklands, behind the all-conquering Delage team.

It was a promising start to a racing career; in 1928, Chiron established himself as one of Europe's leading drivers, with a sensational victory in the European Grand Prix at Monza, averaging a record 99.4 mph over the 373-mile distance, and beating Campari and Nuvolari.

He followed this with victories in the Spanish, Antibes, Marne and Rome Grands Prix, all in the 1928 season. The Monza event was the only one run to the full international formula. Indeed, the two Spanish events, one for full GP cars, the other for sports cars, were won using the same Bugatti, fitted with wings and windscreen for the Touring Car Grand Prix.

Early in 1929, Louis Chiron crossed the Atlantic to compete in the Indianapolis 500. It was reported that four feet of snow had been shovelled from the surface of the Brickyard so that he could try a variety of American cars, but in the end he settled on a Delage, which proved completely outclassed by the Millers and could only manage seventh place.

Back in Europe, Louis le Debonair – his neat light blue racing suit and red-and-white polka-dot neckerchief were smart enough to evoke press comment – was on surer ground, and he proved it by winning the German GP at the Nürburgring and the Spanish GP. And he had also begun to carve his own individual niche in motor-racing history by devising, in conjunction with Anthony Noghès, the Monaco Grand Prix, run through the streets of Monte Carlo. Intended to give the Automobile Club de Monaco international status, the Monaco GP was first run in 1929, although Chiron's local knowledge did not avail him in the original race, won by Williams. In 1930, Dreyfus defeated him by just 22 seconds, but, in 1931, his Type 51 Bugatti did win at Monaco.

The 1930 season had, in any case, been rather disappointing for Chiron, whose record had been one of narrow defeats punctuated by a contrived victory in the European GP at Spa. 1931 was far more satisfactory, with victories in the French Grand Prix (co-driven with Achille Varzi) and the Czechoslovak GP (first of a three-in-a-row series of wins on the Brno circuit) as well as at Monaco.

The 1932 season opened badly for Chiron, who crashed at Monaco, almost rolling into the harbour, but he made up for this uncharacteristic lapse with wins in the Dieppe and Czechoslovak GPs, plus a number of successes with the four-wheel-drive Bugatti type 45. It was, however, increasingly apparent that the Bugatti was becoming outclassed, and Chiron moved over to Alfa Romeo. Initially he and Rudi Caracciola jointly operated the Scuderia CC on a private basis, but he subsequently joined the works-backed Scuderia Ferrari.

Chiron demonstrated that a decade with Bugatti hadn't made him a one-make man, by winning the Brno GP for the third time; he also took first places with the Alfa P3 in the Spanish and Marseilles Grands Prix, and won the 24-hour race at Spa in an Alfa 2.3 sports.

New, more powerful rivals had appeared on the scene in 1934, in the shape of the Nazi-backed Mercedes and Auto Unions, but Chiron managed to pull off one last coup, at Montlhéry, displaying all the gamesmanship that had earned him the nickname of *Le Vieux Renard* (The Old Fox). He made one of his characteristically quick starts that fractionally anticipated the fall of the flag, and forced the pace so hard that the German cars broke down, leaving the way clear for him to win.

In 1934, too, he looked as though he would be the first driver to win two Monaco GPs until, two laps from the end, he overdid things and went into the sandbag barrier, letting Guy Moll through to win. In 1936, Chiron again slid into the sandbags, this time driving a Mercedes, a marque with which he had no success at all.

Indeed, after that win of a lifetime in 1934, Chiron's career seemed to have plunged from zenith to nadir almost overnight – only a win in the sports car-orientated French Grand Prix of 1937, driving a 4-litre Talbot, redeemed the situation, and after that Chiron announced his retirement to the principality of Monaco.

Such a man does not bear inactivity lightly, however, and in 1938 Chiron was out again, driving a Delahaye at Le Mans.

He gave up racing for the war and resumed in 1946, but he did not get into his full stride until 1947, when his victory for Talbot in the French Grand Prix at Lyons was a Chiron classic.

After 135 miles, he had established a lead of 54 seconds, yet every time his Talbot came past the pits it was obvious that *Le Vieux Renard* was touring, apparently to save the tyres and brakes, for he looked happy and confident enough. It turned out that the head gasket had gone and the air of confidence was to bluff his rivals.

His last major victory was, fittingly, the Grand Prix of France in 1949, again driving a Talbot; after that he campaigned a Maserati for a couple of years, won the 1954 Monte Carlo Rally in a Lancia, and then gently faded from active competition, bowing out with a class win in the Mille Miglia at the age of 58.

Thereafter, at the invitation of Prince Rainier, Chiron became *Commissaire Général* of the Monaco Grand Prix and the Monte Carlo Rally, until his death in July 1979.   DBW

JIM CLARK (1936-1968)
Great Britain

Born on 14 March 1936 in Kilmany, Fifeshire, the son of a Border farmer, Jim Clark was widely acclaimed as one of the most complete Grand Prix drivers of all time. Driving Lotus Formula One cars built by Colin Chapman's team, this unassuming young man won a total of 25 World Championship Grands Prix between 1962 and his death in 1968. He was World Champion in 1963 and 1965 and won the Indianapolis 500 race at his third attempt in 1965.

Clark's motor sporting participation actual-ly started a short while after his 17th birthday, when he won a driving test at Winfield and, subsequently, started rallying in local events at the wheel of the family's Sunbeam Talbot 90. His talent was obvious to his many friends in the locality and it was through the generosity of one friend in particular, Ian Scott-Watson, that Jim Clark had his first car race, in 1956. He drove Scott-Watson's DKW saloon at the now-abandoned Charterhall circuit and was subsequently invited to drive in a locally organised team named 'Border Reivers' for 1958. At this time he was still working on the family's farm at Duns, Berwickshire, but during his spare time he managed to win twelve out of twenty races, driving the team's Jaguar D-type that season!

On 26 December 1959, Clark had his first outing at the wheel of a single-seater. He drove a Formula Junior Gemini at the Boxing Day Brands Hatch meeting and his talent was so obvious that he was invited by Reg Parnell to join the Aston Martin Grand Prix team. Unfortunately this project never got off the ground and Parnell released him from his obligations. In consequence, he signed to drive for Colin Chapman's Team Lotus at the start of 1960, the team he was to remain loyal to for the rest of his life.

The Lotus Formula Junior team, contesting an important championship for aspiring newcomers, provided its two drivers with the very effective Lotus 18s, and they were so well-matched that Clark and Trevor Taylor finished the season by sharing the Junior championship. In the meantime, he had the opportunity to drive at Le Mans with Roy Salvadori in an Aston Martin DBRI owned by 'Border Reivers'; they finished third, the best showing the car ever put up while owned by this private team.

Jim Clark's first opportunity in a World Championship Grand Prix came at Zandvoort in 1960, where he deputised for regular team member John Surtees, who had a clashing motor-cycle engagement. He worked his way up to fifth place before gearbox trouble caused his retirement. In the following weekend he took part in the Belgian Grand Prix, at Spa, as Surtees was missing again; this was a tragic weekend for Team Lotus, as Clark's team-mate Alan Stacey was killed during the race and both Stirling Moss and Mike Taylor, who were also driving Lotus cars, crashed very badly. He finished fifth in the Belgian Grand Prix and the French Grand Prix.

By this time, Clark was developing his confidence, the confidence which would elate thousands of racing fans all over the world in years to come. His style became smooth and he developed into an international driver of repute throughout a troubled 1961 season during which the works Lotus team, and most of its rivals, were outclassed by the powerful V6 Ferraris. Clark was sadly involved in the fatal accident that cost Wolfgang von Trips his life and took the lives of several spectators during the opening stages of the Italian Grand Prix at Monza, the Italian authorities bothering him for many years afterwards about this terrible tragedy.

1962 was the second season of the controversial 1½-litre Formula One. None of the British teams really believed that the FIA, the international governing body of motor sport, would change the formula at the end of 1960 from the 2½-litre limit which had been in effect since 1954. However, Ferrari settled down and developed the V6 which dominated the 1961 championship and Coventry Climax, who supplied all the British teams with their motors, came up with their response for the following year.

The great days of Jim Clark started at the beginning of the 1962 season. Colin Chapman designed an ultra-slim Grand Prix car of monocoque construction to house the Coventry Climax V8 and Clark quickly became the man to beat. Stirling Moss had retired from racing following a nasty crash at Goodwood on Easter Monday, leaving Clark to spar with Graham Hill's BRM for championship honours. The Lotus 25 made its debut in the Dutch Grand Prix, but retired, and it wasn't until the Belgian race that Clark scored the first of his 25 Grand Prix wins. The little green Lotus, with its yellow central stripe and blue helmeted driver sitting low in the cockpit, was to become a legend over the next few years. Despite an admitted dislike of Spa, the venue for the Belgian Grand Prix which winds and twists its way round public roads in the Ardennes, Clark was destined to take no fewer than four wins in that race.

In 1962, Clark's Lotus sped to victory at Spa, Aintree (the British Grand Prix) and Watkins Glen (United States Grand Prix) and it seemed certain that he would take his first championship in the South African Grand Prix. Indeed the young Scot was out on his own with his Lotus, half a minute ahead of the nearest opposition, when an oil leak cut short his championship aspirations and Graham Hill took the laurels for the BRM team.

Clark had only to wait until 1963. Again driving the Lotus 25, his tally included first place in the Belgian, Dutch, British, French, Italian, Mexican and South African Grands Prix. In addition to this devastating form, he shook the American establishment by taking a tiny Lotus to the much-hallowed 'Indy 500', finishing second behind Parnelli Jones in a controversial race. Many people felt that Jones should have been disqualified for dropping oil, but the American held on and won. Eventually the USAC establishment had to wake up: although Clark was put out of the 1964 race with broken suspension, he ran away with the 1965 Indy 500 and then finished second behind Graham Hill in 1966.

Back on the Grand Prix scene, his brilliance was undisputed. Inevitably it would be Jim Clark who shot onto pole position with the fastest time in the dying moments of practice, it was Jim Clark who had the uncanny ability of making brilliant starts...consistently. In 1964 it was the same familiar story, with wins in the South African, Dutch, Belgian and British Grands Prix. Then luck deserted him and he didn't win another Grand Prix all season long. Nevertheless it seemed as though he would clinch the championship in Mexico, but his engine broke with just over one lap left to go and John Surtees took the title. It was the second time that Clark had seen a world title slip away in the final moments of the last race of the season.

The Lotus 33, a sophisticated version of the 25, was just the car needed for 1965. On New Year's Day he opened his score by leading the South African Grand Prix from start to finish. Then he won the Belgian, French, British, Dutch, and German Grands Prix. He didn't go to Monaco as he was busy winning the Indy 500 on the same day, but he still clinched the World Championship for Drivers.

Another major change to international regulations came about at the start of 1966, leaving Team Lotus without a proven engine with the advent of the new 3-litre Formula One. With Graham Hill now in the team, alongside Clark, Chapman was forced to use the complicated H16 configuration BRM motor in his Lotuses for one season. Clark won just a single Grand Prix, at Watkins Glen, the only occasion that the H16 BRM engine finished first in any F1 race, championship or otherwise.

The Ford Motor Company commissioned Cosworth Engineering to design and build a 3-litre V8 for Formula One use. This astoundingly successful Cosworth DFV, which won every drivers' and constructors' World Championship from 1968 to 1974, made its debut in the 1967 Dutch Grand Prix, installed in Clark's brand new, equally radical Lotus 49. In time-honoured Clark fashion, the Scot scored a first-time win for the new combination and it was quite clear that Clark and the new Lotus-Ford posed quite the strongest force on the Grand Prix circuits. The Flying Scot was on top again.

Winning the British, United States and Mexican Grands Prix, he just failed to snatch the World Championship from Denny Hulme, but one of Clark's greatest ever drives was in the 1967 United States race where he completed the last three laps with a broken rear suspension, the right-hand rear wheel leaning in at a drunken angle. After a successful Tasman series in Australia and New Zealand, where he won the Australian Grand Prix, he celebrated the New Year in 1968 by winning the South African Grand Prix at Kyalami, racking up his 25th Grand Prix win and beating Fangio's ten-year-old record in the process.

Jim Clark, who by this time had been awarded the OBE, was killed in a mysterious accident in the rain at Hockenheim on 7 April 1968. In a race which didn't matter, on a pointless and featureless circuit, Clark's Formula Two Lotus 48 twitched suddenly in the wet on a flat-out bend and plunged into the tall pine trees which line the long straights. Several explanations for the accident have been offered, a popular one being that the car suffered a blow-out at near maximum speed which pulled the tyre completely over the rim of the wheel. Whatever the cause of the disaster, no satisfactory explanation ever came to light. Chicanes were built on Hockenheim's long, fast straights but it was just a gesture.

In that accident, motor racing lost its pace-setter, the man by whom others measured whether they were competitive or not. He was not just a great driver, but a complete driver as well; utterly versatile, equally at home 'three-wheeling' a Lotus Cortina (in which he won a British Saloon Car championship in 1966) as at the wheel of a Grand Prix Lotus. He set a new standard for his competitors to aspire to, realised his ability, but remained a charming and rather self-effacing individual to the end of his 32-year life.   NB

JOHN COBB *(1899-1952)*
Great Britain

In the early 1920s, it is said, a young man approached Malcolm Campbell in the paddock at Brooklands, and asked him for his autograph. That young man – John Cobb – later rode as passenger in a race, in Ernest Eldridge's Fiat, *Mephistopheles*. Eldridge, no mean driver himself, is reported to have said: 'This man will make a better driver than I.' Cobb's rise to fame was meteoric, and soon it was said: 'For handling really huge and difficult cars, he is already on a par with Parry Thomas, and there is every reason to suppose he will go further, for his time seems only just begun.' They were prophetic words, for Cobb went on to become a highly successful racing driver, the outright Brooklands record holder and the fastest man on earth.

John Cobb was born on 2 December 1899, and educated at Eton and Trinity; he was a city businessman whose wealth came from his fur-broking interests. He first appeared at Brooklands in competition, at the wheel of Richard Ward's 10-litre Fiat, at the autumn 1925 meeting, where he duly won his race. Cobb's victory, however, was overshadowed by another event at that meeting, the long-awaited match between Parry Thomas's Leyland-Thomas and Ernest Eldridge's giant Fiat, *Mephistopheles*.

For the next couple of years, Cobb enhanced his reputation with some stirring performances at the wheel of various powerful cars, including the Leyland-Thomas No. 1, *Babs*, the 10-litre Fiat and Jack Barclay's TT Vauxhall. Then came the chance to acquire one of the fastest cars in the world – one moreover which was admirably suitable for Brooklands. This was the celebrated 10½-litre, V12 Delage, which had first appeared at the Gaillon Hill-climb in 1923, and which the crack Delage driver René Thomas had driven to victory in countless events in France. In 1924, Thomas took this car to Arpajon where he set up a new world speed record of 143.3 mph, soon beaten by *Mephistopheles* at 146.01 mph.

The Delage company decided not to attempt to better Eldridge's record, for they felt that to tune the Delage's engine any further would be 'dangerous', and it was subsequently retired from competition and offered for sale. Seemingly, no-one was interested, until much later, when John Cobb came to hear of the car. He travelled to Paris, and within the space of twenty-four hours had purchased the Delage, complete with a spare engine and a host of extra parts, including a choice of seven rear axle ratios, for the bargain price of £350, shipped it aboard a Seine steamer bound for London, and celebrated his purchase with a champagne dinner. His confidence was not misplaced for, in its opening season, 1929, the big Delage annexed eleven British records, lapping at speeds in excess of 125 mph. Over the next three years, the Delage proved itself a remarkably consistent performer, perhaps the high-point of its career being a close-run match race with Birkin's Bentley in 1932.

In that same year, Cobb carried off the BRDC British Empire Trophy race at an average speed of 126.4 mph. However, he had an even more potent car on the stocks so, after the 1932 season ended, the Delage was sold to Oliver Bertram, a young barrister who was beginning to make a name as a racing driver. Eventually it passed into the hands of the Junior Racing Drivers' Club for the instruction and use of members. With the Delage, Cobb had raised the Brooklands outer circuit lap record to a remarkable 132 mph, but he was already looking ahead to the new season.

Cobb's new car, which was taking shape in the workshops of Thompson and Taylor at Brooklands, was revealed to the public in the summer of 1933, exciting much comment. In many ways, it was a modern equivalent of the aero-engined monsters of the 1920s, being powered by a 24-litre, twelve-cylinder Napier-Lion aviation engine, which had the cylinders set in arrow-head formation in three banks of four. Unlike earlier aero-engined giants, such as *Chitty-Chitty-Bang-Bang* and *Viper,* Cobb's car was a scientifically designed vehicle, having more in common with the sophisticated land speed record cars of the period than the conventional racing car. The chassis, very strong and deep, was typical of the work of the car's designer, Reid Railton, Parry Thomas's ex-assistant (who had also designed Malcolm Campbell's *Bluebird*). Everything about the car suggested solidity and reliability, which was amply borne out by its subsequent career, for among its many feats were numbered two victories in the BRDC '500', in 1935 and 1937, in 1935 the fastest-ever lap of Brooklands (143.44 mph), and the fastest speed (almost 152 mph) recorded at the track. In addition, it had travelled to Montlhéry (where, with Freddie Dixon at the wheel, it left the track and finished in the ditch) and Bonneville Salt Flats, Utah, in an attempt on the 24-hour record,

which was set up, with twenty other world records, in July 1935 at a speed of 134.85 mph. And all this was achieved without a hint of mechanical trouble.

In 1939, the partnership of Cobb and Railton again bore fruit, this time in the shape of a new land speed record contender. This *Railton Mobil Special* used twin 1250 bhp Napier aero-engines, mounted in an S-shaped backbone frame which allowed them to be mounted at an angle. This considerably reduced the car's overall width and frontal area: one engine drove the front wheels, the other the rear. The streamlined body had a frontal area of only 30 sq ft, which gave it a theoretical top speed of 400 mph plus in top gear. From rest, the car could reach 100 mph in ten seconds, still in first gear; Cobb changed into second at 150 mph, and into top at 250 mph. Cobb's enclosed cockpit was set well ahead of the front axle; the entire body shell lifted off to replenish the fuel tank and the ice and water tanks used for cooling so that no filler caps or hatches broke the car's smooth, highly aerodynamic surface.

Cobb successfully broke the record held by George Eyston's massive six-axled, eight-wheeled *Thunderbolt,* recording an average speed of 369.7 mph. After the war, in which he flew for the RAF and the Air Transport Auxiliary, Cobb made another attempt on the record. At Bonneville, he achieved an average of 394.18 mph with a one-way of over 400 mph, making Cobb the first man ever to achieve over 400 mph on land. The extent of that achievement in 1947 may be gauged by the fact that it was not until 1964 Donald Campbell beat Cobb's record.

Like Sir Malcolm Campbell, John Cobb also turned his attention to the world water-speed record. But on 29 September 1952, while travelling at speed on Loch Ness, Scotland, Cobb's jet boat *Crusader* exploded, killing the driver whose 'skill, courage and enterprise had inspired the admiration of the world'.   DBW

PETER COLLINS (1931-1958)
Great Britain

Before World War II, there were few British drivers considered worthy of inclusion in the top Grand Prix teams – in fact, only Dick Seaman had made it as a full works driver. However, out of the post-war boom in motor racing grew a small but talented band of British drivers who showed that they were the equals of the Continental aces. In this group were drivers like Mike Hawthorn, Stirling Moss, Tony Brooks and Stuart Lewis-Evans. Most of them pretended to be high-living playboys, using motor racing as a well paid means of seeing the world at someone else's expense, but behind the wheel they were as dedicated as their Continental counterparts, and all of them gained places in factory Formula One cars, which were all highly advanced.

Peter Collins was born at Kidderminster in 1931, the son of a garage proprietor, so it was inevitable that he should graduate to four wheels very early in life. In fact, at the tender age of 17, he was behind the wheel of a Cooper-Norton 500, the car that started many young men on their motor-racing careers. He soon showed the natural talent that all top drivers seem to possess and he began winning almost immediately. He spent three years in the cut and thrust of Formula 500 racing, a good deal of it on the Continent where he gained valuable experience, including wins in the inaugural International Trophy at Goodwood and Silverstone's first 110-mile race.

In 1951, John Heath and George Abecassis invited Collins, still only 20, to join their HWM Formula Two team, alongside Stirling Moss and Lance Macklin. The cars were not very successful but Collins showed that he was a fast and consistent driver. Subsequently he was signed by John Wyer for the 1952 Aston Martin sports-car team. He won the Goodwood 9-hour race with co-driver Pat Griffith and the following year won the TT at Dundrod, again with Griffith.

Tony Vandervell was beginning his bid to enter Grand Prix racing in 1954 and, while his Vanwall was being developed, he bought a 4½-litre Formula One Ferrari which he christened the *Thinwall Special,* after a type of bearing his company produced. Collins was signed to drive this car, further enhancing his reputation with some brave performances in *formule libre* races against the V16 BRM, very often beating the British car. Collins was asked to drive the 2.2-litre Vanwall in the Italian Grand Prix of 1954, where he finished a good seventh behind the works Mercedes and Ferraris.

Collins made it as a full time Formula One driver in 1955, when he was signed by the Owen Organisation to drive their 250F Maserati at the beginning of the season and then the new 2½-litre BRM. But the BRM wasn't ready until August and, although it was very fast, it had many problems. So, for 1956, Collins joined the Ferrari team to race the modified Lancia cars which had been handed to Ferrari when the Lancia team withdrew from racing. The car proved very much to Collins's liking and in 1956 he won both the French and Belgian Grands Prix as well as sharing the second place car at both Monaco and Monza with his team leader Fangio. In fact Collins's generous act of handing his car over to Fangio at Monza assured Fangio of the World Championship and earned for Collins the undying worship of the Italian motor-racing fans. Collins took third place in the World Championship that year. As well as his other placings in 1956, Collins finished third in the non-championship Syracuse GP and won both the punishing Tour of Sicily and Supercorte maggiore 1000 km races in Ferrari sports cars and finished a fine second in the Mille Miglia.

The year 1956 established Collins as one of the top five drivers in the world and, for 1957, he decided to remain with Ferrari, being joined in the team by his friend Mike Hawthorn. The two were inseparable, referring to each other as *'Mon ami* mate'. Unfortunately, the Lancia-Ferrari was outclassed in 1957 and Collins had to watch Fangio and Moss do most of the winning in the Maserati and Vanwall respectively, but he did finish third in the French GP and won the non-championship Syracuse and Naples Grands Prix. In sports car racing, he won the Venezuelan 1000 km and finished second in the Swedish GP and Nürburgring 1000 km.

With new cars for 1958, Ferrari were once again competitive and Collins remained with them, as did Hawthorn. The season started well with sports car victories at Buenos Aires and Sebring with Phil Hill as his co-driver, and he followed it up with a win in the International Trophy at Silverstone in the Formula One car. Then there was a third place in the Monaco Grand Prix and soon after he fulfilled a long-cherished ambition by winning the British Grand Prix at Silverstone, followed home by team-mate Hawthorn. In his next race at the German Grand Prix, on the difficult Nürburgring, Collins was chasing the leading Vanwall of Tony Brooks when, in attempting to pass the British car, his Ferrari slid into a grass bank and catapulted the driver into the woods bordering the track. Although he was flown to hospital by helicopter, the popular young driver was already dead. MT

EARL COOPER (1886-1965)
USA

Although not as well known as drivers like Barney Oldfield, Ray Harroun and Ralph de Palma, Earl Cooper was one of the most successful racing drivers in the pioneer days of American motor racing. At a time when racing in the USA meant being able to drive on road circuits as well as the ovals, Earl Cooper was three times national champion and very nearly won at Indianapolis too.

Early American professional motor racing was largely confined to track racing, either on small dirt or cinder ovals, or on the bigger half-mile board tracks or even bigger concrete bowls, of which Indianapolis was the first in the USA. However, there was a fair amount of road-racing, which was mostly confined to the east with events like the Vanderbilt Cup, but there were also a number of long-distance races in deserted California in the early days.

Born in 1886, Cooper took up motor racing in his early twenties, and spent several years doing the rounds of the dirt tracks with various cars, mostly in the California area. He was moderately successful and was making a decent living, since track-racing was fully professional right from the early days. Cooper's big break came in 1913 when he was invited to join the up-and-coming Stutz team, an achievement he celebrated by winning the American Automobile Association's national championship that year. His 1913 victories included a pair of wins at the Tacoma, Washington track over 200 and 250 miles, plus wins in the Santa Monica and Corona road races in California. In the Santa Monica race, he averaged an impressive 73.8 mph over a distance of 445 miles. At that time, Stutz used virtually standard production sports cars, so Cooper's wins against aces like Oldfield in much bigger racing cars were impressive feats. In 1914, Stutz announced the Bearcat model which, along with the Mercer Raceabout, became the symbol of American youth during World War I. The Stutz team had little success in 1914, even though Oldfield had joined the team. Cooper retired during his first attempt at the Indianapolis 500 mile race but Oldfield finished fifth.

Harry Stutz, the owner of the Stutz factory, realised that he would have to build a specialist racing car if he was to compete against foreign invaders such as Mercédès, so he built a 4.8-litre, single-overhead-camshaft, 16-valve engine, which gave 130 bhp, and installed it in a new chassis. Three cars were built and the main drivers were Cooper and Gil Anderson, the cars being painted white and the team named the White Squadron. Cooper was immediately successful with this car, winning the national championship for the second time with victories at Minneapolis, San Diego and Elgin, as well as fourth place at Indianapolis. Anderson also did well to finish third in the championship.

Stutz continued racing in 1916, but Cooper had few successes, although he did finish second in the Vanderbilt Cup to Resta's Peugeot. Stutz gave up racing at the end of that year so Cooper bought one of the White Squadron cars and won the national championship for the third time in 1917. At this stage, he decided to retire from racing at the comparatively early age of 31 but, in 1921, he was asked to take the place of an injured driver at a race in Fresno. In storybook form, he shrugged off his four-year retirement and won the race, which resulted in a contract to drive for the Durant team. No great success ensued with the Miller-powered Durants so, for the 1924 season, Cooper persuaded Studebaker to build a car powered by a Miller engine. Cooper finished second at Indianapolis as well as winning at Fresno.

He raced a Miller Special throughout 1925, winning the tough board-track race over 250 miles at Charlotte, North Carolina. Then, in 1926, he was invited to drive one of the legendary new front-wheel-drive Millers which had been developed for the new 1½-litre formula at Indianapolis. With this almost futuristic machine, he made fastest practice lap at Indianapolis, but transmission trouble put him out of the race. However, with the transmission repaired, he won the 200-mile race at the Rockingham board track only a month later. This was his last race victory but, in 1927, he was asked by the Marmon company to build a Miller-powered Marmon which he took to Europe for the European Grand Prix, held that year at Monza in Italy. With fellow American Peter Kreis as co-driver, he finished third in the 311-mile race, behind Robert Benoist's Delage and Morandi's OM.

That was his swan song in motor racing, for he finally retired in 1927 at the age of 41. He kept a close association with motor racing, though, serving as a race official with the AAA for many years and also working as a consulting engineer with the Union Oil Company. He died in 1965 at the age of 79.   MT

PIERS COURAGE (1942-1970)
Great Britain

Piers Courage was born on 27 May 1942, the first son of the Chairman of Courage breweries and therefore destined to inherit the vast fortune of the brewery family. However, like so many sons of wealthy fathers, he turned his back on the family business and began to make his own way in the precarious world of motor racing, with very little assistance from the family.

His upbringing was conventional for someone from his background; after preparatory school at Seaford, he went to Eton. This was an establishment he hated, partly because he was not a great scholar and partly because he disliked most games intensely, especially football and cricket. However, there was a car club at Eton which Piers joined, and through the club his love of motoring began in earnest. Several friends raced sports cars soon after they left Eton and Piers went along to watch, although he showed no early inclination to join them. He went off to Paris to learn French, working in a bookshop, and then went to college in Paris to learn French history, but he was rather rootless and was always taking time off from lectures.

On his return to England, he shared a flat with three motor racing enthusiasts, all of whom took up racing. Piers decided he wanted to join in and persuaded his father to buy him a Lotus Seven, which he built up from a kit of parts. His mechanical ability was not noticeable at that time, for the front suspension was put on upside down and the car had to be towed to the Lotus factory for them to put it right. However, he immediately began to race the Lotus and picked up a few places in club events.

For the following season, 1963, Piers bought an 1100cc Merlyn-Climax which was, at that time, quite a competitive car. He picked up a number of wins in British events and began to rate the odd mention in the specialised motor-racing press.

For two years he had been struggling along as a trainee accountant but he had little interest in the subject, threw it all up and moved to a flat in Harrow which he shared with Innes Ireland, Charles Lucas, Frank Williams, Jonathan Williams and Charles Crichton-Stuart; this flat has become famous in recent motor-racing history, for a succession of tenants were destined for great things in motor racing. For 1964, Courage decided to turn

professional and, together with Jonathan Williams, he formed a team called Anglo-Swiss Racing, bought a pair of Lotus 22s and barn-stormed round Europe taking part in every possible Formula Three race. The pair raced on a shoestring, usually sleeping in their cars and tending to the racing cars themselves, without the aid of mechanics, whom they couldn't afford. Piers never won a race that season but, for 1965, Charles Lucas took charge of the team, furnished Williams and Courage with F3 Brabhams and gave the team a very polished professional outlook. Courage suddenly showed his great potential by winning at a Silverstone international meeting and at Rouen; he also picked up a number of minor successes and began to attract notice from team managers.

In 1966, Charles Lucas was asked to run the factory team of Formula Three Lotus 41s and Courage led the team to a number of impressive victories both in England and abroad. That season he married Lady Sarah Curzon, daughter of Earl Howe, the pre-war racing driver, and she became an avid follower of her husband's career.

Courage's exploits during 1966 impressed the BRM team sufficiently for them to offer him a contract for the Tasman series in Australia and New Zealand during the winter 1966/67. He raced a 2-litre BRM for them but, despite being fast, he tended to spin off the track frequently and, although he was given a couple of Formula One drives by BRM when he returned to Europe, they soon dropped him in favour of Chris Irwin. Courage was signed by John Coombs to race his Formula Two McLaren-Cosworth during 1967, but a series of hair-raising spins and other off-course incidents hardly made up for the few places he gained. He was in a despondent frame of mind at the end of 1967 for it seemed that he was not going to make it to the top, for such was his reputation in motor racing circles that his nickname of 'Porridge' was applied to anyone who spun or did something wrong in a racing car: if anyone spun off, a trackside critic would say 'Fred's made a porridge of it'.

Despite his reputation, he was invited back to the Tasman series, with the McLaren which he had by now purchased from Coombs. This time he showed his true potential, taking three third places and one second, before winning the final race of the series in heavy rain. His 1600 cc car had been up against bigger-engined machines, including the works Lotus-Ford

2½-litre cars of Clark and Hill and such was the impression he made that he was invited to join Team Lotus as number two to Graham Hill after Clark's death, but he turned it down. Instead, he signed for the works-backed Tim Parnell team of BRMs and finished the season with a best placing of fourth in the Italian Grand Prix. He also raced a Brabham BT23 in Formula Two, for Frank Williams, in which he gained one victory.

He returned to the Tasman series in the winter of 1968/69 with a Formula One Brabham BT24, entered by Frank Williams and powered by a 2½-litre Cosworth-Ford engine. He gained a win, together with a second and a third place, and finished up third in the championship. On his return to Europe, Williams bought a Formula One Brabham BT26 for Courage and in this fine-handling car Courage did well, considering that it was privately entered; he took second place in the Monaco Grand Prix and the United States Grand Prix, as well as fifth places in England and Italy. His sixteen points gave him eighth place in the World Championship. He also raced a Brabham for Williams in Formula Two, putting up excellent performances.

For 1970, the Italian De Tomaso factory asked Frank Williams to run their Formula One car and, once again, Courage took the wheel for Williams. The car was not very competitive because it was rather heavy, but it picked up third place in both heats of the International Trophy at Silverstone and was running steadily in seventh place in the Dutch Grand Prix when the car suddenly left the track on a long 150 mph bend and crashed through the fencing. Piers was killed instantly although the car burned fiercely for some considerable time. Coming so soon after the death of Bruce McLaren, this plunged the motor-racing world into a furore about the safety of the sport and many changes were made both to racing cars and the tracks on which they raced as a result of these two crashes.   MT

SAMMY DAVIS (1887-1981)
Great Britain

Nowadays it is quite a common occurrence for a racing driver, flushed with success and equipped with a tape recorder and a ghost writer, to make a token attempt at motoring journalism. But for a writer of very real talent to become, in his 30s, a competition driver of international standard must be unique. Yet that is what happened to Sidney Charles Houghton Davis – otherwise known as 'Sammy' – born in London in 1887 and educated at Chislehurst, where one of his fellow pupils was the young Malcolm Campbell. The pair soon discovered a mutual fascination with wheeled vehicles, which resulted in a spectacular pile-up with a borrowed penny-farthing bicycle.

Soon, Davis was enthusiastically involved with motor vehicles and, after training as an illustrator, he joined Daimler as an apprentice, helping to build a wide variety of machines from Renard Road Trains to racing cars for the 1907 Kaiserpreis. His artistic talents were called into play to produce a series of 'rude little pictures' showing a sleeve-valve man triumphing over a poppet-valve man, with the aim of knocking Daimler's chief carriage-trade rival, Napier.

In 1910, he took up a new job, 'technical illustrator and general dogsbody', on the magazine *Automobile Engineer,* which was being launched by Iliffe, publishers of *Autocar;* soon he was writing about cars as well as drawing them, and laying the foundations of his motor-racing career by competing in trials with light cars.

Motoring played a large part in his World War I career, too, for he was with a Royal Navy armoured division. One of their spare-time activities consisted of climbing and descending a hill, first on a 3½ hp Douglas motor cycle, then in a Talbot truck, next on a Rolls-Royce armoured car and finally in a four-wheel-drive Jeffery Quad truck, the winner being the one who completed the course quickest without mishap.

After the war, Davis became Sports Editor of *Autocar,* in which capacity he helped his pre-war motor-cycling friend, W. O. Bentley, launch his new sports car.

S.F. Edge invited Davis (who managed to combine his sporting activities with the deadlines of his job) to join his Brooklands AC team in 1921, then, in 1922, he helped Aston Martin smash 32 world and class records at the Weybridge track. Around the same time, he began entering trials with an ABC flat-twin light car, which at first had a fantastic ability to seize solid on hills; Waverley, Aston Martin and Frazer-Nash were among other marques which he drove in contemporary road events.

In 1925, he drove a 3-litre, twin-cam Sunbeam at Le Mans with Jean Chassagne, and came within an ace of winning. The following year he was back, at the wheel of a 3-litre Bentley, which he contrived to crash 20 minutes from the end of the race while attempting to take the lead.

He crashed again at Le Mans in 1927, but this time it was an accident that became part of motoring mythology. Davis was driving the 3-litre Bentley known as 'Old Number Seven' into White House Corner when he noticed that the roadside fence had been damaged during his last lap, so he immediately slowed down. Just around the corner was a tangle of crashed cars, into which Davis managed to skid sideways to minimise damage. Even so, when he extricated the Bentley from the wreckage, he found it had a twisted chassis in addition to more superficial damage, yet managed to persuade the car to stay together long enough to win.

Davis was not just a Bentley Boy though for, in 1927, he won the Essex Six-hour race at Brooklands with a 12/50 Alvis, a marque to which he transferred his allegiance for the 1928 Le Mans, coming in ninth at the wheel of a 1500 cc, front-wheel-drive car, partnered by Urquhart-Dykes. Sammy also drove a Riley in that year's Tourist Trophy, while in 1929 he was in the Lea-Francis team, with a 1500 cc Hyper. He came second in the Saorstat Cup at Phoenix Park, Dublin and was also second in the Brooklands Double-Twelve and 500-mile races.

In between times, he acquired an 1897 Bollée tri-car in France, his enthusiasm for such antique vehicles leading him to become one of the three founders of the Veteran Car Club in 1930. Davis, who wrote under the pseudonym 'Casque', and his assistant, L. V. Head ('Caput'), campaigned the Bollée – christened *Beelzebub* – in pre-war Brighton Runs; indeed, Davis continued to drive *Beelzebub* in the Brighton Run until the late 1960s, when he was entering his 80s, his doctor then warning him that this sort of activity was hardly suitable for an octogenarian. The Bollée was sold to the Indianapolis Speedway Museum.

The year 1930 was a vintage, as well as a veteran, one for Davis, for the little Austin Seven he co-drove with the Earl of March won the Brooklands 500-mile race at the astonishing average of 83.41 mph, then added to its fame by carrying off several Class H records, including a flying kilometre at 89.08 mph. On that occasion, Davis's co-driver was Charles Goodacre. Sammy's successes during the season were so numerous that he was awarded a BRDC Gold Star. Off the track, he drove a Double-Six Daimler in the Monte Carlo Rally, an event in which he subsequently entered a Railton tourer, an Armstrong Siddeley and a Sunbeam-Talbot; the Wolseley he drove in this event in 1937, won a special award for being the best equipped vehicle to finish.

Davis's racing career came to an abrupt hiatus at Brooklands in 1931, when the low-chassis Invicta he was driving skidded into a telegraph pole. During his spell in hospital, he wrote the classic book *Motor Racing*.

In 1935, he was driving a Singer Nine in the TT when a ball-joint in the steering fractured, and the car left the road, rolling over on Norman Black's sister car, which had crashed at the same spot for the same reason. Despite the serious nature of the crash, Davis escaped this time without injury, apart from a scratch where his helmet had been knocked off.

Long after his retirement from active competition, Davis – with his habitual beret and pipe – was a familiar figure at motor-sporting venues and, when well into his 80s, the seemingly indestructible Sammy was still writing, drawing and painting with unabated vigour. On his 94th birthday tragedy struck: Sammy suffered a heart attack, apparently knocked over a paraffin heater in his home and died in the ensuing fire.   DBW

EMMANUEL DE GRAFFENREID (b.1914)
Switzerland

Baron Emmanuel De Graffenreid is a fine example of the wealthy, independent amateur racing driver whose heyday was in the pre-war and immediate post-war years, long before sponsorship or factory teams offered drivers the chance to become fully professional. Born in Fribourg, Switzerland, de Graffenreid went into the garage trade and, in 1936 he took up racing with a 1½-litre six-cylinder Alfa Romeo. He won his class in his first-ever race, at Berne, a victory which encouraged him to go in for something more powerful for the 1937 season. Partnered by an old friend, John du Puy, he bought a pair of Maseratis and the two men raced all over Europe, gaining much experience if little success. De Graffenreid kept his 6C Maserati until the war, winning his class at the odd meeting.

Switzerland was neutral during the war and

de Graffenreid stayed there, but as soon as hostilities ceased he was itching to get back into racing, so he bought a new four-cylinder Maserati for the 1946 season and teamed up with fellow countrymen Christian Kautz and Basadonna to race it. He picked up a fifth place at the Grand Prix des Nations at Geneva in 1946 and a third place at Lausanne in 1947. In 1948 he finished third in the Monaco GP and also second in the GP des Nations.

The old Maserati was pensioned off in 1949 to be replaced by a 4CLT/48 Maserati which de Graffenreid drove in a loose sort of team with Prince Birabongse 'Bira' of Siam under the patronage of an Argentinian, Enrico Platé. When the drivers went to the same race they would send their cars in one transporter, thus easing transport costs but the drivers would sometimes go their separate ways or even drive other people's cars when the opportunity arose. De Graffenreid's best ever win came in 1949 when he won the British Grand Prix at Silverstone, benefiting from the retirements of Bira and Villoresi. He later admitted that Silverstone was one of his favourite tracks, partly because it was the scene of his only major Grand Prix win and partly because he disliked racing on tracks bordered by trees and other hard objects. He had an instinctive dislike of tracks like Monaco and his own Berne circuit, especially in the wet, because he knew that a mistake would almost certainly mean injury and a very expensive rebuild, which the team could ill afford. Nevertheless he took second places in the Dutch GP, the Swedish GP and the Jersey Road Race.

The 4CLT Maserati was retained for 1950 and he gained a few minor placings, but the highlight of his career was when Alfa Romeo asked him to drive their legendary Type 158 blown 1½-litre Formula One car at the Geneva GP. He finished a good second and was also asked to drive in the 1951 Swiss and Spanish GPs, where he finished fifth and sixth respectively. It must be admitted that Alfa Romeo's interest was not entirely unconnected with the fact that de Graffenreid had been appointed their agent for the Lausanne area in 1950.

Formula One was abandoned in 1952 in favour of the 2-litre Formula Two, so the Platé team redesigned the 4CLT/48 Maserati by shortening the chassis and removing the supercharger. Although his only Grand Epreuve placing was a sixth at the Swiss GP he took several good placings in minor events.

With a new F2 Maserati for 1953 he took on a new lease of life. In World Championship races he was placed sixth in the Dutch GP, fourth in the Belgian, and fifth in the German GP, while in non-championship events, he won the Syracuse GP, the Eifelrennen at the Nürburgring and both the Freiburg and Ollon-Villars Mountain-climbs. He also won a heat in the International Trophy at Silverstone but jumped the start in heat two and retired when he was penalised by one minute.

In 1954, with a 2½-litre formula now in being, he fitted a 2½-litre engine to the Maserati and took it and a sports 2-litre Maserati to South America; he finished eighth in the Argentinian GP with the single-seater, but with the sports car he won the Rio de Janeiro GP at Gavea and the São Paulo GP at Interlagos. He did not contest many European races, because he knew the car was outclassed, and in 1955 he retired from racing after finishing third in the Venezuelan GP in a 3-litre Ferrari, behind Fangio and de Portago, and second in the Lisbon GP in a 3-litre sports Maserati.

He retired to his garage business in Lausanne, selling Alfa Romeo and Rolls-Royce cars among others, but he made a short return to the track when he drove for the film *Such Men Are Dangerous*. Although long-retired from racing, de Graffenreid has retained close links with the sport and in recent years has acted as a roving ambassador for the Marlboro cigarette company which has sponsored several teams in Formula One racing. MT

RENÉ DE KNYFF (1864-1954)
Belgium

Of all the drivers of the first generation of racing cars, the most successful was the Chevalier René de Knyff, a portly, bearded figure, whose habitual headgear was a yachting cap. Born in Belgium in 1864, de Knyff always raced for France; indeed, he always drove Panhards, for he was a director of that company. Like so many of his competitors, he was originally connected with cycle racing, although as a manager rather than as a rider (Gaetan de Knyff was the racing cyclist of the family), and as early as 1891 he had earned the reputation of being an excellent sportsman.

In 1892 he became a director of the magazine *Revue des Sports,* a position which he held for many years: this was reckoned to be the leading cycling journal.

De Knyff's racing career began in January 1897, in the three-day Marseilles-Nice-La Turbie event, driving a 6 hp Panhard and wearing a large pair of goggles which took the public fancy considerably; he came fourth, having averaged 17.4 mph over the 149 miles total racing distance.

During July of that year, he took part in the Paris-Dieppe event, driving one of the new Panhard racers which incorporated carburettors, gearboxes and lubricators cast from aluminium by Maxime Corbin in order to reduce their all-up weight. Despite this, he could manage no better than fifth in his class and fifteenth overall, well behind his teammates Gilles Hourgières and Fernand Charron. There was further technical innovation in the Paris-Trouville race the following month, for the works Panhards all had the new lightweight Grouvelle & Arquembourg gilled-tube radiators; this time de Knyff did better, recording fourth place in his class and sixth overall.

Then, in May 1898, came his first victory, in the famous 'Criterium des Entraineurs', organised by *Le Vélo* over the 356½-mile course from Paris to Bordeaux and back. He led the two-day event from the start, and won by over two hours, at an average speed of 22.1 mph. Next came the Paris-Amsterdam-Paris contest, which took on a musical comedy air from the persistent interference of one M. Bochet, the Paris police engineer, who raked up an obsolete bylaw, which insisted upon the competing cars having a certificate to prove that they were safe to drive on the roads, and threatened to mow them down with a half-squadron of the 23rd Hussars and two guns placed in the middle of the road if they defied him (for he had refused most of the cars permission to race). The problem was resolved by shifting both start and finish outside M. Bochet's jurisdiction; de Knyff, driving one of the new 8 hp Panhards with wheel instead of tiller steering, came fourth, having averaged 25.4 mph over 889.25 miles.

He came second in the 1899 Paris-Bordeaux event, only eight minutes behind Charron, also driving a 12 hp Panhard, one of the first true racing cars.

The main race of 1899 was the Tour de France, a 1350-mile marathon, starting and finishing at Paris; de Knyff was in front virtually all the way, winning by over five hours at an average speed of 30.2 mph.

He started the 1900 season with a notable victory, too, driving the car with which he had won the Tour de France, but with a bigger engine and with 200 kg taken off the weight. De Knyff led the Circuit du Sud-Ouest, a 209-mile event centred on Pau, with this vehicle, only to have his lubricating pump pack up just before the finish. However, he hurtled across the line in first place, enveloped in an acrid blue cloud of oil smoke, with the engine seized solid, having averaged 43.8 mph, three-quarters of an hour ahead of the next man.

A month later, in March, the Automobile Club of Nice organised a race from Marseilles to Nice and back, for which de Knyff entered his Panhard (doubtless fitted with a new power unit). Before the race, the car was parked beside the road, in gear and with the ignition burners alight. Gilles Hourgières drove up behind it in his Panhard 12 hp, failed to stop in time, and slammed into the back of de Knyff's car – which promptly started, and, driverless, dashed into a barrier before it could be stopped. Fortunately, it was undamaged, and de Knyff was able to start and win, even though bad weather caused the race to be abandoned at the halfway stage.

After the event, de Knyff's car was sold to a young American, Bostwick, who used it to take third place in the Bordeaux-Périgueux race, made an instant reputation as a first-class driver, and then vanished from the scene.

De Knyff was chosen to drive a 20 hp Panhard in the first Gordon Bennett race, but was forced to retire when the gearbox broke. Ill-luck attended him in the Paris-Toulouse-Paris competition that year, too, for his 24 hp Panhard was so plagued with punctures that he retired.

The Paris-Berlin race of 1901, the season's leading event, saw de Knyff at the wheel of a 40 hp Panhard, with which he took third place; but a further power uprating, to 70 hp, for the 1902 Circuit du Nord, brought transmission problems which forced him out of the race. It was gearbox trouble, too, which eliminated him from the combined Paris-Vienna/Gordon Bennett event in 1902, giving the victory to S.F. Edge of Britain.

A broken camshaft put de Knyff out of the 1903 Paris-Madrid, while his last major success was a second place behind Jenatzy's Mercédès in the 1903 Gordon Bennett Cup. From then on he devoted himself to the organisational side of motor sport, as President of the Commission Sportive of the Automobile Club de France from its foundation in 1899 to 1926, and also as president of the Commission

Sportive Internationale from 1922 to 1946.

During his racing career, René de Knyff had not had a single accident. On 13 May 1905, he and the journalist Charles Faroux were driving out to inspect the Gordon Bennett course in a powerful 100 hp Panhard racer when a cow wandered into the road. The peasant woman who owned it rushed after the beast: in trying to avoid her, de Knyff hit the cow broadside on, wrecked the car and disembowelled the cow. He and Faroux hurtled through the air to land on the road with broken ribs, cracked collar-bones and other injuries.

Fortunately, they both recovered and survived to ripe old ages, de Knyff dying in 1954 at the age of 90.   DBW

PATRICK DEPAILLER (1944-1980)
France

Patrick Depailler was born on 9 August 1944 and in fact started his racing career on two wheels, in 1962, at the age of eighteen. At that time, he was backed by Jean-Pierre Beltoise, who also raced bikes and who was also to make a name for himself in Formula One car racing. Depailler campaigned a Norton 500 in those days and proved to be quite successful in national events, although it was not to be too long before he turned his attention to four wheels. In 1966 he represented his province in a novice Lotus 7 championship and at the same time enrolled for a racing-driver course at the Magny-Cours circuit. He finished an encouraging second in the end-of-term Volant-Shell awards and was beaten only by François Cevert, yet another contemporary who was to make the grade in Formula One.

Bitten by the bug, the architect's son from Clermont-Ferrand joined the Alpine Renault team on a three-year contract as mechanic and test driver. He gained some useful experience with the team and took his first major victory at the 1967 Formula Three Paris Grand Prix. As well as completing in single seaters, Depailler was able to drive the team's Gordini-powered three-litre sports cars and took a fine third place in the Monza 1000 km race in an A211 in 1968. Formula Three was the obvious place to be, however, and he concentrated on this formula until 1970 when he accepted a drive with Marius dal Bo's Pygmée Formula Two team. Beltoise and Jabouille also raced those cars that year, but their combined talents and enthusiasm could not make up for a lack of funds and the outfit was disbanded.

It was back to Formula Three in 1971 and, with a well-sorted Alpine-Renault Depailler took that year's French national championship, with some spirited drives. For the next three seasons, Depailler concentrated on Formula Two again and his perseverance paid off when he took the European Formula Two Championship in 1974 with his works March-BMW 742. That championship only confirmed his talent to Formula One teams for back in 1972 he had driven to victory in the prestigious Monaco Formula Three race and greatly impressed Ken Tyrrell, who wasted no time in signing him up for two Grands Prix, the French and the American. But, with both places in the Tyrrell team secured, there was no chance of a regular F1 drive, although Depailler was given the options on the North American races in 1973. A biking accident cost him these races, however, and Depailler thought that he had lost his chance of driving for Tyrrell; but fate was to play a part. François Cevert was killed in practice at Watkins Glen and Jackie Stewart was retiring, so the Tyrrell team had no drivers for the new season. Depailler was contacted, and signed up to drive as number two to Jody Scheckter.

Depailler's best result that year was second place, behind his team-mate, in Sweden. He followed up with some more encouraging drives for Tyrrell in the following seasons with both 007 and the P34 six-wheeler, and again followed Scheckter home in Sweden in 1976. Tyre problems hampered development of the innovative multi-wheeler, and behind new team-mate Peterson in 1977 things were very much on the lean side.

In 1978 Depailler was given a clean sheet with a new Maurice Phillipe-designed four-wheeler, the position of team leader and technical maestro Karl Kempf on hand with computers to work out the car's problems. In South Africa that year, it seemed as though Depailler would improve on his seven Grand Prix second places when he led into the last lap with an ailing car, but he did not reckon on a hard-charging Ronnie Peterson and had to give best to his old team-mate, now with Lotus. It seemed impossible that the amiable French driver could be kept off the winners' rostrum for much longer. Again it was Monaco that provided the setting for a major stepping stone in Depailler's career, and he crossed the finishing line first, comfortably ahead of the Brabham of reigning World Champion Niki Lauda.

Thereafter, the season went downhill and it was apparent that it had been Depailler's determination to overcome a bad-handling chassis that gave him that first win. After a series of retirements and poor placings, a turn away from the Tyrrell camp was needed. Guy Ligier was at hand to snap up the 34-year-old at the end of the season, in the hope that his experience would prove useful and help the team to achieve success with their new Cosworth-powered JS11 car.

South America 1979 was something of a fairy tale for the Ligier team and twice Patrick shared a front row grid position with his team-mate Jacques Laffite. In the two races, in Argentina and Brazil, he scored a fourth place and a second and it immediately became clear that the Ligiers were the cars to beat. After a disastrous performance in South Africa, where he crashed after just four laps, and then a hard fought fifth place at Long Beach, Depailler took the French-blue JS11 to victory in the Spanish Grand Prix at Jarama. The win gave him the joint lead in the World Championship with Gilles Villeneuve. From the front row he led the Belgian Grand Prix, only to crash on the 46th lap. He finished fifth in Monaco and may have been in a position to challenge for the championship, but at the beginning of June he suffered serious leg injuries in a hang-gliding accident which kept him out of the cockpit for the rest of the season and rather soured relations with the Ligier hierarchy.

When Depailler made his comeback at the beginning of the 1980 season it was with Alfa Romeo. He retired from seventh place in Argentina and although the Alfa improved through the year he did not finish another race. Seemingly back on the verge of real success, Depailler was testing at Hockenheim just before the German Grand Prix when his Alfa crashed inexplicably at very high speed into an unprotected barrier. He was killed instantly and motor sport lost a true enthusiast whose results never adequately reflected an immense talent.   BL

RALPH DE PALMA (1883-1956)
USA

Considered by many as the greatest racing driver the United States has ever known, Ralph de Palma was indeed one of the most successful. Over a 27-year period, he participated in approximately 2800 speed events and won over 2500 of them. Above all else, he was a

pleasant, friendly man, always willing to offer advice and assistance, even to rival teams. A true sportsman, he accepted defeat with grace.

De Palma, one of four brothers, was born in southern Italy in 1883, and taken to the United States by his parents ten years later. He soon forgot his native tongue and became accepted as an American. He began racing in 1908, a time when dirt- and board-track racing was prevalent – road-racing was then outlawed and Indianapolis had not been built. From the start, he was a success and was recognised as the leading dirt- and board-track driver. Soon he was competing in sand races, on closed road tracks and, in 1911, in the first Indianapolis 500-mile race.

The 1912 Indianapolis 500-mile race is often cited as an example of de Palma's sportsmanship. Driving his sleeve-valve Mercédès Grey Ghost, de Palma seemed an easy winner when a piston collapsed with only ten miles to run. Running on three of its four cylinders, the Mercédès was nursed round while second man Joe Dawson's National began to make up its five-lap deficit. As de Palma completed his 198th lap, Dawson was only three laps behind and racing at twice the speed. Three-quarters of a lap later the Mercédès coughed its last and de Palma said to his riding mechanic, Australian Rupert Jeffkins: 'I guess it's time to start walking, and we might as well take the car with us.'

As the pair pushed their heavy Mercédès, the National completed its three laps to win the victor's laurels. However, the crowd's cheering was shared between Dawson and de Palma, who took defeat like a man. Utterly exhausted, de Palma went up to his young rival, shook his hand and warmly congratulated him.

Also that year, de Palma had his most serious accident. In the 1912 Grand Prize road race near Milwaukee, he crashed on the last lap, while attempting to overtake a rival, Caleb Bragg. Seriously injured and bleeding, he was brought back to race headquarters in the ambulance. In being taken out, he saw press reporters and whispered to them: 'Boys, don't forget that Bragg wasn't to blame. He gave me all the road.'

In 1914, the French Peugeot team arrived in America for the Indianapolis 500-mile race and team manager W.F. Bradley told de Palma that his drivers didn't know the turns well. De Palma said to them: 'Just tuck yourself in behind me for a few laps and I will show you the best place to enter the bends.'

De Palma's most meritorious victory came in 1914. The previous year he had been appointed captain of the Mercer team, but the American cars were frail and it was only early in 1914 that they began to show reliability as well as speed. The Vanderbilt Cup race, run around the roads at Santa Monica, was to be held at the end of February and, for this event, Mercer executives went behind de Palma's back and hired Barney Oldfield. This so upset de Palma, who was not consulted until after the deal, that he resigned on the spot.

What car was he to race? His old friend E. J. Schroeder brought de Palma's Mercédès Grey Ghost out of retirement, hastily prepared it and rushed it to California where practice had already commenced. De Palma's practice laps were 40 secs slower round the 8-mile circuit than Oldfield or the other Mercer drivers; prospects looked poor.

In the early stages, de Palma was well out of the reckoning, but steady and reliable driving was rewarded with fifth place as the race progressed. Then the leader crashed; Oldfield had to stop for oil and tyres; a broken propeller shaft eliminated another leader. De Palma and the Mercédès Grey Ghost were ahead! On the 25th lap, with ten to go, Oldfield's superior speed told, and he retook the lead. He didn't draw away, however, as de Palma used every tactic in the book to remain in contact, slipstreaming to great advantage.

De Palma had not made a pit-stop, but he could see Oldfield would probably have to, as his wild driving was causing the tyres to wear rapidly. On one lap, knowing that Oldfield was watching him, de Palma slowed as if to come into the pits, Oldfield felt that the race was now his, reckoned he had a comfortable lead and, to play safe, decided to stop next time round for new tyres. As he sat in the pits the old Grey Ghost raced by into the lead. De Palma had never stopped; he had eased off to lure Oldfield into thinking he had! Try as he might, Oldfield could not reduce the deficit and had to be content with second place.

European racegoers saw de Palma compete in the 1912 and 1914 French Grands Prix. Driving a Fiat, he was disqualified on the first occasion owing to his being unfamiliar with the refuelling regulations. In 1914, as a member of the Vauxhall team, gearbox trouble put him out. He also went to Germany (only a few days before the outbreak of World War I) to purchase a new Mercédès. He took it back to the United States where he won several

important races, which included the 1915 Indianapolis 500-mile race.

In 1919, working at Packard, de Palma developed the well known Liberty engine; also, with a 15-litre V12 Packard, he smashed the measured-mile record at Daytona Beach at 149.87 mph. The following season saw de Palma become a member of the French Ballot team. After some American events, he raced for the team in the 1921 French Grand Prix at Le Mans, finishing second to his compatriot Jimmy Murphy in the American Duesenberg. However, Ballot and de Palma had their disagreements, one of them concerning the French race.

De Palma and his nephew Peter de Paolo, his riding mechanic, devised a system of which Ballot disapproved. Not quite automatic transmission – de Palma arranged a neat gear-change manoeuvre whereby he would signal and declutch while de Paolo changed gear! This enabled de Palma to keep both hands on the steering wheel and, perhaps, gain a fraction of a second here and there. Ballot happened to witness these actions and insisted the gear lever be moved to the right-hand side, out of de Paolo's reach.

Back in the United States, de Palma continued racing until 1934, still winning and establishing records although well into his 40s. He drove for Duesenberg, Packard and Miller in major races and then concentrated on 'exhibition' races on the smaller tracks, such as those on which he had started his career. He also peformed record-breaking and endurance trials for Chrysler.

The Depression of the 1930s, however, meant that it was no longer profitable to race and, at the age of 51, de Palma finally retired. He became a consultant engineer to the Mobil Oil Co and was busily employed by them until his death in 1956. He was 73.   MK

MARK DONOHUE (1937-1975)
USA

Mark Donohue, who died after a practice accident at the Austrian Grand Prix in 1975, was one of the most distinguished of the United States' large number of racing drivers who began to invade the world's race tracks in the 1960s.

Born in Summit, New Jersey in 1937, Donohue soon showed an aptitude for things mechanical, and graduated from Brown University in mechanical engineering.

He went into industry, but soon his interest in motor racing began to lure him away from his chosen career. He started off with a Chevrolet Corvette which gave him victory in his first-ever event in a hill-climb. He soon moved on to circuit racing in the amateur SCCA (Sports Car Club of America) events and, in 1961, he won the production car category in class E of the SCCA national championships, with an Elva Courier. He seemed destined to remain in the ranks of the amateurs despite his undoubted talent, but by 1965 he had transferred to single seaters and, when he won the Formula C championship in a Lotus 20, he came to the notice of Walt Hansgen, then one of America's top sports-car drivers.

Hansgen obtained a drive for Donohue in John Mecom's Ferrari, alongside Hansgen, but the pair gained no great success. However, his drive led to an invitation to join the Ford works team and drive the big 7-litre Mk II sports cars in 1966. Partnered by Hansgen, Donohue drove the Ford into third place at the Daytona 24 hours of 1966 and followed it up with second place in the Sebring 12 hours. Tragically, Hansgen was killed at the Le Mans test weekend, but Donohue drove at Le Mans, only to retire.

By this time, Donohue had come to the notice of Roger Penske, the very successful ex-racing driver who had built up a busy Chevrolet dealership in Philadelphia. Penske was running a racing team of his own, and asked Donohue to drive in the new Can-Am championship for sports cars in a Lola-Chevrolet which was dubbed the Sunoco Lola after the team's sponsor. Donohue was immediately successful, for he finished fifth in his first outing at Bridgehampton, then won the Mosport round and followed up with two fourth places at Laguna Seca and Riverside and a third place at Las Vegas. His points total brought him second place to John Surtees in the Can-Am championship.

For 1967 Donohue stayed with the Penske team, but less success came his way because the McLaren team was beginning its annihilation of the American stars. However, he placed the Lola second at Road America and third at Riverside, and was leading the final round at Las Vegas when his car ran out of fuel. He also drove for the Ford team in a few of the World Sports Car Championship races, but his only finish was at Le Mans where he came in fourth, partnered by Bruce McLaren. During 1967, he

also won the less prestigious US Road Racing championship in the Penske Lola.

By 1968, Penske and Donohue had discovered that they worked well together, for Donohue, with his engineering background, had become a fine test driver, while Penske insisted on immaculate preparation of his cars. Penske had been nicknamed 'God' by American journalists while Donohue became known as 'Captain Nice' because of his unfailing good manners and pleasant outlook, as well as his 'all-American boy' chubby good looks and crew-cut hair style. Such was the bond between the two, that Donohue stayed with the Penske team until his death.

The 1968 season was busy for Donohue, as he drove the Penske Chevrolet Camaro in Trans-Am saloon car races, winning no less than ten of the thirteen events, which gave him the championship. He also raced a McLaren M6A in the Can-Am series, winning the Bridgehampton round, finishing second at Riverside and third at both Edmonton and Road America. If he had won the final round at Las Vegas he could have clinched the Can-Am title, but his car refused to start on the grid. As well as winning the US Road Racing championship again in the Lola, he took the Penske Camaro to the Daytona 24 hours and finished 12th, then finished third at Sebring, both times co-driven by Craig Fisher.

By 1969, Roger Penske had decided he could not hope to beat the McLaren team in Can-Am racing, so he decided to switch his attention to Indianapolis. Donohue drove the new Lola T 152 four-wheel-drive car, powered by a turbo-charged Offenhauser engine. Despite never having been to Indianapolis before, he qualified fourth fastest and finished the race in seventh place to win the Rookie of the Year award. He also drove a Camaro to six victories in the Trans-Am series, to clinch the title for Chevrolet again, and teamed up with Chuck Parsons to win the Daytona 24 hours in Penske's Lola coupé.

The Penske team transferred their allegiance to the American Motors Javelin for the 1970 Trans-Am series, and Donohue picked up three wins and three seconds to take second place to Parnelli Jones's Mustang in the championship. At Indianapolis, he drove a Lola T 153-Ford and finished in a fine second place on the same lap as the winner, Al Unser, earning over £30,000 for the team. Noting the increasing interest in Formula A racing in America, which was the equivalent of

Europe's Formula 5000, Penske entered a Lola T192-Chevrolet for the last few races of the Continental championship. Donohue showed that he was perfectly at home in a big single-seater on a road course by winning at Sebring and Mosport, and finished third at Mid-Ohio.

For 1971, the Penske team took on a new project by rebuilding a 512M Ferrari sports car. This was immaculately prepared to Penske's high standards and, co-driving with Britain's David Hobbs, Donohue finished third at Daytona and sixth at Sebring, but retired at Le Mans when the engine seized. In the Trans-Am series, Donohue again drove the Javelin, and this time won the championship for American Motors.

Penske acquired a McLaren M16 for Indianapolis, and with it Donohue led the race, but eventually had to retire with gearbox trouble. However, the team took in more USAC Indianapolis-style races and Donohue won the Pocono 500-mile race in the McLaren, but ran out of fuel while leading the California 500 race. To get a taste of Formula One racing, Donohue drove a McLaren M19 in the Canadian Grand Prix towards the end of 1971, and finished a comfortable third in his first ever Formula One race.

For 1972, Roger Penske arranged to use the very powerful turbocharged 917/10 Porsche in Can-Am racing. Donohue started off with a second place at Mosport, but was then injured in a practice crash which kept him out of racing until October. However, before the crash, he had taken part in the Indianapolis 500 and won the race in an exciting finish when he took the lead with only 13 of the 200 laps left. He was driving the Penske Sunoco McLaren M16B, powered, once again, by a turbocharged Offenhauser engine.

After recovering from his injuries, Donohue showed that he had lost none of his skill, for he won the Edmonton Can-Am race and followed up by finishing second to team-mate George Follmer at Laguna Seca and third at Riverside. Even though he missed five Can-Am races, Donohue still finished fourth in the championship table.

In 1973, the Penske team, affectionately known as the 'Penske Panzers', had the use of improved Porsche 917/30 turbocharged Can-Am cars, the 5.4-litre engines of which gave over 1000 bhp, making them almost certainly the most powerful road-racing cars ever used. Donohue ran away with the Can-Am championship, winning the races at Watkins

Glen, Mid-Ohio, Elkhart Lake, Edmonton, Laguna Seca and Riverside. It was said that the 917/30 was so fast that Donohue purposely drove 'slowly', just to make the races more interesting. He would have won the remaining two races, but a collision in one race dropped him to seventh and a fuel leak in the other slowed him slightly and he finally managed to finish second.

Mark also contested Indianapolis again that year in an Eagle-Offenhauser, but he retired with piston failure. He also had a few races in a Formula A Lola, powered by an American Motors V8, but the engine was not very powerful and his best place was second at Seattle. With George Follmer as co-driver, he took a Porsche 911 Carrera to sixth place in the Watkins Glen six-hour race and, driving a standard Porsche 911 Carrera, he won the special Race of Champions series laid on at the top US circuits for top racing drivers, in late 1973 and early 1974.

That should have been Donohue's last race, for in November he had announced his impending retirement. However, when Penske made his first forays into Formula One, late in 1974, Donohue relinquished his role as team manager and returned to the driving seat. Penske's first home grown Formula One car, the PC1, made its first appearance in the Canadian Grand Prix in late September. Donohue's return was not a particularly happy one, he started the race from the penultimate row of the grid and finished 12th, two laps down on the leaders. In the final race of 1974 he qualified the Penske in the middle of the Watkins Glen grid but lasted only until a rear suspension bracket broke on the 27th lap.

1975 started with seventh place in Argentina, retirement in Brazil and eighth place in South Africa. He was out of the shortened Spanish Grand Prix after only three laps and only two further results brightened the gloom. At Monaco he crashed, and he finished eleventh in Belgium before scoring the team's first championship points, for a fifth place in Sweden. After finishing eighth in Holland, another retirement, in France, prompted the team to acquire a March 751 to try some comparative testing.

The team raced the March for the first time at Silverstone, where Mark was placed fifth, though he had fallen victim to one of the race's infamous aquaplaning accidents. His last race was at the Nürburgring where he completed only one lap before retiring with a puncture.

A week before going to Austria Donohue had the highlight of his return to racing when he took the Porsche 917/30 Can-Am car to Talladega and set an all-time closed circuit lap speed record, at 221 mph.

Lifted by this success, the team went to Austria in high spirits. On Sunday morning, the circuit was swept by rain and in the unofficial morning practice session Donohue apparently had a front tyre burst in a flat-out top gear corner. The car ploughed straight off the circuit, demolishing rows of catch fence which rolled into a ball and launched the disintegrating March over the very low Armco barrier, into the supporting posts of an advertising hoarding. The forward roll bar bracing on the March had apparently saved the driver from serious head injuries and although he was unconscious he appeared to recover before being taken to hospital.

His injuries were much more serious than was thought and he developed brain haemorrhages. Two days later, on 19 August 1975, this most popular and talented driver, who simply could not give up racing, succumbed to his injuries in Graz Hospital.   MT

PHILIPPE ETANCELIN (b.1896)
France

Philippe Etancelin, or 'Phi Phi' as he was nicknamed, was one of the few drivers who raced in the top flight of motor racing both before and after World War II and, although he was a successful driver, his main claim to fame among racing enthusiasts was his curious habit of wearing a cloth cap back to front when racing. This was quite common in the early days of racing but he persevered with the cap even when crash helmets were compulsory – he simply wore it over the crash helmet!

Born in 1896 in Rouen, Etancelin began his motor-racing career in 1926 with a Bugatti, taking part in local hill-climbs and other small events, but the following year he took up circuit racing and was immediately successful, winning the Grand Prix de la Marne at Reims and finishing third in the Coppa Florio at St Briac.

He retired temporarily in 1928 but returned in 1929, once again in a Bugatti, winning the Marne GP for the second time, ahead of the similar cars of Zenelli and Lehoux. He also won the Grand Prix de la Baule and the Prix de Conseil Général at Antibes.

In 1930, Etancelin, still driving a Bugatti,

won the Algerian Grand Prix on handicap, again from his friend Lehoux. He then won the *formule libre* French Grand Prix at Pau from Sir Henry Birkin's Bentley, won the Circuit de Dauphine at Grenoble and finished third in the Lyons GP.

For the 1931 season, Etancelin placed an order for an Alfa Romeo, but commenced the season with his old Bugatti, with which he finished second to Czaykowski in the Casablanca Grand Prix on the Anfa circuit. He also won the minor Estorel Plage race at St Raphael.

Several of the major races of 1931 were for *formule libre* run over a time of ten hours rather than a specific distance. This was too much for a single driver to manage, so Etancelin teamed up with his friend Marcel Lehoux. They started well in both the Italian and the French Grands Prix but were forced to retire. However, when Etancelin took delivery of his Alfa Romeo, he finished fourth in the Marne GP, then went on to win the four-hour Dieppe Grand Prix from Czaykowski's Bugatti and Earl Howe's Delage. This was followed by victories at Grenoble and St Gaudens, where he won the Comminges GP.

Etancelin had reached the top ranks of private owners by now but, with very few places in factory teams available at that time, he was forced to remain an independent. His 1932 season was unrewarding because he was always beaten by the factory cars, but he did manage a win in the Picardy Grand Prix at Péronne.

The Alfa Romeo was retained for 1933 and, with it, Etancelin came within an ace of winning the prestigious French Grand Prix. After a furious battle with Giuseppe Campari's Maserati, he had to be content with second place. However, he won the Picardy GP for the second year running, beating the formidable Raymond Sommer. He then finished second in the Nîmes GP to Tazio Nuvolari and finally won the Marne GP again, beating Jean-Pierre Wimille.

The 750 kilogram formula was introduced in 1934, and with it came the all-conquering Mercedes-Benz and Auto Union monsters which tended to overshadow everyone else until the war. Etancelin bought a Maserati for the new formula and, in 1934, he finished second at Casablanca, Montreux and Nice and won the Dieppe GP. However, his best victory was a win in the Le Mans 24-hour race when he partnered Luigi Chinetti in an Alfa Romeo.

The German cars were dominant again in 1935 and all Etancelin picked up was a third place at Tunis. However, in the Monaco GP he fought a tremendous duel in a 3.7-litre Maserati against the unwieldy Mercedes of Caracciola, but dropped back to fourth place when his brakes faded.

Etancelin used one of the new V8 4.4-litre Maseratis in 1936 but this was no match for the German cars. He won the Pau Grand Prix on the tight street circuit against modest opposition but retired in virtually every other race.

Lacking a competitive car, Etancelin did not race again until 1938 when he drove one of the new Talbot sports cars at Le Mans with Chinetti, without success. In 1939, he occasionally drove a Talbot, finishing third at Pau behind the Mercedes of Lang and von Brauchitsch and fourth in the French GP.

After the war, Etancelin took part in the first French motor race, held in the Bois de Boulogne in 1946, where he drove an Alfa Romeo, but failed to finish. New racing cars were few and far between and it was not until 1948 that he was able to buy a new 4½-litre Talbot, with which he finished second to Villoresi's Maserati at the Albi GP. He did well in 1949, finishing second to Fangio at the Marseilles GP, second to Ascari in the European GP at Monza and second to Peter Whitehead's Ferrari at the Brno race in Czechoslovakia. He also won the Paris GP at Montlhéry that year.

By 1950, he was 54 years old but he continued to race until 1953, picking up good placings. He was third at the Rouen GP of 1953 and third in the 12 hours of Casablanca, but the Talbot was only usable in a few *formule libre* races as Formula One was temporarily abandoned. He decided to retire at the end of 1953 but he still retained an interest in the sport, occasionally appearing at meetings to drive an historic car in displays by the 'Anciens Pilotes' even in his eighties. MT

GEORGE EYSTON *(1897-1979)*
Great Britain
Possibly the most versatile driver in racing history is George Edward Thomas Eyston, a Briton, whose successful machines ranged from 750cc racers to 73-litre land-speed-record contenders. Born in 1897, Eyston was initiated into motor sport at an early age, as he recalled to the author many years later.

'Long before World War I, I often stayed with my father at the Weybridge residence of Mr Cox, then Editor of *The Field*. He well knew the Locke Kings who built Brooklands, and hence I was often taken to the track.

'Among my earliest remembrances were the three Sunbeam cars in laurel wreathed stalls in the Paddock, fresh from their victory in the Coupe de L'Auto at Dieppe. Little did I then know that I should own one of these cars!

'Motor cycling was more in my line, with my cloth cap reversed and, at BARC meetings, a jockey sash round my waist.

'I was at the start of the Round England Air Race in 1911, and watched Commander Porte stall at the take off in his Deperdussin monoplane. Afterwards, I helped his mechanic to smash up the machine to obtain the maximum insurance payment.

'I started to race motor cars at Brooklands in 1923 with Aston Martin.'

That was following a distinguished wartime service as a Captain in the Royal Artillery, when Eyston was awarded the Military Cross; after the Armistice, Eyston went to university to take his BA, then established his own engineering company.

During the 1920s, he concentrated mainly on track events, both in England and on the Continent. He won his class in the 1923 Boulogne Motor Week driving an Aston, after a rapid dash to England to collect spares for repairing damage inflicted on his car in a crash during practice.

'I won the Brooklands Gold Cup and Gold Vase in a Bugatti, and the British Empire Trophy in an MG,' added Captain Eyston. 'Then there was my duel in the sleeve-valve Panhard-Levassor with John Cobb's Delage (which Cobb won by just one fifth of a second) in the 1932 British Empire Trophy Race.

'To the three-quarter distance, I twice led the JCC 200-miles race. I led the BRDC 500-mile event for the same distance in a 2-litre Sunbeam. I won quite a few BARC races, including two first and one second in an OM on the same day.

'Coming straight from Ascot in a top-hat, I drove for the first time the reverse way round the track in record breaking time. This was a special occasion, as I was achieving nearly 115 miles in the hour in a Rolls-Bentley from Derby.'

Certainly, by the 1930s, it was Eyston's record-breaking activities which had come to dominate his sporting career: he was the first man ever to exceed 120 mph in a 750 cc car, in his famous MG *Magic Midget,* in December 1932. The same year he covered 130 miles in an hour then, in 1933, turned his attention to the hitherto unexplored field of diesel-engined record runs, averaging 104.86 mph over the flying kilometre at Brooklands in a streamlined 'Safety Saloon' compounded from a Chrysler chassis with an 8.9-litre AEC diesel engine identical to that used in London's buses.

In 1935, he took his 25-litre Rolls-Royce-engined *Speed of the Wind* to the Bonneville Salt Flats in Utah and averaged 140.52 mph (aided by C.S. Staniland and Bert Denly) over 24 hours; the following year, he raised the figure to 149.19 mph and also took the world 48-hour record at 136.34 mph.

Eyston's most fantastic machine was the *Thunderbolt,* built in 1937 to challenge Campbell's land-speed record of 301 mph. *Thunderbolt* had twin Rolls-Royce R-type aero-engines, developing 6000 bhp from a total of 73 litres, and six wheels, of which the front two pairs steered, and the rear pair drove. Gulping down five gallons of petrol every minute, the *Thunderbolt* rushed over the twelve-mile record course at Bonneville at an average speed of 312 mph. Modified, the car achieved 345.49 mph in August 1938. In September, John Cobb's *Railton-Mobil-Special* raised the record to 350.2 mph but, the next day, Eyston capped this with a speed of 357.5 mph, his highest land speed. Although he nudged 400 mph during testing, Thunderbolt was at its limits and a new car would have been needed to raise the record any further.

Awarded the OBE in 1948, Eyston took his last record in 1954, with a streamlined MG works car consisting of a 1500cc TF engine in an MGA chassis, fitted with similar stream-lined bodywork to that of fellow record breaker Goldie Gardner's speed car. Once again at Bonneville, Eyston and his co-driver, Ken Miles, captured seven international and 25 American records with this car; their achievements included twelve hours at an average of just over 120 mph.

Eyston kept in touch with the speed business by masterminding all MG's subsequent record attempts up to 1959, when they withdrew from this field. He died in July 1979.

The hundreds of speed records set up by Eyston during his long career constitute a unique achievement; certainly their sheer variety makes it highly improbable that Eyston's speed successes will ever be equalled.   DBW

JUAN MANUEL FANGIO (b.1911)
Argentina

The question 'Who was the world's best racing driver?' is often discussed by motor-racing enthusiasts. The man who constantly tops the poll is Argentina's Juan Manuel Fangio, the five-times World Champion who did not make his bow in European Grand-Prix racing until he was 37, and who finally retired at the end of 1958 when he was 47. Over his seventeen-year career as a racing driver, Fangio competed in over 180 races in 23 countries and won eighty of them.

Fangio was born on 24 June 1911 – San Juan's day, hence his name – at Balcarce, a small town 200 miles from Buenos Aires. His father, Loreto Fangio, an Italian immigrant, was a house-painter by trade. At school, young Juan Manuel was not a brilliant pupil, but a terrific footballer. He earned the nickname 'El Chueco' (bandy legs) for his magnificent goals.

Aged ten, Fangio began his interest in items mechanical. He did odd jobs after school for a local garage man. Later, his father found him employment at Señor Viggiano's garage.

At seventeen, by now a qualified mechanic, Fangio was approached by one of Viggiano's customers, Señor Ayerza, to be his riding mechanic in a race for Model T Fords. Fangio readily accepted and managed to participate without his parents' knowledge. Initial fear turned to exhilaration and a thirst for more.

After a lengthy bout of pneumonia, during which he almost died, Fangio was called up for military service. Upon his return to Balcarce, he obtained a loan from his father and went into partnership with his friend, José Duffard, to start a small garage. In December 1934, however, there came the chance Fangio had been waiting for: a borrowed Ford Model T for him to race.

It was an inauspicious debut; 23-year-old Juan Manuel Fangio seized a big-end and had to fix it for nothing before returning the machine. The bug had well and truly bitten now and Fangio began collecting parts to build his own Ford Model T.

After some races with the Model T, Fangio built a V8 special, inserting an 85bhp Ford V8 into a Ford chassis and wrapping the ensemble with a home-made two-seater body. Its first race at Necochea in March 1938 was eventful. Fangio out-accelerated Carlos Arzani's 3.8-litre Alfa Romeo 8C-35 Grand Prix machine off the grid, but eventually power told and Arzani shot ahead. Fangio was third.

The highlight of the Argentinian calendar was the *Gran Premio Nacional,* an annual race of around 6000 miles, run in stages of between ten and fifteen hours each, for modified production cars. Fangio could not afford one of the cars used in this classic event, but he competed as a riding mechanic, in 1938, for Luis Finocchietto; they finished seventh. In September 1939, Fangio's supporters in Balcarce organised a collection to buy him a car – a Chevrolet coupé. In the *Gran Premio,* held in flooded conditions, Fangio was fifth despite an accident. This secured him a place in the official Chevrolet team and he won the race in 1940. For the next two years, Fangio won many major endurance races with his Chevrolet, but racing ceased in 1942, owing to the war, and Fangio took a job as a taxi driver.

Fangio had kept his reactions sharp by relentlessly practising on the road, but when racing resumed in 1947 he wondered if, at 36, he was too old to be a serious contender. Far from it. His results with track- and road-racing Chevrolet specials resulted in the loan of a European car in a series of international races run early in 1948. Driving a Maserati 4CL and a Simca-Gordini, Fangio impressed the visiting Europeans.

The Argentine Government, headed by Juan Perón (a motor-racing fanatic), decided to send a group of drivers to Indianapolis and then to Europe in the summer of 1948 to see the current trends for themselves. Fangio received a telegram from Amedée Gordini, asking him to drive at Reims. However, the little Simca-Gordinis were outclassed and Fangio's European debut was hardly noticed.

For the international races in 1949, the Argentine Automobile Club lent Fangio an old Maserati 4CL and later a brand new 4CLT/48 model. With the latter he scored a great victory; beating all the European aces, Fangio won the Mar del Plata Grand Prix. A few days later came news that the club were to send Fangio and Benedicto Campos to race in Europe.

Admittedly, the Argentine team chose the lesser Grands Prix, but their jubilation knew no bounds when Fangio's blue-and-yellow Maserati 4CLT/48 won at San Remo, Pau, Perpignan and Marseilles. Then funds began to run low and when Fangio retired with piston failure on the first lap of the Belgian Grand Prix it was utter disaster. However, a textile firm offered financial support, a new Formula

Two Ferrari 166C was ordered and Fangio put things right by winning the Monza Autodrome Cup with it, beating the three works-entered cars. The prize money from Monza meant that the team's Maseratis could be rebuilt at the works. Fangio won at Albi, but failed at Reims in both the Formula One and Formula Two races. By the end of July, the cars were in a poor state and Fangio decided to cut his losses and return home.

For 1950, the FIA brought new glamour to Formula One racing by instigating the World Championship series. This attracted the Alfa Romeo team back into racing after a year's retirement and they signed up Fangio to partner Giuseppe Farina and Luigi Fagioli. It was the underlining of Fangio's prowess and, to back this up, one of the previous season's Maseratis, plus a Formula Two Ferrari had been prepared for the minor races. After warming-up with a third at Marseilles in the Ferrari and victory at Pau in the Maserati, Fangio made his debut for Alfa Romeo in the non-championship San Remo Grand Prix. He quickly recovered from a poor start to win by a minute in the pouring rain.

Victories followed in the Monaco, Belgian and French Grands Prix plus the non-championship Grand Prix des Nations in Geneva and the Pescara Grand Prix. Fangio was also third in his first Mille Miglia, a road race he hated, and participated unsuccessfully in his first Le Mans 24-hour race. Before the final Grand Prix, in Italy, Fangio led the World Championship table with 26 points to Fagioli's 24 and Farina's 22. In the race, Fangio blew up his engine; he took over Felice Bonetto's Alfa Romeo 158, but broke down yet again. Farina won and took the championship honours.

In 1951, Fangio was once more contracted to Alfa Romeo for Formula One, although in the early-season Argentine free formula races he had his first acquaintance with the Mercedes-Benz, driving their famous pre-war 3-litre W163 model, albeit without success. In Europe, it was Fangio's year: he won the Swiss, European (French) and Spanish Grands Prix to clinch the World Championship for himself, in the face of tough opposition from Ferrari's Alberto Ascari. It was Alfa Romeo's swan-song in Formula One and, for 1952, Fangio signed with Maserati for Formula Two (which replaced Formula One for two years for the World Championship series) and with BRM for the few (non-championship)

Formula One racing events that still remained.

Fangio's year started on top form with six wins in South America in the Argentine Automobile Club's old Ferrari 166C equipped with a 2-litre supercharged engine. The BRM P15 broke down at Albi and at Dundrod in Northern Ireland, and then came the Monza Grand Prix on 8 June, the day after Dundrod. Fangio had flown to France immediately after the race, but bad weather caused his flight to Italy to be cancelled. Undaunted, he borrowed a car and drove through the night, arriving two hours before the start of the race. Starting his Formula Two Maserati A6GCM from the back of the grid, he began to climb through the field when he lost control and crashed. His car touched a straw bale at Lesmo Corner, slewed all over the road and finally somersaulted in mid-air. Fangio was thrown out, brushing past the branches of a tree to land on the grass. His vertebrae were damaged and he spent 42 days in hospital and five months in plaster.

January 1953 saw Fangio back in the cockpit, driving a Maserati A6GCM at the new Buenos Aires Autodrome in the first Argentine Grand Prix. He had lost none of his skill, taking the lead on lap three and holding it until the transmission failed. The Maseratis were fast but fragile, and it was not until the end of the year, the Italian Grand Prix in September, that Fangio won a World Championship race with the newer A6SSG model. Highlight of the year, however, was surely his performance in the Mille Miglia when he took his Alfa Romeo Disco Volante into second place, with the steering only working on one wheel!

In 1954, Fangio began the year driving Maserati's new 2½-litre 250F Formula One car, winning the Argentine and Belgian Grands Prix. He had signed, however, to drive the new Mercedes-Benz W196 and, when the German team made its debut in the French Grand Prix in July, Fangio continued his winning run. He added the German, Italian and Swiss Grands Prix to his list, to win his second World Championship with ease. In 1955, it was a repeat performance. He won the Argentine, Belgian, Dutch and Italian Grands Prix to claim the title again.

With Mercedes-Benz withdrawing from racing at the end of the year, Fangio moved to Ferrari to collect his fourth World Championship in 1956, but he did not enjoy his season with this team and returned to Maserati for 1957. His fifth and last World Championship that year was again clear-cut: he won the

Argentine, Monaco, French and German Grands Prix, the last being his most famous victory. His Maserati 250F risked rear-suspension failure on the bumpy Nürburgring if it started on full tanks, so Fangio elected to start on half-tanks and stop midway through the race. This he did, but as he set off from a bungled pit-stop, what had been a 27.8 secs lead had evaporated into a deficit of 28 secs. Slowly but surely, Fangio began to overhaul the Ferraris of Peter Collins and Mike Hawthorn ahead. Breaking the lap record no fewer than nine times, Fangio drove as never before, overtook his rivals and won by 3.6 secs. Afterwards, he revealed that his seat had broken – he had wedged himself in by bracing his knees on the side of the cockpit – and he confessed, 'I never want to drive like that again.'

In 1958, now approaching 47, Fangio turned down offers to lead works teams and decided to run as an independent. For the first time since 1954, he failed to win the Argentine Grand Prix, finishing fourth with a sick engine; but he won the non-championship Buenos Aires Grand Prix two weeks later. Fangio hit the headlines during a visit to Cuba for a sports-car race, when he was kidnapped by Fidel Castro's guerillas, to be released safely after the event. After an abortive attempt to enter the Indianapolis 500-mile race (the cars offered were uncompetitive and he withdrew), Fangio came to Europe for the Monza 500-mile race round the banked circit, for Indianapolis-type machines. Sadly, his American car retired with fuel-pump problems after establishing good times in practice. Fangio's last race was the French Grand Prix at Reims, scene of his first European appearance some ten years before. Driving a new but underpowered Maserati 250F, Fangio was handicapped by an inoperative clutch, but struggled on gamely to finish fourth.

It was the end of his last competitive season before he retired to attend to extensive business interests in his native Argentina.

Why did Fangio retire? Was it due to the deaths of his great friends and rivals Eugenio Castellotti, Luigi Musso and Peter Collins that year? Had he passed his peak as a driver? It was none of these things. He had fulfilled his ambitions. He had won the World Championship five times and he felt a sixth title would mean little more.

Even in his late sixties, Fangio was still a charismatic figure on his occasional appearances at races around the world, but it was his infrequent outings in 'demonstration' events that gave just a glimpse, to those who never saw him in his heyday, of the Fangio who ranks as one of the all-time great drivers; time did not hide his outstanding natural talent. MK

GIUSEPPE FARINA (1906-1966)
Italy
Giuseppe Farina was the first official World Champion, gaining the title in 1950. Also Italian champion in 1937, 1938 and 1939, he is best known as the driver who set the style of modern motor-race driving. Farina's trademark was to control his machines with arms outstretched and head held back. Ironically enough, although he gave an impression of smoothness and precision, during his thirty-year racing career he suffered a series of accidents. Burns, fractures, cuts and abrasions were part and parcel of the life of Giuseppe ('Nino') Farina.

Farina hated publicity. After winning the World Championship, he refused to allow photographs of him to be taken at home or to allow the press to probe his private life. Possibly, part of the reason was that his wife would have nothing to do with his racing activities.

He was born on 30 October 1906, in Turin. His father was the eldest of the Farina brothers whose car coachbuilding company (known as Pininfarina) has won world acclaim. Giuseppe began driving at the tender age of nine, handling a two-cylinder Temperino machine. He was a brilliant student and became Doctor of Political Science, he also excelled at skiing, football, horse riding, athletics and cycling. A career as a cavalry officer in the Italian army was cut short in order to fulfil ambitions in another direction – motor racing.

While a student, Giuseppe Farina purchased his first car, a second-hand Alfa Romeo, and ran it in the 1925 Aosta-Gran San Bernardo Hill-climb. He crashed, breaking his shoulder and receiving facial cuts, while trying to beat his father, who was fourth. In 1933 and 1934, he returned, racing privately-entered Maseratis and Alfa Romeos, and began a friendship with Tazio Nuvolari who, to some extent, guided Farina's early career.

In 1935, he raced a works Maserati and the following year joined Scuderia Ferrari, the team which ran works-backed Alfa Romeos. He finished second in the Mille Miglia, driving

through the night without lights, and took several other places in important races that season.

In 1938, the official Alfa Romeo team returned to motor racing and Farina was a member. Driving the new Alfa Romeo 158 *voiturettes* – the legendary 'Alfettas' – in 1939, Farina won the Antwerp Grand Prix, the Coppa Ciano and the Prix de Berne to become Italian champion for the third year in succession. In 1940, he won the Tripoli Grand Prix and finished second in the Mille Miglia for the third time.

After World War II, Farina returned to drive the Alfa Romeo 158s, winning the Grands Prix des Nations at Geneva and at St Cloud in 1946. Then he left Alfa Romeo after a disagreement over team leadership, sat out the following season and returned in 1948 with privately-entered Maseratis and works Ferraris. In 1950, Farina rejoined Alfa Romeo. He won the European (British), Swiss and Italian Grands Prix to clinch the World Championship at the age of 43. He continued with Alfa Romeo in 1951 but had to give best to Fangio who took the championship. Farina was fourth in the table with only one championship race victory – the Belgian Grand Prix at Spa Francorchamps.

Farina joined Ferrari in 1952, but had to take second place to team leader Alberto Ascari. He won the non-championship Monza Grand Prix and secured a string of seconds. Driving Tony Vandervell's *Thinwall Special* – a modified 4½-litre Ferrari 375 Formula One car – he was second in the end-of-season Goodwood Woodcote Cup free formula race. In 1953, the highlight of Farina's year was victory in the German Grand Prix; he took up the challenge against the works Maseratis when Ascari's Ferrari lost a wheel. Other victories came at Bordeaux, Buenos Aires, Naples, Rouen, Silverstone, Nürburgring and in the Spa 24-hour race when he shared a 4.5-litre Ferrari 375MM with Mike Hawthorn.

Although he was now a veteran at 47, a golden opportunity arose in 1954 when Ascari quit the team to join Lancia, and Farina emerged as Ferrari team leader. After some impressive results – including victory in the Buenos Aires 1000 km sports-car race, the Circuit of Agadir and the Syracuse Grand Prix – he crashed heavily in the Mille Miglia when leading in a 4.9-litre Ferrari 375 Plus. Seven weeks later, his right arm still in plaster, Farina raced in the Belgian Grand Prix, dicing with

Fangio's Maserati for the lead before his Ferrari broke down. Then practising for the Supercortemaggiore Grand Prix sports-car race at Monza the next weekend, a rear universal joint broke, a drive-shaft punctured a fuel tank, and his Ferrari was engulfed in flames. Farina jumped clear, but was out of racing for the year recovering from severe burns.

It seemed nothing could keep the man out of the cockpit of a racing car. In 1955, he was back with Ferrari in Argentina, taking morphine injections to kill pain. He was second there, fourth at Monaco and third in Belgium before 'retiring' in mid season, owing to continued pain and the death of his friend, Alberto Ascari. He failed to start in the Italian Grand Prix in September after his Ferrari-entered Lancia D50 threw a tyre tread at 170 mph in practice and was withdrawn. The car spun wildly, but Farina stepped out unhurt.

In 1956, he planned to enter the Indianapolis 500-mile race. A six-cylinder Ferrari engine was installed in a Kurtis Kraft chassis, but the project was a failure. The following year Farina, now 50, elected to race a 'conventional' Indy car, but withdrew after it crashed in practice, killing test driver Keith Andrews.

Farina became involved in Alfa Romeo and Jaguar distributorships and later assisted at the Pininfarina plant. In 1966, on his way to the French Grand Prix, he lost control of his Lotus-Cortina road car in the Savoy Alps near Chambéry, hit a telegraph pole and was killed instantly.

The man who had survived countless accidents on the track ironically perished on the road.　　　　　　　　　　　　　MK

EMERSON FITTIPALDI (b.1946)
Brazil

The story of Emerson Fittipaldi is almost one of the classical rise to fame stories which Hollywood used to inflict on the public. Certainly it parallels the history of Juan Manuel Fangio, who, coincidentally, started from humble beginnings and rose to become a multiple World Champion. It is not co-incidence, though, that both men come from South America, where chronic poverty often inspires young men to fight their way out of their environment to reach the top of their chosen profession.

Not that Fittipaldi was born into a poor family, for his father, Wilson, was a well

known journalist who had reported on motor racing for many years, and had taken part in motor-cycle racing himself. Born in São Paulo on 12 December 1946, Emerson, like his elder brother Wilson, was soon being indoctrinated with motor-racing lore. At the age of fifteen he was taking part in 50 cc-motor-cycle racing, while his elder brother was participating in kart races. It was not long before Emerson graduated to karts and by 1965 he had won the São Paulo Kart championship.

He was noticed by several people at this stage; he was still only nineteen, yet he was given a place in the Renault Gordini team which raced in Brazilian events. He won the Brazilian Novices championship in the Renault and then moved into a Formula Vee car with which he was again successful, winning the Brazilian championship in 1967. However, there was little real opposition, largely because Brazil possessed no proper motor-racing industry unlike most European countries, so cars were few and far between, while strict import regulations restricted the sale of racing cars. Most cars had to be built from production parts, so the Fittipaldi brothers began building up their own cars, using mostly Volkswagen components. They built and raced an Alfa Romeo GTA and a Karmann Ghia Volkswagen powered by a 2-litre Porsche engine. With the latter Emerson finished second to Carlos Pace in the 1967 Brazilian GT championship. A much more sophisticated car was built up for 1968, again powered by the Porsche engine, but it was unreliable and did not finish many events.

By the end of the 1968 season Emerson knew that if he was going to get anywhere in international motor racing he had to go to Europe to discover if he was as good as the Europeans. He decided to go to England and arrived in March 1969. He had enough money for a Formula Ford car, so he bought a Merlyn Mk IIA, which was quite a successful car at the time. With a good engine, tuned by Denny Rowland, Emerson started on a storybook trail of victories, which led to numerous mentions in the motoring press. He soon came to the notice of Jim Russell, the former racing driver who ran a racing school at Snetterton, and Russell offered him a drive in his new Lotus 59 Formula Three car. The extra power of the Formula Three car did not worry Fittipaldi and he again won a string of races, taking the Lombank F3 championship with no less than eight straight wins.

There was no looking back after that, for Colin Chapman of Lotus quickly snapped him up for the 1970 season to drive a Formula Two Lotus 69 alongside Jochen Rindt. He was not as outstanding in the Formula Two car as he had been in the FF and F3 machines, but the Lotus 69 performed no better for Rindt, who had a multitude of problems. However, Fittipaldi finished second at Imola, and third at Barcelona and Rouen, to take third place in the European F2 Trophy.

Other team managers were beginning to woo Fittipaldi, but Chapman forestalled them by offering Fittipaldi a drive in the Formula One team alongside Rindt and John Miles. Fittipaldi was given a type 49 to test and race while the others were using the new type 72. Chapman already suspected that Miles was not suited to Formula One and was looking for a replacement. Fittipaldi's first F1 race was in the British GP, where he finished a creditable eighth, following this with a good fourth place in the German GP at Hockenheim. For the Italian GP he was given a Lotus 72, but he made one of his rare mistakes and crashed in practice shortly before Rindt also crashed and was killed. The team withdrew from the race, but returned for the United States GP, when Fittipaldi was promoted to team leader, for Miles had left and had been replaced by Reine Wisell. There was great pressure on Fittipaldi, for he was leading the team in only his fourth F1 race and the car had the suspicion of weak brake shafts hanging over it – for there was a possibility that these caused Rindt's crash. However, Fittipaldi overcame these problems and coolly drove the car to victory.

The following year Fittipaldi remained as team leader, but the Lotus 72 was uncompetitive, probably as a result of Emerson's lack of experience, although he had a bad crash on the road which kept him out of racing for a few weeks. However, he finished second in the Austrian GP, third in both France and Britain to take sixth place in the World Championship.

In 1972 everything came right for Fittipaldi and Lotus, for the Brazilian won the Grands Prix of Spain, Belgium, Britain, Austria, and Italy, finished second in South Africa and France and third at Monaco, to run away with the World Championship. He also won the £50,000 Rothmans race at Brands Hatch, as well as the Race of Champions, the Silverstone International Trophy, the Republic GP at Vallelunga and a string of Formula Two races.

For 1973, Fittipaldi was joined in the Lotus team by Ronnie Peterson, the brilliant Swedish driver. They were designated as joint number one drivers, which many pundits forecast would bring trouble to the Lotus team, whose 72s were being raced as John Player Specials. Fittipaldi won the opening events in Argentina and Brazil, much to the delight of his countrymen, then he won the Spanish GP and finished second in the Monaco GP, but from then on his luck ran out as he retired in a number of events. Both Fittipaldi and other observers felt that Colin Chapman favoured Peterson towards the end of the season. At Monza, this equal number one driver status problem reared its head. A win for Emerson would have kept his championship hopes alive, but Ronnie Peterson, having led the race throughout, with Emerson running second, was allowed to win the race. To be fair, Ronnie had waved Emerson by to lead the preceding Austrian Grand Prix. Jackie Stewart's fourth place at Monza was sufficient to win him the title.

Although Chapman offered Fittipaldi handsome terms to stay with Lotus for 1974, he was disenchanted with the team and accepted an offer to drive for the Texaco-Marlboro team.

Emerson won his home Grand Prix at Interlagos, the Belgian and the Canadian Grands Prix, which together with second places at Brands Hatch and Mosport, ensured him of his second World Championship. 1975 saw a repeat of his previous successes in South America with a win in Argentina and a second in Brazil. Second at Monaco, Monza and Watkins Glen, Emerson's other win was in the shortened Silverstone race, when he was in the right place with the right tyres when nearly everyone else was aquaplaning off the circuit. Emerson finished second in the championship, and there was speculation to see whether he could maintain his impressive scoring rate: 1972, 1st; 1973, 2nd; 1974, 1st; 1975, 2nd. The motor racing world was most surprised to find that Emerson had elected to join brother Wilson's Fittipaldi Racing Team which was handsomely financed by the Brazilian state-owned sugar producers, Copersucar. The Copersucar-Fittipaldi had been designed by Emerson's friend Richard Divila, and the car looked promising as Emerson qualified it fifth fastest at Buenos Aires for its first race. Unfortunately for Emerson, that was its best showing all year, and try as he might, he was unable even to qualify for some races. 1977 looked brighter, however, for Emerson scored fourth place in both South American races. The third generation car, designed by Divila and Dave Baldwin, and built close to the Interlagos circuit, gave some cause for optimism.

His season did not maintain this early promise, although he scored further points with fifth place at Long Beach and fourth in Holland to finish twelfth in the championship. The old flair was demonstrably still present, but Emerson continued to pay the penalty of his faith to Copersucar.

Nevertheless, the car was improving – albeit slowly – and no-one was surprised when Emerson stayed put for 1978. Again, things started well and with the F5A he scored a rousing second place in Brazil and also remained much more competitive than of late throughout the season. He netted fourth places in Germany and Austria, fifth in Holland and the USA (East) and sixth in Sweden, climbing to ninth place in the championship.

Emerson continued to race for Brazil and started 1979 encouragingly with sixth place in Argentina. However, his hopes of consistent front running seemed to dwindle when the long awaited F6 chassis, designed by Frank Bellamy, proved slower initially than its predecessor. Emerson's gritty determination carried him to more middle-of-the-field running as the opposition developed their cars further. He reverted to the F5A chassis in mid-season, finishing only in Spain and Belgium, in disappointing ninth and eleventh places, before struggling to the end of the season with the F6A. As the season ended, Fittipaldi Automotive took over the redundant equipment of the disbanding Wolf team, plus Keke Rosberg as a talented number two driver, and the controversial Copersucar dollars were replaced by sponsorship from Skol.

Few people doubted Fittipaldi's raw ability but yet again in 1980 his machinery was simply not good enough to reflect his true stature. Pending the arrival of the Harvey Postlethwaite-designed F8, the team struggled on with the outclassed F7. Emerson was in the points with third place (from last on the grid) at Long Beach, fifth in the controversial Spanish Grand Prix (helped by a partial boycott and much attrition) and sixth in Monaco.

Although the F8, which made its debut at Brands Hatch just ten years after Emerson's own Grand Prix debut, improved the team's qualifying pattern from back row to mid-grid, the rest of the season was blighted by mechanical problems. As Rosberg signed on for another two years with the team, the rumours flew that Emerson was about to retire and Emerson, still only 34 years old, confirmed them at the beginning of 1981.   MT

A.J. FOYT (b.1935)
USA

A.J. Foyt is one of the most colourful and successful characters ever to have entered motor racing, as well as being one of the most durable, for, at the age of 45, he entered his 27th year of professional motor racing in 1980. Born on 16 January 1935 at Houston, Texas, Anthony Joseph Foyt Jnr entered motor racing almost as soon as he was able, taking part in his first race at Houston in 1953. He drove in a rough-and-tumble midget-car event. This type of racing is held on cinder-tracks of ¼, ⅓ or ½-mile, and the bravest man invariably wins. He soon began to attract notice and quickly moved up into sprint cars, which are bigger, more powerful versions of the midget racers and which sometimes race on the paved ovals as well as cinder tracks. By 1958, he was good enough to take second place in the Sprint Car championship of the United States Automobile Club (USAC) and he took part in his first Indianapolis 500 race in the Dean Van Lines Special, spinning off the track, but being placed sixteenth. He took part in the 1958 Race of Two Worlds event at Monza in Italy, finishing sixth after taking over another driver's car.

For the next few years, he concentrated on events run by USAC, taking part in almost every type of racing they organised. Even when he became a highly successful and wealthy driver he still took part in midget, sprint and stock-car races, sometimes driving three or four races in a week. He won his first national championship in 1960 and the following year he won Indianapolis for the first time, driving the Bowes Seal Fast Special, also taking the national championship for the second year.

As he became more successful, Foyt became a controversial spokesman for the type of racing enjoyed by the USAC drivers, and when the European 'sporty car' drivers arrived at Indianapolis, he was openly contemptuous of the tiny, mid-engined cars. Even when they showed their high speed and incredible cornering ability, he still maintained that the front-engined 'Dinosaurs' would blow off the little European cars. He did manage to win Indianapolis again in 1964 in a front-engined car of the old type and, as he passed the finish, he made a rude gesture at the Ford and Lotus people in the pits, whose car he had just beaten. As he later commented, his win 'wasn't bad for a li'l ole antique car'. Foyt was no fool, however, and, within three months of Indianapolis, he was racing one of the Lotus-Fords about which he had been so contemptuous. For the 1965 Indianapolis race, he had the use of a Lotus and a Lola, which did not bring him any luck, and he eventually decided to turn constructor, building his own Coyote-Fords. He won Indianapolis for the third time in 1967 in his Coyote and took the USAC national championship for the third time.

Foyt was contracted to Ford for a number of years and in 1966 they invited him to drive the Mk II 7-litre Ford GT in long-distance endurance races. He teamed up with Ronnie Bucknum in the Sebring 12-hour race where they finished twelfth. In the following season, he again drove the Ford, finishing second at Sebring, then winning the Le Mans 24-hour race, with Dan Gurney, in a Mk IV Ford GT. As well as all this activity, Foyt found time for a full season of stock-car racing and sprint and midget races.

A.J. Foyt won the USAC Stock-Car championship in 1968, and continued winning in most other categories, until he was eventually credited with more race wins than any other American driver in history. He did not win Indianapolis between 1967 and 1976, but he made pole position in 1974 and 1975 with his Ford V8-engined Coyote. His 1974 season was marred by non-finishes but in 1975 the Coyote repaid A.J's faith with a string of good results to capture another USAC championship. Foyt won the California 500 at Ontario but was robbed of his elusive fourth Indy win after hitting accident debris while leading; he finished second after a pit stop. He was second again in 1976's rain-soaked Indy and abandoned NASCAR racing after being disqualified for allegedly cheating in Daytona practice.

He was soon back in circulation, of course, and vowing not to retire before his fourth Indy win came, and come it did, with a well-earned win at the Brickyard in 1977. Thereafter, rumours that A.J. would retire were rife, but he was back in the hot seat in 1978. He struggled with outdated machinery to win the Texas Grand Prix in August, and the Silverstone event when the USAC trail moved to England in October. A brief excursion into NASCAR, with a Buick, netted third place in the Winston 500 at Taladega. Far from being ready to retire, A.J. was already busy with plans to run a new Parnelli-Cosworth in 1979, with his sights set firmly on Indy. As one Indy veteran said of him during qualifying for Indianapolis, 'Ole A. J. gets himself so psyched up, he could turn a 180-mile-an-hour lap on foot'; this may be true.

1979 was the year of the big political split between USAC and CART – Championship Auto Racing Teams Inc. – each with its own rules, own championship and own contenders, who raced 'head to head' only once, at Indy. After being in at the birth of CART, Foyt rejoined the depleted USAC ranks with his Parnelli 6C and cleaned up the championship with six wins from eight races, plus second (to CART champion Rick Mears) at Indianapolis. The USAC/CART split was eventually resolved to form the Championship Racing League in 1980, with hybrid rules and Foyt as a board member. The bitterness lingered however and in mid-season, after a disappointing showing at Indy and some barely disguised nose-thumbing at the unpopular new regulations at Pocono, A.J. announced his retirement. He qualified his departure by saying he might run the odd race in support of the election campaign for his long time friend and sponsor, Jim Gilmore. When he made a 'one-off' return to the dirt tracks in September, many sceptics wondered just how long 'olc A.J.' could stay away.   MT

PETER GETHIN (b.1940)
Great Britain
Many young men tend to be influenced by the chosen career of their fathers but Peter Gethin, born on 21 February 1940, the son of Ken Gethin, the famous flat-race jockey, ignored the turf and chose tarmac instead.

Like so many sons of famous fathers, his academic career was not notable, and he led a rather rootless life until he moved into motor racing. He soon found the excitement he was looking for, and in 1962, at the age of 22, he took up racing with a Lotus 7. He soon decided that single-seater racing was the only path to the top though, and he switched to a Formula Three Brabham. He took part in many races in Britain and Europe, joining the circus of drivers who toured the Continent living from hand to mouth and often sleeping in their cars. This way of life continued for several years with no great success coming his way. He moved to a B7 Formula Three Chevron in 1967, and began to pick up a few good placings. By 1968, he had moved into Formula Two, racing both a Brabham and a Chevron, but there were many Grand Prix drivers taking part in Formula Two at that time and Gethin made only a modest impact against the tough opposition.

The breakthrough came when he decided to desert the established formulae and take a chance with the fledgling Formula 5000 for single seaters powered by 5-litre stock-block engines. He was given the opportunity of driving the factory-supported McLaren M10A run by Church Farm Racing. These cars were as powerful as the current Formula One machines, and Peter showed that he could handle the power and cope with the difficult handling of the big cars by winning three races in a row – the Guards F5000 race at Oulton Park, the Kent Messenger F5000 race at Brands Hatch and the Guards race at Mallory Park. He took his car to the USA for a spell of racing in their equivalent Formula A but returned to take a fourth place at Hockenheim and win the Guards F5000 championship from ex-Formula One Lotus driver Trevor Taylor who had also turned to F5000.

His victories naturally brought him to the attention of the McLaren team, and it seemed they would eventually give him a chance of driving in Formula One, but his chance came much earlier than he anticipated, for Bruce McLaren was tragically killed in a testing accident at Goodwood and then Denny Hulme received badly burned hands during a testing accident at Indianapolis. He took over the works Formula One McLaren M14A at the Dutch Grand Prix where he crashed the car, but he began to get the hang of F1 racing and he finished tenth in the Austrian GP, ninth in the Italian, sixth in the Canadian and fourteenth in the USA event. His sixth place in Canada earned him his first World Championship point.

Gethin also raced for the McLaren Can-Am team midway through the season when Dan Gurney was forced to leave the team because of contractual difficulties. He showed that he was equally at home in the McLaren M8D by winning the Road America race and finishing second at Edmonton and Donnybrooke. This put him third in the Can-Am championship.

In Formula 5000 races Gethin was often unbeatable. If his car was going well, he would win. Out of twenty F5000 races, he won no less than eight and finished second in two others. His victories came at Zandvoort, Castle Combe, the Silverstone Martini race, Mallory Park, Zolder, Anderstorp and Brands Hatch (twice), while he took second places at Oulton Park and Mondello in Ireland. His McLaren M10B had been immaculately prepared and run by Sid Taylor who was working on behalf of the factory.

McLaren retained Gethin in the Formula One team for 1971, firstly with an M14A then with the new M19 model. He had very little success, although neither did his team leader, Denny Hulme, but McLaren decided to drop Gethin from the team before the Austrian GP in August. He was immediately snapped up to drive a P160 BRM by the factory and, in only his second drive with the team, he won the Italian Grand Prix in a classic finish in which he led a screaming five car group of cars across the line by mere inches. He also won the Rothmans Victory race at Brands Hatch which was stopped due to the crash which killed Jo Siffert.

Earlier in the season, Gethin had taken second place in the two-heat International Trophy race driving an F5000 McLaren, and he also took in several Interserie races using an ex-Can-Am McLaren. Against modest opposition, he won at Zolder and finished second at Keimola and the Norisring.

For 1972, he was retained by BRM but had a miserable season, hardly ever finishing a race. His only championship point was for sixth at Monza. In Formula Two, he drove a Chevron-BDA in which he put up some fine performances, notching up a victory at Pau and taking fourth place at Salzburgring.

Gethin lost his place with the BRM team for 1973 and, as no other Formula One team wished to sign him, he returned to Formula 5000 with a Chevron B24. He notched up several wins with the Chevron, none more welcome than when he outpaced all the Formula One cars in the Race of Champions at Brands Hatch.

The Belgian Team VDS recruited Gethin to join Teddy Pilette in an attack on the 1973/1974 Tasman series in Australia and New Zealand. They proved to be the most competitive team in the series; Gethin scored in every round allowing him to take the championship comfortably.

Gethin continued to race for VDS in European F5000 races until the end of 1977 when he finally retired from active racing.   MT

RICHIE GINTHER (b.1930)
USA

For a long spell in the late 1950s and early 1960s, America's Richie Ginther was one of the world's leading Grand Prix drivers, offering formidable opposition to the European aces, along with his countrymen Phil Hill and Dan Gurney, who showed that the 'colonies' could provide racing drivers of the highest calibre.

Born in Los Angeles in 1930, Paul Richard Ginther was given a grounding in motor engineering and began work as a motor mechanic. He moved to Santa Monica where his interest in motor racing led him into a friendship with Phil Hill who, in 1950, was just beginning his international career. With Hill's encouragement, Ginther himself took up racing with an MG TC, but two years of National Service as an aircraft merchanic kept him off the tracks until 1953. In that year, Hill invited Ginther to ride with him as mechanic in his Ferrari on the famous Mexican Road Race. They crashed, but Ginther's enthusiasm was not dampened and he returned for a further spell in the passenger's seat the following year when Hill drove a 4½-litre Ferrari into second place.

Ginther returned to his work as a car mechanic when he left the services but he chose to work for dealers who ran racing teams and, before long, he was being invited to race the machines he prepared. He handled sports cars like the vicious 4.9-litre Ferrari and an Aston Martin DB3S, but it was with a Porsche Spyder that Ginther's name really came to public notice, for he won several races in Sports Car Club of America events.

Phil Hill was firmly entrenched as a works Ferrari driver in the late 1950s and it was no doubt his persuasion that caused Enzo Ferrari to invite Ginther to Europe. He had, in fact, already made a trip to Europe to drive a 2-litre Ferrari for Luigi Chinetti in the 1957 Le Mans race without making any great impact, but Ferrari was well disposed towards American drivers since he felt that this encouraged sales of his road cars in the USA.

Ginther joined the Ferrari team in 1960 and, despite having famous team-mates like Phil Hill, Wolfgang von Trips, Willy Mairesse and Cliff Allison, he showed that he was a first class driver. He finished second in the Buenos Aires 1000 km race with von Trips, then took sixth place in the Monaco GP on his Grand Prix debut and followed up with second place in the Italian GP at the Monza circuit.

Ferrari soon appreciated Ginther's engineering talent and he was given the task of track testing all new Ferrari models as well as being a team member of both the sports-car and Grand Prix teams. With the new 1½-litre Ferrari in 1961, Ginther usually had to give best to his more experienced team-mates but he finished a memorable second at Monaco when Stirling Moss's underpowered Lotus outwitted the Ferraris; only Ginther could get within striking distance of the maestro. He also took third place in the Belgian and British GPs and a fifth in the Dutch GP to end up with fifth place in the World Championship. In sports-car racing, he co-drove with von Trips to second place in the Sebring 12 hours and then third place at the Nürburgring.

Ferrari did not pay their drivers very well in the early 1960s, so Ginther defected to BRM in 1962 where he again had to play second fiddle, this time to Graham Hill who won the World Championship. However, Ginther finished second in the Italian GP, third in the French GP and third in the Natal GP in South Africa with the 1½-litre V8 BRM. He remained with BRM in 1963, taking second place at Monaco and Monza and third in the French GP, to tie with team leader Hill for second place in the championship. He also finished second in the non-championship Oulton Park Gold Cup.

For his final season with BRM, Ginther finished every World Championship race he started, although once again the elusive victory did not come his way. He finished second at Monaco again, eleventh in the Dutch GP, fourth in the Belgian, fifth in the French, eighth in the British, seventh in the German, second in the Austrian, fourth in the Italian, fourth in the US and eighth in the Mexican.

For the 1965 season, Ginther was invited to join the Honda team, but the 1½-litre V12 Japanese car was a troublesome machine and he usually finished well down the field. But in the final race of the 1965 season, the Mexican Grand Prix, the Honda held together and Ginther recorded his first and only GP victory.

Ginther had also raced for Ford in long-distance races but his only good finish was a third place in the 1965 Daytona 24-hour race.

Ginther stayed with Honda in 1966 for the

first season of the new 3-litre formula but as the V12 car was not ready he drove a Cooper Maserati occasionally, taking fifth place in the Belgian Grand Prix. Ginther crashed the Honda during its debut at the Italian GP but he finished fourth in the Mexican GP.

For 1967, his countryman Dan Gurney asked Ginther to join him in running the Eagle Weslake Formula One cars but they were very troublesome and, although Ginther practised several times, he never got into a race, and midway through the season he decided to retire.

The tiny, crew cut, carrot-haired Ginther was a much admired member of the Grand Prix circus, who was on the fringe of greatness. After his retirement, he concentrated on acting as team manager for various teams, notably the American Porsche importers' team.   MT

FROILAN GONZALES (b.1922)
Argentina

José Froilan Gonzales was one of the most popular and talented of the bunch of South American drivers who invaded the European motor-racing scene in the 1950s. He never matched the almost clinical tidiness of his countryman Juan Manuel Fangio, because his technique at the wheel of a racing car was to hurl it at every corner as fast as it would possibly go, sorting out the slides with lightning movements of his enormous arms.

Like Fangio, Gonzales, who was born in 1922, raced the primitive cars used in Argentinian road races, but these powerful old cars with poor roadholding helped him to achieve a great deal of skill in controlling slides on the dirt roads often used in local races. The Argentinian Government under President Perón was amiably disposed towards motor racing in the late 1940s and early 1950s, so in 1950 Gonzales was given the opportunity to join Fangio in Europe. He was given a drive in the Scuderia Argentina team of 4CLT Maseratis, taking the place of Fangio, who had gone to the works Alfa Romeo team. He soon showed his skill, with a heat victory in the Albi GP and second overall on total time.

In early 1951 he returned to Argentina for the early-season races, taking a 2-litre Ferrari to Buenos Aires, where he gained the ecstatic admiration of his countrymen by beating the pre-war 1939 blown 3-litre Mercedes-Benz Grand Prix cars, although the German cars were by no means running well.

Back in Europe he drove one of the big 4½-litre Talbots in the Paris GP, where he finished second, and he also drove a sports version at Le Mans, with his countryman Onofre Marimon, but they retired. He was offered a place in the Ferrari team of 4½-litre Formula One cars later in the season, when Taruffi was taken ill, and in his first race, the French GP at Reims, he was holding second place when he was obliged to hand over to his team leader Ascari.

He stayed with Ferrari for the rest of the 1951 season, winning his first Grande Epreuve at Silverstone when he won the British GP after an initial battle with Fangio's Alfa Romeo. This spirited drive earned Gonzales the affection of the British motor-racing public who christened him the Pampas Bull, because of his 18-stone figure and his hard-driving tactics.

He took third place in the German GP, followed by second places at Barcelona and Monza, and finished third in the World Championship, behind Fangio and Ascari. He also took second place at Bari and at Modena in a Formula Two race.

For 1952 Gonzales was signed by Maserati to drive their 2-litre car in World Championship races; he had little luck against the rapid Ferraris and he preferred to blow up his engine rather than finish in a low position. His only placing of note was a second at the Italian GP. He also handled the 1½-litre BRMs in races at Silverstone, Albi and Goodwood and put up some brave performances in these difficult cars, with a couple of minor wins at Goodwood to his credit. He also drove the *Thinwall Special* to victory at Goodwood. Gonzales stayed with Maserati for 1953 but again he played second fiddle to the Ferraris, although he took third places in the Argentine, Dutch and French GPs and fourth in the British GP. Another brave display in the Albi GP with a V16 BRM almost brought victory, but tyre failure caused him to settle for second place.

With the coming of the 2½-litre Formula One in 1954, he joined the Ferrari team. This change brought him more success, for he won the British GP again – his second and final GP win – and finished second at the German and Swiss GPs, third in the Argentinian and Italian GPs and fourth in the Belgian GP. His British GP win at Silverstone was taken at the expense of countryman Fangio in the all-conquering new Mercedes 'Silver Arrow', so his victory was all the more popular in Britain. He took second place in the World Championship for 1954 and also won the Le Mans 24-hour race in a 4.9 Ferrari, co-driving with Maurice Trintignant. He was none too successful in long-distance sports-car races because he tended to break the cars rather quickly.

His career was interrupted by a bad crash during practice for the 1954 TT race at Dundrod in a 3-litre Ferrari. He had a broken shoulder and other injuries and decided to retire from racing, but he took part in the Argentine GP of 1955, sharing the third placed Ferrari with Farina and Trintignant. However, he decided not to come to Europe for the remainder of the 1955 season and restricted himself to local events. He drove a 3-litre Maserati with Jean Behra into third place in the 1956 Buenos Aires 1000 km race and was temporarily lured back to Europe later in the year to drive a Vanwall at his favourite circuit – Silverstone. The car broke its transmission at the start, however, and he went back to Argentina never to return.

From then on Gonzales took part only in South American events, usually with a Chevrolet-engined Ferrari, but he did enter the 1957 Argentinian GP, where he drove a Ferrari with the Marquis de Portago, finishing fifth.

The burly Argentinian gradually eased himself out of racing to concentrate on his garage business. There is little doubt that he would have won far more races and probably taken the 1954 World Championship, had it not been for the skill of Fangio.   MT

MASTEN GREGORY (b.1932)
USA

Motor racing is rich in 'characters', and few greater characters ever existed than America's Masten Gregory. Yet Gregory could not have looked less like a racing driver had he tried. He was short and skinny, wore thick horn-rim spectacles and spoke with a slow Kansas City drawl that seemed to come from the depths of his cowboy boots. Nevertheless, he had a long and varied racing career and was one of the first Americans to establish himself on the European motor-racing scene.

Gregory was born on 29 February 1932 to reasonably wealthy parents. At the age of fifteen, he unofficially began his motor-sport career by borrowing one of the family cars late at night and drag racing it through the streets of Kansas City. Two years later, he married and set up home in Mission Hills, Kansas. It was here that his interest in motor racing was fully developed. His brother-in-law, Dale Duncan, was involved in racing midget cars and it was he who introduced Gregory to the sport. Shortly afterwards, Gregory's father died, leaving him sufficient capital to begin a racing career.

His debut, driving a Mercury-engined Allard J2X in a SCCA 50-mile event, was hardly successful. After five hair-raising laps (a typical Gregory trademark throughout his career), the engine blew a gasket and he retired. However, the racing bug had bitten hard and the Mercury engine was soon exchanged for a 325 bhp Chrysler motor. Together, he and Duncan set off to race in the 1953 Sebring 12-hour event. Again the car failed and he returned home with the Allard and a brand-new Jaguar C-type in tow. Driving the Allard, he gained his first victory at Golden Gate Park in 1953, before switching to the C-type in which he scored several good placings during the season.

At the beginning of 1954, he decided to campaign in Europe and bought a 4.5-litre Ferrari. Co-driving with Biondetti, he was fourth in the Reims 12-hour, third at Lisbon and first at Aintree and Nassau. His success inspired him to remain in Europe and for 1955, he acquired a 3-litre Ferrari. He followed thirds at Bari and the Eiffelrennen with a first at the Lisbon Grand Prix and also scored a class victory at the TT, co-driving a Porsche Spyder with fellow American Carroll Shelby. His best showing the following year was a class victory at Nassau.

Up to this stage, Gregory's career had been concentrated around the European sports-car racing scene. In 1957, however, he turned his talents to single-seaters and signed for the Italian Scuderia Centro Sud team. Driving their Maserati 250Fs, he had his best season ever, finishing fourth at Pau, fourth at Pescara, fourth in the Italian GP and third in the Monaco GP. He completed every race he started in and finally gained sufficient points to be classified fourth in the World Championship table. He did not neglect his sports-car career, however, and finished second to Fangio in Portugal.

The following year, 1958, Gregory joined the Scottish Ecurie Ecosse team, but had a dismal season. He finished few races and showed little of the previous season's form and was lucky to survive a huge accident at Silverstone in which he managed to destroy the team's Lister Jaguar. In spite of this, he was signed to drive as number three to Jack Brabham and Bruce McLaren in the works Cooper F1 team for 1959. This was the year that saw the tiny rear-engined Coopers victorious, the World Championship title eventually going to the Australian, Brabham. Despite being eclipsed by his two team-mates, Gregory managed a third in the Dutch Grand Prix. The problems of running a three-car works team, however, proved to be too much for the cooper organisation and so, at the end of 1959, Gregory was dropped. By this time, Gregory had acquired a reputation for crashing and none of the leading Formula One teams would have him on their books, so he rejoined the Scuderia Centro Sud. Success eluded him, however, and he returned to his first love, sports-car racing, signing for the American Camoradi Racing Team to drive their new, but unreliable, Maserati Tipo 61s. His greatest success during these lean years was a superb victory at the 1961 Nürburgring 1000 kilometre event, co-driving the 'Birdcage' Maserati 61s with Camoradi patron 'Lucky' Casner. In 1963, he captured the Players 200 at Mosport Park, but the interim year, spent driving a Formula One Lotus for the UDT Laystall team, proved frustrating and fruitless.

Perhaps his greatest victory was his win in the 1965 Le Mans 24-hour endurance race, an event he had been given little hope of winning. His co-driver was a young Austrian, Jochen Rindt, who, like Gregory at that time, was burdened with a reputation as a car wrecker. Their machine was a private Ferrari 275LM, entered by the North American Racing Team, a team whose reputation for reliability and efficiency was, until then, conspicuous by its absence. Nevertheless, the two held their car together and outlasted all the more highly fancied works runners to take a surprise victory. Gregory's critics were silenced. Their allegations of poor eyesight and dangerous driving were further battered by Gregory's superb drive in the 1965 Indianapolis 500, a form of racing unfamiliar to the by-now 'Europeanised' American. After qualifying 31st on the grid, he electrified the huge crowd by moving up to fifth place by lap 43, eventually being forced to retire through engine failure.

Thereafter, Gregory returned to Europe, but his appearances became fewer and further between. In 1969, he won the Österreichring sports-car event in a Porsche 908 and in 1970 he and Toine Hezemans drove a works Alfa Romeo T33 to third place in the Sebring 12-hour race. His last year of racing was 1971, when he drove for the Alfa Romeo team. Gregory, who speaks several European languages fluently now concentrates on his business interests in private life.　　　MW

KENELM LEE GUINNESS
(1887-1937)
Great Britain

It was said of Kenelm Lee Guinness, that he was a driver who seldom made the headlines, but always did a job well. That was only part of the story, however, for this modest, retiring man, who drove so unspectacularly, could always be relied upon to finish well to the fore in any race in which he took part.

He had received his baptism of fire – literally – as riding mechanic to his elder brother Algy (Sir Algernon Lee Guinness, Bart) in the notorious V8 200 bhp Darracq, whose 22.5-litre engine boasted only the most minimal of exhaust stubs, and which threw great spurts of flame back over the occupants of the car's two tiny bucket seats causing many anxious, and probably heated, moments.

Kenelm – more familiarly known as Bill – took over where his brother had left off, first coming to the public notice with his victory in the 1914 Isle of Man Tourist Trophy, in which he drove a Sunbeam. He also achieved fame as the creator of the KLG sparking plug, which he originally developed for his racing cars. He subsequently founded the KLG sparking-plug factory, Robinhood Works, on Putney Hill, where, incidentally, Segrave's 1929 land-speed-record car, *Golden Arrow,* was built.

After World War I, Bill Guinness rejoined the Sunbeam works team as leading driver. He was reported as lacking the fire that had distinguished his brother's driving, but he compensated for this with the regularity with which he could be relied upon at consistent high speed. 'It has been said of many people,' wrote Sammy Davis in *Autocar,* 'that if you were to place a halfpenny on a corner during a race, and one front wheel ran over it on the first lap, the same wheel would pass over the coin again on every other lap. But of very few people is this as true as it was with Bill.' Coming from a journalist of Davis's calibre, this was praise, indeed.

Guinness enjoyed his greatest successes with Louis Coatalen's 1.5-litre Talbot-Darracq *voiturettes,* which on their very first outing,

1 Left: In 1979 Mario Andretti added the World Championship to a list of achievements which place him among the sport's great all-rounders. Andretti could also number victory at Indianapolis and in the Daytona 500, three USAC titles and numerous sports car classics among his successes.

2 Below: Alberto Ascari followed in the footsteps of his famous father, Antonio, and like his father he was killed by the sport he loved. Alberto was twice World Champion, in 1952 and 1953, and in 1954 he won the Mille Miglia.

3 Above: When Jean Behra won the 1952 Reims GP for Gordini his name went into motor racing history but thereafter hard results bore scant witness to his true stature.

4 Left: Among his three World Championships, Sir Jack Brabham numbered the unique distinction of winning the title in a car bearing his own name.

5 Right: Jim Clark was, quite simply, one of the greatest racing drivers ever seen. His record of two World Championships, 25 Grand Prix wins and winning at Indianapolis is perhaps inadequate testimony to his real dominance and what might have been.

7 Right: 1950 was the first year motor racing boasted an official World Championship for drivers. That first championship was dominated by the two drivers seen here after that year's French Grand Prix, at Reims. Juan Manuel Fangio, in the car, won the race for Alfa Romeo and Dr Giuseppe 'Nino' Farina, with the goggles, went on to win the championship for the same team. Farina was a prolific winner almost to the end of his career in the mid 'fifties, but it was Fangio who reaped the lion's share of the glory, with an unlikely to be emulated tally of five World Championships between 1951 and 1957. The Argentine was master of his craft, capable of winning on any type of circuit and of transcending inadequacies of machinery as few other drivers. He was loved and feared by his own generation and revered by those who followed.

6 Left: Three years after Ralph De Palma was photographed at Indianapolis in 1911 at the wheel of this Simplex, he won the 500-mile classic. During his career he won some 2000 races, on dirt, on boards, in the Vanderbilt Cup and virtually anywhere else he raced, gaining a reputation along the way as a true sportsman.

8 *Left:* Like many before him, Emerson Fittipaldi paid the price of patriotism. With two World Championships won he struggled valiantly but vainly with his own team until his retirement.

9 *Right:* There was tragic irony to Graham Hill's death in an air crash. Having survived many contempories and his own share of pain, Hill, twice World Champion, Le Mans and Indianapolis winner, had recently retired to the role of team patron.

10 *Below left:* Long before his name went on the Borg Warner Trophy for the fourth time, A.J.Foyt was an institution in USAC.

11 *Below:* In the space of a year, Mike Hawthorn became World Champion, announced his retirement and died in a road accident.

12 *Left:* Phil Hill was the first American to win the World Championship, his victory for Ferrari in 1961 laying the lie that Americans were just 'roundy-round racers'.

13 *Below left:* Driving for fellow Antipodeans Brabham and McLaren, Denny Hulme won the World Championship, two Can-Am championships and the affectionate nickname 'The Bear'.

14 *Below:* James Hunt after the final rain-soaked race of the dramatic 1976 Grand Prix season, when he crowned a colourful career with a hard-earned World Championship.

the 1921 Grand Prix des Voiturettes, at Le Mans, scored a one-two-three victory over the Bugattis which had hitherto dominated this capacity class. Guinness came in second in this event, as he did in that year's Junior Car Club 200-mile race at Brooklands, his team-mates being Henry Segrave and Malcolm Campbell.

In the 1922 '200', however, the Talbot-Darracqs were up against stiff opposition, especially from the new Gremillon-designed twin-overhead-camshaft Aston Martins, as well as the Brescia Bugattis. However, although it was Kensington Moir's Aston and the Bugattis which made the initial running, Segrave's Talbot-Darracq soon took over the lead. Guinness, who had lost a tyre on the sixth lap, was a lap behind. The third member of the team, Jean Chassagne, was eliminated when a burst tyre sent his differential-less car over the top of the Brooklands banking (he and his mechanic were unhurt, but by some freak, Chassagne's shoes were deposited neatly in the centre of the track). Then a burnt-out valve slowed Segrave, and it was up to Guinness, the Aston menace having dwindled to Stead's side-valve car, the famous *Bunny,* which was lapping at 88 mph. Guinness's car was faster, though, and could average 94.5 mph for the Brooklands circuit: so the finishing order was Kenelm Lee Guinness, who had averaged 88.06 mph for the entire distance, G. C. Stead and H. O. D. Segrave.

Guinness took the next two races for which, with the Talbot-Darracq, he was entered, in his stride. These were the GP des Voiturettes at Le Mans and the Penya Rhin 1.5-litre Grand Prix and he carried his lucky penny, which had saved a soldier's life by stopping a bullet, had belonged to a man who broke the bank at Monte Carlo, and then had gone to the winner of an international motor-boat race.

His good fortune was not confined to *voiturette* events, for he also took the land-speed record, with the 350 hp V12 Sunbeam, at Brooklands; his speed was 133.75 mph, it being the last time the world record was ever broken on a proper, established race circuit.

The Talbot-Darracqs were not entered for the 1923 200 miles, but brand-new cars, copies in miniature of the successful GP Sunbeam, appeared for 1924. They dominated the event, lapping neatly in line abreast at record-breaking speed, 10 mph faster than their rivals – over 100 mph on the first lap, 106 mph on the second, 108 mph on the third – a performance which was maintained to the end. Guinness

was first at 102.27 mph, then came George Duller, then Henry Segrave.

However, Bill Guinness's luck ran out in the 1924 Spanish Grand Prix at San Sebastian. Momentarily distracted, he crashed severely, wrecking his Sunbeam and killing his mechanic. The accident affected him greatly, and he increasingly became prey to bouts of depression, which were, it seems, the direct cause of his death in 1937.   DBW

DAN GURNEY (b.1931)
USA

Daniel Sexton Gurney was one of the United States' most successful racing drivers in Grand Prix racing during the 1960s, winning four major Grands Prix as well as a host of other events. He also had the distinction of being the first American driver in an American car to win a Grand Prix race since Tommy Milton won the 1921 French Grand Prix in a Duesenberg.

Born in New York in 1931 Dan Gurney was the son of an opera singer who moved to southern California after World War II. The young Gurney soon became involved in hot rodding and was often harried by the police for the impromptu drag races he and his friends started on the streets. He was drafted into the forces and served mostly in Korea, but on his return he gravitated once more to the motor-racing scene, buying a TR2 which he raced with moderate success in 1955.

In the next couple of years Gurney drove various sports cars, including a Chevrolet Corvette, a Porsche Speedster and a 4.9-litre Ferrari. With the Ferrari he showed that he was more than competitive with the top American drivers and in 1958 he was invited to go to Europe to drive a privately entered Testa Rossa Ferrari at Le Mans. He impressed everyone with his fast, smooth driving of the car in the early stages of the race (his co-driver later crashed the car) and he was asked to drive a GT Ferrari in the Reims 12-hour race with André Pilette. Again they failed to finish, but Enzo Ferrari was impressed with the lanky, fair-haired Gurney. Since Ferrari was conscious of the need to sell Ferrari road cars in America, he gave Gurney a contract for the 1959 season to join one of his countrymen, Phil Hill, in the sports-car team. He shared the winning Ferrari in the Sebring 12-hour race and showed his versatility by leading the Targa Florio before the Ferrari broke.

He was also invited to drive the big, 2½-litre front-engined Formula One Ferrari by mid-season and he celebrated by taking a close second place to team-mate Tony Brooks in the German Grand Prix at Avus. He followed this with a third place in the Portuguese GP at Lisbon and fourth in the Italian GP at Monza.

The pay for a Ferrari driver was very poor in 1959, so he decided to accept a more lucrative contract from BRM for 1960. It was a disastrous year, for he seldom even finished a race in the troublesome new rear-engined BRM, his only placing of note being a second in a *formule libre* race in Cordoba. However, in sports-car racing he drove a 2.8-litre Bird-cage Maserati for the Lucky Casner team and, partnered by Stirling Moss, he won the Nürburgring 1000-kilometre race. He also led several other races in the Maserati, but it was a fragile machine.

Gurney drove for BRM in Australia and New Zealand in the winter of 1960-61. He won his heat at Ballarat and finished third in his heat of the New Zealand GP, but he decided to leave BRM and join the new Porsche Formula One team at the start of the new 1½-litre Formula One. Although his car could not match the speed of the new Ferrari, he had a good season, taking second place in an exciting photo-finish with Baghetti's Ferrari at the French GP, plus a fifth at Monaco, sixth in Belgium and two more second places at the Italian and US GPs. This gave him joint third place, with Stirling Moss, in the World Championship. He also drove a 2-litre Porsche in sports-car races, taking second place in the Targa Florio, with Jo Bonnier as co-driver.

Gurney remained with Porsche for 1962, driving their new flat-eight F1 car. It was not really competitive with the new British V8-engined cars, but in the French GP he benefited from retirements to give Porsche their first and only Grand Prix win, as well as taking his own first championship victory. In the remainder of the season he took a third place in the German GP, and fifth at the US GP. He also took part in his first Indianapolis 500 in 1962, driving one of Mickey Thompson's Harvey Aluminium Specials, which eventually dropped out with gearbox failure.

In 1963, Porsche withdrew from Formula One, so Gurney moved to the Brabham team. The V8 Climax-engined Brabham suited Gurney and he was always among the leading five drivers in Grand Prix races, but he was often sidelined with mechanical problems. However, he was third in the Belgium GP, second in the Dutch GP, fifth in the French GP, sixth in the Mexican GP and second in the South African GP. To prove his versatility he drove a Lotus-Ford to seventh place at the 1963 Indianapolis 500 and won the Riverside 500-mile stock-car race.

Gurney stayed with Brabham in 1964 and once again proved that he was among the fastest three or four drivers in the world, although mechanical problems and poor team-work robbed him of vital places, such as at the Belgian GP when he ran low on fuel while in second place; he called at his pit for more fuel only to find that they didn't have any, so he returned to the race and his tanks ran dry. However, he won the French GP, which followed, to give Brabham their first ever Grand Prix victory. Later in the season he also won the Mexican GP, but his only other championship placing was a sixth at Spa. He also won the Riverside 500, in a Ford again, and at Indianapolis he drove a Lotus-Ford, but was withdrawn from the race when team-mate Jim Clark suffered from chunking tyres.

For the final year of the 1½-litre Formula One, Gurney stayed with Brabham, finishing second in the United States GP, and the Mexican GP, and third in the Dutch, German and Italian GPs, to finish fourth in the World Championship. He once again won the Riverside 500 and again retired at Indianapolis.

In 1964, Gurney had teamed up with Carroll Shelby to form All-American Racers, but for 1966 he acquired sole ownership of the team and also formed Anglo-American Racers to build his own Formula One car at Rye in England, using a new V12 engine designed and built by Harry Weslake. In the 1966 season he was obliged to use a four-cylinder Coventry Climax 2.7-litre engine as the V12 was not ready. His new car was called the Eagle and the only places of note he obtained in 1966 were a couple of fifth places in the French and Mexican GPs.

He was signed by Ford to drive their 7-litre Mk II cars in sports-car racing for 1966. In his first race he took second place in the Daytona 24-hour race, co-driving with Jerry Grant, but he retired in his other races for Ford. He also won his fourth successive Riverside 500-mile race in a Ford saloon. He entered his own Eagle-Ford at Indianapolis, but it was damaged in a first lap crash which put him out of the race. He took part in the Bridgehampton round of the Can-Am series in his Lola Ford, fitted with Weslake cylinder heads, and he won the race in a close finish.

The Weslake V12 was ready for Formula One in 1967 and he started the season well with a victory in the non-championship Race of Champions at Brands Hatch. He followed this with an epic victory at the Belgian GP, making him the first US driver of a US car to win a European classic for 46 years. It also established Spa as the fastest track in Europe, for he put in a fastest lap at 148.8 mph. However, although the Eagle car was beautifully made, the engine was unreliable and Gurney's only other place of note was a third in the Canadian GP. He had some consolation, for he won the Le Mans 24-hour race, with A. J. Foyt, in a Mk IV Ford.

He persevered with the Eagle in Formula One for 1968, but the engine was still unreliable and he seldom even finished a race. He borrowed a McLaren for the United States GP and finished fourth, but at the end of the season he decided to abandon Formula One racing because it was too expensive and unrewarding. He was fast becoming a successful constructor of Indianapolis cars and in 1968 he sold several cars to customers. He drove an Eagle in the race himself finishing a fine second in a car powered by a stock-block Ford engine. The race was won by another Eagle, driven by Bobby Unser, with a further Eagle in fourth place, driven by Denny Hulme.

Gurney also won two other USAC races, at Mosport and Riverside, in 1968 with Eagles, but he had no luck in the Can-Am series. However, he did win the Riverside 500-mile race for the fifth time.

For 1969, Gurney decided against driving for another team in Formula One and he concentrated on Indianapolis, Can-Am and Trans-Am events in the USA. He again finished second at Indianapolis in his stock-block Ford-engined Eagle; he also won the Donnybrooke 200, was second in the Rocky Mountain 150, third in the Rex Mays 300 and fourth in the Dan Gurney 200, a race at Seattle which had been named after him. This gave him fourth place in the USAC championship. He occasionally drove in Can-Am events, taking a third at Michigan in the spare works McLaren car and fourth in the Los Angeles Times in his own M6B McLaren. Eagle cars also swept the board in the American Formula A championship, the equivalent of Britain's Formula 5000.

Gurney made a short return to Formula One racing in 1970, when McLaren asked him to drive an M14 model following Bruce McLaren's death. He took sixth place in the French GP, but he felt out of touch with Formula One and did not drive in the latter part of the season. He drove a works McLaren in the early part of the Can-Am series, winning the opening events at Mosport and Mont Tremblant, but contractual difficulties with rival sponsors forced him to leave the team after a few races.

At Indianapolis, Dan finished third in an Eagle with a turbocharged Offenhauser engine and, with a Ford-engined Eagle, he won the Golden Gate 150 at Sears Point Raceway. Gurney's protégé, Swede Savage, won the Bobby Ball Memorial 150 race at the end of the season, but shortly before this race Dan Gurney announced that he was retiring as a driver to concentrate on his role as a constructor. His success as a driver would soon be repeated as a car builder.

After 1971 Gurney concentrated almost exclusively on building cars for the USAC Championship Trail series in the USA, running a factory team and also selling cars to private owners; he was also constructing cars for Formula A racing. Bobby Unser was particularly successful in an Offenhauser-engined Eagle during 1972, winning four of the USAC championship races. In the 1973 Indianapolis 500, no less than sixteen of the starters were in Eagles and they took five of the first ten places, including the first and second-placed cars of Gordon Johncock and Billy Vukovich. In 1974 they did even better, with eight of the first ten cars using Eagle chassis, while nineteen of the 33 starters were Eagles. However, they missed victory, which went to Johnny Rutherford's McLaren; the best-placed Eagle was the car of Bobby Unser, which finished second.

Gurney was running a team of cars in Formula A during 1974. He originally intended to modify one of these for Formula One, but decided that the design would not be competitive and built a fresh car for Formula One in 1975. He eventually forsook Formula One entirely in favour of USAC. In 1980 he made a 'one-off' comeback in a NASCAR race, just for the fun of it. After a sensational performance he was sidelined by mechanical problems and retired for good with the satisfaction of knowing that he could still run with the very best.   MT

MIKE HAILWOOD (1940-1981)
Great Britain

Stanley Michael Bailey Hailwood was born on 2 April 1940 at Oxford, where his father, Stan, a former motor-cycle racer, owned a motor-cycle business which developed into a prosperous series of dealerships in post-war years. Mike, as he became known, was educated at Nautical College, Pangbourne and was then apprenticed to Triumph Motor Cycles in Coventry. Encouraged by his father, he took up motor-cycle racing almost as soon as he was legally able, at the age of seventeen. His first race, on a 125 cc MV, resulted in thirteenth place at Oulton Park, but within four years he had obtained the first of his nine World Championships. Between 1961 and 1968, he won 75 motor-cycling Grands Prix and no less than twelve Isle of Man TT races, which are still regarded as the greatest test of any motor cyclist.

There were many precedents for successful motor cyclists moving into motor racing, and Hailwood's dominance of the two-wheeled world convinced him that he stood a good chance of following other great motor cyclists-turned-motor racers like Tazio Nuvolari, Piero Taruffi, Jean-Pierre Beltoise and John Surtees. In 1963, he bought himself a Formula Junior Brabham, finishing fifth in his first race and doing reasonably well in the few races his motor-cycling commitments allowed.

For 1964, Reg Parnell invited him to join his team of Formula One Lotus-BRMs in Grand Prix racing, but little success came his way because the Lotus 25s were already three years old when Hailwood started to drive them and their engines were unreliable. He took part in the occasional race in sports cars and kept his hand in by driving cars such as E-type Jaguars, various Ferraris and an Iso Grifo on his journeys across Europe and Britain.

At the end of 1967, he decided to bring his motor-cycling career to an end, at which time he was honoured by the award of the MBE. He switched to full-time motor racing, taking part in the South African Springbok series by co-driving Ed Nelson's Ford GT40.

For 1969, he was signed by the John Wyer team to drive Ford GT40s and Mirage-BRMs in the World Sports Car Championship races. He often led races, but was invariably forced to retire, while the rivalling 3-litre Porsches often proved too fast for the Fords. However, he and co-driver David Hobbs finished a good third in the Le Mans 24-hour race. He also drove a factory-sponsored Lola T142 in the Guards Formula 5000 championship, taking third place in the championship despite having an ill-handling car.

Mike remained in Formula 5000 for 1970, driving the works-backed Lola T190 entered by Jackie Epstein. After the chassis had been improved, he really made the Lola competitive, winning at the Salzburgring in Austria and at Silverstone, and taking second place at Brands Hatch, Mallory Park, and Snetterton. This gave him fourth place in the Guards championship. He also drove a Gulf-Porsche 917 at Le Mans, but spun in torrential rain and shattered the front of his car against the Armco railing.

Ex-motor cyclist John Surtees recognised Hailwood's potential at the end of 1970, so he signed him to drive the Surtees TS8 in the Rothmans F5000 championship. The car was very competitive and Hailwood picked up victories at Mallory Park (twice) and Silverstone (twice), together with several other placings, to take second place in the championship. Towards the end of the season, John Surtees gave him a drive in a Formula One Surtees at the Italian GP, where he led the race on occasions and eventually finished fourth. This resulted in a full-time contract with Surtees for 1972 to race both Formula One and Two cars. In the Matchbox Toys-sponsored Surtees TS10, Hailwood had a fine year in Formula Two, winning races at Rouen, Österreichring, Mantorp Park, Salzburging and Hockenheim to take the European F2 Championship very easily. In Formula One, he finished only four races in his Surtees-Ford TS9B, but he scored World Championship points on all four occasions by finishing second in the Italian GP, fourth in the Belgian and Austrian GPs and sixth in the French GP to come eighth in the World Championship, with thirteen points. He also finished second in the Race of Champions at Brands Hatch and was leading the exciting International Trophy race at Silverstone until he was forced to retire.

He stayed with Surtees for 1973, but the Formula One car was not very competitive and Hailwood either retired or finished well down in all his races. In long-distance events, he drove the Mirage Cosworth V8, winning the prestigious Spa 1000 kilometres with Derek Bell as co-driver. He also finished fourth in the Austrian 1000 km race and fifth in the Dijon 1000 km and Watkins Glen 6-hour races.

For 1974, he left the Surtees team and joined

the Yardley-McLaren team to race a McLaren M23, in the colours of Yardley toiletries. He started the season well, but in the German GP at Nürburgring, on the 12th lap, Hailwood's car crashed heavily, breaking the driver's leg in three places, and putting him out of racing for the remainder of the season.

Mike Hailwood retired from racing in 1976 to concentrate on his boat building company in New Zealand. He never achieved his ambition to add a motor-racing World Championship to his motor-cycling ones. That his bravery is not in doubt was shown when he pulled Clay Regazzoni from his blazing car in South Africa in 1973, a feat for which he earned the George Medal.

By 1978 the craving for action was getting stronger and as well as taking in a couple of Australian saloon car races, 'Mike the Bike' made a sensational return to the Isle of Man, winning the Formula One race on a Ducati to add another World Championship to his tally. For 1979 he committed himself to a full season of Formula One 'bike racing and a return to living in England. Once again he had a successful Isle of Man TT outing, winning the Senior TT and finishing second in the Classic TT. By this time, however, Hailwood was publicly admitting that his desire to race had gone. After an unhappy post-TT meeting at Mallory he decided to quit racing once and for all and concentrate on a motor-cycle dealership that he and fellow-racer Rod Gould had opened in Birmingham during mid-1979. In March 1981 Mike Hailwood crashed tragically while driving in Warwickshire with his two young children: all three were killed.   MT

DUCAN HAMILTON (b.1920)
Great Britain
For many motor-racing enthusiasts, Duncan Hamilton epitomises the sort of carefree, wealthy, amateur racing driver of the 1950s who treated motor racing as a well paid sideline to the more serious business of high living, hard drinking and chasing girls. Duncan Hamilton enjoyed good living, as his ample waistline revealed, but beneath the external veneer of a *bon viveur* lay a dedicated racing driver of great skill, exuberance and, above all, stamina, for he was able to drive many long-distance races without showing signs of tiredness.

Born in 1920 in Ireland, Hamilton learned to drive in the ubiquitous Austin Seven, and was soon immersed in the atmosphere of Brooklands. He was too young to take a serious part in pre-war motor racing, but after war-time service with the Fleet Air Arm he bought an R-type MG, followed by a Type 35 Bugatti. These he used mostly in local sprints and hill-climb events before he invested in a 60 Maserati which he used for gaining experience in circuit racing. The Maserati was not particularly competitive and Hamilton was already indulging in the tail-out driving technique which gained the crowd's attention, but often ended in a spin.

Hamilton really came to public notice in 1950, when he drove a Healey Silverstone in the 1950 Production Car race at Silverstone and soundly beat the works Aston Martin team, led by Reg Parnell. This led to an invitation to drive a Nash-Healey at Le Mans in 1950. Partnered by Tony Rolt, he finished fourth and followed up in 1951 by taking sixth place with the same driver. He also purchased from the Belgian Johnny Claes a Formula One Talbot Lago, with which he had a great deal of amusement, although not much success. He drove one excellent race with the Talbot; he was holding second place in the rain-lashed British GP, at Silverstone, when it was stopped after only six laps. Hamilton also occasionally drove a Formula Two HWM in 1951, taking second place in Dublin. He also drove for HWM in 1952, but he preferred big-engined sports cars and did not get on too well with the small HWM and its 2-litre Alta engine.

In 1952, Hamilton bought a C-type Jaguar from the Coventry factory and began a long association with the marque which lasted until his retirement from racing in 1958. A second place at Turnberry in Scotland was his only decent placing with the car, but he was invited to join the works team at Le Mans and for the Goodwood Nine hours. The cars failed ignominiously, but Hamilton gained valuable experience.

For 1953, Jaguar again signed Hamilton to drive a C-type and, although he retired in most races, he had the satisfaction of winning at Le Mans, partnered by his long time co-driver Tony Rolt, leading a Jaguar 1-2-4 rout of the Ferraris. Hamilton also drove his own C-type in various races, but injured himself at Oporto when he collided with an electricity pylon. In typical Hamilton fashion, the pylon he chose was a vital link in the city's electrical system, with the result that the electricity was cut off for several hours.

Hamilton again drove for Jaguar in 1954, this time using the new D-type model. The Hamilton/Rolt car held second place in the early hours of the morning at Le Mans and Hamilton was put into the car in streaming wet conditions to try and catch the leading Ferrari. He drove frantically to finish only three miles behind. He and Rolt finished second in the Reims 12 hours, but retired from the TT. Hamilton had also acquired a D-type of his own, which he raced in many club events with gay abandon.

He was once again in the Jaguar team for 1955, but did not have much success, for this was the year of the Le Mans tragedy and there was little international racing after June. He and Rolt both retired at Le Mans, but in his own car he won the Coupe de Paris at Montlhéry, as well as various smaller races at Goodwood and Silverstone, and finished third in both the Dakar GP and the Portuguese GP.

For 1956, he remained with Jaguar. He started off the season by winning the Coupe de Paris again, followed by second place in the Frontières GP at Chimay. Then he and Ivor Bueb won the Reims 12-hour race, but the irrepressible Hamilton was sacked from the team after the race because he had refused to slow down to orders when holding a clear lead. He was signed on by Ferrari, but had little luck with them, apart from a third place in the Swedish GP.

It was back to his own D-type Jaguar for 1957, together with outings in a 3.4-litre Jaguar in saloon-car events. He once again won several club events and picked up places in foreign events. At Le Mans, where he entered his own car for himself and Masten Gregory, they finished sixth behind a string of other Jaguars.

It was yet another Jaguar season for Hamilton in 1958 with the usual crop of good places and wins in both the D-type and Jaguar saloons. At Le Mans he fitted a 3-litre engine to the D-type he shared with Ivor Bueb, but after getting into the lead during the night Hamilton overturned the car at Arnage, while avoiding a slower car, and received severe injuries. Long before he was completely fit he took sixth place in the Tourist Trophy but his will to race was shattered by the death of his close friend Mike Hawthorn.

Upon his recovery he decided to hang up his helmet and retire to his garage business in Byfleet, Surrey, although he was still seen at many race meetings.   MT

RAY HARROUN (1879-1968)
USA

There are few more pervasive myths found in motoring history than the half-baked chestnut that Ray Harroun, who won the first Indianapolis 500-mile race in 1911, was the first man to fit a rear-view mirror to a car. Even Harroun, who was born in 1879, was quick to deny the statement: 'Hell, no. We had them on horsedrawn carriages,' he would growl 50 years later. But what is true is the fact that Harroun was the first·man to use a rear-view mirror as a substitute for the riding mechanic who was employed on early racing cars as much to keep a look-out for following cars as to attend to the vehicle.

Harroun started racing in a small way in 1905, competing in a ten-mile dirt-track event in Chicago. In 1908 he joined the Marmon car manufacturing company at Indianapolis, where businessman Carl G. Fisher was proposing to build a banked motor racing circuit to rival Britain's Brooklands.

And when the Indianapolis track eventually opened, in August 1909, Harroun, who was both engineer and racing driver to the Marmon company, was there.

Though the Buicks of Bob Burman and Louis Strang dominated the inaugural meeting, Harroun took third place in the strongly contested 100-mile trophy race, as well as winning several minor events.

He repeated his Indianapolis form three months later at the opening of another famous circuit, the two-mile dirt-track at Atlanta, Georgia, with five first or second places.

The following season opened well for Harroun, who took two first places on a new banked board circuit at Playa del Rey in California, though his performance in the United States Grand Prize at Savannah was disappointing, for he was the last of six finishers (though to have finished was in itself an achievement, for no less than 50 per cent of the entry had fallen by the wayside during the gruelling 415-mile race).

Again, it was Atlanta and Indianapolis which saw his most impressive victories: he won a 200-mile event at Atlanta, while a ten race meet at Indianapolis saw four first places, two seconds and three thirds. His Indianapolis victories included the 200-mile Wheeler-Schebler trophy, donated by one of the circuit's founders, won in the face of stiff opposition from several of the leading racing teams, such as Buick and National.

This was the *annus mirabilis* of the Marmon team, which took 25 first places, 24 seconds, and 13 thirds in the 93 races for which they were entered: but one failure deserves to be recorded, for the car that Harroun drove in the Vanderbilt Cup, which retired with a broken crankshaft, was based on the new Marmon six-cylinder model, which would achieve lasting fame the following year. Indeed, the Vander-bilt could still have seen a Marmon victory, for Harroun's team-mate Joe Dawson would have come first had he not stopped to report a trifling incident – a collision with a spectator who had strayed on to the course.

In any case, Harroun's showing during the year was sufficient to win him the title of National Driving Champion: and that, he decided, was time enough to quit, and he therefore announced his intention to retire.

Howard Marmon, however, had other ideas and eventually managed to persuade the reluc-tant Harroun to take part in the year's major event, the first 500-mile race at Indianapolis, driving the bright yellow Marmon Wasp six-cylinder single-seater. Indeed, the Marmon just had to do without the weight of a riding mechanic, for it was, at 7.3 litres, well outclassed by the other entries, which were built right up to the maximum capacity allowance of 9850 cc. Harroun rigged up the famous mirror when the other competitors complained of the danger inherent in a car with no rear lookout, but it seems that his heart wasn't entirely in the race for which he had so unwillingly entered.

Forty of the opening laps were driven by one Cyrus Patschke, an unknown who proved his worth by keeping the relatively diminutive Marmon well up with the leaders; then Harroun took over, and consolidated Patschke's performance. This swapping of drivers was quite permissible under the rules of the race, and in fact Patschke, annoyed at having been pulled out of the race when he was doing so well, took over Joe Dawson's four-cylinder Marmon and brought it up level with the leaders, until a leaking radiator spoiled his chances. Cyrus, cheated of his chance to make motoring history, handed the car back to Dawson (who finished a creditable fifth).

Harroun, closely pressed by Ralph Mulford's Lozier, held the lead and finished first. His average speed was 74.59 mph, and he had taken 6 hours 42 minutes 8 seconds to cover the 500 miles, beating Mulford by 1 minute 43 seconds.

Both Marmon and Harroun retired from racing after that; three years later Harroun designed two Indy racers for Maxwell, one of which, running on paraffin fed through a Harroun-designed carburettor, finished ninth in one race.

Harroun's subsequent career was as a consultant engineer specialising in car accessories, though he recreated his 1911 Indianapolis victory with the Wasp in a commemorative film in the 1940s and drove the same car in the track's golden jubilee cele-brations in 1961, at the age of 82. He died seven years later.   DBW

GWENDA HAWKES
Great Britain
Of that small, select band of lady drivers who could compete in terms of sheer speed with the racing motorists of the inter-war period, one of the most successful was Gwenda Hawkes.

She was, it seems, almost destined to achieve fame, for her father was Sir Frederick Manley Glubb CB, KCMG, DSO, who served with distinction during both the Boer War and World War I, while her brother John was Glubb Pasha of the Arab Legion. Gwenda herself had a war record of some note, for she drove ambulances on the Russian and Ruma-nian fronts in the 1914-18 hostilities, and was awarded the Crosses of St George and St Stanislaus and mentioned in official war despatches.

After that, peacetime seemed somewhat of an anticlimax, and Gwenda looked around for an activity which offered some of the excite-ment of her wartime career. She found it in motor cycling, and during the harsh winter of 1921 she set up a 1000-miles record on a Ner-a-Car under official ACU scrutiny.

Then, in 1922, she rode a 249cc Trump-JAP at Brooklands to break 'Double-12' records (local protests had caused a ban on 24-hour events at the Weybridge track); her average speed was 44.65 mph. Soon after this, Gwenda, who had been Mrs Janson, married Lieutenant-Colonel Stewart, who was her co-driver on long-distance records. Finding the ambience in France to their liking, the Stewarts set up home there, and Gwenda began setting up records with Morgan three-wheelers; her most notable achievement was a fantastic 118 mph at Arpajon.

Helping her prepare her cars was Douglas Hawkes, who had made his name at

Brooklands driving vehicles as diverse as a 1914 Tourist Trophy Morgan, a sports Hoestmann and the 15½-litre Grand Prix Lorraine-Dietrich *Vieux Charles Trois.* Hawkes had come to France to take up his controlling interest in the Derby car factory, near Paris.

Gwenda Stewart was a stickler for immaculate preparation of her racing cars: this was probably a legacy of her military background. Two hours before any record attempt, her car had to be lined up on the track for inspection, immaculate and ready to go in all respects. The mechanics, too, had to be impeccably turned out, dressed in spotless white overalls, for which Gwenda gladly footed the laundry bills. It was a policy which paid off time and again in broken records.

In 1930, Mrs Stewart began racing the Miller which Douglas Hawkes was using as a mobile testbed for Derby front-wheel-drive designs; her first notable achievement with this car was a batch of records at Montlhéry, covering a mile at over 118 mph, and breaking hour and 200 km records, too, while the car shattered the world 100 km record several times.

In 1931, the Derby-Miller (now bored out to take it from the 1500 cc into the 2-litre class) lapped Montlhéry at 141.37 mph, a new record.

The Montlhéry lap record fell to Mrs Stewart several times, her fastest speed being recorded in 1934, when the Derby-Miller achieved an extremely impressive 147.79 mph.

She also set up the all-time ladies' lap record of 135.95 mph at Brooklands with this car, which seems to have been almost a good-luck mascot for her, as she escaped from death when this tricky vehicle went out of control at 150 mph at the Montlhéry circuit in France.

She had less success with the second Derby fwd racer, which Hawkes (whom she married in 1937) built for her: this slim single-seater was independently-suspended all round, and had a twin ohc supercharged 1500 cc Maserati engine; it survives today, in superb condition, in Tom Wheatcroft's single-seater collection museum at Donington Park, near Leicester.

Away from the banked tracks, Gwenda seems to have been less fortunate, for she entered fwd Derby sports cars at Le Mans in 1934 and 1935, but was forced to retire in both events.

But her exploits with the Morgans and the Derby-Miller have secured her place in motoring history, a place made all the more remarkable because few women racing drivers have ever achieved universal fame in the field of motor racing. And this was at a time when women's liberation was unheard of!   DBW

MIKE HAWTHORN (1929-1959)
Great Britain
Mike Hawthorn was something more than a successful racing driver to the youth of the 1950s for, in some intangible way, he epitomised the aspirations of young people who were recovering from the gloomy after-effects of a world war. In the early 1950s Britain had little to be cheerful about, but this tall blond young man, with his happy countenance, ever-present pipe and horribly battered cloth cap, took on the best that the mighty Italian motor racing world could offer – and beat them. He was not a clinical driver in the Fangio and Moss mould, for he only drove well if the world was right with him, but when it was he was almost unbeatable.

John Michael Hawthorn was born on 10 April 1929 at Mexborough in Yorkshire, but in 1931 his father Leslie Hawthorn went into partnership in a garage business at Farnham, in Surrey. Hawthorn senior was a keen racing motor cyclist and the major reason for the move was to be near the Brooklands track at Weybridge. Naturally, the young Hawthorn was taken to Brooklands and he was soon being steeped in the traditions of motor racing. Like so many racing drivers Hawthorn soon got behind the wheel of a car – unfortunately it was a customer's Jowett which the eight-year old Hawthorn managed to trundle round a field behind the family's TT Garage at Farnham.

Schooling took place at Ardingly College in Sussex during the war years, while father was away working as a ferry pilot, and it was while he was still at school that Hawthorn acquired his first motor cycle. A succession of bikes followed and he took up trials and scrambling on a competitive basis, winning several events. After leaving school he was apprenticed to Dennis Brothers of Guildford, the commercial vehicle builders, and then he went on to Kingston Technical College and the College of Automobile Engineering at Chelsea. His father wanted him to get a good grounding in engineering theory and practice but the only practice the young Hawthorn wanted was to drive cars as fast as possible.

His father gave him a Fiat 500, but youthful

exuberance was a little too much for the tiny Italian car which broke frequently under high cornering stresses, so an indulgent father replaced it with a decrepit Riley 9 which served well until a Lancia Aprilia took its place. This fine car impressed Hawthorn and reinforced his desire to become a racing driver.

Leslie Hawthorn encouraged his son in this ambition and in 1950 he bought a Riley Ulster Imp, a pre-war 1100 cc machine which was still impressively fast. It was completely rebuilt and Mike Hawthorn took part in his first motoring competition, the Brighton Speed Trials, where he won his class. His second and last ever speed trial was at Gosport soon afterwards when he finished second in class.

For the 1951 season the Imp and a 1½-litre TT Riley Sprite were prepared for racing and Hawthorn began notching up wins in club races around England; he took part in the 10-lap handicap race which preceded the Ulster Grand Prix at Dundrod, and with a favourable handicap he won the race with ease, then followed up by winning the Leinster Trophy at Wicklow.

Hawthorn knew that he would have to get into single seaters if he was to progress much further in motor racing and he had test drives in Formula Two Connaughts and HWMs. He spun the Connaught at Goodwood and HWM selected Peter Collins, but a family friend, Bob Chase, offered to buy a Cooper-Bristol if Leslie Hawthorn would prepare and run it for Hawthorn junior. The Hawthorns accepted immediately and they rushed to get the car ready for the Easter Monday meeting at Goodwood. After engine bothers and a night without sleep, Hawthorn justified Bob Chase's choice by running away with his first race in the car. Later in the day he came up against the great Fangio, who was also in a Cooper-Bristol, but Hawthorn ran away from the great man and won again. In the third race of the day Hawthorn was up against Froilan Gonzales in the *Thinwall Special* 4½-litre Ferrari, a combination which proved unbeatable, but he finished second and the press went mad about the new English hope.

For the rest of the season Hawthorn captured headlines with his driving of the Cooper, for he invariably won or led the race until the car broke down. He won a heat of the International Trophy at Silverstone against top opposition but broke down in the second heat. His first Continental race was in the Belgian Grand Prix at the difficult Spa circuit, where he finished a fine fourth after various dramas. He followed up with another fourth at the Dutch Grand Prix, against the might of the works Ferraris and after this race he was invited to test a Ferrari later in the season. Before that he had finished third in the British GP, had won a Coupe des Alpes in the Alpine Rally and had won the Turnberry F2 race in a works Connaught.

He tried the Ferrari at Modena and found it a very fast and pleasant car to drive, but after testing the Ferrari he went out in his own Cooper-Bristol to compare it, crashed into some straw bales and was put in hospital for several weeks. Despite this, Ferrari signed him on for the 1953 season which proved to be pretty successful for Hawthorn. In the F2 Ferrari he won the races at Pescara, the Ulster Trophy, the Daily Express Trophy and the French Grand Prix at Reims which he won after a race-long duel with Fangio, beating the maestro to the line by a few yards. The victory was a turning point for British motor racing because it showed that British drivers were able to mix it with the accepted masters and win. As well as his French GP win, Hawthorn finished third in the German and Swiss GPs, co-drove to victory with Farina in the Spa 24-hour race and picked up other good places.

Hawthorn stayed with Ferrari for the 1954 season but it was much less successful. At the start of the year he was attacked by the press and many MPs for not doing his National Service, although kidney trouble prevented him joining up anyway, and then in April he crashed in the Syracuse GP and was badly burned when the car caught fire. He was out of racing until June, but then his father was killed in a road crash and he had to assume control of the family business.

However, he returned to racing with a fourth place at Spa, then finished second in the British GP, second at the Nürburgring, second at the Italian GP and wound up the season with a win at the Spanish GP. But the new 2½-litre Squalo Ferrari was not a good handling car and the Ferrari drivers merely hoped that the Mercedes would retire, which they seldom did. His only other major victory of 1954 was to win the Supercortemaggiore GP in a Monza Ferrari with Maglioli, but he and Trintignant finished second in the TT race at Dundrod.

With the need to spend more time in England to look after his garage business, Hawthorn signed for the Vanwall team in Formula One and Jaguar in sports cars for 1955.

Unfortunately the Vanwall was not yet raceworthy and Hawthorn resigned from the team and rejoined Ferrari in mid season, but the Ferrari was no more competitive than the previous year and he was seldom placed. He did win Le Mans in a D-type Jaguar with Ivor Bueb but there was little happiness in it for Hawthorn because he was blamed by many people for the crash which killed 80 spectators. He also won the Sebring 12-hour race in a D-type and fought a tremendous race in a D-type against the works Jaguars at the TT on the Dundrod circuit and was leading them until the crankshaft broke.

He wanted to continue with Ferrari in Formula One in 1956 and stay with Jaguar in sports cars, but Ferrari would not agree, so he signed for BRM in Formula One. However, the new rear-engined 2½-litre BRMs were having a poor season and Hawthorn suffered a number of expensive blow ups and spectacular accidents. His season with Jaguar was little better, his only placing of consequence being a second in the Reims 12 hours.

Although Hawthorn was intensely patriotic and wanted to beat the foreign cars in a British machine he knew that the British manufacturers were still finding their feet so he returned to Ferrari for 1957 to handle the V8 Lancia-Ferrari. These were difficult cars to drive well and Hawthorn needed to be fully confident in a car to give his best, so he contented himself with several good placings, such as fourth at the French GP, third at the European GP held at Aintree, second at the German GP, and sixth at the Italian GP. He also finished third at Sebring in a D-type Jaguar and took in various saloon car races with a 3.4 Jaguar, winning the production car race at the Daily Express Silverstone meeting.

For 1958 Hawthorn again stayed with Ferrari who had introduced a new Formula One car, the Dino V6 which was a much better car. Hawthorn was always well placed during 1958 and although he couldn't always match the speed of Brooks and Moss in Vanwalls he picked up many high placings, finishing third in the Argentine GP, fifth in the Dutch GP, second in the European GP at Spa, second in the British GP, second in the Portuguese GP, second in the Italian and second in the Moroccan. He also won the French GP for the second time at Reims. Although both Brooks and Moss had won more races than him, Hawthorn became World Champion because of his consistency. In sports car racing he had finished third in the Targa Florio and second in the Nürburgring 1000 km. He had become the first British driver to win the World Championship and as such he was widely fêted both in Britain and on the Continent, where he had become very popular. But his triumph was tinged with sadness for during that season he had lost team-mates Luigi Musso and Peter Collins (who was his inseparable 'mon ami mate') and Stuart Lewis-Evans. Racing had always been fun to Mike Hawthorn and with the deaths of so many friends the fun had gone, so he announced his retirement from racing.

He spent the winter of 1958 rebuilding his old Riley Sprite and a 2.3-litre Alfa Romeo as well as attending to the now prosperous Jaguar dealership in Farnham. But one day in January he had some business in London, so he set off across the Hog's Back and down the Guildford by-pass in his 3.8 Jaguar. On the way he passed ex-racing driver Rob Walker in a 300 SL Mercedes who acknowledged him as he passed. No one knows whether Hawthorn decided to show a clean pair of heels to the Mercedes but halfway down the steep hill into Guildford, the Jaguar suddenly shot across the dual-carriageway and smashed into a tree. By the time Walker had stopped and run across to the spot, the World Champion was already dead.

MT

GRAHAM HILL (1929-1975)
Great Britain

To many people, Graham Hill was the man who epitomised their image of a racing driver – a sort of Bulldog Drummond, Biggles and James Bond all rolled into one. Tall and handsome, with long hair, a thin moustache and a superb dry sense of humour, he almost seemed to act the part of the racing driver, but in the cockpit he was as dedicated as any of his rivals, more successful than most.

Born on 15 February 1929, and christened Norman Graham Hill, he was the son of a comfortably off stockbroker who could not drive and had no wish to, so the motor car did not play any significant part in Graham Hill's development. Like so many other top racing drivers, Hill's schooling, undertaken mostly at Hendon Technical College, was borne grudgingly, but he took refuge in sport by playing football and cricket and becoming a very competent oarsman with the London Rowing Club. Upon leaving school he was apprenticed to Smiths the instrument makers in

Cricklewood. They despatched him to Birmingham, where he bought a motor cycle and took part in one or two minor scrambles and trials with no great success. Returning to London one day on the motor cycle he was involved in an accident which left him with a slightly shortened left leg after it had been badly broken. This left him with a permanent limp and the slightly rolling gait which became almost a hallmark. He was able to practise the rolling gait in 1950 because he was called up for National Service and joined the Navy as an engine room artificer, a period in his life which he enjoyed immensely.

Back in Civvy Street he rejoined Smiths in their development department, turning his spare time attention once more to rowing. The London Rowing Club of 1953 had a first class eight and Hill stroked them to victory in the Grand Challenge Cup at Henley – the rowing equivalent of the British Grand Prix. Hill's attachment to rowing became famous, for he wore their blue and white stripes on his crash helmet.

It was in 1953, at the age of 24, that he first learned to drive a car. He bought a 1934 Morris 8 Tourer and set off home in it, although he had never driven a car before and had no licence. Despite never having taken a driving lesson he took his test soon afterwards and passed. Later that year he spotted an advertisement in a magazine which offered lessons in a racing car at the Brands Hatch track for five shillings a lap. Although he had no real intention of becoming a racing driver at the time he thought that it would be interesting so he set off for Brands Hatch and the Universal Motor Racing Club which owned a pair of rickety 500 cc Formula Three cars. Hill paid up £1 for four laps and thoroughly enjoyed the experience although the car had little resemblance to the only car he had driven to date. At the end of the four laps he knew that he had to become a racing driver. Since he had no money with which to buy a racing car he had to inveigle his way in somehow, so he offered his services to the racing school as an instructor! Since his experience consisted of those four laps he had few qualifications for the job, but the school was none too choosy and he was given the job so long as he maintained the cars and did not require any salary. Hill's dedication to motor racing was so great that he threw up his job at Smiths and took the 'job', although he was now on the dole. His Morris had been written off in a crash so he had to catch a train or bus to Brands Hatch each day.

He had been promised that one of the perks of his job would be to drive in a race, and on 27 April 1954 Graham Hill took part in his first motor race, driving a Mk IV Cooper-JAP. To his surprise he surged into the lead of the race but was eventually overtaken by another driver, so he finished second in his first event. Later in the day he finished fourth in another race.

It was obvious that the cars in the racing school would never set the tracks alight so in August of 1954 Hill obtained a job with Lotus at £1 a day. He helped to build cars for customers and on occasions was loaned out to owners who needed a mechanic. In 1954 he worked for Dick Steed and the following year he looked after Dan Margulies's C-type Jaguar in return for the occasional drive. He also worked for Lotus owners Jack Richards and Peter Lumsden, who allowed him to drive their cars occasionally. At the end of 1955 Lotus held a test day with a Mk 9 sports car for prospective customers and right at the end of the session Hill was allowed out for a few laps, putting up second fastest time of the day. Lotus could not afford to give Hill a works drive but they offered him a full time job at £9 a week and told him that he could build up a Lotus XI at the factory and race it himself. This appealed to Hill and he put a lot of work into the Lotus, which was painted yellow and quickly dubbed the *Yellow Peril*. With this car he performed extremely well during 1956, winning a number of club races. However, he is principally remembered for spinning the car on four consecutive laps on a streaming wet track at Brands Hatch, eventually earning the black flag and a stern lecture from the Clerk of the Course. Lotus retained Hill as a mechanic during 1956, working on gearbox development, but they would not let him drive works cars, so he left to join Speedwell Engineering, the tuning company, of which he later became Chairman.

During early 1957 he drove for whoever would have him but, after Cooper had given him a drive in a Formula Two car, Colin Chapman of Lotus had second thoughts and invited Hill back as a fully fledged driver to handle the new front-engined F2 car. The car was not very competitive against the rear-engined Coopers but Hill gained useful experience and in 1958 he was asked to drive the new front-engined Lotus 16 in Formula One races. Unfortunately, the cars were rather fragile and Hill seldom finished a race, but he scored his first World Championship point when he finished sixth at the Italian Grand Prix. He did have the slight consolation of winning the Silver City Trophy at the same circuit in the type 15 sports car.

The 1959 season proved to be no better for Hill, as the front-engined Formula One and Two Lotuses were uncompetitive against the rear-engined cars, so for 1960 Hill joined the BRM team to drive the new rear-engined car. Again he had little luck, for the BRM was a poor handling car, but he picked up third place in the Dutch Grand Prix. He stayed with BRM for 1961, when they were forced to use a Coventry-Climax engine as their own V8 was not ready for the new 1½-litre Formula One. All he had to show for the season was a sixth at the French GP and a fifth at the US GP, but the new V8 was looking promising.

Hill's painstaking attention to detail was already becoming apparent and, although his mechanics often complained, they realised in 1962 that he knew what he was talking about when he began to win races with the V8 BRM. He won his first F1 race at Goodwood at Easter 1962, followed up with a breathtaking victory over Jim Clark at the International Trophy at Silverstone when he broadsided the BRM across the line inches ahead of the Lotus and then won his first World Championship race by taking the Dutch Grand Prix. He followed this with sixth place at Monaco, second at the Belgian GP, fourth at Aintree, first at the German GP, first at the Italian GP, second in the US GP and then, needing to beat Jim Clark at the South African GP for the World Championship, he had to sit behind the Lotus in second place. But Clark's engine gave up and Hill drove on to victory and the World Championship. Prior to 1962 he had never won an F1 race and had scored but a single championship point. In 1962 alone he won four championship GPs and had scored 52 points to become World Champion.

He adapted well to his new role as World Champion and soon became an articulate speaker, accomplished raconteur and a splendid ambassador for a sport which boasted few characters at that time. Naturally, he stayed with BRM for 1963, but this year Jim Clark was at his brilliant best and Hill had to settle for second place in the championship despite winning the Monaco GP and the US GP as well as finishing third in the French, third in the British, fourth in the Mexican and third in the South African GPs.

Hill remained with BRM once more in 1964, winning the Monaco and US GPs, but Ferrari and Lotus were very competitive and his string of second places at the French, British and German GPs just kept him out of the title, and he was rammed out of the final race in Mexico by Bandini's Ferrari, which allowed team-mate Surtees to take the title. Hill also drove Ferraris in sports car races, winning the Reims 12 hours and Paris 1000 km, with Jo Bonnier as co-driver, and the Tourist Trophy.

The BRM was not developing as well as its rivals and in 1965 Hill's BRM did not quite match Jim Clark's Lotus although he again won the Monaco and US GPs. However, several other good placings brought him second place in the championship.

Hill's final year with BRM was 1966, the year the new 3-litre formula arrived. He picked up a few good places early in the season, such as third at Monaco and the British GP and second at the Dutch GP in a 2-litre BRM, but when the 3-litre H-16 BRM engine was used it proved very unreliable and Hill never finished a race. Earlier in the season he won both the New Zealand and Australian GPs in a BRM and in May he won the Indianapolis 500 mile race driving a Lola T90 with a Ford V8 engine. His win was much disputed as many people thought that his friend Jim Clark had won the race.

For 1967 Hill joined Clark in the Lotus team to drive the new Lotus 49-Ford F1 car. Although the cars were fast Hill had a good deal of trouble, with the result that his only placings of note were second at the US GP, second at Monaco (in a 2-litre Lotus-BRM) and fourth in the Canadian Grand Prix.

One of the saddest days in motor racing occurred when Jim Clark was killed at Hockenheim early in 1968, elevating Hill to number one place in the Lotus team. He realised that some good victories might pull Lotus through this tragedy and immediately he won the Spanish GP, followed by yet another win at Monaco and a victory at Mexico right at the end of the season. Added to second places in the German and US races this gave him his second World Championship, a heartening win which renewed Colin Chapman's appetite for motor racing.

The 1969 season should have been equally successful but a broken aerofoil wing on his Lotus at the Spanish GP destroyed his car and although he won his fifth Monaco GP he was seldom placed in other races. In the United

States GP he suffered a severe accident when his Lotus somersaulted several times after suffering a puncture. He was thrown out and sustained a broken right knee, dislocated left knee and severely torn muscles and ligaments. Many friends and racing enthusiasts hoped that Hill would retire after recovering from the crash, for he was now 40, but he subjected himself to a strenuous series of exercises and, although still hobbling painfully, he drove Rob Walker's Lotus in the South African GP in March 1970. He finished an incredible sixth despite being unable to press the brake pedal properly. However, the rest of the season was not as happy because he was still unable to regain full control of his leg muscles, but his fourth place in the Spanish GP showed that he was certainly not finished.

Far from retiring in 1971 he took over the place of retiring Jack Brabham in the Brabham team, driving the 'Lobster Claw' Formula One car. He showed how well he could still drive by winning the International Trophy race at Silverstone after a duel with hard charging Pedro Rodriguez. He also won the Formula Two race at Thruxton on Easter Monday to the delight of motor racing enthusiasts. But the Brabham was temperamental and all he had to show at the end of the season was a couple of points for fifth place in the Austrian GP.

Hill remained with Brabham for the 1972 season but he seemed to have lost much of his old fire and the season was one of lowly placings and retirements, although it was punctuated by a glorious win at Le Mans together with Henri Pescarolo in a Matra, thus giving him the distinction of being the only driver to have won Indianapolis, Le Mans and the drivers' World Championship.

Again, many supporters hoped that Hill would retire, especially after his Le Mans win but he had no intention of retiring for he still enjoyed his racing. He was not signed by any of the major teams in 1973 so he decided to purchase his own car and settled on the new American financed Shadow. This proved to be uncompetitive both in his hands and those of the works drivers and he seldom finished a race.

For 1974 he made more ambitious plans, persuading Eric Broadley of Lola to build a special Formula One car for him. With sponsorship from Embassy cigarettes, Hill ran a two-car team during 1974 with Guy Edwards as his number two driver.

In July 1975, Graham Hill OBE, finally stepped down from driving to assume a new and still more challenging role with a racing team of his own. His formidable race-craft and track experience could now become the inspiration and life-blood of a team with the potential to take on and beat the established might of Ferrari, Lotus and Tyrrell-Ford on the World Championship Grand Prix scene. He even constructed his own team-car, the GH1, which was designed with the help of Andy Smallman.

That obvious and refreshing optimism, the ambitions and expectations, hopes and plans of both team and followers were, tragically, never to be fulfilled.

On Saturday 31 November 1975, a light aircraft crashed into a golf course on the outskirts of Elstree Aerodrome; poor weather conditions had caused a fatal error of judgement from its pilot. When the first people arrived at the scene all that remained of the plane and its occupants was charred debris scattered over a wide area.

Some hours later, an announcement was broadcast on television and radio that Graham Hill had been killed, along with members of his team, while piloting them from a test session at the Paul Ricard circuit in France. The team included Hill's number one driver, the young and talented Tony Brise.

It was a tribute to Graham Hill's strength of personality, his immense courage and determination and, not least, his brilliance as a racing driver that motor racing folk represented only a small number of the total who mourned his death throughout the world. His death, and the death of his team, will be remembered as one of sport's saddest losses.   MT

PHIL HILL (b.1927)
USA

In the year after World War II sports car racing began to gain a hold in the United States. Prior to the war most motor racing was on banked ovals or on the cinder speedway tracks, and the drivers did not aspire to race on European road circuits. However, many American servicemen discovered the sports car when they visited Europe during the war and the delights of open air motoring were soon being exercised in the US. The drivers of these cars began to race them and, before long, organised races were held. European racing drivers and other enthusiasts were openly contemptuous of the American racing scene because they felt that

Europeans were far more suited to road racing, but the first of many Americans to surprise Europe was Phil Hill, who became the first American driver to win the drivers' World Championship.

Born in Miami, Florida, in 1927, Philip T. Hill moved to Santa Monica, California, where his father became head postmaster. California was the centre of the sports car boom in the late 1940s and early 50s and Phil Hill soon joined in with the almost mandatory MG TC, which he began to race to good effect. By 1952 he was coming to the notice of sports car enthusiasts and in that season he won his first race at the famous Pebble Beach Course at Monterey in California. He joined forces with Richie Ginther in 1953 for the Carrera Panamerica race, with Hill driving and Ginther acting as mechanic in a Ferrari. Hill crashed in this race but the next year the Hill/Ginther duo finished second behind the works Ferrari of Umberto Maglioli. Hill was already receiving sponsored drives by 1953, because importers of sporting machinery saw the value of competition success as a sales booster. He visited Europe in 1954 to drive an OSCA with Fred Wacker at Le Mans but the car retired after leading its class comfortably.

In 1955 Hill drove a 3-litre Ferrari Monza sports racing car for wealthy private owner Alan Guiberson and, partnered by Carroll Shelby, he finished second in the Sebring 12-hour race, although many people felt that faulty lap scoring had robbed the pair of victory.

By 1956 the American Ferrari importer, former racing driver Luigi Chinetti, had persuaded Enzo Ferrari to give Phil Hill some drives in the works team and his first drive with them was the Buenos Aires 1000 kilometre race where, partnered by Olivier Gendebien, he finished second. He finished third in the Nürburgring 1000 km race and then ended the sports car season with victory in the Swedish Grand Prix, partnered by Maurice Trintignant in a 3½-litre Ferrari. He also won the non-championship Messina five-hour race and finished second in the Porto GP at Boavista.

Hill stayed with the Ferrari sports car team for 1957, winning the Venezuelan GP with Peter Collins in a 4.1-litre Ferrari, finishing second in the Reims 12 hours and the Swedish GP, and winning the Palm Springs race back home in California. By now Hill was regarded as a fast, consistent driver, who was ideally suited for long distance races as he usually managed to bring the car home, but in 1958 he joined the Ferrari Formula One team, finishing in excellent third places at the Italian and Moroccan Grands Prix. But it was in sports car racing that Hill shone, for he captured no less than three long distance races, the Argentine 1000 km, the Sebring 12 hours, and the Le Mans 24-hour race. This enabled Ferrari to run away with the World Sports Car Championship for the third year in succession.

In 1959 Hill drove the big front-engined F1 Ferrari against the fleet little rear-engined cars and had little luck apart from second places in the French and Italian GPs and a third at the German GP. In sports car racing Aston Martin were all-conquering during 1959, so Hill had to take a back seat for a change, but he and Gendebien won the Sebring 12 hours again as well as taking second place in the Nürburgring 1000 km. Hill also won the Riverside sports car race in a Ferrari.

The 1960 season gave Phil Hill his first victory in a championship F1 race, with a win at the Italian GP, but the rest of his Formula One season was uneventful, his only other placings of note being a third at Monaco, and a fourth at the Belgian GP. He was still driving for Ferrari in sports car races but his only win in 1960 was the Argentinian 1000 km with Cliff Allison as co-driver; however, he finished second in the Targa Florio with von Trips and third in the Nürburgring 1000 km.

The 1961 season saw the introduction of the 1½-litre Formula One, a step with which the British teams disagreed. The Ferrari team got on with the job of designing new cars for the formula while the British hesitated, so that at the opening meetings of the season the Ferrari drivers were comfortably faster than their rivals – all except Stirling Moss who sometimes managed to beat them with his outdated Lotus, by sheer skill. Wolfgang von Trips was the fastest of the Ferrari drivers but Hill was consistent, finishing third at Monte Carlo, second at the Dutch GP. Then he won the Belgian GP at Spa, finished second at the British GP and then third at the German GP. At the Italian GP it seemed that von Trips could clinch the world title but on the second lap he touched Jim Clark's Lotus and his car shot up a bank into the crowd, killing six spectators and the driver. This left Phil Hill to cruise on to an easy and unhappy victory which gave him the World Championship in most unpleasant circumstances. He was even denied the opportunity of racing in front of his home crowds as Ferrari withdrew from the United States GP which ended the season. In sports car racing Hill helped Ferrari to another manufacturers' championship victory with wins at Sebring and Le Mans again, partnered once more by Gendebien.

The British constructors had caught up with Ferrari by 1962 and Hill's successes were less numerous that season. He picked up a third place at the Dutch GP, second at Monaco and third at the Belgian GP, but after that the Ferrari challenge faded away and Hill did not score another point. In truth, Hill was not a natural Formula One driver, for he preferred the challenge of sports car racing where he and Gendebien formed the most outstanding partnership of all time. Together, they won the Nürburgring 1000 km and Le Mans yet again in 1962 and finished second at Sebring in a Ferrari GTO to give Ferrari another sports car world title.

Relations between Hill and Enzo Ferrari deteriorated during 1962, for the dictatorial Ferrari blamed Hill for the lack of success in Formula One racing; the American fell out with Ferrari over this and decided to join the new ATS concern for 1963. This Formula One venture was disastrous, for the car was badly made and the engine unreliable, so that Hill hardly ever finished a race. The car was not ready at the start of the season, did not qualify until the Belgian GP and was never really competitive.

For 1964 Hill joined the Cooper team for Formula One races to drive the Cooper-Climax 1½-litre but Cooper were in decline and his only championship placing was a sixth at the British GP. In sports cars he won the Daytona Continental race with Pedro Rodriguez in a Ferrari then switched to the new AC Cobra and Ford GT40, neither of which brought him any success.

In 1965, Hill retired from Formula One racing to concentrate on sports cars. He drove factory Ford GT40s and Mk1 models in championship events but he retired in all but one event.

For 1966 Hill decided to join the Chaparral team in sports car racing, the Chevrolet V8-engined coupé drawing attention wherever it appeared. Partnered by Jo Bonnier, Hill showed the quality of the car by leading several races before retiring. But victory eventually came in the Nürburgring 1000 km race. Hill also drove an open Chaparral with a huge free-standing aerofoil in the first Can-Am series in

1966; the car proved to be very fast and he won the Laguna Seca round, finished second at Mosport and seventh at Las Vegas, to wind up fourth in the championship.

Hill stayed with the Chaparral team in 1967 to drive the new coupé 2F model with large rear-mounted aerofoil. Again the car was very fast, putting in a number of fastest laps, but it was not until the BOAC 500 at Brands Hatch that victory finally came to Hill, partnered this time by the British driver, Mike Spence.

It proved a fitting end to Hill's career, for he retired at the end of the 1967 season. He had suffered from poor health for some time which had limited his performances at times. It was discovered that he had been suffering from stomach ulcers and when he was operated on his health improved considerably. There is no telling how well Hill would have done if his health had been perfect, but he was content to retire, keeping in contact with the sport by doing commentaries on TV.   MT

TED HORN (1910-1948)
USA

In these days of the international Grand Prix circus, with drivers and cars jet-setting all over the world, it is difficult to realise just how parochial the American racing scene used to be. In his day, for example, Eylard Theodore 'Ted' Horn was reckoned to be one of the USA's greatest-ever racing drivers. It would be difficult to find anyone in Europe who agrees with this verdict or, indeed, who had actually heard of someone called Ted Horn.

At the age of 21, Ted began racing on the Californian dirt tracks, and within a couple of years was kicking up the cinders all over the United States. He visited Indianapolis as a spectator in 1934, returned as a competitor in 1935 at the wheel of a works-sponsored Ford V8 – and dropped out of that race.

In 1936, driving a Miller-powered car, he battled for first place in the Indy '500' with Lou Meyer; Meyer won, but Horn was well up with the leaders when the flag fell. The following year, Horn briefly took second position on the 130th lap of the Indianapolis event when Wilbur Shaw, who was leading, made a brief pit stop; but the race ended as a close-run thing between Shaw and Ralph Hepburn, who made record time and finished a fraction over two seconds behind. The 1939 race saw Horn finish in fourth position, behind Wilbur Shaw's Maserati, Ted Snyder and Cliff Bergere; he was always among the first finishers at Indy, taking third place in 1941.

His run of Miller-powered Indianapolis cars finished in 1941, when racing ended 'for the duration'. When he appeared on the starting line for the first post-war '500', in 1946, Ted Horn was at the wheel of Wilbur Shaw's old Maserati, which had won the race in 1939 and 1940. The car had been rebuilt after a major crash in 1941, in which Shaw had been seriously injured while leading the field at Indianapolis. The car started in the No. 7 position in the 1946 race, and Shaw, who had become President of the Indianapolis Speedway in the interim, remarked that he would have gladly traded his official position as starter and pace-car driver for Horn's place behind the wheel of his old car. However, Horn was soon forced to make a pit stop with magneto trouble and, despite rapid work by his mechanic, Cotton Henning, was held up for five laps. However, once the car was mobile again, Horn moved steadily up through the field, finishing in third position behind George Robson and Jimmy Jackson. This placing was just one of the racing successes that contributed to the 750-point-plus score that assured Ted Horn of the title of America's champion racing driver for the 1946 motor-racing season.

The following year, the Indianapolis 500 was jeopardised by a drivers' boycott from members of the American Society of Professional Automobile Racing, but Horn did not belong to ASPAR, and his presence at the qualifying trials was a major factor in the resolution of the dispute. Horn started in the premier position with the Maserati, and stood a very good chance of winning; this went out of the window when he turned the tricky oil-control valve on his car the wrong way and filled the crankcase with oil. The pit stop that was necessary to drain the sump of excess lubricant cost him the race, but he still finished third. The winner Mauri Rose had had a less troubled run to take the chequered flag for his own second Indy win.

Once again, he gained enough points during 1947 to secure the American championship. He repeated the feat the following year, in which he also took fourth place at Indy but, towards the end of the season, Ted Horn entered a meeting at Duquoin, Illinois, and was driving with his customary speed and precision when a stub-axle sheared, the car crashed and he received fatal injuries.   DBW

LORD EDWARD HOWE
(1884-1964)
Great Britain

'If the ship of State were a car,' said Sir Henry Birkin in a praising speech in 1932, 'Lord Howe would have been Prime Minister long ago . . . of all racing motorists with whom I have ever come in contact, he is, I think, the keenest; he brings to any·subject with which cars are remotely concerned an application that nothing will deter.'

Yet, Lord Howe, who was one of Britain's best-known racing drivers of the 1930s, did not take up competitive motoring seriously until 1928, when he was 44. That was, commented Birkin, 'after visiting almost every police court in the land'. Howe, it seems, decided to practise his speed where it would be more appreciated, and exact from the constabulary of the track a licence he had been refused on main roads.

Edward Richard Assheton, Viscount Curzon (he had not succeeded to the title when he started racing), had followed in the wake of his illustrious forebear, the first Lord Howe, victor of the Glorious First of June in 1794, and served with distinction in the Navy during the Great War aboard HMS *Queen Elizabeth* in the Dardanelles campaign.

His light-hearted manner concealed a determination to succeed, inspired by his intense patriotism; his cars were always meticulously prepared, because he felt that to start in a race with a scruffy car would be letting the side down. Indeed, Howe's cars always stood out on the starting line because of their driver's brilliant blue helmet and racing overalls, and the huge Oxford blue umbrella that he always affected in the rain, virtually to the fall of the starter's flag.

The first race of note in which Lord Howe appeared was the 1928 Irish TT at Newtownards; he drove with great skill for the first 150 miles at almost 68 mph, then speeded up his Bugatti until it was averaging over 70. By the halfway mark, he had lapped all the back markers and was gaining rapidly on the smaller cars – which had had a considerable start under the handicap system - with a good chance of winning the race, when his petrol tank burst. The Tourist Trophy remained a regular commitment for Howe: 1930 saw him at the wheel of an ex-Caracciola SSK Mercedes, while the following year he drove his Alfa Romeo. Indeed, 1931 was a very good year for Howe: he won the Gold Star handicap at the Whitsun meeting at Brooklands, beating Cobb and Birkin, then within the month shared an Alfa at Le Mans with Tim Birkin. Because of a last-minute decision to run on pure benzole, the car's pistons had to be replaced, and the work was not finished until 5.30 am on the morning of the race. At first, the car was slowed by plug trouble, but by the end of the sixth hour Howe had moved up through the flying Talbots, Aston Martins and Mercedes to take second position. Then, as midnight struck, he slipped into the lead, a position which the two co-drivers comfortably maintained until, at the end of the 24 hours, Birkin thundered across the line at over 90 mph. It was the fastest *Vingt-Quatre Heures* that had yet been held, and the Howe/Birkin combine's average speed of 78.13 mph had broken all records. A couple of weeks later, Howe was at the French Grand Prix, with a different car (Bugatti) and a different co-driver (the Hon Brian Lewis); but this time his luck was out, for an hour and a half was wasted in the pits trying to discover the cause of a mysterious ignition fault, which turned out to be nothing more serious than a chafed-through sparking plug lead. Once this had been rectified, the Bugatti was the fastest car in the race; but it was too late to catch the leaders, and Howe had to be content with twelfth place.

By this time, Lord Howe had acquired one of the famous 1.5-litre Delages from Malcolm Campbell and with this he won his class at the 1931 Grand Prix de Dieppe, despite narrowly missing being involved in a pile-up which eliminated seven Bugattis. Indeed, he could have won the race outright with his five-year-old car, had it not been for a burst tyre caused, it seems, by an act of sabotage.

The Delage's successful career, however, was cut short at Monza in 1933: Howe entered a bend fast, only to find the track blocked by three slower cars. He braked hard and the servo jammed. With all four wheels locked, the car spun right around and skidded off the road backwards, into the trees lining the track. All Howe could do was duck. 'The next moment,' he recalled later, 'the car was among the trees, and I saw one tree cut a front wheel off like a knife. Then the car turned on its side, something hit me hard on my crash helmet, and we came to rest with an almighty bump. I was still sitting in the car, holding the steering wheel, but the car, on its side, was wrapped clean round the tree, with the front wheel and the rear wheel only six inches apart.'

Although his car had been sliced and wrapped, Howe was unhurt and the remains of the car were pushed into his purpose-built Commer Invader car transporter van, eventually to be dumped in his mews garage near the Dorchester hotel.

In any case, the Delage was not Howe's only car: in 1932, he had driven a 2.3-litre Bugatti into fourth place in the Monaco Grand Prix, beaten only by Nuvolari, Caracciola and Fagioli; his green Bugatti, moreover, had beaten the official team cars, whose drivers numbered just about every immortal name in the Bugatti canon.

Summing up Howe's drive, *The Motor* commented: 'He is incontestably to be classed among the world's greatest drivers, and may be ranked with the Continental champions whose names are household words.'

To prove this point, Howe led the 1934 Le Mans 24-hour race in his Alfa until the failure of his lights and clutch put him out of the running.

Howe, let it be noted, only drove foreign cars because he was convinced that there was not a British car that was truly competitive with the Continentals, although he did essay a few races with an MG Magnette. Leading his class in the Mille Miglia with this car, he slid off the road on a waterlogged S-bend, and knocked down a telegraph pole.

After 1936, however, he seems to have revised his opinion of British cars, for he acquired an ERA, and also drove as a member of the Fox & Nicholl Lagonda team.

His last significant track achievement was a 108.27 mph lap of Brooklands at the wheel of a Lagonda V12, in 1938: no mean achievement for a 54-year-old man. Although his racing days were over after World War II, he continued to support motor racing, both in committee and organisational work and in the House of Lords. He also became President of the British Racing Drivers' Club; his death in 1964 removed one of the last great gentleman amateurs from the racing scene.   DBW

DENNY HULME (b.1936)
New Zealand
Some racing drivers show an intuitive ability at the wheel of a racing car almost as soon as they step into their first racing machine. Others need to work away for many years, gradually honing their skills until they eventually reach the upper echelons of the racing profession.

Examples of the former are Jimmy Clark and Jackie Stewart, but a prime example of the latter is Denny Hulme who had been a racing driver for nine years before he was given a Formula One car. However, after that, progress was rapid, for he became World Champion within two years.

Born on 18 June 1936, Denis Clive Hulme (pronounced 'Hulm' rather than 'Hume') was the son of Clive Hulme, who gained distinction by winning the Victoria Cross during World War II, and his home town was Nelson in New Zealand. As with so many other racing drivers, schooling was suffered rather than enjoyed and much of his youth was spent on his grandparents' tobacco farm at Motueka on New Zealand's South Island. After the war, Hulme's family moved to Te Puke on the Bay of Plenty in the North Island, where his father started a small haulage business. After leaving school, Denny went to work in a garage where he soon showed an aptitude for engineering which he used to good effect when working on his father's fleet of trucks, tractors and cars. His father also paid him for delivering materials to farmers and Denny saved hard to buy his first car, a brand new MG TF.

The MG was kept for three years and, during that time, he joined a car club, taking part in his first event, a local hill-climb in 1956. He showed a liking for racing and often beat his rivals in events on the North Island. After three years with the TF, he graduated to an MGA, then to a 2-litre Cooper-Climax which was bought with the help of his parents. This was potentially one of the fastest cars in New Zealand at the time and, after he had rebuilt it, he began to win races in great numbers. So successful was his 1959/60 season that he was nominated by the New Zealand International Grand Prix Association for their 'Driver to Europe' scheme, which each year financed a promising young driver for a year's racing in Europe. The previous year, Bruce McLaren had been the winner, and for 1960 the NZIGPA picked both Hulme and George Lawton to go to Europe. Hulme chose a Cooper-BMC Formula Junior car and barnstormed around Europe, racing every weekend, gaining experience all the time. However, his friend Lawton was killed in Denmark and Hulme almost decided to give up racing, but he returned to New Zealand with a 2½-litre Cooper-Climax in 1961 and later that year he went back to Europe again to rejoin the Formula Junior circus. There was little money to be made in Formula Junior so, to make ends meet, he worked as a mechanic in Jack Brabham's garage in Chessington, Surrey. He was invited to drive a works Abarth at Le Mans in 1961, finishing an excellent fourteenth overall with countryman Angus Hyslop. In 1962, he was asked to drive Ken Tyrrell's FJ Cooper on occasions and then, later that year, he was invited to take over the works Formula Junior Brabham after Gavin Youl retired from racing. Brabham's manager, Phil Kerr, persuaded Jack Brabham to give Hulme a chance; Kerr and Hulme then worked together almost continuously until Hulme's retirement.

Hulme's first full season with the Brabham was in 1963, when he won seven races out of fourteen starts, but he was still not a full professional as he had to work in the garage and prepare his own car. By now, he was married to Greeta, a fellow New Zealander, who travelled with him to races around the world.

The successes of 1963 spurred Jack Brabham to invite Hulme to join him in the all-conquering Brabham Formula Two team for 1964, and between them they cleaned up most of the F2 races on the calendar, Brabham winning the championship with Hulme second. For 1965, the F2 Brabhams were powered by Honda engines, which were far more powerful than the Cosworth engines used by most of the opposition, so both Brabham and Hulme picked up some easy wins over the 1965 and 1966 seasons.

Jack Brabham gave Hulme occasional drives in non-championship Formula One races during 1964, but Brabham himself – and Dan Gurney – did most of the F1 driving. However, Hulme took Gurney's place at Monaco in 1965, finishing eighth, and later in the year he finished fourth in the French GP and fifth in the Dutch GP. He also won the Tourist Trophy in a Brabham BT8 sports car.

When Formula One changed to 3 litres in 1966, Gurney left the team to build his own cars and Hulme was given the second seat alongside Jack Brabham. The team ran what were considered underpowered Repco V8-engined Brabhams, but they proved ideal and, in 1966, Brabham won the World Championship. Hulme picked up a second place in the British GP and also took third places in France, Italy and Mexico to end up fourth in the championship.

At long last, Hulme had reached the pinnacle of motor racing and, the following season, he outstripped his boss by taking the

World Championship, winning the Grands Prix of Monaco and Germany, finishing second in the French and British GPs and third in Holland, the United States and Mexico. That season, he also finished fourth at Indianapolis in an Eagle and second in the Can-Am championship where he drove a McLaren M8 to victory at Road America, Bridgehampton and Mosport.

For the 1968 season Hulme was wooed away from the Brabham team by McLaren, where Phil Kerr was now general manager. He drove the M7A in Formula One and the M8A in Can-Am events, winning another three Can-Am races as well as the Italian GP, the Canadian GP and the International Trophy at Silverstone. With other good placings, he took third place in the World Championship. He also drove a Lola T70 for Sid Taylor in British sports-car events, winning the Tourist Trophy and the Martini race at Silverstone.

By 1969, the McLaren F1 car was less competitive and his only victory came right at the end of the season in the Mexican GP. However, he won no less than five Can-Am races in the works M8B McLaren-Chevrolet to finish second in the championship to McLaren.

Early in the 1970 season, Bruce McLaren was killed while testing a Can-Am car at Goodwood, but the remaining directors decided to carry on with the team. Hulme himself received badly burned hands when his car caught fire at Indianapolis, which put him out of racing for several weeks, but he won no less than six Can-Am races, to clinch the title again. He picked up a number of good placings in Formula One such as second in South Africa, third in England, Germany and Mexico, together with fourth places in Monte Carlo, France and Italy, but victory eluded him.

By now, he was a public figure in several continents, but, like his old boss Jack Brabham, he was basically shy and introverted; he hated giving speeches and was seldom good for a quote after a race. If anyone rubbed him up the wrong way he would give them his opinion in colourful language, a reputation which soon earned him the nickname of the 'old bear', because bears often have sore heads! However, with friends and colleagues, away from the spotlight of the circuits, he was invariably more relaxed and excellent amusing company.

The 1971 season was very disappointing, no doubt because the McLaren team was still feeling the reaction from the loss of Bruce

McLaren and Hulme picked up a meagre nine points in the World Championship. He was partnered in Can-Am races by Peter Revson and, although Hulme won at Mosport, Edmonton and Riverside, he had to take second place to his team-mate, who won five races.

With the M19 McLaren, Denny Hulme had a much better 1972 season in Formula One, winning the South African GP, as well as finishing second in Austria and Argentina and third in Belgium, Italy and the USA. This gave him 39 points and a fine third place in the World Championship.

The new M23 Formula One McLaren was ready for most of the 1973 races, but Hulme had very little success with it, although he did win the Swedish Grand Prix. His best places apart from that win were a couple of third places in Brazil and England. He was overshadowed by his team-mate Peter Revson who won the British and Canadian GPs. McLaren had, by now, withdrawn from Can-Am racing due to the overwhelming superiority of the Porsches, so Hulme contented himself with Formula One racing.

He was joined in the McLaren team for 1974 by Emerson Fittipaldi, the young Brazilian proving somewhat quicker than the 38-year-old New Zealander. However, Hulme showed that he was by no means finished by winning the Argentinian GP and taking a well earned second place in the Austrian GP. Nevertheless, with his team-mate winning the World Championship, it was eventually announced that the taciturn Hulme would retire at the end of the 1974 season and he returned to the more peaceful life in New Zealand, punctuated by occasional outings, 'for fun', in saloon car races around the world.   MT

JAMES HUNT (b.1947)
Great Britain

Few seasons in the history of the World Championship for Drivers have had the kind of cliff-hanging finish which distinguished 1976. After a season-long struggle against Niki Lauda, on the track, and the sport's governing body on the sidelines, James Hunt won the title by a single point. In Hunt the sport found a champion with the kind of modern image which pushed motor racing into a new market and attracted thousands of new followers.

In true jet-setting style, James Simon Wallis Hunt's rise to stardom was rapid and spiced with front page news.

Hunt was born on 29 August 1947 in Belmont, Surrey. His father was a stockbroker in the City of London and James's home background was comfortable, if not ostentatious. His early education included prep school at Wellington College (whose colours he later wore on his helmet) and was geared to a career in medicine. When he was eighteen, he saw his first motor race. From that day he had only one ambition: to drive racing cars.

Being an eighteen-year-old with no personal finances and few prospects meant that James had to work his way into the sport the hard way. He initially approached his father and explained that if he were to go to medical school it would cost some £2500 but he was willing to accept £2500 and settle. His father was not impressed by the deal so James's first racing car was a Mini which he built himself. To finance it he worked as a labourer, a night porter in a hospital, a day porter in a supermarket and a van driver for the Civil Service. The van was often pressed into use for collecting pieces for the Mini, which was built in the family garage.

The Mini was finally readied towards the end of the 1967 season and Hunt's first race entry was made at Snetterton. The scrutineers, however, were not impressed by the lack of a windscreen in the car and James was not allowed to race. When the car eventually did get onto a circuit there was more disappointment for the budding driver as it was soon apparent that it was hopelessly uncompetitive against more expensively prepared machinery – and that included almost everyone else's.

His break came early in 1968 when he saw an advertisement offering Russell-Alexis Formula Ford cars on hire purchase terms. It was not long before the sale of the Mini provided most of the deposit for one of these cars. At the time, the man to beat in Formula Ford was Australian Tim Schenken and he was using a Chris Steele prepared engine in his Merlyn, so it was to be a Steele engine for the Alexis. Unfortunately, installation of the dry-sumped unit proved a problem and the engine was badly damaged, even before the car's first race, when welding swarf from inside one of the oil carrying chassis tubes was ingested by the engine. At Steele's the rebuild resulted in a bill for £90 and, of course, James was broke.

The desire to race again won the day and, with the help of his mother and the promise of some sponsorship from a local Ford dealer, Hunt persuaded his father to bring forward payment of his 21st birthday present by some four months. That £100 put the Alexis back on the road and James, at last, proved his worth.

His sponsorship arrangement at first brought in less than the cost of his racing but, after he had won his second race in their colours, and set a new lap record, the deal was improved. Eventually James's racing became self-supporting.

It was in 1969 that James took the next step up the ladder to Formula One, by moving on from Formula Ford to Formula Three. Having been sponsored by Gowrings during the early part of the season he found backing from Mike Ticehurst of Motor Racing Enterprises who entered him first in an MRE Formula Ford and then in an MRE Brabham BT21 Formula Three car. With the Brabham, James's first result in an International race came at Cadwell Park, where he finished fourth. Ahead of him were Tim Schenken and Ronnie Peterson – both destined for future Grand Prix careers. James had several more good results, was generally quite well behaved and earned the second place Grovewood Award – and a cash prize of £300.

1970 had its ups and downs. Hunt was again driving regularly in Formula Three, now with a Molyslip sponsored Lotus, and he scored his first international victory at Rouen, plus many other good results. Unfortunately he also showed a flair for being in the wrong place at the wrong time and had a number of accidents – not all of his own making – earning himself the nickname, and reputation, of 'Hunt the Shunt'.

At the end of the 1969 season James had been co-opted into the works March Formula Three car, when Ronnie Peterson had been injured, and for 1971 he was back in a semi-works March 713M, sponsored by Baty. He also made a tentative move in the right direction with a one-off drive in the Formula Two March 712M, at Brands Hatch. There was the promise of more Formula Two in the future which probably influenced James in his move to the works STP-March Formula Three team for 1972. However, he was less than happy at March and finally split with them on the weekend of the Monaco Grand Prix. It was probably the most significant decision of his career; also at the seafront circuit was a team owned by one Lord Alexander Hesketh, managed by 'Bubbles' Horsley, and with a seemingly endless supply of cash. What the team lacked was a fully competitive car. At the time they were running Dastles instead of the more universal Marches and consequently were having difficulty in recruiting a reputable driver. James ran briefly with the French La Vie Claire team, but at Chimay in Belgium he met Horsley and agreed to drive for Hesketh.

Alexander, less than used to failure, soon tired of Formula Three and another major accident (again caused by someone else) for James, at Brands Hatch, was the final straw. On the horizon was a highly publicised 'Super-Libre' race in which any kind of car was to be allowed to contest a £50,000 prize fund. Hunt rapidly negotiated the loan of a March Formula Two chassis, Bubbles persuaded Lord Hesketh to provide an engine and James finished fifth. Alexander, watching on TV at his stately Northamptonshire home was suddenly committed to motor racing, just as Hunt had been seven years earlier. The prize money financed the rest of the Formula Two season and James made a name for himself with some stirring drives against high class opposition. He earned a front row position on the grid at Salzburgring and set fastest lap at Albi, as well as giving Ronnie Peterson a very hard fight at Oulton Park. Hesketh's team was on the map and plans were made for 1973. They were to have centred around Formula Two again, with occasional forays into Formula One 'just to test the temperature', but James totally destroyed the team's Formula Two Surtees in a spectacular testing accident and it was back to the drawing board. Working on the premise that if something is worth doing it is worth doing properly, the team took the plunge into Formula One.

For the Race of Champions at Brands Hatch in March they hired a Formula One Surtees and despatched James to do battle with the 'Cream'. He acquitted himself well with a fighting third place.

Initially the team were to purchase a Surtees TS14 but the deal did not come to fruition and a March 731 was purchased. Then came Hesketh's big coup; the transfer of designer Dr Harvey Postlethwaite from March to Hesketh to work on the development of the car. James's first Grand Prix was at Monaco, exactly one year after his split with March. He finished ninth, after having been as high as sixth during the race. The team's well publicised flamboyance hid a true professionalism and James's first season netted a second, a third, a fourth and a sixth place from eight starts. Also in 1973, he won the inaugural Tour of Britain Rally in a Camaro, finished second twice in

ETC races with a BMW and drove in long distance sports car and Can-Am races.

For 1974 the team had their sights set on winning with their own car and James did indeed score his first Formula One victory, albeit in the non-championship International Trophy Race at Silverstone in April. It was a popular win as Hesketh's headquarters are almost on the circuit's doorstep and it made James a national hero with many enthusiasts. His Grand Prix record included third places in Sweden, Austria and the United States and a fourth place in Canada. Otherwise, the season was marred by breakdowns.

In 1975, James made the grade with his first Grand Prix win, at Zandvoort in Holland. It was a classic victory won as much by tactics and maturity as by sheer speed. At last the ghost of 'Hunt the Shunt' was laid. Sadly, the rest of the season was not so good and James could only finish fourth in the World Championship. Hesketh were in financial difficulties and the team was disbanded.

When Emerson Fittipaldi left McLaren Teddy Mayer, McLaren's manager, was quick to sign up James. It was to be the beginning of a thrilling season. His early season headlines came from off the tracks when his wife, Susy, met Richard Burton and suddenly James was single again. Meanwhile, Ferrari were scooping the first three race wins and, although Hunt had scored a second place in South Africa, the pundits still forecast that Niki Lauda would retain his title. Amid acrimony off-stage which disqualified him from victory in Spain and then reinstated him, disqualification from first place in Britain and harsh treatment at Monza for alleged fuel infringements, James rose above the problems and scored six Grand Prix wins. He won in Spain (where he later lived), France, Germany, Holland, Canada and the United States and took the title three laps from the end of the rain soaked Japanese Grand Prix; he finished third as his only rival, Niki Lauda, watched from the pits having declined to race in the appalling conditions. It was a memorable finish to a championship marred by the rule book and Lauda's near-fatal accident in Germany, but James was a worthy victor.

For 1977 he stayed with McLaren but had a miserable start to the season with good performances let down by mechanical failures. In the second half of the season, however, his fortunes picked up – largely through sheer determination. To his second place in Brazil, third in France and fifth in South Africa Hunt added three fine wins, in Britain, at Watkins Glen and in Japan, to haul himself to fifth place in the championship – won by his arch rival, Niki Lauda.

Strangely, the M26 was comprehensively out-classed during 1978 and although Hunt fought hard his best results were third place in France, fourth in Brazil and sixth in Spain. He suffered nine retirements, including more than one controversial first lap shunt, and the ignominy of being disqualified (for taking a short cut back to the pits following a puncture) in Germany.

With his confidence in McLaren shaken and with the avowed intention of retiring at season's end, Hunt moved to Wolf and the promise of individual attention and a new ground effect car for 1979. The first half of the season suggested that, try as he might, James was not going to go out in a blaze of glory, for the Wolf was simply not competitive. In the first seven races Hunt retired six times. Although he began to qualify reasonably well, mechanical problems and two minor indiscretions limited his finishes to just eighth place in South Africa.

The Monaco Grand Prix was to be his last race. In Monte Carlo he was sidelined by drive shaft failure after only four laps and a few days later he announced that he was retiring from the sport forthwith. He made no secret of his concern for his personal safety, and memories of pulling the critically injured Ronnie Peterson from his blazing car at Monza were obviously still in his mind. With the Wolf proving sadly uncompetitive, James could no longer balance the results against the risks and he prepared to vent his need to excel on the somewhat less hazardous pursuits of squash and television commentating.   BL

JACKY ICKX (b.1945)
Belgium

Jacky Ickx became recognised as one of the world's outstanding drivers when he joined the Grand Prix circus in 1968. On occasions, he would show the sort of skill that marked him down as an almost certain World Champion, but he would often be let down by his cars and, like one or two other drivers, he would change teams just when the team he was leaving produced a race-winning car.

Born on 1 January 1945 in Brussels, Jacques Bernard Ickx was the son of a well known motoring journalist, and the younger brother of Pascal Ickx who began a promising career as a motor-cycle racer. However, this close involvement with cars left no great impression on young Jacky, and he confessed to having been thoroughly bored by racing cars when taken to meetings by his father. Nevertheless, he soon learned to ride a motor cycle and began to show a natural flair for competitions. By the age of sixteen, he was showing up well in local trials, and the Belgian concessionaire for Zundap offered him works rides on trials and road-racing machines. Then Ickx was snapped up by the Japanese Suzuki firm who entered him in 50cc racing events. The young Ickx won race after race and became a public figure in Belgium before he was eighteen. He was offered a BMW 700 car for hill-climb events and, once again, he showed great skill and speed in such a tiny car, although his main claim to fame came when he rolled it spectacularly in front of TV cameras. He was offered a drive in a works-entered Ford Cortina as a result of his BMW exploits, but the intervention of National Service prevented any serious development of his potential for a couple of years, although he was often given time off from being a tank instructor to race at Belgian meetings.

Returning from the army in 1965, he once again began racing saloon cars, but after two years of local success with BMWs and Lotus Cortinas, which included successive wins in the Spa 24-hour race, he was spotted by Ken Tyrrell who gave him a drive in one of his Formula Three Matras. Ickx was fast, but the car often broke; however, he impressed Tyrrell enough to gain a few drives in his Matra-BRM Formula Two car. Although the Brabham-Hondas were winning everything in sight, Ickx put up fastest lap at Reims and finished fourth in the Albi GP, towards the end of the 1966 season. This persuaded Tyrrell to give the young Ickx a full-time F2 drive in the Matra, for 1967; he showed that this confidence was not misplaced by winning three races, including the Crystal Palace event in England, and taking the European Championship for non-graded drivers.

Ickx really came to the fore during the German Grand Prix of 1967 when his tiny F2 Matra qualified third fastest, behind two of the new 3-litre F1 cars. The F2 cars had to start behind the F1 cars, but Ickx shot through the field and reached an incredible fourth place before retiring with a broken front suspension. This single drive ensured that he would soon be among the ranks of Formula One drivers, for team managers were clamouring for his signature at the end of the race. He drove an F1 Cooper into sixth place in the Italian GP, but he signed with Ferrari for 1968. During 1967, he had driven the Mirage-Ford sports cars to four wins and he stayed with the Gulf-John Wyer team for 1968.

In Formula One, he soon showed his prowess by winning the French Grand Prix which, together with a string of third and fourth places, carned him fourth place in the World Championship. In the Gulf-Fords, he won the BOAC 500 at Brands Hatch, the Watkins Glen 6 hours and the Spa 1000 km race, which he had also won in the previous season. He broke his leg whilst practising for the Canadian Grand Prix, but he was soon back in action and, for 1969, he decided to drive for the Brabham team. The Brabham was very fast in Ickx's hands and only the brilliance of Jackie Stewart kept him in second place in the World Championship. He won the German and Canadian GPs, as well as taking second places in the British and Mexican races. He also won the Oulton Park Gold Cup race and took a thrilling last lap victory at Le Mans in the technically outclassed Ford GT40, against Hans Herrmann's faster Porsche.

In 1970, Ickx returned to Ferrari for Formula One with the new 312B but, although he won the Grands Prix of Austria, Canada and Mexico, he once again had to take second place, this time to the late Jochen Rindt. He also drove the 5-litre Ferrari in sports-car races, but fared poorly, his only good finishes being second place in the Spa 1000 km and third in the Daytona Continental. During 1970, Ickx became disenchanted with the Grand Prix Drivers' Association, because he disagreed with their policy on circuit safety which led to the loss of his home circuit at Spa as a championship track.

He stayed with Ferrari during 1971, but his only victory was in the Dutch Grand Prix, although he was placed fourth in the World Championship. In sports-car racing, Ferrari tested their new 3-litre car against the 5-litre machines and Ickx picked up only one place of note – second in the BOAC 1000 km. In 1972, the well tested Ferrari 312P swept everything before it and Ickx won the Daytona Continental, Sebring 12 hours, BOAC 1000 km, Monza 1000 km, Austrian 1000 km and the Watkins Glen 6 hours, as well as taking second place in the Spa 1000 km, to give Ferrari a runaway win

in the World Sports Car Championship. In Formula One, he was less fortunate, winning only the German Grand Prix and dropping out of other races while leading.

Once again Ickx opted to stay with Ferrari for 1973, but the team deteriorated even further because of the great load of work in running both sports-car and Formula One teams. A series of poor results forced Jacky to make a withdrawal from the F1 teams and he drove a McLaren at the German Grand Prix, finishing a comfortable third. Later in the season, he also drove an Iso-Marlboro without success. In the sports Ferrari, he was more successful, winning the Monza 1000 km and the Nürburgring 1000 km, as well as taking second place in the Dijon 1000 km and Watkins Glen 6-hour races.

Ickx was thoroughly disenchanted with the Ferrari team and gladly signed for Lotus in 1974, but Ferrari made a brilliant come-back and Lotus went into decline as their new 76 car failed to come up to expectations, forcing them to revert to their old Lotus 72s. Whilst the Ferraris were winning, Ickx retired from many races, his best GP placings being a couple of thirds at the Brazilian and British GPs. Jacky did, however, win the non-championship Race of Champions at Brands Hatch when his wet-weather driving technique (something he is renowned for) was enough to show the other cars, including the Ferraris, the way home in torrential conditions.

For 1975 Ickx stayed with Lotus, but his only points came at the shortened Spanish Grand Prix in which he finished second. He withdrew from the last five races of the season. The high spot of his year was another win at Le Mans, driving John Wyer's Gulf Mirage.

On the Formula One front 1976 was even worse. He drove the Williams Hesketh 308C and the Ensign, both with a conspicuous lack of success. He ended the season with a huge fiery accident at Watkins Glen, in the Ensign, from which he was lucky to escape with bad leg injuries. His sports car exploits were again more successful: he drove for Porsche, winning at Mugello, Vallelunga, Monza and twice at Dijon. He also won his third Le Mans, with Jochen Mass.

In 1977 he was fit enough to resume driving for Porsche and scored his fourth Le Mans win in June. Three weeks before Jacky had made his return to Formula One at Monaco, deputising in the Ensign for Clay Regazzoni who was qualifying for Indianapolis. Ickx finished tenth, despite problems from an old back injury. In the World Championship of Makes he won three races for Porsche, at Silverstone, Watkins Glen and Brands Hatch.

Ickx had another sortie into Grand Prix racing in 1978, driving Mo Nunn's Ensign once again. He finished twelfth in his native Belgium, retired in Monaco and Spain and failed to qualify in Sweden. In sports car racing his successes were limited to winning the Silverstone six-hour race with the latest Porsche 935. At Le Mans he was into the pits after two laps, back two laps later and, in spite of some incredibly hard driving after another tactical change of cars, he saw his fifth win slip away. He eventually salvaged second place.

Although, little by little, he was cutting his commitments, he was back at Le Mans in 1979 with the works Porsche 936, looking for yet another victory in the world's most prestigious sports car race. Sadly, he suffered the ignominy of disqualification after receiving outside assistance when he came to a halt on the circuit. After Patrick Depailler's hang-gliding accident Ickx also returned to Grand Prix racing, in the number two Ligier seat, scoring points in Great Britain and Holland plus half a dozen retirements. Although the ability was demonstrably still there, perhaps the hunger had gone.

Life was easier in the States where Ickx scooped the Can-Am title, with five wins, after a titanic struggle with Elliot Forbes-Robinson, and, of course, yet again in 1980 Jacky contested Le Mans. This time he settled for a close second to Jean Rondeau, after leading with Jöst's Porsche before gearbox bothers intervened. It was another near miss for a remarkable fifth victory but, in spite of his annual 'retirement', few observers had yet ruled out the possibility that one day he would make it.   MT

INNES IRELAND (b.1930)
Great Britain

Innes Ireland was one of the last of the great characters of motor racing, for after he gave up racing in 1966 the amount of sponsorship money hanging on race results precluded any of the all-night pre-race parties and escapades in which Ireland often indulged. Although he was a professional racing driver, his approach was that of a gentleman amateur to whom the sport was simply a well paid means of assisting him to enjoy life.

Born Robert McGregor Innes Ireland at Kirkcudbright, Scotland, in 1930, he was the son of a veterinary surgeon who attempted to give him a good education. However, Innes was more interested in sport and motor cycles, so his father bowed to the inevitable and apprenticed him to the Rolls-Royce aero-engine division in Glasgow. His engineering talent was obvious, but he went to great lengths to hide this by becoming involved in various pranks and other anti-establishment activities. His departure from Glasgow was precipitated when he managed to blow up an expensive aircraft engine during power tests, so he was switched to the car division in London. In London, he met various people interested in motor racing, and before long, he was working on vintage cars, which naturally introduced him to the race track. His first race, at Boreham in 1952, was in a 4½-litre Bentley but before his racing career could develop any further he was called up for military service, joining the Parachute Regiment, where he was commissioned as an officer.

On his discharge from the army, he went into partnership in a garage business and soon got back into racing with a pre-war Riley, with which he scored several wins and good placings. He really began to come to public notice when he acquired a Lotus 11 for the 1957 season. He picked up several wins with the car, principally at Goodwood, finally winning the Brooklands Memorial Trophy as a result of his success in club racing at Goodwood in 1957. Already, he was developing a reputation as a 'hairy' driver, for his Lotus spun quite regularly on its way to victory. By now, his rather long name had been shortened by race reporters and public alike to Innes Ireland, and that is the way it remained.

In 1958, he drove both his own Lotus and those of other entrants in a large number of races, winning the 3-hour Circuit of Auvergne race in France as well as a number of other minor events. By 1959, he had been invited to join Team Lotus as a works driver both in Formula One and sports cars, although he also drove an Ecurie Ecosse Jaguar at Le Mans. In Formula One, he was number two to Graham Hill, but the front-engined car he drove was not very competitive and his only result all season was a fourth place at the Dutch Grand Prix. However, he picked up several wins in the 1½-litre Lotus sports car.

He stayed with Lotus in 1960 when they produced the new rear-engined Mk 18 F1 car.

With it, he won the Glover Trophy at Goodwood and the International Trophy at Silverstone but, in Grand Prix races, he was less fortunate because the car often broke down, and his only places of note were second in the Dutch and US GPs. In the F2 Lotus, he won the Lavant Cup at Goodwood and the Oulton Park Trophy race.

Staying with Lotus in 1961, Ireland had another poor year, partly because of a crash in the Monaco Grand Prix when he changed into the wrong gear in the famous tunnel, receiving serious leg injuries. However, he came back to top form later in the year, winning a furious battle for the Solitude GP in Germany, following up with the non-championship F1 race at Zeltweg in Austria, and then, in October, he won the United States Grand Prix; not only was it his first, and only championship win, but it was also the first championship win for Lotus.

Despite his success in the US GP, he was dropped from the Lotus team in favour of Jim Clark, a decision which rankled with Ireland years after. He joined the private UDT-Laystall team which ran Lotus-BRMs but, from then on, he was equipped with out of date machinery and, although he drove particularly hard in 1962, his only major win was in the London GP at Crystal Palace. He had more luck in the team's Lotus 19 sports car with which he won the Nassau Trophy in the Bahamas and a whole string of British sportscar races. He also won the Tourist Trophy at Goodwood in a Ferrari 250GTO.

The UDT team was renamed BRP for 1963, and Ireland stayed with them, winning the Glover Trophy at Goodwood, in their Lotus-BRM. When he switched to their new BRP-BRM car, he was often fast, but the car seldom lasted the distance. However, he was put out of racing for a long while when he crashed a Lotus-Ferrari in America; he received multiple injuries, including a very badly smashed hip. He returned to racing in 1964 with the BRP once more, winning the Daily Mirror Trophy at Snetterton, but, in Grand Prix races, he either crashed or retired in most events.

By now, he was unable to command a place in a works team and, in 1965, he drove a rather uncompetitive Lotus-BRM for the Parnell team which brought him no success at all. In 1966, he raced only spasmodically, taking in the last two races of the season in Bernard White's old 2-litre BRM. His last race was the Mexican Grand Prix of that year.

Ireland retired from the sport soon afterwards to take up farming, but he was tempted by *Autocar* magazine to come back into the sport as their sports editor, reporting on Grand Prix racing. He also wrote an amusing autobiography called *All Arms and Elbows* and, later on, returned to competition in such events as the London to Sydney Marathon, about which he also wrote a book. MT

JEAN-PIERRE JABOUILLE (b.1942)
France

Jean-Pierre Jabouille's first Grand Prix success was a long time coming, but when it came it was very special: Jabouille won the 1979 French Grand Prix in an all-French car, the turbocharged Renault. His win was just reward for the dedicated effort he had put into developing the unconventional car from the very beginning of the project. Moreover, Jabouille was much more to Renault than simply a very talented driver, he was also an outstanding development engineer and his record of previous success has often been sadly underestimated.

He was born in the Auvergne on 1 October 1942 and made his racing debut in 1966 with, appropriately, a Renault 8 Gordini saloon. The following year he moved on to the French Formula Three championship, scoring his first single-seater win at the daunting Reims circuit. His mechanic during his Formula Three days was Jacques Laffite, who was destined to become not only a rival and then team-mate in Grand Prix racing but also Jean-Pierre's brother-in-law.

Jabouille stayed in Formula Three for several years, taking the runner-up spot in the national championship in 1968, 1969 and 1971. In 1972 he progressed into Formula Two where he began the successful development of the Renault-powered Elf 2 cars, which culminated in 1976 with his winning the European Formula Two Championship. By this time the Elf was largely 'Jabouille' in all but name. He won at Vallelunga and Mugello and trailed René Arnoux by three points going to the final round at Hockenheim. A superb tactical race, aided by his team-mate Michel Léclere, eventually brought overall victory in the series by a single point over Arnoux.

Alongside his exploits in Formula Two, Jean-Pierre also built a successful career in sports car racing, finishing third at Le Mans in

1973 and 1974 for Matra and third in the 1974 European 2-litre Sports Car Championship for Alpine. His sports car successes and his obvious talents as an engineer made him a natural choice for Renault's onslaught on Le Mans. When the team won the 24-hour classic in 1978 it was Jabouille who led the engineering operation, the driving strength and, for twelve hours, the race itself, although the eventual winners were Jean-Pierre Jaussaud and Didier Pironi.

Jabouille in the meantime had made tentative sorties into Formula One, failing to qualify the Williams-run Iso and the Surtees during 1974, before making his Grand Prix debut for Tyrrell in the 1975 French Grand Prix, where he finished twelfth.

His real break into Grand Prix racing, however, came with the entry of Renault onto the World Championship stage with their ambitious turbocharged car in 1977. Jabouille did a prodigious amount of testing and development on the new car, but only had four races in Britain, Holland, Italy and Watkins Glen – none of which brought a finish. By 1978 Renault, helped by Jabouille, were making real progress but just three championship points, for fourth place at Watkins Glen, did not really reflect that progress. Once again, lack of reliability dogged the team.

1979 saw Renault (Jabouille now joined by former Formula Two rival René Arnoux) equipped with the new, twin-turbo, ground effect RS10, after early races with the older cars. Jabouille now began to show that he was more than just a hard worker; during the year he sat on pole position four times and it was a poor reflection of his performances that the only points he scored during the year were the nine for his famous and commanding victory in the French Grand Prix. Nevertheless, it was entirely appropriate reward for his efforts that it should be Jabouille who gave Renault their first laurels.

In 1980 Jean-Pierre was to some extent overshadowed by his young team-mate, Arnoux, but he was often among the front runners. Justice was done when he scored a well-judged win in Austria, nursing rapidly deteriorating tyres, avoiding the valve spring problems which had of late plagued the yellow cars and resisting a determined last minute challenge from eventual World Champion, Alan Jones.

Jean-Pierre's season came to a catastrophic end in Canada, where he was lucky to survive a huge accident caused by suspension failure,

suffering badly broken legs. It was a sad end to what proved to be his last race for Renault; for 1981, he joined his brother-in-law and former mechanic in the Talbot-Ligier team.

He was surely seen as a valuable asset, as the team set out to develop its brand new car and engine, and perhaps that was at least part of the reason why Jabouille accepted the new challenge.   BL

CHARLES JARROTT (1877-1944)
Great Britain
'Finish at all costs.' That was the racing motto of Charles Jarrott, one of Britain's greatest drivers in the first decade of motor sport, who took part in just about every race that mattered, up to 1905. Yet out of all those events, he had just one major victory, although he was often well up with the leaders. Jarrott's creed, recalled Arthur Bray (one of his racing contemporaries), was that it was always much better 'to race clean and lose, than to win by foul driving'.

Jarrott was born in 1877 and originally planned to make the law his career. He was articled to a solicitor, but gave this up for motoring. He started racing with a De Dion tricycle at the old Crystal Palace cycle track and drove a Panhard, fitted with a prototype Napier engine, in the 1900 Thousand Miles' Trial.

He first competed in an international event in the 1901 Paris-Berlin race, driving a 40hp Panhard. Its racing number was 13, so he had it painted green to cancel out the bad luck; he finished tenth.

In the following year, he took part in the Circuit du Nord, driving a new 40hp Panhard. For this race, the cars had to run on alcohol, which the French Government was trying to promote as a fuel; this reduced their speed by around twenty per cent, and they were further slowed by torrential rain, which caused Jarrott's car to misfire. Nevertheless, he soon took second position behind Maurice Farman's sister car. For much of the race, he was challenged for second place by Marcellin's Darracq and the cars were running hubcap to hubcap right up to the finish, when Jarrott put on a spurt, hurtled over the line at top speed and knocked the Police Commissaire of Paris for six. Fortunately for all concerned M. le Commissaire was only shaken.

The 1902 Paris-Vienna race saw Jarrott at the wheel of one of the new 70hp, 13.8-litre Panhards built to the 1000 kg maximum-weight formula; he finished eleventh, having repaired the car's broken wooden chassis-frame with wood taken from a bedstead in his hotel room and smuggled out to the car in his trouser-legs.

Jarrott was now anxious to enter this car for the Welbeck Speed Trials, but the car was in Vienna with a broken gearbox and its chassis tied together with string, the Panhard company seeming not at all anxious to repair it. Jarrott's team-mate, Pinson, suggested that if the car were to be entered for the Circuit des Ardennes, to be held in Belgium a week or so before the Welbeck event, Panhard certainly would overhaul the car. The organisation of the Ardennes race left a lot to be desired – Jarrott and his mechanic even found themselves without hotel rooms, and had to accept the hospitality of a chance passer-by – and huge dust-clouds made it almost impossible to follow the road. However, Jarrott, fortified by a bottle of champagne handed to him en route by a spectator, roared through the field, eliminating the crack Mors racers one by one, to win the event – the first-ever closed circuit race – at 54 mph. During the following week in torrential rain, Jarrott achieved the fastest time then recorded in Great Britain – 64 mph over the flying kilometre.

In 1902, Jarrott went into partnership with William Letts, acquiring the sole British agencies for Oldsmobile and De Dietrich (Crossley was a later addition).

He drove as leader of the De Dietrich team in the 1903 Paris-Madrid, and finished third, after an epic drive which he vividly recounted in his autobiography *Ten Years of Motors and Motor Racing* (which was, in fact, ghost-written by A.B. Filson Young).

Jarrott's De Dietrich failed to last more than a couple of laps in the Circuit des Ardennes, held a month after the Paris-Madrid event; a few days later, he was driving a Napier in the Gordon Bennett held in Ireland, and crashed when the steering gear broke on the second lap, breaking his collarbone.

He drove a 96hp Wolseley Beetle in the eliminating trials to choose the British team for the 1904 Gorden Bennett – and an 89hp De Dietrich in the French eliminating trials! – and took twelfth place in the actual Gordon Bennett Cup, held on the German Taunus circuit, driving the Wolseley. Strangely, perhaps, it was his only major race in a British car.

After that, Jarrott retired from the international racing scene, although he did compete in some of the first Brooklands meetings, and also set up records for the London-Monte Carlo run, in a 40hp Crossley. His last major racing success was a dead heat for first place in the De Dietrich at Brooklands in 1907.

In 1905, he was one of the founders of the Automobile Association. In fact, Jarrott's mechanic, H. P. Small, clearly recalled fitting the first-ever AA badge on Jarrott's De Dietrich. Jarrott became the AA's chairman in 1922. He was also chairman of the Junior Car Club, founder member and vice-president of the Society of Motor Manufacturers and Traders, and one of the seven men who founded the Olympia Motor Show. He sold his interest in Charles Jarrott & Letts Ltd in 1910, but continued in the motor trade for some considerable time after that.

During World War I, he was Inspector of Transport to the Royal Flying Corps, and was three times mentioned in despatches; he was also secretary of the Royal Society of St George.

Lieutenant-Colonel Charles Jarrott died on 4 January 1944, and was mourned as 'Britain's finest racing driver of the old school'.   DBW

CAMILLE JENATZY (1868-1913)
Belgium

Camille Jenatzy, born in 1868, was a Belgian civil engineer turned motor manufacturer who made his competition debut in 1898 at the controls of one of his own electric vehicles, in the Chanteloup hill-climb organised by *La France Automobile*. Although heavy rain had affected the road surface, Jenatzy made the fastest time of the day, covering the 1800-metre course at an average speed of 17 mph.

Three weeks after this, on 18 December, *La France Automobile* held a second speed trial, this time over a standing-start, two-kilometre course on a deserted stretch of level road at Achères, to the west of Paris. Jenatzy could not take part, and the event was won by the Comte de Chasseloup-Laubat driving an electric car built by Jeantaud, Jenatzy's manufacturing rival. The following day, Jenatzy wrote to Chasseloup-Laubat challenging him to a duel of speed, to be held within the month.

So, on 17 January 1899, the two men met at Achères. Jenatzy recorded a speed of 41.1 mph, but Chasseloup-Laubat clocked 43.7 mph, despite having the motor of his car burn out 200 yards from the finish.

Ten days later, there was a return match.

This time, Jenatzy reached 50 mph over the flying kilometre, but Chasseloup-Laubat's motor burned out before he had even started. So his run was postponed until 4 March, when the Jeantaud achieved 57.6 mph. This was a phenomenal speed for the period, all the more remarkable for the fact that Chasseloup-Laubat's car was a standard touring vehicle fitted with a special body.

Not in the least discouraged, Jenatzy set about building a new car with the express purpose of regaining the speed record.

This was the famous *Jamais Contente,* a wonderful metal cigar on wheels which was the first real racing freak built. Its bullet-shaped body was made by Rheims & Auscher and was of partinium, a primitive aluminium alloy. To eliminate friction losses in the transmission, the electric motor was mounted directly on the driving axle. As a result, the car was fitted with the smallest wheels and tyres yet seen.

The low, streamlined effect was somewhat nullified by the fact that Jenatzy had to sit on top of the body, with only his nether regions inside the cockpit; nevertheless, after one false start, the car achieved his ambition of being the first vehicle to exceed 100 kph, his actual figure being 105 kph (65.8 mph).

Not everyone was impressed, though. W. Worby Beaumont wrote in his massive *Motor Vehicles and Motors:* 'This is without doubt a higher speed than any other human being has ever travelled on roads, but it was only for about three-quarters of a mile that it was maintained. This vehicle was of no use in any way as a guide for any other class of vehicle.'

Because of the extremely limited range of the battery electric vehicle, especially if it was to have any sort of speed, Jenatzy soon turned his attention to petrol-electrics; he was also seen driving a Mors in three of the principal races of 1899 – the Tour de France, the Paris-St Malo and the Paris-Ostend – attracting public notice by his sporting effort in driving through the night in the Tour de France to make up for time lost.

In the 1900 Gordon Bennett, Jenatzy drove a Bolide petrol-electric of his own design, but lost his way and gave up in despair; the later Jenatzy petrol-electrics were equally unsuccessful, and his patent magnetic clutch, used by Pipe and Rochet-Schneider, enjoyed only a limited vogue.

Jenatzy dropped out of motor sport during 1901, and his return in 1902 was hardly auspicious. During the Circuit des Ardennes, he had a fearful smash at the beginning of the second lap, the car going into one ditch and all four wheels into the other. With his usual good fortune, he escaped with a few bruises.

Because of his red hair and beard, and his flamboyant driving style, Jenatzy earned the nickname *Le Diable Rouge* (The Red Devil), although there was nothing diabolic – apart from a liking for practical jokes – about his personality.

In 1903, he transferred his allegiance to Mercédès, driving one of the new 90hp racers in the Paris-Madrid. Early in the race, he overtook 16 competitors, despite the unfavourable road conditions, and at Chatellerault, the big grey Mercédès was lying seventh. By Angoulême, Jenatzy was third, and was being tipped as a possible winner but, at the top of the Pétignac hill, he pulled up, with a mysterious fault in his engine. He eventually discovered, of all unlikely things, that the misfire was caused by a fly in the carburettor. This had cost him the race, for the delay had caused him to fall back into eleventh place, a position which he maintained until the race was halted at Bordeaux.

Then came the Gordon Bennett, held in Ireland. A fire at the Mercédès factory having destroyed the special 90hp models built for this race, the Mercédès team – Jenatzy, Baron de Caters and Foxhall Keene – used 60hp tourers borrowed back from customers and fitted with racing bodywork. Ironically, as the two drivers chosen by Emil Jellinek (Werner and Heironymus) were not *hochwohlgeborene* (of high birth), the Deutsche Automobil Club refused to allow them to compete, on social grounds – only gentlemen could take part in the Gordon Bennett – so the honour of Germany was upheld by two Belgians and a Briton.

From the second lap, Jenatzy, driving the wealthy American Clarence Gray Dinsmore's stripped Sixty Mercédès, led the field, and his victory by nearly 12 minutes brought the Gordon Bennett Cup back to Germany.

He represented Germany in the 1904 Gordon Bennett, too, but was outclassed by Léon Théry's Richard-Brasier, and had to be content with second place. As he reputedly had a narrow shave of epic porportions with a train at Wehrheim, where the line from Usingen to Frankfurt crossed the road, this was no mean achievement!

A month later, for the Circuit des Ardennes, Jenatzy transferred his allegiance to the Belgian Pipe marque, but his 60hp car only lasted two laps in this arduous race before breaking down.

In the 1905 Gordon Bennett, the Red Devil drove a 120hp Mercédès, but although he made a spectacular start, the car only completed half the distance at an average speed of 40.5mph. Having sworn to bring the Cup back to Germany whether he finished dead or alive, Jenatzy was somewhat embarrassed. Nor did he fare any better in the Circuit des Ardennes, where his Mercédès was forced out after a rim collapsed following the loss of its frail tyre.

He concluded an unsuccessful season by failing to finish in the Vanderbilt Cup, retiring on the fourth lap after dropping from second to sixth position in the preceding three rounds with the 120hp Mercédès.

Jenatzy drove a Mercédès in the 1906 French Grand Prix. At the end of the first day's racing, he was lying 16th, having averaged 47.4 mph, finishing well over two hours behind the leader, Szisz in a Renault. On the second day, he shared the car with Burton; the Mercédès started 16th and finished 10th, the first German car to complete the course.

There was a tenth place for Jenatzy's Mercédès in the Circuit des Ardennes, too, while he came fifth in the Vanderbilt Cup that October. The race was stopped after he had finished, as the crowd had become uncontrollable, and hundreds of people were swarming on to the track.

The next season saw Jenatzy's Mercédès come 14th in the Kaiserpreis, but the combination failed to finish in the French Grand Prix, falling out on the eighth lap after working up through the field from 20th to 12th position.

As in 1904, Jenatzy drove a Pipe in the Circuit des Ardennes. Again, the car failed to last the distance in the Belgian event.

The year 1908 saw Jenatzy back with his original petrol-powered love, Mors. He drove a steady race to finish 16th at an average of 56.8mph. However, both Mors and Jenatzy were past their prime, and this was the Red Devil's last appearance in international racing.

He drove a 180hp Mercédès in sprint and hill-climb events in 1909 and 1910, but thereafter devoted himself to his tyre company, whose factory in Brussels was one of the biggest in Belgium.

It was not Jenatzy's love of fast driving which caused his violent death in 1913, but his propensity for practical joking. He was entertaining a party of friends at his shooting box in the Ardennes, and one night decided to frighten them. Jenatzy crept outside, hid behind a bush, and imitated the fearsome grunt of an enraged wild boar. Whereupon one of his guests leaned out of the window and shot the supposed wild animal dead.   DBW

ALAN JONES (b.1946)
Australia

In a world notorious for its share of prima donnas, 1980 World Champion Alan Jones brought to Formula One racing an air of easy-going casualness that made him popular with spectators and competitors alike.

Jones, born in Melbourne, Australia, in 1946, has been a motor racing enthusiast all his life. His father, Stan Jones, was one of Australia's most successful drivers during the 1950s – he won the Australian Grand Prix of 1959 in a Maserati 250F – and it was inevitable that young Alan would follow in his footsteps.

Alan Jones started his racing career in karts and by 1963 he was the Australian champion. Then followed a period during which he raced a Mini and this in turn led to Alan talking his father into lending his 2.2-litre Cooper Climax for the 1964 racing season. That season, however, was Alan's last for some time because at the end of the year his father ran into severe financial difficulties as a result of the squeeze being experienced throughout the motor industry.

Alan's brief racing experiences only served to whet his appetite further and in 1967 he arrived in Britain, set on securing a future in motor racing. Unfortunately for the young Australian nothing went right and he returned to his homeland frustrated and disillusioned. Nevertheless he refused to give in, and by 1970 he was back in the UK ready to fight his way to the top. The fact that he eventually made it is a credit to his stamina, for the path was never easy.

By 1973, Jones had enough money to compete in Formula Three where he raced the works GRD 373 model with some good results. At the end of the season, however, Jones's sponsor withdrew and for 1974 he was left looking for a drive. Happily help came by courtesy of wealthy enthusiast Harry Stiller, who offered Jones a Formula Atlantic drive. Driving Stiller's March 74B, Jones won three of that year's John Player Formula Atlantic championship rounds to finish fourth in the final points table. Suitably encouraged by his young driver's promise, Stiller then purchased an ex-works Formula One Hesketh for use during the 1975 season.

Jones made his Formula One debut at the International Trophy event at Silverstone where he put up a steady and impressive drive to finish seventh. He drove the car in four Grands Prix, even qualifying at Monaco, before Stiller withdrew from racing to retire to America for tax reasons. Once again Jones was left with a racing career that seemed to be heading nowhere. As fate would have it, however, the German driver Rolf Stommelen was injured in an accident and Jones was invited to take his seat in the Embassy-sponsored Graham Hill Racing team. Jones responded to the opportunity in fine style, his best result being fifth place in the German Grand Prix. Things were beginning to look up for the stocky, dark-haired Australian at this time because he also secured a drive in the RAM Racing Team Formula 5000 March with which he gained several successes.

With the death of Graham Hill at the end of 1975, Jones was again forced to look for another drive and this time his saviour appeared in the guise of John Surtees and his Durex Surtees team. For the first time in his career Jones started a season as a fully sponsored works Formula One driver. Unfortunately, however, Jones and Surtees never quite saw eye to eye and in spite of some good placings during the '76 season – a fourth in Japan and fifth places in Belgium and Britain – Jones finished the season vowing to quit Formula One rather than drive for Surtees again. To keep his hand in, he signed for Teddy Yip to race in some Formula 5000 and USAC events but withdrew from his USAC commitments after failing to get to grips with this most specialised of sports. During the early months of 1977, fate again came to the rescue of Jones, once more at the expense of an established Grand Prix driver. Following the horrible accident at Kyalami which claimed the life of Tom Pryce, the Shadow team contacted Jones to offer him a contract. So once again he took his place among the Formula One stars and this time fortune was to smile more favourably. Following sixth place in Monaco and fifth in Belgium, Jones piloted the white and red Villiger-sponsored Shadow DN8 to a superb win in the wet and windy Austrian Grand Prix at the Österreichring. Starting from the seventh row of the grid, Jones relentlessly worked his way forward, finally winning the race by twenty seconds from the Ferrari of

Niki Lauda. It was the first Grand Prix win for both Jones and Shadow and, while the result was a surprise to most, no-one begrudged the likeable Australian his win. Jones followed up this victory with a third place in Italy and fourth places in Canada and Japan, to finish the season with 22 points, placing him seventh in the final World Championship table.

At the end of the season Jones was offered another drive, this time with the revitalised Frank Williams team, who had a new car plus a bagful of sponsorship money from the Saudia Airline company.

Jones's 1978 results, however, were a little disappointing. He was always a threat, always very fast and polished – he took fastest lap at the Canadian Grand Prix – but, apart from a fourth in South Africa, a fifth in France and a very impressive second at Long Beach in America, he failed to find the consistent reliability to make him a championship contender. He ended the season with eleven points and in joint eleventh place in the title table. In spite of his mechanical misfortune in Formula One, 1978 wasn't a total disappointment because he managed to win the valuable Can-Am championship in America using one of Jim Hall's immaculately prepared Lola T333CS machines, proving that given the machinery he was capable of winning in any class of racing.

For 1979, Jones again teamed with Frank Williams, both men hoping for better things, and it soon became apparent that the decision was a wise one. Williams began the season with the old FW06 (and a new team-mate for Jones in the person of Clay Regazzoni) and Alan started with tyre troubles and ninth place in Argentina. He retired from fifth spot in Brazil and crashed heavily in South Africa before driving another inspired race at Long Beach to finish third, to the Ferraris of Villeneuve and Scheckter.

In the wings at Long Beach was the new Williams FW07 ground effect car and Jones gave this its debut in Spain a few weeks later, only to retire with gear linkage problems. Next time out, in Belgium, the combination of Jones and the FW07 was a sensation, leading the race quite comfortably until a minor electrical fault brought a sudden halt on lap forty. In Monaco Jones was again challenging for the lead when failing tyres helped him into the barriers at the chicane (leaving Regazzoni to prove the Williams's potential with a storming second place).

That Jones could run with the world's best

was no longer in doubt. He finished fourth at the French Grand Prix, before Regazzoni put the Williams in the winners' circle for the first time, at Silverstone, after 'Jonesy' retired from the lead. He waited only until the next race – the German Grand Prix – for this first win for Williams, in spite of a puncture towards the end and Regga dutifully breathing down his neck!

That was the beginning of a hat-trick, with dominant wins in Austria and Holland following. He won again in Canada and might have done so too at Watkins Glen had a wheel not fallen off following a fumbled pit stop. In spite of scoring more wins than either World Champion Scheckter or second place man Gilles Villeneuve, Jones had to settle for third place in the drivers' championship.

The message was clear for 1980: Jones and the Williams were the combination to beat. His championship-winning year was full of drama. It started well enough, with a win from pole position at the Argentine season opener, in spite of a spin and a pit stop. In Brazil he was third as René Arnoux's turbo Renault romped away. Arnoux took the championship lead with more of the same at Kyalami where Alan retired with a broken gearbox. At Long Beach, having been eliminated from second place in an incident with Bruno Giacomelli, Jones watched from the sidelines as Nelson Piquet took his first-ever win and began a challenge that would last throughout the season.

Jones won in Spain but saw his points discounted as the race was declared void following political wrangles within the sport. He won again in France and Britain and, having survived a huge accident during testing at Donington, he fended off Piquet by less than a second for third place in Germany after a last minute pit stop with a puncture. He was a very close second in Austria, closing rapidly on Jabouille's Renault, but in Holland he made an uncharacteristic error which dropped him out of the points as Piquet stormed to a very valuable win. The young Brazilian beat Jones fairly and squarely into second place in Italy, throwing the championship wide open in the last two races, in North America.

The complicated scoring system meant that Piquet had to win in Canada to stay in the hunt. In the event the race was stopped after Jones and Piquet came together at the first corner, involving the whole grid. At the restart, Piquet, in his spare car, rushed away in the lead only to see his title hopes blow up with his engine. Jones won the race and the championship with one Grand Prix to spare, but, if anyone thought that he would end the season gently at Watkins Glen, they were in for a surprise. After falling right back thanks to a first corner excursion, Jones drove his heart out to win his sixth Grand Prix of the year. In the closed season he also won the non-championship Australian Grand Prix and a British saloon car race. His performances underlined once and for all that Jones is an outstanding talent with a single-minded desire to win and a worthy World Champion.   MW/BL

PARNELLI JONES (b.1933)
USA
In the typically rough and tumble world of American stock car and Indianapolis-style racing, Parnelli Jones has been one of the most outstanding performers, winning many races and being involved in many controversies.

Born Rufus Parnell Jones, on 12 August 1933, the young Californian soon gravitated towards racing cars; at the age of nineteen he took part in his first race, a stock car event in Los Angeles. For the next four years he took part in practically every stock-car race organised by the California Racing Association, gaining a number of victories. He then turned to sprint car racing, the small speedway cars which race largely on ¼ and ½-mile cinder tracks. Despite joining in half way through the 1959 season, he drove so well in these unfamiliar cars, that he finished fifth in the Sprint-Car championship.

He joined the United States Automobile Club 'circus' in 1960 and set the lap record at Houston in his first event, in which he finished third. During the remainder of the season he won no less than seven of the thirteen races he contested. He also attracted a great deal of attention by putting in the fastest lap at Milwaukee in his sprint car, which beat the lap record of the bigger-engined Indianapolis-type cars.

This naturally brought Jones to the notice of the wealthy car owners who virtually controlled Indianapolis racing. He came under the wing of the flamboyant J. C. Agajanian, the cowboy-hatted millionaire, who entered him for Indianapolis races in his Willard Battery Special. Jones took in a few minor championship races late in 1960, his best placing being second at Sacramento. However, in 1961, he was given a full season of championship racing and in the Indianapolis 500 he qualified fifth fastest. In the race he was running well, until the engine went off tune, and he finished twelfth. Late in 1961 he gained his first championship win, the Phoenix 100 and was voted as 'Rookie of the Year'. In sprint-car racing he won nine races to become champion for the second year running.

For 1962, he again drove the Willard Battery Special, showing his skill by becoming the first man to lap the 2½-mile Indianapolis track at over 150 mph, in qualifying, to give him the coveted pole position for the race. He led for 120 laps but vibration broke a pipe line which slowed him to an eventual seventh place. His only victory that year in championship cars was in the Hoosier 100 at Indianapolis, but his consistent placings gave him third place in the USAC championship. In sprint-car racing he won the championship yet again to become only the third man to win the title three times.

By 1963 the rear-engine revolution at Indianapolis was well under way with Jim Clark driving a Lotus-Ford, but Jones stuck with his old fashioned 'Dinosaur', as the front-engined Indy cars were called, and he won the race in a very controversial finish. His car was leaking oil towards the end of the race, an offence which normally calls for the car to be flagged into the pits at Indianapolis, but the Stewards allowed Jones to carry on to victory, with Clark slipping and sliding in second place on the oily surface. The Europeans angrily disputed the 'home town' decision, but Jones was confirmed as winner.

Jones had now turned back to stock-car racing as a sideline to the Indianapolis-style events; he raced in USAC events with a Mercury, picking up three wins in 1963.

Although the mid-engined cars were beginning to swamp the 'Dinosaurs' at Indianapolis, Jones continued with Agajanian in 1964, this time with a Bowes Seal Fast Special. The Indy 500 race developed into a battle between Jones and A. J. Foyt, both in 'Dinosaurs', but Jones's fuel tank caught fire during a pit stop and he had to abandon the car, leaving Foyt to win. Despite the speed of his and Foyt's old-fashioned cars, he knew that time was running out for the front-engined machines so, later in 1964, he switched to a Lotus-Ford for several races, winning the Milwaukee 200 and Trenton 200 to wind up sixth in the USAC championship. The versatile Jones continued with a Mercury in stock-car races, winning seven of the fourteen races he entered, taking the

USAC Stock Car championship. He won the Pikes Peak class again and for good measure won the Riverside sports-car race in a Cooper. Although he reduced his participation in sprint and midget races, he still won seven midget races and one sprint race.

Jones was now fully established as one of the greats of American motor racing, able to pick and choose the cars he drove. For 1965, he drove a revamped 1964 Lotus-Ford for Agajanian, under the name of Hurst Special, but the car proved to be troublesome, suffering several chassis failures, one of them causing the Lotus to hit a wall at Indianapolis. However, in the 500 the car ran well and he finished a comfortable second place, behind Jim Clark's Lotus. He also won the Milwaukee 100 with the Lotus, but the rest of the season provided him mostly with retirements. For 1966, Agajanian decided on a Shrike chassis, powered by a supercharged Offenhauser engine for Indianapolis racing, and with this car, known as the REV 500 Special, Jones qualified fastest at Indianapolis at 162.484 mph, but his engine gave up after 87 laps of the race.

Jones at last deserted Agajanian in 1967 in favour of the exciting new STP Special from Andy Granatelli. This gas-turbine-powered car proved to be a sensation at Indianapolis, for it was streets ahead of anything else, allowing Jones to lead the race with ease, until, with only three laps to go, a drive-shaft bearing failed and he coasted to a stop, being credited with sixth place.

The Indianapolis rules were changed for 1968 to make the turbine engines less competitive. However, Jones was entered in an STP Lotus turbine car for the Indy 500 but he withdrew before the race, saying that the cars were not competitive enough. At this point Jones decided to retire from single-seater racing, but throughout the rest of 1968 he took part in USAC stock-car events, winning several more races.

By 1969, Jones was beginning to run down his racing participation to concentrate on his thriving businesses as a Firestone tyre distributor in California and as a Ford car dealer, but he continued to drive in stock-car events. In 1970 he organised and drove in the Trans-Am Ford Mustang team; he won no less than five races to give Ford the championship.

Together with a well known tuner and car builder, Bill Stroppe, Parnelli Jones formed an organisation to run various types of car, principally for Ford. They ran the Trans-Am cars and also built four-wheel-drive Ford Bronco pick-ups, which ran very successfully in the Baja 1000 and other off-road events in southern California. Parnelli Jones himself drove in these events, showing his versatility once again by winning the Baja 1000. However, he gradually tapered off his own competition activities and formed a new company to build racing cars, principally for USAC Indianapolis races. Their first effort at an Indianapolis car was a very radical design which performed poorly to start with. However, driver Joe Leonard picked up three major wins in 1972 USAC races. Little success came to the team in 1973 or 1974 in USAC racing, despite using top drivers like Mario Andretti and Al Unser. In late 1973, it was announced that the Vels Parnelli team would build a Formula One car powered by the Ford DFV engine. The car was driven by Mario Andretti but development was hampered by a lack of finance and time. The car was forced to run on Goodyear tyres after Firestone withdrew from racing in 1975. In 1976 Andretti contested only the Long Beach Grand Prix – from which he retired after fifteen laps – and the Formula One team was disbanded.

Jones had more success with his other racing operations. In 1975 Andretti and Al Unser won all eight races in the US Formula 5000 championship and in 1976 Unser, using a turbocharged Cosworth DFX engine developed by the team, won three USAC championship races, including the prestigious Pocono 500. Unser also finished second in the 5000 championship.

The team continued to develop the Cosworth engine in their USAC racing programme successfully. The tall, lean Parnelli Jones, with his striking crew-cut hair style, was used to winning and his lean years as an entrant in USAC racing made this likeable Californian all the more determined to keep his team right at the top.   MT

ELIZABETH JUNEK (b.1900)
Czechoslovakia

One of the great Bugatti drivers – perhaps the greatest lady driver of all time – was Elizabeth Junek from Czechoslovakia, who, in a few crowded seasons in the mid 1920s, showed that she had the ability to meet and beat the world's racing elite.

Born in 1900, she first heard of the Bugatti in Paris, where, at the age of 21, she met her future husband, Cenek Junek, a Prague banker. That was shortly after Bugatti's famous victory in the Circuit di Brescia: Type 13 Bugattis were on show in the Champs-Elysées, and Elizabeth and Cenek determined that they would buy one of these cars, a resolve strengthened by Haimowitch's impressive showing in the Zbraslav-Jiloviste race in 1922.

That year the Juneks were married, and in the autumn they returned to France to buy one of the 2-litre Bugatti team of cars, which had finished second, third and fourth in the French Grand Prix at Strasbourg. Their car was delivered by racing driver Pierre Marco in November 1922, and as soon as it had been rebuilt, after travelling on the atrocious main road to Prague, the Juneks began trials.

As a result, Elizabeth drove the car back to Molsheim the following spring to have a new, cigar-shaped body fitted; after the Tours Grand Prix, the Juneks acquired another racing Bugatti, one of the 'Tanks' with aerofoil-section bodywork, but its road-holding proved inferior. The Juneks complained to Ettore Bugatti, who told them that after the 1924 Lyon GP they could take their pick of any of his new racing cars taking part. That was how the Juneks acquired one of the first Type 35s.

Between 1924 and 1926, Elizabeth competed in a number of Czech events, but thought that she would like to try international racing. So, in 1926, she took part in the Klausen hill-climb in Switzerland, achieving second place in her class. However, she had determined to take part in road racing, and in the following year the Juneks set sail for Sicily, to compete in the Targa Florio. Their preparation for the event was thorough – for the month preceding the race they practised daily over the course, which they also walked on foot to memorise its many twists and curves.

At the end of the first lap, Elizabeth was lying fourth, 34 seconds behind the leader, Minoia, who was closely followed by Dubonnet and Materassi. However, steering trouble developed, and put her out of the race on the second lap. Nevertheless, her performance had so impressed the organisers that she was awarded a special gold medal as a reward.

Later in the season, the Juneks achieved a unique victory in the Moravian Circuit of Praded, in which Cenek finished first and Elizabeth second; then Elizabeth won the 2-litre class in the first Grand Prix of Germany to be held over the newly opened Nürburgring. She also won two ladies' races at Montlhéry, and finished second in the Karlova Studanka event despite the fact that two broken con-rods were hanging through the side of the crank-case!

The following year, Elizabeth was determin-ed to make an all-out attempt to win the Targa Florio – or at least the Ladies' Cup. She prac-tised relentlessly, even driving the full five-lap, 500 km distance to ensure that she had suffi-cient stamina for the event.

Her performance in the actual race proved a sensation. At the end of the first lap she was ly-ing fourth, then on the next lap her pit signall-ed that she was in the lead, ahead of drivers such as Divo, Nuvolari, Materassi, Campari, Minoia and Conelli!

She dropped back to second place on the third and fourth laps – then, in the fifth lap, disaster struck. The water pump began to leak violently, and she had to slow down until she could top up the radiator. As a result, Elizabeth Junek finished fifth, behind Divo, Campari, Conelli and Chiron, but she still won the Ladies' Cup, as well as the Izolatti class award. Had the car held up, she might have won the entire event.

That was the climax of Madame Junek's rac-ing career, for in the German GP later that season, her husband crashed and was killed; she abandoned competitive driving at once, although her infrequent appearances in old-car events in later years showed that she had lost little of her ability in a Bugatti.   DBW

JACQUES LAFFITE (b.1943)
France

After a period during which British drivers dominated Grand Prix racing, the success of the numerous and prestigious domestic cham-pionships in France suddenly threw a galaxy of new French stars into the ascendancy in the middle and late 1970s. One such product of the French racing machine is Jacques-Henri Laf-fite, a driver who worked his way to the top by the classic route and who is totally dedicated to his sport.

Laffite, the son of a leading Paris lawyer, was born on 21 November 1943, in Magny-Cours. While at school he began to take an in-terest in motor racing and, almost as soon as he could, he abandoned his studies to become a racing mechanic, looking after Jean-Pierre Jabouille's Formula Three cars in the late 1960s and later working for the highly res-pected Winfield racing school.

Jabouille narrowly missed winning the Euro-pean F3 title in 1968 and Laffite began to race in the formula the following year. That, how-ever, was a very expensive way to start motor racing and Jacques soon switched to Formule Renault, already proving to be a superb yard-stick for stars of the future. He soon made his mark in that formula and in 1972 he won the national championship, the Critérium de For-mule Renault.

With that success behind him, he was able to move back into F3 as a works driver for BP Racing, with a Martini. He was spectacularly successful in the highly competitive world of F3 during 1973, winning the French champion-ship most convincingly, and finishing fourth in the British championship in spite of missing several crucial rounds. He won the all-import-ant Monaco event – which always lists a large number of Grand Prix team managers among its most avid spectators – and at one stage in the season he went ten races without defeat.

F3, however, was passing through hard times, and in 1974 it was dropped completely in France. By now, though, people were begin-ning to take note of the young Frenchman's progress and he was able to move up another rung in 1974 to contest the European F2 Championship. With his Martini-developed March-BMW he maintained his rapid pro-gress, taking second place 'round the houses' at Pau and scoring his first win in the formula at Salzburgring. He was second again at Hockenheim, third at Karlskoga and second at Vallelunga. Had it not been for a spate of engine failures, he might have improved on his third place in the championship – behind Depailler and Stuck.

That Laffite's talent had not gone unnoticed was confirmed when Frank Williams put him into one of his Iso Formula One cars for the last five races of the 1974 season, starting with the German Grand Prix. Although he scored no points (his best finish was fifteenth in Canada) he signed for a full season with Williams in 1975.

It was to be a busy year: as well as contesting the full Grand Prix season he found time to win the European F2 Championship outright, taking six wins with his Martini-BMW. Five victories came in the first six races and although the season then turned sour – with only two finishes in the last eight rounds, thanks to mechanical failures – he was comfor-tably champion. In F1 he finished a dogged se-cond at the Nürburgring but was generally hampered by the Iso's lack of speed and reliability. He also co-drove to three World Championship of Makes wins, with Arturo Merzario, in an Alfa Romeo 33TT12 – at Dijon, Monza and Nürburgring – making him Group 6 World Champion. Towards season's end he somehow found time to test the new Ligier-Matra Grand Prix car, leading him to sign for the team for 1976.

His performances in developing the car during 1976 were ample justification for Ligier's choice. His best result of the year was second place in Austria, but he also scored third in Italy and fourth in both Long Beach and Sweden, for seventh place in the championship.

Laffite's efforts in the often underfinanced car brightened the team's future and he was quite content to stay with the much improved Matra-engined car for 1977. Despite the preponderance of Cosworth-powered machinery, Laffite made the most of his team's reliance on the gloriously musical V12. He was invariably competitive, but was usually just on the wrong side of the real breakthrough. When the 'circuit' moved to Sweden, Laffite had still to collect his first point. In front of an unusually large crowd he went the whole hog and scored an immensely popular win for himself and the marque Ligier. True, Mario Andretti led most of the race, ducking into the pits for fuel only two laps from home, but Laffite fought hard to carve through the field from as low as eleventh place. The first-ever all-French championship Grand Prix win spoke volumes both for the country's motor racing structure and for Laffite's own raw talent.

Sadly, he was unable to recapture the same form for the rest of the season and his remaining points came from second place in Holland, fifth in Japan and sixth in Great Britain. Eighteen points gave him tenth place in the championship, though many observers placed him higher in their driver ratings.

For 1978, Laffite stayed with Ligier and Ligier stayed with Matra, frustrating once again direct comparison of the driver's talents with his Ford-powered contemporaries. 1978 was the year of the Lotuses and although Laffite was, justifiably, one of the favoured Goodyear runners at most races, he was never really in the hunt. His best results were third places in Spain and Germany, which he backed with fourth place in Italy and fifth places in South Africa, Long Beach, Belgium and Austria. He achieved the remarkable record of

fourteen finishes from the season's sixteen Grands Prix, netting eighth place in the championship.

For 1979, the break that many people had long predicted came when the Ligier team finally capitulated to the need for Ford-Cosworth power, if the car was ever to be a real challenger for the world title. The V8-powered Ligier JS11 was an instant and spectacular success. In the opening race of the 1979 season, Laffite started from pole position, a full second ahead of the next quickest runner, his own new team-mate, Patrick Depailler. After Laffite had taken the lead on the eleventh lap, the result was in little doubt, and he romped away to a supremely convincing win.

Two weeks later he repeated the performance with consummate ease in Brazil, Depailler completing a Ligier one-two. Many now predicted that Laffite would run away with the championship but in South Africa he crashed, following a puncture, after 45 laps. At Long Beach Jacques started from the back of the grid in the spare car, after gearbox failure sidelined the race car on the warm-up lap, but succumbed to overheating brakes after just eight laps. From pole position in Spain he retired from second place with a blown engine – the legacy of a missed gear change – but he ended his run of bad luck in Belgium, with second place behind Jody Scheckter, which might have been first had his battle with Depailler not taken the edge off his tyres.

Laffite went to Monaco as joint championship leader (with Scheckter) but a recurrence of an old wrist injury, plus a loose wheel and gearbox problems made for a particularly fruitless weekend. In spite of all his problems he put in a memorable drive, leaving no doubts about his championship aspirations.

Shortly after Monaco, Depailler was seriously injured in a hang-gliding accident, sidelining him for the rest of the season and Ligier (with Jackie Ickx as a stand-in number two) lost their direction somewhat. At the French Grand Prix, modifications to the JS11 made it totally uncompetitive. Things improved a little and Jacques took third places in Germany, Austria and Holland but he never again looked quite a winner. Fourth place in the championship was rather less than the opening races had seemed to augur.

Still, Laffite is one of those drivers who races for the love of it and, joined by countryman Didier Pironi, he stayed faithful to Ligier for 1980. It was a mixed season; Pironi frequently proved quicker, if rather more impetuous, but Jacques showed he could still run at the front, particularly in mid-season when the car was at its best. He won in Germany when Alan Jones had a puncture on his way to the flag, and he scored second places in South Africa and Monte Carlo, third in France and Holland (both times after leading), fourth in Austria and a gritty fifth at Watkins Glen, nursing a damaged neck after a big practice accident.

He could look back on some bad luck stories too. In Canada he ran out of fuel while in fourth place. He collided with Reutemann and Villota while challenging (a little too hard perhaps) for the lead in Spain, and he crashed out of the lead in the British Grand Prix with a puncture.

Once again, fourth place in the championship might have been so much more but 1981 as leader of the Talbot-powered Ligier team offered another chance for the ever enthusiastic Jacques.   BL

NIKI LAUDA (b.1949)
Austria
At the end of 1973, Marlboro BRM team-mates Niki Lauda and Clay Regazzoni withdrew from the BRM team and signed for Ferrari. It did not cause much excitement in the motoring press, for Ferrari were experiencing a difficult time, following a walk-out by Jacky Ickx, and Lauda and Regazzoni had finished the season in joint sixteenth place with two points apiece. A year later, Regazzoni had scored 52 points, and lost the World Championship to Emerson Fittipaldi by only three points, while Lauda finished in fourth place with a total of 38 points. In addition, Lauda had established himself as one of Formula One's fastest drivers. Obviously, a lot of credit went to the Ferrari cars, but no one could deny the contribution made by the slightly-built young Austrian himself, Nicholas von Lauda.

Lauda was born in Vienna on 22 February 1949, the son of a successful paper-processing executive. Lauda's introduction to motor sport came when he was taken to see the 1966 German Grand Prix. He immediately caught the racing bug and decided to trade his Mini Cooper S for a racing car. Shortly afterwards, Niki became involved with local racing hero Fritz Baumgarten, and purchased the latter's racing Mini. Because of parental opposition, the car was kept in Baumgarten colours and

Lauda told his parents he was storing it for Fritz!

Baumgarten and Lauda went hill-climbing together in 1968 and this, in turn, gave way to circuit racing the following year. By this time, Lauda's talent had earned him a factory ride with the Austro-Kaimann Formula Vee team. His debut with the team was something of a disaster, though. At Hockenheim in his first F Vee race, he led for most of the distance but spun off on the last lap. The following day, he took the car to Aspern airfield and destroyed it in a monumental cartwheel during practice. Nevertheless, the factory provided another car and Lauda's career was thankfully saved. His enthusiasm and determination triumphed, and soon he held the F Vee lap record at the difficult Nürburgring. Following this, Lauda enjoyed a brief flirtation with Formula Three, driving for Francis McNamara, before purchasing a Porsche 908 sports car. Using the Porsche, he competed in a number of events gaining experience and having some success.

At this stage, Lauda's career had arrived at the crossroads. He was determined to make motor racing his living but no team seemed prepared to employ him. Niki decided to 'rent' better drives and approached his bank for sponsorship. Surprisingly, they agreed to the deal, provided that Lauda's family guaranteed the loan which, even more surprisingly, they agreed to do. If nothing else, the deal emphasised Niki's almost fanatical determination to go motor racing. With this sponsorship, he bought a March Formula Two ride for the 1971 season. That year, however, F2 was dominated by his team-mate Ronnie Peterson, but Niki did enough to impress. 1971 also saw his Formula One debut, in a March 711, at the Austrian Grand Prix.

Lauda's spell in the world of big-time motor racing had made him even more determined to succeed. At the beginning of the following season, 1972, Lauda negotiated an even more elaborate sponsorship deal. It was the biggest gamble of his life. At the age of 23, he approached the bank and secured an overdraft of $100,000, 85 per cent of which was repayable over three years. It was an awesome responsibility for the frail-looking young Austrian, but he was determined not to let it cripple him. The money bought a Formula One drive with the STP-March team as number two, again to Ronnie Peterson. He began the season with an 11th place in the Argentinian GP and followed this up with a promising seventh place in the

South African GP. He also won an F2 event at Oulton Park and scored a second at Mallory Park. However, thereafter, his season began to run downhill. The radical F1 March 721X proved unsuccessful and was abandoned halfway through the season. Engine problems also plagued his F2 rides and, at the end of the season, it looked as though Lauda's bank manager was due for a prolonged bout of nail biting. Nevertheless, Niki's loan still had two years to run and he was not about to go down without a fight.

For the 1973 season, Lauda joined the Marlboro BRM team as number three to Regazzoni and Beltoise. By mid season Lauda was proving quicker than his supposedly more capable team-mates. He had some fine drives, notably at Monaco, Silverstone and Mosport and, but for two stops for tyres, might have won the Canadian GP. His enthusiasm, however, got the better of him occasionally and a crash, resulting in a broken wrist, caused him to miss his own Austrian GP. Although it was not a successful season in terms of points and placings, it had proved that Lauda had a great deal of potential.

So, for 1974, Niki Lauda joined the Ferrari team. Ferrari, after several years in the doldrums, suddenly produced a winning car and Niki, now more desperate than ever to succeed, was not slow in taking the opportunity. In fact, the Lauda/Ferrari combination proved to be the sensation of the season. He now became *the* man to beat. Of the fifteen GP races in the championship season, he won pole position nine times. He won two GPs, the Spanish and the Dutch, and would have won the British GP but for a puncture in the closing laps which forced him into the pits. As Jody Scheckter won the race Lauda was prevented from rejoining the fray by the crowds in the pit lane. He was eventually awarded fifth place after long legal arguments. It was a turning point in the season after which Lauda's luck deserted him. Although he continued to set pole positions and fastest laps he also fell victim to mechanical failures and several minor accidents: in the last five rounds of the season he failed to score a single point and finished the championship in fourth place. Nevertheless, he had made the big breakthrough; suddenly he was the man to beat. The gamble had succeeded and even Niki's bank manager could rest a little easier.

1975 was the year when everything clicked for the young Austrian and all his promise finally reaped the sport's ultimate reward. Lauda announced that he had again signed to drive for Ferrari and declared his intention to become the second Austrian to win the World Championship – following in the footsteps of his idol, Jochen Rindt. Not only did Lauda fulfil his promise but he did it in dominant fashion.

The season began with Emerson Fittipaldi, the man who had eventually clinched the 1974 title, winning the Argentine Grand Prix. Niki, who put his 1974-model Ferrari on the second row of the grid, fought hard against poor handling to score a single point for sixth place. It was virtually the same story for Lauda in Brazil where he finished fifth, again starting from the second row and again fighting handling problems.

In South Africa Ferrari introduced their new car – the transverse-gearboxed 312T – and, in spite of a practice accident, Niki showed the car's potential with yet another second row grid position. It was some reward for long periods of testing which Lauda had carried out on the car over the preceding weeks, but in the race he was forced to settle for fifth place and just two more points for his title chase. The Spanish Grand Prix which followed had the makings of a *tour de force* for the Ferrari team as Niki put the 312T on pole position and his team-mate, Clay Regazzoni, emphasised the car's superiority by sitting alongside him on the front row. This was not a happy race however; throughout practice the drivers had been troubled by the safety arrangements at the Montjuich circuit and in the race Rolf Stommelen was to crash and take the lives of four bystanders. For the Ferrari team however the race was over long before that accident caused it to be stopped. Lauda and Regazzoni were involved in a bumping match in the first corner and Lauda's race went no further.

It was apparent that his luck must change and change it did. He won from pole position in Monaco, repeated the performance in Belgium and went on to do the same in France and the United States later in the year. He also won the Swedish Grand Prix and scored second place in Holland (to James Hunt), third in both Germany and Italy, sixth in Austria and eighth in Great Britain. The rain-shortened British race was the only one of the season other than the Spanish in which he did not score points. That Lauda clinched his championship at Monza (a race which Regazzoni won) was just icing on the cake for the Italian team in a season in which Lauda had won five Grands Prix and sat on pole position nine times. He also won the non-championship International Trophy race at Silverstone in a memorable championship year.

1976, too, was a year which Lauda was unlikely to forget – but for much less happy reasons. He began his defence of the title in style, with victories in Brazil and South Africa. Regazzoni, again Lauda's team-mate at Ferrari, won the United States Grand Prix (West) at Long Beach. Then the problems began: James Hunt, now with McLaren and rapidly establishing himself as Lauda's main rival, won the Spanish Grand Prix – only to be disqualified for a technical infringement, handing the official result to Lauda, but eventually being reinstated. After that the season took on an aura of open hostility between Ferrari and McLaren, with protests flying thick and fast. Niki dominated the Belgian Grand Prix to take a huge lead in the championship and added further with a narrow win in Monaco. At that point in the season he was 36 points ahead of his nearest challenger, Regazzoni, and it seemed the retention of his title was a mere formality. However, Niki's next win did not come until the British Grand Prix in July and that was gained at Hunt's expense. Regazzoni precipitated a multiple accident in the first corner and the race was immediately stopped, with several cars (including Hunt's) in various stages of disarray around the circuit. Hunt, his McLaren hastily repaired, won the restarted race only to be excluded on the grounds that he was not actually running when the first 'heat' was stopped. Niki was declared the winner.

All animosity was forgotten two weeks later when the 'circus' moved to the Nürburgring in Germany. Again the race was stopped in its opening stages, but this time it was Lauda who had crashed. On the second lap his Ferrari crashed heavily and inexplicably at Bergwerk and burst into flames. Brett Lunger and Harald Ertl both crashed into Lauda's car which was ironically fortunate as it was they who had to remove the critically injured Lauda from his blazing car – there being no marshals close by.

Lauda's recovery was typical of his fighting spirit: from near death caused by breathing flames and toxic fumes he forced himself back to racing in time for the Italian Grand Prix at Monza, just six weeks after his accident, and he finished fourth! The battle for the championship was still not over.

By the time Niki returned, Hunt, who had won in Holland, had caught up to within two points. James won in Canada and America while Niki managed only one third place, at Watkins Glen. The two drivers went to the final round, at Mount Fuji in Japan, with Lauda leading by three points. He was then forced to make one of the bravest decisions of his career; the decision *not* to race. Conditions as the cars left the grid were truly appalling and Lauda went no further than the end of the second lap, climbing out of the car with the comment: 'There are more important things to me than the World Championship.' He watched from the pits as Hunt finished third in an exciting race to clinch the title by a single point.

Lauda stayed with Ferrari for 1977, in spite of cruel jibes from the Italian press and regular rumours of his departure. By mid-season he had shown that he was back on his top form and after the British Grand Prix, in which he finished second to Hunt, he was leading the championship. He had scored a win in South Africa, finished second in Monaco, Belgium, Britain and at Long Beach, third in Brazil and fifth in France. He missed the Spanish Grand Prix with a recurrence of a rib injury gained in a tractor accident one year earlier and retired in disgust from the Swedish Grand Prix when his Ferrari would not behave properly.

Although it was apparent that the Ferrari did not now enjoy its previous outright superiority Lauda's determination proved that it takes more than a good car to be a true champion: it takes courage and determination, qualities which the young Austrian still possessed in abundance. His greatest satisfaction probably came from the German Grand Prix, held at Hockenheim owing to the Nürburgring's safety problems; just one year after his near fatal accident Niki stormed to victory, extending his championship lead to ten points.

By the end of the season he was World Champion once again, having added another win, in Holland, second places in Austria and Italy and fourth in the USA. When Ferrari brought Gilles Villeneuve into the team in Canada, Lauda – already taunted by jibes from the Italian press – walked out of his contract in disgust and headed for Brabham, taking with him his Parmalat sponsorship and chief mechanic Ermanno Cuoghi. Between them they helped the Brabham-Alfa a little further along the road to competitiveness, but it took Gordon Murray and a liberal interpretation of the rules to give Niki his only 'on the road' win of the season, in Sweden. The car which did it was the Brabham 'fan' car – using an engine-driven fan to suck the car onto the road. The car was banned in fairly short order, although the Swedish result was allowed to stand.

Lauda's other 'win' also came in controversial circumstances. He finished third on the road at Monza, but with Mario Andretti and Gilles Villeneuve penalised for jump starts he inherited first place points. True to form he also picked up three second places, in Argentina, Monaco and Great Britain, plus third places in Brazil and Holland. He lost the lead at Brands Hatch through a rare moment of indecision while lapping Bruno Giacomelli near the end of the race. Carlos Reutemann took advantage of their near miss to relegate Lauda to second place. He also had an uncharacteristic total of nine retirements.

For 1979, Lauda stayed with Brabham who had been treated to an all-new V12 engine from Alfa, enabling them to build a ground effect car. Various problems with the radical Gordon Murray-designed car hampered results, and it was not until Monaco that Niki Lauda regained his status as a consistent front runner. But nothing really went right for Lauda after that. The V12 Alfas lacked reliability, Niki was less than happy with team patron Ecclestone and he was often slower than his raw team-mate Nelson Piquet. He finished fourth in the Italian Grand Prix and actually won the non-championship race at Imola in September.

That was his last race. Brabham introduced the promising, Cosworth-powered BT49 for the Canadian Grand Prix but Lauda came into the pits during practice and announced his retirement, on the spot. He no longer wanted, he explained, 'to drive a racing car round in circles'. He left his helmet and overalls on the pit counter and never looked back at the shocked public as he went off to pursue his new passion as an airline proprietor. MW/BL

FRANK LOCKHART (1902-1928)
USA

The history of motor racing is dotted with tales of brave and skilful drivers. None was more courageous, technically adventurous or skilful than Frank Lockhart, who won the Indianapolis 500-mile race at his first attempt, and who died in his attempt to wrest the land speed record from Sir Malcolm Campbell.

Born in California in 1902, Frank Lockhart soon gravitated towards motor engineering and racing. He began racing a Fronty Ford in track races, showing a good turn of speed against the all-conquering Duesenbergs and Millers. After a couple of seasons' racing he was invited along to Indianapolis as a relief driver, but another driver, Peter Kreis, was taken ill and Lockhart was offered a drive in his Miller. Despite his lack of experience, Lockhart took the lead after 150 of the scheduled 500 miles and increased it all the way until he was two laps in front when the race was stopped at 400 miles because of rain.

This win established Lockhart as a leading driver and he drove Millers for the rest of the 1926 season, notching up a number of wins on the board tracks. He had also developed into a talented engineer, pioneering the use of intercoolers for the supercharged Miller engines. For 1927 he returned to Indianapolis with his own car, the Perfect Circle Miller Special with which he took pole position at 120.1 mph, some 7 mph faster than the previous year's pole winner. Once again he led the race with ease, only to retire with a damaged engine after 120 laps.

Next, Lockhart turned to record breaking. He built a 1½-litre supercharged Miller single seater which he took to Lake Muroc in California, a flat bed of a dried up lake. With this tiny car he set a two-way 1-mile record of 160.01 mph, topping 171 mph during the runs.

In 1927 this was an incredible speed for such a tiny engine and it gave Lockhart the idea that a small car might well be able to take the land speed record. Only a short while earlier the land speed record had stood at a modest 174.883 mph to Malcolm Campbell's *Bluebird,* but in March 1927 Sir Henry Segrave raised it to 203.792 mph with his Sunbeam. However, Lockhart still felt that a small car might do the job, although Segrave had used a pair of 22½-litre aero engines which produced up to 1000 bhp.

Lockhart was working for the Stutz company as a development engineer at that time so he asked them if they would assist him in building his record breaker. They agreed to supply engines and some other parts if he financed the rest of the project. Lockhart decided to use a pair of Stutz 1½-litre twin overhead camshaft engines which he mounted together at an angle of 30 degrees, gearing the two crankshafts together to provide a 3-litre, 16-cylinder engine. The secret of the power output came from Lockhart's twin centrifugal superchargers which were driven off the rear of the engines. With these installed the engines gave around 380 bhp at 7500 rpm.

The car was covered in an aluminium skin and the wheels were completely faired in to reduce wind resistance; there was not even an opening at the front of the car for Lockhart dispensed with a radiator.

The machine was named the *Stutz Black Hawk,* after the town in Indiana where Stutz had their factory, and early in 1928 Lockhart took the car to Daytona Beach and began trials. He was delayed with clutch and carburettor problems until he had only two hours of his allotted time left. Despite falling rain he decided to go for the record, but on his first run the car suddenly veered off course at top speed and somersaulted into the sea, landing back on its wheels. Amazingly Lockhart had stayed in the cockpit and suffered only one or two cuts and shock.

On 25 April 1928 Lockhart was back at Daytona with the car, although in the meantime his American rival Ray Keech had raised the record to 207.552 mph in his brutal 81-litre Triplex Special. After a couple of warm up runs at around 198 mph, Lockhart decided to go for the record despite the fact that the beach was badly ridged. His first run was completed at 203.45 mph which meant that his return run would have to average over 212 mph to take the record. He hurtled back along the beach, entering the mile at around 220 mph, but suddenly a rear tyre blew out and the car somersaulted to destruction, throwing Lockhart to his death. It later transpired that a sea shell had probably cut the tyre on his first run, the cut going unnoticed in the rush to prepare the car for the second run.

So ended the short but meteoric career of the talented young engineer who had taken on the brutal monsters with his 3-litre car and had come so near to vanquishing them.   MT

JOCHEN MASS (b.1946)
West Germany

Jochen Mass could not be considered the luckiest of drivers; people forecast great things for the curly-haired German but his undoubted ability was too often thwarted by circumstance.

Jochen Richard Mass was born in Munich on 30 September 1946. Although his early interest was in flying, he followed in the foot-

steps of his grandfather, a former sea captain. Leaving school at the age of seventeen, Jochen joined the German merchant navy as a trainee officer. His love of the sea did not last long and he returned to dry land to work in a bank. After just a few months he left. With no job and no prospects he now faced the possibility of being taken into the army. While he had been in the navy he had developed an interest, as a spectator, in motor sport and when offered a job as a competition mechanic by an Alfa Romeo dealer in Mannheim he took it.

It transpired that he was also to drive in hillclimbs and minor races, although his only previous racing experience had been with bicycles, as a schoolboy! In 1968 he won his debut outings on both hill and circuit, driving an Alfa Giulia Super. Further successes in 1969 brought Mass to the attention of Ford Motorsport boss Mike Kranefuss and before long Jochen was campaigning a Ford in the European Hill Climb Championship, taking second in class with the 2.4 Cologne Capri. By 1971 he was a fully fledged works driver and won the prestigious German Touring Car Championship.

Mass also gained his first single-seater experience in 1971, in Super Vee. Of the six races he contested with his Kaimann he won two, impressing Ford sufficiently for them to back him in a Formula Three Brabham BT35 at the end of the season. He finished second on his debut and scored one win, in Britain. In 1972 he was much in demand and raced both Formula Two and Formula Three for March, as well as continuing his Ford associations. It was a good year; Mass won the European Touring Car Championship, was second in the Springbok series and won the Formula Two Eifelrennen at the Nürburgring.

Not surprisingly he led the Ford team in 1973 but he transferred his Formula Two allegiance to the Matchbox Surtees team. Two wins, at Hockenheim and Kinnekulle, helped Jochen to second place in the European Championship and prompted Surtees to give him a Grand Prix drive. His debut was very brief; he was involved in the infamous first lap accident at Silverstone which claimed all Surtees cars. He also drove at Watkins Glen but retired.

He signed for a full Grand Prix season with Surtees in 1974 but had a frustrating season, plagued by mechanical problems. His best result was fifteenth place, at the British Grand Prix. In August, after no less than eight retirements, he walked out of the team. After

Mike Hailwood's enforced retirement Mass was drafted into a McLaren for the American races, finishing the season with a fine seventh at Watkins Glen and a McLaren contract for 1975, as team-mate to Emerson Fittipaldi.

It was a much better year but, having scored third place in Brazil and sixth in South Africa, Jochen was unfortunate that his win in the Spanish Grand Prix was clouded by tragedy and bitterness. From the start of practice the drivers condemned the Montjuich circuit as unacceptably dangerous. The race started, under protest, with a multiple first lap accident and on the 25th lap Rolf Stommelen's Hill, leading, crashed heavily when a wing support failed. Three officials and a photographer were killed and Stommelen badly injured. When the race was stopped, four laps later, Mass's McLaren was in the lead. He was awarded half points for his win but there were no celebrations. He finished the year with third places in France and at Watkins Glen, fourth in Austria and sixth in Monaco for seventh place in the championship.

He stayed with McLaren for 1976, alongside James Hunt, but it was a bad year. While Hunt took the championship Jochen picked up a string of places for ninth in the series. He was unlucky not to win the German Grand Prix, running away with the race before it was stopped due to Niki Lauda's near fatal accident.

The following year was much as before; he was second in Sweden, third in Canada, fourth in Spain, Monaco, Britain and Italy, fifth in South Africa and sixth in Austria, but again a win eluded him. He did, however, win World Championship for Makes rounds at Silverstone, Watkins Glen and Brands Hatch, sharing a Porsche 935-77 with Jacky Ickx.

In 1978 Mass joined German industrialist Günter Schmid's ATS team. It was a disastrous season in which he didn't score a single point, his best result being seventh place in Brazil. He failed to qualify in Austria and Holland and ended the season with a badly broken leg following a big testing accident at Silverstone.

Recovered, he joined the controversial Arrows team for 1979 but struggled throughout the year, scoring just three sixth places. He showed touches of inspiration but the cars were simply outclassed. Nevertheless, he stayed with Arrows in 1980 but initial promise with the new A3 was not fulfilled and he was never a real front runner. His best result was a lucky second in the outlawed and partially boycotted Spanish Grand Prix but he was a good fourth at Monaco and sixth in South Africa. A big practice accident in Austria injured his back and kept him out of action until the American finales.

Over the closed season, as Arrows fought sponsorship problems and the sport itself fought unseemly political battles, Mass spoke to Lotus about a 1981 contract but then in November, while holidaying on his boat he broke his leg in just the same position as in his Silverstone accident. Disillusioned by recent events and struggling to recover yet again, Jochen began to voice serious doubts about his keenness to continue racing.   BL

RAYMOND MAYS (1899-1980)
Great Britain

Raymond Mays was one of the most prominent British racing drivers of the between-war years. However, not only did he race cars successfully, he also developed the ERA during the 1930s and, after World War II, was responsible for instigating the BRM project.

Born in 1899 at Bourne, Lincolnshire, Raymond Mays was the son of a pioneer motorist who used to enter his Napiers and Vauxhalls in early speed events. The young Mays became infatuated with the motor car, and schooling at Oundle and Cambridge was impatiently suffered while schemes were laid to get into motor racing. He persuaded his father to buy him a Speed Model Hillman whilst at Cambridge and, together with his school friend, Amherst Villiers, he modified the engine considerably. His first event was the Inter-Varsity hill-climb at Aston Clinton in 1921 where the Hillman made best time of the day, a victory which inspired him to modify the Hillman even further so that it could take part in circuit races. His first race was at Brooklands late in 1921, where he won one handicap race and came second in another.

The post-war slump in his father's wool business forced Mays to take a job with another wool firm, but in 1922 he part-exchanged the Hillman against a Bugatti Brescia, paying the balance in instalments. Together with Amherst Villiers, he modified the Bugatti engine until it was the fastest Brescia around, giving Mays victories in countless hill-climbs. The success came to the notice of Ettore Bugatti who rebuilt the car at the end of the 1923 season free of charge and also gave Mays another Brescia – entirely free. For 1924, these two cars were named *Cordon Bleu* and *Cordon Rouge* after the champagnes of those names, and Mays had another successful season.

In 1925, Mays was offered a works assisted AC by S.F. Edge. Unfortunately, the car gave considerable trouble and Mays had to use most of a £1000 win on a Victory Bond to pay off the debt on the car. He worked in his father's wool business during 1926, but in 1927 was asked to drive for Mercedes-Benz of Great Britain, taking the 2-litre Targa Florio model to several victories. In 1928, Mays used a highly modified 1922 TT Vauxhall, which was tuned by Amherst Villiers to give nearly 300 bhp. This car and an Invicta were kept for several years, bringing him many wins in British events. Both Villiers and his other long-standing friend, Peter Berthon, helped with the development of these cars.

Then, in 1933, Mays turned to a Riley. He felt that a suitably modified 1½-litre Riley-engined car would be very competitive. Fitted into a racing Riley chassis, the 1½-litre engine, with a Murray Jamieson supercharger and tuning by Peter Berthon, proved to be extremely fast, so much so that Humphrey Cook suggested the car would form the basis for a fine single-seater racing car in the *voiturette* class. Mays agreed and, with financial backing from Cook, English Racing Automobiles was formed, with premises at Bourne. After a disappointing first outing, the new ERAs began to win race after race, with Mays himself winning all over Europe as well as at Brooklands and Donington. He also won the Shelsley Walsh hill-climb with special ERAs every year from 1934 to 1948 with the exception of 1937. Perhaps his best known victory was his win in the 1935 Eifelrennen at the Nürburgring, against top Continental opposition.

In 1939, Mays left ERA, taking with him his Zoller-blown car, known as R4D, together with 1½ and 2-litre engines. With this car, Mays won at all of Britain's major circuits, putting up lap records, and new best times at hill-climbs. The success of the ERA in *voiturette* racing (the equivalent of today's Formula Two) fired Mays with a passion to develop a world-beating Grand Prix car, so he and Peter Berthon formed Automobile Developments Ltd, to try and achieve this ambition, but the intervention of the war put the project on ice for six years. However, Berthon began design work on the V16 1½-litre engine during the war and, as soon as the war finished, Mays began canvassing British industry for financial and material assistance. This was forthcoming and Mays eventually formed British Racing Motors to build and race the car. At the same time, he was still heavily involved in the family wool business as well as running a garage business in Bourne where he sold Bentley, Rover and Ford cars. He also raced his old ERA R4D mostly in hill-climbs, where he was still very successful, but the demands of the BRM project soon forced him to bring his own career to a close.

The BRM story was one of almost continual failure and humiliation over many years but, when Sir Alfred Owen took control, the team gradually improved until Graham Hill won the World Championship in 1962. Raymond's involvement in the day-to-day running of the BRM team gradually lessened, but he was still retained by the Owen organisation in an advisory capacity and even in his late seventies was still attending the occasional race meeting. Mays died in January 1980.　　MT

BRUCE McLAREN (1937-1970)
New Zealand

For many years McLaren cars have been one of the most respected and least glamour-ridden makes in top-class motor racing. The man whose name the cars bear, Bruce McLaren, was a driver with a similar reputation; his youthful brilliance was maintained throughout the 1960s in a notably unflurried style, and he was very seldom guilty of an error in driving or in tactics. His cars, his driving and his manners were all of the same no-nonsense style – quiet, polished, fired by enthusiasm and tempered by seriousness to emerge utterly convincing and effective.

Bruce McLaren was born on 30 August 1937, in Auckland, New Zealand, the son of a garage owner who was devoted to motor sport and who with his brothers was active and successful in motor-cycle races and hill-climbs. As a child Bruce had ambitions to pursue a two-wheel career, but these were dashed when at the age of 9 he contracted a hip malady known as Perthes disease. It was two years before he walked again, and it left him with a legacy of a permanent limp and the hyperdeveloped shoulders and arm muscles of one whose mobility has depended on wheel-chairs and crutches. His hankering for a livelier kind of mobility eventually led him into motor sport with the aid of an Austin 7, provided for his sixteenth birthday by his father. While he studied engineering Bruce went from strength to strength in New Zealand's motor sporting events, culminating in a very successful season in 1957 in a 1500 cc Cooper-Climax sports car and a 1750 cc single-seater of the same make. At that time the organisers of the New Zealand Grand Prix had come up with the bright idea of lending financial encouragement to the most promising young driver in their country, offering him the chance to go to Europe to pursue his career further. The first New Zealand Driver to Europe Scholarship was won by McLaren, and he came to England to buy a Formula Two Cooper to race in 1958. His first event was at Silverstone in a borrowed car, where he finished ninth; soon after, he made a tremendous impression on all concerned, not least the Coopers themselves, by finishing fifth overall in the German Grand Prix at the Nürburgring while driving a Formula Two Cooper, the winner of the class for the smaller cars (which was added to the tail of the Formula One list in order to enlarge the field). This was the first of several impressive drives that led the Coopers to offer McLaren a place in the works Formula One team as second string (alongside the American Masten Gregory) to the Australian Jack Brabham.

This was a mixed blessing. McLaren always turned in a good performance, but it was No 1 driver Brabham who did all the winning, to become World Champion in 1959, and the press and public were so concerned with the novelty of rear-engined cars in Grand Prix racing, and with the challenge presented by Brabham to the popular idol Stirling Moss, that very little attention was paid to the young New Zealander who was assumed to be simply a good back-up driver – even when, just after his 22nd birthday, he won the US Grand Prix at Sebring and became the youngest man ever to win a race of that status. In 1960 he won another Grand Prix, that of the Argentine, but usually he finished second to Brabham in the Cooper team, and second or third in the overall results, which actually left him as runner-up in the drivers' championship at the end of the year, only his second of big-time Formula One motor racing.

With two World Championships and plenty of experience of the Cooper mentality behind him, Brabham then left the team to plough his own furrow, doubtless realising that the Coopers were incapable of pursuing the early advantage they had taken with their pioneering rear-engined cars. As time passed by, McLaren

began to realise it too, but his loyalty to the Coopers who had given him his start would not allow him to leave them, and he led their team until the end of 1965. The fact that he won the Grands Prix of France and of Monaco in 1962, and ended the year third in the championship placings, reflects more credit on his persistence and reliability at the wheel than on the effectiveness of the Cooper, which grew sadly more ineffectual as the years went by and other designers made progress while the Coopers did not. McLaren was very frustrated during these years, because he was allowed no say in the design and engineering of the cars that he was required to drive. Only when he became involved in a privately entered team of Coopers for the low season of races in Australia and New Zealand could he compound his driving talent with his engineering ability, and in these events he was notably successful.

Thus emboldened, he formed his own team to campaign in the Tasman series of 1964/5, with a brace of specially designed and lightweight Coopers to be driven by himself and a young American called Tim Mayer, the nephew of a former Governor of Pennsylvania and a recent addition to the Tyrrell Formula Junior team. The firm of Bruce McLaren Motor Racing Limited was incorporated to undertake the enterprise, Bruce financing the construction of his own car while the cost of the other was borne by Tim and his brother Teddy. Alas, Tim Mayer met his death in an accident at Longford in Australia; but despite the tragic loss of this polished young driver the team was successful, Bruce becoming the first New Zealander to win the New Zealand Grand Prix, and going on to win the first Tasman championship. It was a gratifying way of justifying the faith that had been reposed in him those few years earlier, but McLaren wanted to go ahead and do more, being now convinced that the proper course would be to create a team to build and race his own cars.

He made a start by buying a sports car (based on a 2.7-litre Cooper-Climax) in which Roger Penske had scored some notable successes in the USA. The transaction was carried through by Teddy Mayer, who was entrusted with the business management of the young McLaren company, which had established a workshop conveniently near London's Heathrow Airport. The car's engine was soon replaced by an aluminium-blocked V8 Oldsmobile, the chassis was suitably stiffened, and McLaren embarked on a successful season with what for political reasons he called a 'Cooper-Oldsmobile', during that stimulating period when in England and the USA a new class of racing for high-powered two-seaters was being developed, leading to the eventual birth of the Can-Am series of sports-car races.

The blossoming of American motor sport at this time led to a further important American connection for McLaren. In 1965 Firestone were preparing to widen their motor racing horizons and enter the European fray in sports-car and formula racing and McLaren was given an important contract to help them develop the tyres that were being designed for this purpose. McLaren built a V8-engined racing car chassis specifically for tyre testing, and supplemented his own considerable talents as a development and test driver/engineer with those of his young compatriot Chris Amon. A great deal of valuable work was done during the summer of 1965 and the ensuing winter, and it brought McLaren to the notice of Ford, who engaged him to assist in the development of their GT 40 sports-racing coupé and its derivatives Mk2 and Mk4. All this was extremely profitable for McLaren, in more ways than one: it vastly amplified his experience and technical knowledge, it brought him due and merited fame as the winner (with Amon) of the 1966 Le Mans 24-hour race in a Mk2 Ford and it provided a very considerable fillip to his finances, enabling him to embark on the production of his own racing car.

To assist him in the design of this first Formula One McLaren, Bruce engaged Robin Herd. This car, which was ready for the first classic Grand Prix of 1966 at Monaco, was technically the most interesting machine there, being unique among Formula One cars both in engine and chassis; but though the latter was a brilliant piece of aviation-inspired Herd work, it did no more than make the unconvincing best of the former, which was a bad job indeed. The substitution in mid-season of the V8 Serenissima engine proved equally fruitless, this being just as feeble as the modified Ford engine it replaced.

The inauguration of the Can-Am series of sports car races, supported during 1966 by a number of events for broadly similar cars in Britain, saw little more success for the two-seater McLaren, which fared less well than its ancestor. In 1967 things changed considerably, and although in Formula One the new slimmer and more conventional McLaren cars still suffered the want of a competitive engine, making

do with BRM V8 and V12 engines that earned them no distinction, Herd's new M6 sports car was right from its very first test runs. The two McLarens in their new orange livery won five of the six Can-Am races that year. Bruce McLaren earned the championship, and his new co-driver (fellow New Zealander Denis Hulme) was runner-up. The M6 was then put into production by the Trojan firm, who had been building Elva sports cars, and was sold to customers as the McLaren Elva at £6000 a time, a run of twenty being built for private entrants both in Europe and in the United States.

This profitable business was maintained during the ensuing years when the continued success of McLarens in the Can-Am championship made them the cars that all serious contestants wanted to buy. The continuation of that success was ensured by McLaren keeping his works cars one jump ahead of the customers' as well as of the rest of the opposition. The opposition facing the McLaren M8s in the 1968 season was very strong, several other teams having the same lightweight Chevrolet engine. Nevertheless, McLaren and Hulme completely dominated the series as the McLaren team was to continue to do until the end of the 1971 season. In those four years the McLaren team won 32 of the 37 Can-Am races which were run.

During these gilded years of sports car racing (Can-Am victories were very lucrative) Teddy Mayer concentrated his efforts more and more on the transatlantic campaign. To look after the other racing categories, which included not only Formula One but also Indianapolis and USAC single-seater racing, not to mention Formula Two in which a few cars were built spasmodically but never achieved much, McLaren added to their staff another New Zealander, Phil Kerr – erstwhile rival of Bruce in his Austin 7 days.

The arrival of Kerr coincided with – or was possibly the explanation for – a new competitiveness on the part of the Formula One team, which he strengthened by the addition of Hulme, and which was now able to rely on the Cosworth Ford V8 engine. The want of real success in the F1 Grands Prix might still be attributed to the priority enjoyed by the Can-Am cars; and in the course of development trials on a new one, the M8D, Bruce McLaren was killed at Goodwood when the rear bodywork became detached and the car crashed at high speed. It was June 1970; he was not yet 33.

Mayer and Kerr carried on the activities of

the company while Bruce's widow assumed control of the board, and over the years, in spite of changes, the McLaren name has remained at the forefront in Grand Prix racing.   LJKS

OTTO MERZ (1889-1933)
Germany
Even in an era of heroic larger-than-life racing drivers, Otto Merz stood out from his contemporaries. Not simply because he was physically a giant, but also because of his phenomenal strength – he was reputed to be able to drive six-inch nails into a plank of wood with his fists, and when, during the 1929 Ulster Tourist Trophy, a damaged front wing impeded his Mercedes, he ripped it off with his bare hands.

But Merz, who was born in 1889 at Cannstatt, had another claim to fame. Following a period as a mechanic with Mercédès (whose factory was, after all, in his home town) in which he rode with Willy Poege, 'the gentleman driver', Merz became a chauffeur in the service of the Archduke Franz Ferdinand of Austria. He was driving the car which was following the Gräf und Stift carrying Franz Ferdinand and his morganatic wife Sophie Chotek when they were shot by the assassin Gavrilo Princip at Sarajevo. And it was Merz who carried the dying Archduke into a nearby house; after which, having lost his employer, he returned to Mercédès.

After the war, he joined the Mercédès racing department, and began to score successes in local events. Merz first came to the attention of the international motor-racing public in 1924, when he secured first place at both the Solitude and Klausen hill-climbs. In 1925, he won the race on the narrow, winding, Solitude Ring, a tortuous circuit of closed public roads which circled the Schloss Solitude near Stuttgart at the wheel of a 2-litre, four-cylinder Mercedes; not content with this feat, he repeated it the following year, averaging a hair-raising 57.29 mph in his new, Porsche-designed, Mercedes 2-litre straight-eight, a car which was hardly renowned for good handling (the model had already caused Count Louis Zborowski's death at Monza).

Then, in 1927, the new Nürburgring circuit in the Eifel mountains was officially opened; the first German Grand Prix was held that July over a distance of 316 miles, resulting in a victory for Merz's Mercedes.

But the following year the German GP acquired full international status. If 1927 had

seen the Mercedes pitted against a motley selection of stripped touring cars (including a brace of Hanomags with 499 cc single-cylinder engines), 1928 saw them ranged against a formidable array of foreign vehicles, including 2.3-litre Type 35B Bugattis, and top drivers like Chiron, Varzi and Nuvolari. On top of this, the weather was swelteringly hot, and the drivers were rapidly overcome by heat exhaustion. Mercedes driver Christian Werner collapsed, and his car was taken over by Walb, who had crashed at Wehrseifen; then Caracciola flaked out and Werner, recovered, took over *his* Mercedes, which eventually won. As Walb had taken third place, Werner had the confusing distinction of featuring as joint winner and joint third place.

But the savage heat had not beaten Otto Merz, who drove the entire distance single-handed, to come in second, the steering wheel of his Mercedes sticky with blood from his hands, chafed raw by his gruelling drive.

The 1929 Ulster TT saw the Mercedes of Merz/Caracciola finish 13th and this partnership also contested the 1931 French Grand Prix, in which year Merz took fifth place in the German GP at the Nürburgring.

Merz had an enforced break from racing in 1932, for that year Mercedes-Benz decided to forsake motorsport because of Germany's financial crisis (though it was only a temporary abandonment); but the driver Manfred von Brauchitsch made a gallant freelance effort in winning the Avusrennen in an antiquated SSK Mercedes endowed with a streamlined cigar-shaped body developed in the Zeppelin wind-tunnel by the aerodynamicist von Koenig-Fachsenfeld. The car was thus endowed with a greater speed potential than either the Alfas or the Bugattis, lapped at 125 mph in practice (beating Caracciola's existing record for the circuit), and won the race at over 120 mph.

A repeat performance was planned for 1933, with Merz as driver, but a few days before the race, practising on the track in heavy rain, Otto Merz overturned the big car and was killed instantly.   DBW

LOUIS MEYER (b.1904)
USA
In the long history of the Indianapolis Motor Speedway, only four men have ever won the celebrated 500-mile race three times – Louis Meyer, Wilbur Shaw, Mauri Rose and A.J. Foyt. The first man to achieve the coveted

treble was Louis Meyer, born in 1904.

Meyer was a comparatively unknown mechanic from California who helped racing driver Frank Elliott prepare a straight-eight Miller for the 1926 Indy 500 by reducing the stroke to bring the swept volume within the 91½ cu in limit for the race. The Miller was, indeed, a car of ill-omen, for it was the 'death car' in which Jimmy Murphy had crashed fatally at a meeting at Syracuse, NY, in 1924, and when it was resold to Fred 'Fritz' Holliday of the Holliday Steel Company in 1927, its new owner renamed the racer 'Jynx Special'. Meyer, who had hoped to drive the car in the 1927 '500', went with the deal, acting as mechanic for the Miller's new driver, Wilbur Shaw.

During the race, Meyer drove 40 laps while Shaw rested, and managed to take the car from seventh to sixth place.

The following year, Meyer got his first big break. Wilbur Shaw was negotiating to drive a new Miller Special in the Indy for Phil Shafer, who was promoting a new type of automatic fuel pump. However, when tests proved that the pump was less efficient than the conventional handpump, Shafer put the car on the market. Shaw could not afford to buy it, but Meyer persuaded Alden Sampson to buy him the car, fitted it with a hand fuel pump, started 13th in the race, took the lead in the 181st lap and won by 45 seconds at an average speed of 99.5 mph.

That same season Meyer also took first place in a 200-mile race on the Altoona 1¼-mile board speedway at 117.02 mph in his Stutz-Miller, and was placed in sufficient events throughout the season to ensure him the American championship, which he also won in 1929 and 1933.

Meyer was beaten into second place at Indianapolis in 1929 by Ray Keech, who drove the Simplex Piston Ring Special Miller – in which Keech was killed a fortnight later while leading the 200-mile event at Altoona. Meyer won the season's second Altoona 200-miler at 110 mph.

The 1931 Indianapolis 500 saw Meyer up against strong opposition; he could manage no better than fourth place in the event, which was dominated almost from the start by Billy Arnold. Racing was sharply cut back during the Depression, and Meyer was forced to move into dirt-track racing.

After a couple of years in the doldrums, the US racing scene recovered, and in 1933 Meyer was entered for the Indianapolis at the wheel of a Tydol Special Miller. Thanks to good pit work, he was able to take the lead on the 129th lap, and from then on he was unassailable, drawing a little further away from the rest of the pack each lap. With two laps to go, he was confident enough to be able to slow down and pull alongside Shaw's car, four laps behind to shout: 'Are you going to make it?' through cupped hands. And to wait for Shaw's reply!

Despite this voluntary slackening of the pace, Meyer's time for the event was a record, for he won at an average of 104.16 mph, a victory which was to ensure his place in the exclusive 'Hundred-Mile-an-Hour Club' a couple of years later (the club was for those drivers who had averaged over 100 mph in the Indy 500).

He was also one of the top ten drivers who, in 1935, formed Champion Drivers Inc, a promotional group intended to boost racing at the tail-end of the Depression, but which proved an expensive mistake as adverse weather conditions caused repeated cancellations of races.

Meyer had another successful season in 1936, however, which started with a second place in the 200-mile event on the tricky Ascot track in California and culminated in his victory in the Indy 500 with his Ring Free Special Miller at an average of 109.1 mph. He then went on to win on the board track at Altoona.

Meyer was all set to take his fourth Indianapolis victory in 1939 when, battling for the lead with Wilbur Shaw just four laps from the end, he overcooked things on the North Bend and spun off. He was unhurt, but it was his last race. His Bowes Seal Fast Special went to Rex Mays the following season, while Meyer decided to revert to his original status as a mechanic – but on a more ambitious scale than before.

In 1946 he and Dale Drake bought the Offenhauser engine plant, which was the successor to Harry Miller's company – and for the next 18 years the Meyer-Drake Engineering Company provided the power for every Indianapolis winner, until Jim Clark and his Lotus-Ford created motoring history by winning the 500.

By that time Meyer himself was part of the Ford racing organisation, having accepted a 1964 offer to take over the assembly and help with the development of the Ford racing V8, which powered four Indy winners during the five years that Meyer worked there.   DBW

TOMMY MILTON (1893-1962)
USA

Tommy Milton was, along with drivers like Ralph de Palma, Barney Oldfield and Peter de Paolo, one of the outstanding drivers in the early days of American track racing. Born in 1893, Thomas W. Milton had no sight in his left eye, but this handicap did not deter him from an early ambition to become a racing driver, because he simply memorised the standardised eyesight test cards of the day! He had earlier shown promise as an automobile engineer and worked as a builder and tuner of racing cars. At the age of 17, he joined a barnstorming exhibition team driving a Mercer, but the ambitious Milton soon tired of the fixed results of the races in which he took part and was eventually sacked for disobeying team orders. He then joined the Duesenberg team which was enjoying considerable success at that time in the hands of drivers like Eddie Rickenbacker, Jimmy Murphy and Wilbur D'Alene. He was to have driven in the 1916 Indianapolis 500-mile race, but his car was not ready in time. However, he soon began to show that he was a driver of some skill by picking up many good placings on the board tracks, which were becoming popular in the USA at that time. Although he did not manage to win a race, he was placed 7th in the American championship in 1916.

America's intervention in World War I kept him out of action until 1919 but he was made captain of the Duesenberg team for that season. He soon scored his first major victory by winning the 300-mile road race at Elgin, Illinois, at 73.9 mph; he had previously retired from the Indianapolis race after only 50 laps. Soon after his Elgin victory, he was badly burned in a crash on a board track which put him out of racing until early 1920, but during his convalescence, he designed and helped to build a twin-Duesenberg engined car using a pair of the 5-litre, single-overhead-camshaft, straight-eight engines which were redundant because the Indianapolis rules were changed for 1920, reducing the limit to 3 litres. The engines were simply mounted side-by-side and drove by separate propeller shafts to a rigid rear axle fitted with two differentials. The 'Double Duesy' was tested at 151 mph by Milton's team-mate Jimmy Murphy, and then Milton took it out on Daytona Beach and clocked up 156.03 mph over the measured mile. Milton claimed that this was the average of a two-way run, making it eligible for the land speed record, which stood at that time to Horsted's Benz at a very modest 124.10 mph. Unfortunately, the governing body of motor racing in Europe, the AIACR, refused to recognise the run as it had not been carried out under their jurisdiction, but it was certainly recognised in the USA. Milton's speed was not officially bettered in Europe until six years later.

The rest of Milton's 1920 season was very successful, for he won three major long-distance races, finished third at Indianapolis and won the American national championship.

For 1921, Tommy switched to a Frontenac for Indianapolis, although he also attempted to qualify a Durant-Duesenberg without success. The Frontenac went perfectly to give Milton his first Indianapolis victory at 89.62 mph. Although his other successes were not so frequent as in 1920, he picked up enough good places to win his second American national championship.

In 1922, Milton's Leach Special only lasted 44 laps at Indianapolis, but he picked up several victories and many places at the board tracks. He switched to Millers and Miller-powered cars after that and, in 1923, he won his second Indianapolis 500 in his HCS Miller Special at an average speed of 90.95 mph, to become the first man to win two Indianapolis 500 races.

Milton gradually began to wind down his own participation in races, but he still won a number of races in Miller-powered Specials. His 1924 Indianapolis race lasted 110 laps, but in 1925 he finished fifth. On this note, he decided to retire from driving at the age of 32, but he kept his association with racing by designing and building a front-wheel-drive Miller-powered Special for Cliff Durant to drive in the 1927 Indianapolis race. However, Durant was taken ill and was unable to drive, so Milton took over the car, qualified it and finished eighth in the race, despite severe overheating problems which obliged him to use a relief driver.

Like his former Duesenberg team-mate, Jimmy Murphy, Milton took in one major European race during his career. He drove a Duesenberg in the 1925 Italian Grand Prix at Monza, leading the race at one stage, but eventually dropping back to fourth place after suffering a broken oil pipe.

Milton retired for good after the 1927 Indianapolis race, taking a job with Packard before forming his own company. He also remained active in racing as chief steward at Indianapolis and as a member of the American Automobile Association Contest Board. He died in 1962 at the age of 69.   MT

GUY MOLL (1910-1934)
Algeria

In the early 1930s, motor racing was becoming increasingly popular throughout Europe. Although Italy and France still dominated the majority of major events through Bugatti and Alfa Romeo, a number of young drivers were attracted into motor racing from countries which were not normally strongholds of the sport. Even Britain had seldom provided winners in international races but, with the arrival of the Bentley at Le Mans, British cars and drivers soon gained acceptance. For drivers from less well developed countries, however, it was more difficult to break into racing, because there was seldom any native motor industry and very often no surfaced roads at all to race or even practise on.

For Guy Moll, a young Algerian with a Spanish mother and French father, the way was smoothed to a certain extent by his friendship with Marcel Lehoux, who had already established a reputation in North Africa, where he had won such events as the Casablanca, Algerian and Tunisian Grands Prix. Moll began racing in Algeria with a Lorraine-Dietrich, taking part mostly in small local events. By 1932, his friend Lehoux was an experienced and successful driver in European events, and he invited the young Moll to race his Bugatti in the Marseilles Grand Prix at the featureless Miramas track. This was Moll's first race in Europe and he finished third behind the Alfa Romeos of Raymond Sommer and Tazio Nuvolari, a performance which attracted much attention from other drivers and team managers.

For 1933, Moll began in Europe, by driving a Bugatti in the Pau Grand Prix, which was run in appalling snowstorm conditions. Lehoux won the race, but Moll got through into second place in very unfamiliar conditions. Later in 1933, Moll bought a Monza Alfa Romeo. This was the Grand Prix version of the 8C 2300 sports car, although it was not as fast as the P3 Grand Prix car which some other drivers were able to use, especially those under contract to Scuderia Ferrari. Despite this handicap, Moll finished third in the Nimes GP, behind Nuvolari and 'Phi Phi' Etancelin. He

then followed up with more third places at Nice, Comminges and Miramas, and a second place in the Monza GP.

Moll's skill was recognised by Enzo Ferrari in 1934, and he was asked to join Scuderia Ferrari to drive the 2.9 litre P3 single-seater Alfa Romeo which Ferrari was racing on behalf of the works, who had withdrawn from racing following nationalisation.

Moll immediately began to shine in the P3, even though the more powerful and larger Mercedes and Auto Unions were joining in the Grand Prix circus. His greatest victory was in winning the Monaco Grand Prix, but he also won the Avusrennen on the banked Berlin circuit in a streamlined 3.2-litre version of the P3 which developed 265 bhp. He also finished third in the French GP at Montlhéry behind team-mate Chiron, and was second in the Coppa Ciano behind team-mate Varzi's P3, beating Nuvolari's Maserati into third place.

The young Moll's career had been meteoric, for even when the powerful German cars were eclipsing the Italians he was still able to race on level terms with them.

However, his meteoric career came to a tragic end in 1934 during the Coppa Acerbo. Moll was dicing for the lead in his P3 with Luigi Fagioli's Mercedes when his car suddenly flew off the road at near maximum speed when both were lapping the Mercedes of Henne. Moll was killed immediately, the cause of the crash never being satisfactorily explained. Only two years later his mentor, Marcel Lehoux, was killed in an ERA.

In later years, Enzo Ferrari commented that, had Moll lived, he would have become one of the greatest drivers of all time.   MT

STIRLING MOSS (b.1929)
Great Britain

Over the years, motor racing enthusiasts and journalists have expended many thousands of words over exactly who was, or is, the greatest racing driver ever. Was it Tazio Nuvolari, Rudolf Caracciola, Alberto Ascari, Juan Manuel Fangio, Jim Clark, Jackie Stewart, Jochen Rindt, Mike Hawthorn, Graham Hill or Giuseppe Farina? Or could it have been Stirling Moss?

Stirling Moss admits only one peer among his contemporaries – Fangio – with whom he was teamed for Mercedes-Benz in 1955 and who kept the World Championship away from Moss on several occasions. There are those, however, who will rightly claim that Moss was a better all-rounder than Fangio, who was not happy in sports cars or anything other than Formula One.

Born Stirling Crauford Moss on 17 September 1929, he was the son of Alfred and Aileen Moss who had both taken part in motoring competitions. Indeed, Alfred had driven a Fronty-Ford into 14th place at Indianapolis in 1924, while Aileen Moss had driven in many rallies and trials, winning several of them, too.

Although the Moss family was not in the motor trade – his father was a dentist and a farmer – sporting machinery was much in evidence and the talk was all about motor racing, so Stirling Moss grew up indoctrinated with racing lore. Education was undertaken unwillingly, largely at Haileybury public school and the youthful Moss was destined, it seemed, for the catering trade. However, when he let it be known that he fancied a spot of motor racing, the family immediately offered help in the shape of a Cooper-JAP, then the car for any up-and-coming driver who had his eyes set on the big time. His debut was made at a hillclimb in Stanmer Park, Brighton, and in that first season in 1948, at the tender age of 18, he showed that indefinable natural ability by picking up ten class wins.

The die was cast and in 1949 he took on a 1000 cc Cooper-JAP as well as the 500 cc car, gaining his first victory abroad when he won an F3 race at Zandvoort in Holland. Hillclimbing was soon forgotten, as he knew that only in pure motor racing would he rise to the top. His talent was soon recognised by others and in 1950 he was asked by John Heath to drive the 2-litre HWM Formula Two car, beginning a long and mutually rewarding liaison with Polish-born mechanic Alf Francis who was then chief mechanic for HWM. The HWM was not very reliable, but he gained a lot of experience and picked up several wins when the car lasted the race distance. He also drove a works Jaguar XK120 in production-sports-car events, taking his first major victory when he won the Tourist Trophy at Dundrod. The British Racing Drivers' Club awarded him a Gold Star for his performances during 1950.

For 1951, he stayed with HWM in Formula Two and with Jaguar in sports cars, picking up three good wins in the HWM, as well as winning the TT again in a C-type Jaguar. He also won the British Empire Trophy on the Isle of Man – then an important event – driving a Le Mans Frazer-Nash. He stayed faithful to Formula Three as well during 1951, mostly using a Kieft.

In 1952, the restless Moss, who could barely sit still long enough to consume a meal, also took up rallying. He was asked to drive for the Rootes team in a Sunbeam Talbot 90 and in his first event, the Monte Carlo Rally, he finished a close second to the winner, Sydney Allard. Later on in the season, he won a coveted Coupe des Alpes in the Alpine Rally, a feat he repeated in 1953 and 1954 to win one of the only two gold Coupes ever presented for three unpenalised runs.

Moss was intensely patriotic and wanted to drive only British cars, but in the early 1950s there were few British Grand Prix cars with any chance of success. However, Moss turned down an offer from Ferrari in 1953 in order to build his own Cooper-Alta, with Alf Francis as mechanic. This car was not very successful and Moss had another Cooper-Alta built which was a much better car. At the 1953 Italian Grand Prix, he had the car fitted with fuel injection and powered by nitromethane fuel which enabled him to get the green car in amongst the Italian Ferraris and Maseratis which were dominating Formula One racing at that time. In 1953, Moss had his first serious mishaps in racing cars, first when he overturned a C-type Jaguar at Silverstone without serious injury and then when he overturned his Cooper-JAP at Castle Combe.

Moss was now a fully professional driver, even to the extent of employing a manager, Ken Gregory, who negotiated contracts for Moss. Gregory heard that Mercedes were planning to re-enter Grand Prix racing in 1954 and went to the factory to ask if they would sign on Moss. Team manager Neubauer commented that Moss was indeed a promising driver but that he should buy a fully competitive car for the 1954 season to show just how good he was. Moss agreed and his family rallied round to help buy a 250F Maserati. Although he was unable to use the full performance because his budget restricted the number of engine rebuilds that could be undertaken, the green Maserati put up a number of good performances in F1 races, winning the Aintree 200, Oulton Park Gold Cup, the Goodwood Trophy and the Daily Telegraph Trophy at Aintree.

Moss's performances in 1954 were good enough to persuade Mercedes that he should join them and for 1955 he drove the Mercedes W196 as number two to Fangio as well as handling the big 300SLR sports/racing car. Although he had to take second place to Fangio, Moss was allowed to win the British GP at Aintree and he also finished second in the Belgian and Dutch GPs to take second place in the World Drivers' Championship. He also gained three memorable victories in the 300SLR at the Mille Miglia, the Targa Florio and the Tourist Trophy, as well as winning the Oulton Park Gold Cup in his Maserati 250F. In the sports Mercedes, he proved beyond doubt that he was a faster driver than Fangio, who was content to finish second to him in all three races.

The Mercedes team withdrew from racing at the end of 1955 and, although several British teams vied for his services, Moss decided that they were not yet competitive in Grand Prix racing and signed for the Maserati team in both F1 and sports-car events. It was an outstandingly successful season, for he won more than twenty major events during the season. In Formula One racing, he won the Monaco GP and the European GP at Monza, finished second in the German GP, third in the Belgian GP and fifth in the French GP. He again wound up in second place in the World Championship, only three points behind Fangio. He also won the Australian and New Zealand GPs, the Aintree 200 and the Richmond Trophy at Goodwood. In sports cars, he drove the 300S Maserati to victory in the Argentinian 1000 kilometres and the Nürburgring 1000 kilometres, as well as the non-championship Venezuelan GP, Bari GP, Nassau Trophy, the Australian TT and the BRDC Trophy at Silverstone. He also drove Aston Martin DB3S, Porsche Spyder, Cooper-Climax and Vanwall cars to victory, the latter being the F1 Vanwall with which he won the International Trophy at Silverstone.

Moss decided in 1957 that at last Britain had a worthy challenger for the World Championship and he signed to drive for the Vanwall team. The car proved to be very fast but rather temperamental and, although Moss won the Italian GP, the Pescara GP and the European GP at Aintree, he was again relegated to second place in the championship behind Fangio. In sports-car racing, Moss won the Swedish GP in a 4½-litre Maserati and was second at Sebring in a 3-litre Maserati. For the rest of the season, his big V8 Maserati proved fast but fragile.

Moss remained with Vanwall in 1958 and the car won no less than six of the ten championship races. Unfortunately, Moss only drove it to three of these wins – at the Moroccan, Portuguese and Dutch GPs, backing up with a win in a 2-litre Cooper-Climax in the Argentine GP and second place in the French GP. In sports-car racing, he drove in the World Championship for Aston Martin, winning both the Nürburgring 1000 kilometres and the TT at Goodwood. Moss also won a mixed bag of other races in Cooper, Maserati, Ferrari, Lister-Jaguar and Aston Martin sports cars.

A long term contract with a fuel company meant that Moss had difficulty in reaching agreement with works teams who raced on other products so, for the remainder of his career, he drove mostly privately owned cars. In 1959, he drove Rob Walker's Formula One Cooper-Climax in F1 races, retiring on many occasions but, towards the end of the season, he won the Portuguese and Italian GPs. Earlier, he had driven a BRM into second place in the British GP at Aintree. Moss again drove for Aston Martin in sports-car races, taking a memorable victory in the Nürburgring 1000 kilometre race together with yet another TT victory. These wins helped Aston Martin to take the World Championship. Moss also drove a Cooper-Borgward in F2 races and a Cooper-Monaco at non-championship events.

Moss again drove a Cooper-Climax at the start of the 1960 season, taking third place in the Argentine GP, but Rob Walker purchased a Lotus 18 for Moss to drive which he immediately drove to victory at the Monaco GP, followed by fourth place at the Dutch GP. However, in practice for the Belgian GP, the Lotus broke a rear hub carrier and Moss was thrown out of the car, receiving hairline cracks in both legs as well as breaking his nose and damaging his back. Despite these injuries, he was back on the track within seven weeks, winning a sports-car race in Sweden with a new Lotus 19. Later in the season, he won the United States GP with a Lotus 18 to finish third in the championship. In sports-car racing, Moss drove the 2.9-litre Maserati type 61 to victory at the Nürburgring 1000 kilometres. He also picked up a number of other victories, including the Oulton Park Gold Cup with the Lotus 18 and the TT once again with a Ferrari 250 GT.

Formula One changed from 2½ litres to 1½ litres for 1961, leaving the British teams entirely unprepared, while Ferrari built brand new

V6 cars which were far more powerful than the ageing Coventry Climax engine. It was during this season that Moss showed his ability at its best for he did not even have the latest model Lotus all season, yet on circuits where pure straight-line speed was not of paramount importance, Moss was more than a match for the Ferrari drivers. He put in a memorable drive at the Monaco GP, holding off all the Ferrari drivers to take a narrow victory. He followed this with a fourth place at the Dutch Grand Prix then he won another victory at the Nürburgring.

Stirling notched up a whole string of other victories in the Lotus 18 and 19, as well as with a 2½-litre Cooper. He also won the TT yet again with a Ferrari 250GT and gave the new four-wheel-drive Ferguson-Climax its first victory at the Oulton Park Gold Cup.

The 1962 season started as successfully as ever with three victories in the Tasman series of races in Australia and New Zealand and then he went to the USA where he took a class victory in the Daytona 3 hours, driving a 250GT Ferrari.

He returned to England to drive a Lotus Climax V8 in the F1 Goodwood Easter Monday meeting but, after making two pit stops which left him well down the field, his car suddenly veered off the track after Fordwater bend and crashed heavily into an earth bank. He was trapped in the car for a long while and suffered severe head injuries which necessitated several operations. His matchless sense of timing and first-class vision had been affected and, although he recovered fully, he felt that he was unable to match his previous high standards and decided to retire from the sport.

After his retirement, Moss concentrated on various business ventures, as well as acting as technical and public-relations adviser to various companies. Having contested a number of historic single seater races, Moss demonstrated that even at the age of fifty he was still a competitive driver, returning in 1980 for a full season in both historics and the British Saloon Car championship, with a works Audi. He proved his point, that he was still a race winner, and, more importantly perhaps, he enjoyed his reborn career.

Perhaps the most lasting memorial to his achievements is the immortal phrase uttered by police-car drivers as they pull up a driver for exceeding the speed limit: 'Who do you think you are – Stirling Moss?'   MT

JIMMY MURPHY (1894-1924)
USA

Jimmy Murphy was a hero in American motor racing during the early 1920s – the 'Golden Age' of the sport in the United States. He was twice US champion, he won the most famous race of all, the Indianapolis 500 miles, and he became the first American driver to win a European Grand Prix. Murphy's race-driving career spanned but five seasons before he was fatally injured in a crash, yet this was enough for him to become a legend. A dance was named after him, the Jimmy Murphy Fox Trot.

James Anthony Murphy, of Irish parentage, was born in San Francisco in 1894. His mother died when he was a baby and at the age of 10 he was orphaned when his father was killed in the San Francisco earthquake. He was raised by relations, Judge Martin O'Donnell and his wife, and was timid by nature. O'Donnell gave Murphy a motor cycle to ride to school and quickly he learned how it worked and became interested in mechanics. Murphy left school early to start a small garage business in Los Angeles.

Murphy's small size – he was 5ft 7in and weighed 10½ stone – played an important part in his introduction to motor sport. At the age of 21, in 1916, he was offered the place of riding mechanic with Omar Toft in the Corona races. However, on race morning Toft's car was disqualified and Murphy's dream-come-true .hopes seemed vanished for ever. Fortunately, Eddie O'Donnell, veteran driver of the crack Duesenberg team, offered Murphy a ride as his own riding mechanic was ill. And they won.

This led to a permanent seat alongside O'Donnell or Duesenberg team members Tommy Milton and Eddie Rickenbacker. At the end of 1919 Murphy was offered what he considered beyond expectations, a chance to *drive* a Duesenberg at Uniontown. However, he crashed, injuring his riding mechanic, and Fred Duesenberg decided Murphy would never drive again. However, Fred and his brother August Duesenberg were blackmailed into giving Murphy another chance by their top driver, Tommy Milton. Murphy had gone to visit Milton in hospital (following a fiery accident in that same race) and, feeling utterly depressed, told him he was going back into the garage business. Milton urged Murphy to postpone his decision and dictated to the

Duesenbergs that Murphy should be given another chance, or Milton would quit them.

First race in the 1920 season was at Beverly Speedway and with O'Donnell absent with an arm injury Murphy took his place. He took pole position, led off the line and was never headed throughout the 250 miles. Luck was certainly on his side, for seconds after crossing the line the Duesenberg ran out of petrol. After another win at Fresno it was discovered his car's back axle was hanging by the single thread of the last nut – all the other team cars had failed. At the end of the year, however, Murphy's friendship with Milton turned very sour. Milton had helped design and build a new land-speed-record Duesenberg and was due to run it at Daytona following a race in Havana, Cuba. Meanwhile Fred Duesenberg sent Murphy off to Daytona to 'test' the new machine...and the 'test' developed into a new record of 152 mph. To say Milton was furious was an understatement.

Jimmy Murphy was selected to drive a 3-litre Duesenberg in the 1921 French Grand Prix (Grand Prix de l'ACF) at Le Mans. The car was fitted with hydraulic four-wheel brakes, yet they were not perfect in practice a week prior to the race when a wheel locked and Murphy crashed. Jimmy was thrown out, cracked several ribs and was admitted to hospital. The car was quickly repaired and the brake problem solved, but could Murphy compete? He was determined he would and arranged to be tightly bandaged from his hips to his armpits, to be driven to the circuit and lifted into the car. Driving in agony for over four hours, and with the added problem of stones being hurled from the wheels of the cars ahead (one of which pierced the Duesenberg's radiator with two of the 30 laps to complete), not to mention a puncture which meant driving most of the last lap on the wheel rim, Murphy won. He became the first American to win a European Grand Prix, a record no one was to equal until Phil Hill, a fellow Californian, won the Italian Grand Prix in 1960.

For 1922 Murphy contested the Indianapolis 500-mile race with a Le Mans-type Duesenberg equipped with a Miller engine. He won at a record average speed of 94.48 mph and with added victories in long-distance board-track races at Beverly, Uniontown and Tacoma he also gained the American Automobile Association's national driving championship. The following season saw Murphy head the newly-formed Durant team and he won at Beverly

and Fresno, also taking third place at Indianapolis.

Murphy's second championship year was in 1924 when he won two major board-track races at Altoona, another at Kansas City plus a dirt-track event at Readville. The second-to-last event of the season was a dirt-track race at Syracuse. Murphy did not like dirt races, preferring hard surfaces which suited his very smooth driving style. But he had been wrongly led to believe his title might be in jeopardy and entered the race.

Near the end, when about to pounce for the lead, Murphy's car slid wildly on oil and headed towards the inside fence. Others had walked away from similar accidents in the past, but Murphy died. A piece of splintered fencing pierced his heart and, at the age of 30, Murphy's brilliant career was over. Ironically, none other than Tommy Milton took Murphy's body back to Los Angeles and made the funeral arrangements.   MK

LUIGI MUSSO (1924-1958)
Italy

Luigi Musso was, temporarily, the last of a line of famous Italian Grand Prix drivers. The death of former World Champion Alberto Ascari in 1955 left two young Italians, Castellotti and Musso, to fight for the honour of being their country's champion driver at a time when Grand Prix racing was utterly dominated by the two Italian teams, Ferrari and Maserati. Then Castellotti was killed before the 1957 season, leaving Musso as Italy's only world-class driver. The deeply religious man, who in his youth excelled at shooting, fencing and horseriding, knew he had the honour of Italy at stake, but it was a terrible burden to bear. On 6 July 1958, he crashed fatally in the French Grand Prix at Reims. He had been following his Ferrari team-mate Mike Hawthorn round the difficult corner after the pits at a speed in excess of 130 mph, when he lost control and crashed.

Musso was born in Rome on 27 July 1924, the youngest of three brothers. His was a wealthy family, his father having served as a diplomat in China, and a sporting one. Speed interested young Luigi as a child, and by the age of 10 his passion was cars. His elder brothers Lucietta and Giuseppe had sports cars, but they refused to allow Luigi to drive them so he bought his own, a very second-hand 750 cc Giannini. He entered it for the

1950 Tour of Sicily, but during a lapse of concentration lost control and crashed into a monument of Garibaldi. This damaged the gearbox and the only way the car could tackle steep hills was to ascend in reverse.

Later Musso crashed in the Mille Miglia, but he won his class in the Tour of Calabria and won on handicap at Naples. The 1951 season brought retirements in the Tour of Sicily and Mille Miglia, but for 1952 he persuaded his brother Giuseppe into lending him his 750 cc Stanguellini with which he notched up several placings but no wins.

Luigi Musso's big chance came in 1953. The Maserati factory offered their new 2-litre A6GCS sports car to three young Italians on terms which involved the purchase of the cars. Out of a long list of applicants were chosen Sergio Mantovani, Emilio Giletti and . . . Luigi Musso. The outcome was Musso being hailed as the Italian 2-litre champion after numerous wins.

Maserati were quick to test Musso in one of their new 250F Formula One cars in 1954. In sports cars he won at Naples and Senigallia and took class wins in the Tourist Trophy and Buenos Aires 1000 km. His first Formula One victory came in the non-championship Pescara Grand Prix, while he was second in the Spanish Grand Prix after a first-rate drive. The following year he shared the winning Maserati with Jean Behra in the Supercortemaggiore Grand Prix for sports cars at Monza, was second in the Bari, Caserta and Naples sports-car races, second in the Syracuse Grand Prix and third in the Dutch Grand Prix. That year, Musso was proclaimed Italian champion.

In 1956 Musso joined Scuderia Ferrari. The season started reasonably well when he 'won' the Argentine Grand Prix, his only World Championship Formula One victory. But in reality Musso was running in fourth place shortly after one-quarter distance and was called in by his pit to hand over to team-leader Juan Manuel Fangio who went on to win. Whether Musso would have won if he had continued driving is open to doubt. After a second in the Sebring 12-hours and a third in the Mille Miglia, Musso was injured at Nürburgring during the 1000 km sports-car race. He returned in time to compete in the Italian Grand Prix matched against arch-rival Eugenio Castellotti (also a Ferrari team driver). It was inevitable that the pair should disobey team orders and instead of playing a waiting game on the dangerous 6.21-mile banked Monza circuit

they rocketed ahead of the opposition in their personal duel. After four laps both had tyre failures. They stopped at the pits and continued well back. Castellotti was soon out with tyre failure and broken steering, while Musso climbed to second place. During a routine tyre-change Musso was asked to vacate his seat in favour of Fangio, as in Argentina, because the Argentinian needed valuable championship points and his own car had broken down. But Musso refused and roared back into the race, to cat-calls from the crowd. When Stirling Moss's leading Maserati stopped for fuel Musso snatched the lead. The crowd cheered wildly now, but it only lasted a lap. Musso suffered tyre failure coming off the banking before the pits and his steering also broke. Wheels askew, the car skidded to a halt in front of the pits; Musso climbed out – and wept.

In 1957 Musso won the Buenos Aires 1000 km sports-car race and the non-championship Formula One Reims Grand Prix. He was second in the French and British Grands Prix and, at the wheel of the new Formula Two Ferrari, second in the Naples Grand Prix against a field of Formula One cars. In 1958 his long-awaited genuine World Championship Grand Prix race victory seemed close at hand. He won the non-championship Syracuse Grand Prix and the Targa Florio sports-car race and was also second in the Argentine and Monaco Grands Prix. He escaped from a frightening crash in the Belgian Grand Prix, but returned to drive superbly in the Monza 500-mile race, an event which matched European cars against Indianapolis-type machines around the banked oval, finishing a brave third.

A week later Musso arrived to compete in the French Grand Prix at Reims. He crashed at 130 mph on the 10th lap, his Ferrari Dino 246 striking a ditch and overturning, hurling out the driver. Thirty-three-year-old Musso was killed instantly and Italy was left with the best racing cars but no world-class drivers. MK

FELICE NAZZARO (1880-1940)
Italy

'A quiet man, ruddy of face, swart of hair, almost languid of manner. Only a steady, deep-set eye, and a resolute, clear-cut chin to distinguish him from the ruck of his fellows. A mishap to his engine had raised doubts as to the possibility of the start. A staff of men slaved at the work of repair. And Nazzaro had lent a quiet hand – gloved delicately. Now he was ready; and with a shattering roar as of heaven's artillery, and a fierce belching of heavy fumes from the exhaust, the great engine started up. Nazzaro and his mechanician slipped into unobtrusive seats dwarfed by the monstrous bonnet, the crowd fell away, and 180 horsepower transmitted its fierce force to the road wheels as the car fled down the track.'

Thus Alegra, a contemporary motoring journalist, described Felice Nazzaro in 1909, when the driver was at the peak of his international fame. Nazzaro was then 28 years old, and had been a racing driver for nine years. The son of a well-to-do coal merchant, Felice had been apprenticed to Ceirano, who were acquired by Fiat at the turn of the century; his abilities as a driver were soon realised by the new owners, and in 1900 he was entered in the Padua – Vicenza – Padua race with a 6 hp Fiat, and came second (his friend Vincenzo Lancia won the event, although one report claims that both men 'and a dozen other drivers' were disqualified for pushing their cars up one of the hills on the course).

Nazzaro's first racing victory came the following year when, driving one of the new Mercédès-inspired, front-engined, 3.8-litre, four-cylinder Fiats, he won the Giro d'Italia at an average speed of 27.7 mph.

Shortly afterwards, Nazzaro became chauffeur to Vincenzo Florio; Florio's taste for high-powered touring cars and his love of automobile sport ensured that the new appointment was not devoid of interest for Nazzaro, who was able to take part in various local competitions. In 1904, however, with an old 70 hp Panhard, he came fifth in the first Coppa Florio (which was won by Lancia at the wheel of one of the new Gordon Bennett Fiats), beating such crack drivers as Cagno.

This performance earned Nazzaro a place in the Fiat team for 1905, and he responded with a spectacular second place in the Gordon Bennett, beaten only by Léon Théry driving a Richard-Brasier. He achieved sixth place in the Coppa Florio that year, and came second in the first French Grand Prix in 1906.

Which brings us to 1907, the *annus mirabilis* for both driver and car, in which Nazzaro carried off the unequalled feat of winning the season's three major races, all run under entirely different rules, with cars ranging from 7363 to 16,286 cc.

It was a period of flux in international motor sport, with organisers and manufacturers at-

tempting to break out of the straitjacket of the old 1000 kg maximum-weight formula. So, the Targa Florio was run on a 1000 kg minimum weight limit, with cylinder bore diameter restricted to between 120 and 130 mm for a four-cylinder engine. The Fiats for this race had 7363 cc engines, four-speed gearboxes and chain drive, and the old Great Madonie course was one which would test the transmission to the full, for in its serpentine progress through the Madonie mountains, the ill-surfaced circuit at one point rose 1600 ft in eight miles, then dropped 3400 ft in ten miles. There were 44 entries for this, the second Targa Florio, including the previous year's winner, Cagno, with his Itala. On the first 90-mile lap, Lancia's Fiat took the lead, closely followed by Cagno, Trucco (Isotta-Fraschini) and Nazzaro, but a leaking fuel tank slowed Lancia on the second round; and Nazzaro went into the lead, challenged by Louis Wagner (Darracq), who skidded off the road in his eagerness to take the race from Nazzaro. On the third and final lap, the order was Nazzaro – Lancia – Fabry (Itala).

Then came the Kaiserpreis, sponsored by the German Emperor, and nominally for medium-powered touring cars of less than 8 litres (though the 92 cars which entered were all stripped racers). Because of the high entry, the event was divided into two heats and a final, and only those cars which finished in the top twenty in each heat would go through to the Kaiserpreis proper.

The first heat (which was run off in pouring rain at 4 o'clock in the morning) was won by Lancia, the second by Nazzaro; in the final, Nazzaro beat his own record for the 73-mile circuit on the first lap and led the field, though he lost ground second time round, with the orange-coloured Pipes of the Belgians Hautvast and Deplus coming through ahead of him. Nazzaro rallied on the next round, pushed Deplus back into third place, and set off in pursuit of Hautvast. Under this determined attack, Hautvast failed to hold the lead, and at the finish, Nazzaro was five minutes ahead of his rival, averaging 52½ mph for the race; third and fourth were the Opels of Jörns and Michel.

Then came the first French Grand Prix. On the face of it, this was a *formule libre* event, for there was no restriction of engine size: but there was a catch, for the cars had to achieve a better fuel average than 9.5 miles per gallon, for the petrol allowance was strictly measured.

The race took place at Dieppe only two weeks after the Kaiserpreis, and it seems as though Fiat were tardy entrants, for the single fee lists had closed before ex-racing cyclist Dominic Lamberjack, Paris concessionaire for the marque, announced that he was entering a team of three cars which 'he had had constructed at his own expense' at double fees – £400 each car.

Fiat drew first place in the ballot for positions on the starting line, and Nazzaro was driving car F-2. These Fiats had 16,286 cc engines which had originally been designed for the 1905 Gordon Bennett, with overhead inlet and exhaust valves set at an angle in a hemispherical cylinder head; power output was 120 bhp.

The chassis, indeed, apart from a few added holes to reduce weight where it would do least good – mainly in the drop arm and gear and brake levers – was on the face of it identical to the 1905 model apart from lowered steering and different seats and fuel tank. Fiat seem to have used the same design of chassis on their racing cars over a period of six or seven years, for the underpinnings of the 1912 Grand Prix Fiat were apparently identical, too.

The race was dominated by a ding-dong Fiat–De Dietrich battle, with first Wagner, then Lancia contesting the lead with Arthur Duray's De Dietrich; but Nazzaro, driving a steady, less exhibitionist race, had been quietly gaining ground, and when Wagner and Duray had fallen out and Lancia had fallen back, he took the lead, winning by seven minutes with little more than the smell of petrol in his tank, having averaged 70.5 mph over 778 miles.

After this display of virtuoso versatility, Nazzaro's performance in the first major event of 1908, the Targa Florio, proved a disappointment, for his car was forced to retire. June 1908 saw one of motoring history's most famous challenge matches, run off at Brooklands between Frank Newton's L48 Napier *Samson* and Nazzaro on the Fiat *Mephistopheles,* which was similar to the 1907 Grand Prix cars, but bored to 18,146 cc. It was a case of Samson Agonistes, for the dreaded 'power rattle' caused the Napier to break its crankshaft, and the Fiat won at a speed which has remained the subject of controversy ever since. 'Ebby' Ebblewhite the Brooklands timekeeper claimed it had achieved 107 mph; the new-fangled electrical timing apparatus showed a less believable 120 mph . . .

Perhaps it was poetic justice, but in that year's French Grand Prix, Nazzaro was eliminated when *his* crankshaft broke.

In September, Nazzaro won the Coppa Florio at Bologna in convincing manner, averaging 74.1 mph for the 328 mile event; and he might have won the Savannah Grand Prize had not a tyre burst when he was leading on the last lap.

Because of the cessation of major international motoring competition in the period 1909-1912, Nazzaro made few appearances, apart from his record attempt at Brooklands in the summer of 1909 with the sister car to *Mephistopheles,* which was suffering from porous cylinder castings and only achieved 105 mph; then, in 1912, he sought to emulate his former colleague, Lancia, by turning to car manufacture.

There was more than a hint of Fiat about the appearance of the new Nazzaro car, which was built in Turin. In fact, for a car sponsored by a racing driver, the Nazzaro was a rather stolid-looking machine, with a 4.4-litre side-valve engine and a four-speed gearbox.

In the 1912 Targa Florio, Losa and Catalano drove a Nazzaro into 12th place; but the following year saw the marque's first competition success, when Felice himself won the two-day event, run on a 652 mile circuit round Sicily. Then in 1914, he won the Coppa Florio, too.

But an attempt on the French Grand Prix that year with a team of specially-built 16-valve overhead camshaft 4½-litre cars proved an expensive fiasco, for none of the Nazzaros lasted the course.

Felice severed his connection with the company in 1916, but the name was revived in 1920 by a Florence-based firm.

The last Nazzaro cars appeared in 1922, with an overhead camshaft actuating the two exhaust valves fitted to each cylinder.

Meanwhile, Felice Nazzaro was back with his old company, Fiat. He won the 1922 French Grand Prix at Strasbourg with a 2-litre Fiat, a victory which underlined the 'Lucky' Nazzaro legend, for his two team-mates crashed during the race, one of them, his nephew Biagio, receiving fatal injuries.

When the cars were examined, it was found that all the rear axles were flawed, and that had the race continued much longer, it would have been almost inevitable that Felice would have crashed, too.

This was really his last successful race, for the new 1923 Fiats, as is well known, retired hurt in that year's French Grand Prix, having ingested a rich diet of road grit through their innovatory supercharging systems. Nazzaro managed a second place with one of these cars in the Monza Grand Prix (a fitting achievement, for he and his team-mate Pietro Bordino had performed the opening ceremony at the Autodrome).

In 1924, Nazzaro crashed in the Coppa Florio and retired from the French GP with plug trouble; the following year he became head of Fiat's competition department, staying until his death in 1940.
DBW

GUNNAR NILSSON (1948-1978)
Sweden

Occasionally in motor sport there appears a driver who is obviously destined for great things. Gunnar Nilsson was one such driver but fate intervened and he died of cancer in 1978 before he could reap the full rewards of his obvious talent.

Nilsson was the second son of a building contractor and was born in Helsingborg, Sweden, on 20 November 1948. He went to school in his home town and subsequently served as a submarine radio officer in the Swedish Navy. For a while it seemed that he would follow the family business. He studied engineering for four years and gained a degree from the University of Stockholm but eight months of working as a supervisor in the construction industry were as much as he could tolerate. He left his job in Stockholm to return home and start his own business. In spite of his background and training, construction held no attraction and he and his associate, Dan Molim, aimed to establish a transport business. The business flourished and even when he became a full-time racing driver Gunnar continued as a partner in the company.

Sweden's motor racing scene in 1972 gained much publicity through the exploits of Ronnie Peterson and Reine Wisell and, suddenly, Nilsson knew that he too wanted to be a racing driver. He wasted no time in acquiring an RPB Formula Vee car and setting forth to learn the trade. His first season took in only about ten races and included one win, at Mantorp Park.

The following year Gunnar graduated to Formula Super Vee, driving a Lola T252 for Ecurie Bonnier. His team-mate for many races throughout Europe was seasoned campaigner Freddy Kottulinsky and although Nilsson won no races he learned many valuable lessons. One

of the most valuable was that if he were to reach the top his next step must be into Formula Three. Nilsson's experience was growing rapidly; in September he drove a Formula Two GRD for the Swedish Pierre Robert team at the Norisring and, mainly due to the misfortunes of others, he finished a remarkable fourth overall. Also during 1973 he tried his hand at rallying with a series of BMW 2002 Tiis, several of which sustained heavy damage.

Nilsson's most important break in 1973 came during a Super Vee outing at the Nürburgring. At the time Gunnar did not know where the finance for a season in Formula Three might be found but at that meeting he was approached by a man from Västkust-Stugan, a firm which manufactured prefabricated buildings in Sweden, who offered sponsorship for 1974. With their help a March 743 with a Toyota engine was acquired, with which to contest the Polifac Formula Three championship. In terms of results it was not a very good year for the team. Gunnar scored some second places but not a single win and his season was punctuated by many spins and minor accidents. He was the first to admit that most of the problems were a result of trying too hard, but that was the quickest way to learn. Certainly, he did not go unnoticed and towards the end of the season he was given Formula Two drives. In one of these cars he scored a fourth place (and a more convincing one than his Norisring performance) at Hockenheim.

For 1975 March acknowledged the Swede's talent by putting him into their works Formula Three car. With the advantage of adequate pre-season testing and a growing self-confidence, Gunnar scored his first win in the formula at the season-opening supporting race at the Thruxton Formula Two meeting. It was the beginning of a run of success which netted the BP Formula Three championship and included wins at Aintree, Silverstone, Knutstorp, Snetterton and again at Thruxton. In winning the Formula Three round supporting the British Grand Prix, at Silverstone, Nilsson attracted all the right attention and was soon signed by Ted Moore of Rapid Movements to drive his company's Formula Atlantic Chevron. In Formula Three Gunnar had interspersed his successes with some spectacular accidents but in Atlantic he made no mistakes. He managed fourth in his first race and then scored an outstanding run of five wins, including four from pole position. The queue for Gunnar's services for 1976 was a long one.

He eventually signed to drive for March, with a promise of a BMW-powered Formula Two drive. He then became the pawn in the bargaining between Lotus and March for Ronnie Peterson's contract. In the end Ronnie went to March and Gunnar to Lotus; it was the start of a happy union. Nilsson had briefly tried Formula One power in testing for Frank Williams's team at Goodwood, now he was thrown in at the deep end – racing the Lotus in the South African Grand Prix. His debut was not an auspicious one: he started from last place on the grid, in what was known to be a bad car, which had caught fire during practice!

His next race, the non-championship Race of Champions at Brands Hatch, was more promising: he started from the second row of the grid and stormed into an immediate lead, which sadly lasted only until his engine shed a plug lead. In the other British non-championship race, the International Trophy at Silverstone, Gunnar finished sixth. In between these two races he had survived a huge first lap accident at the US Grand Prix West, where he had again started last on the grid. In Spain Andretti re-joined the team and Gunnar finished a fighting third. He scored third place in Austria, fifth in Germany and sixth in Japan (where Andretti won) but the rest of the season was marred by accidents – in Belgium, Sweden and Holland – and by car failures – in Monaco, France, Great Britain, and at Watkins Glen. Nevertheless, he had impressed sufficiently to stay with Lotus for 1977 and Mario was staying too. Once again Gunnar had a true professional to lead him in the right direction.

In 1977 the Lotus 78 was regularly the fastest car on the circuits in Andretti's hands and the American won more races than any other driver during the year. Gunnar proved his worth as a back up driver to Andretti and wrote his name firmly in the record books with a fine win in the Belgian Grand Prix after his team-mate had been eliminated in a first lap accident. Nilsson mastered appalling weather conditions before driving around the outside of Niki Lauda's Ferrari with twenty laps to go, thereafter building up a sizeable lead and cruising gently to victory.

Nilsson also scored a third place in Great Britain, fourth in France and fifth places in both Brazil and Spain, to finish the championship in eighth place with a total of twenty points. He might have scored more but for a whole catalogue of minor accidents (and one not so minor one, in Canada), mechanical failures and punctures. On several occasions, notably in Austria, he drove extremely hard even after pit stops, proving that he was not a man to give up easily.

Gunnar was versatile too; having driven a BMW saloon for the Luigi team in 1976, he joined Dieter Quester in the Alpina BMW 3.2CSL to contest some rounds of the 1977 European Touring Car Championship and took the car to victory at Salzburgring in April and at the Nürburgring in July. He also sampled American style oval racing in the International Race of Champions series, scoring a sixth place at Riverside in October and expressing much enthusiasm for that form of racing.

Towards the end of 1977 Nilsson's relationship with Colin Chapman of Lotus deteriorated to some extent and, even though Andretti openly said there was no one he would sooner have as team-mate than Gunnar, his place at Lotus was taken by fellow countryman Ronnie Peterson. Although Nilsson's name was linked with many teams, the popular and immensely talented young Swede looked set to drive for the Ambrosio team in 1978.

In fact, Nilsson was to lead the Arrows team, born from Shadow under the direction of Jack Oliver and with many of Shadow's former personnel, including designer Tony Southgate. Alas, Gunnar was never to drive the controversial car. For some time he had been suffering pain in his lower abdomen and had even had to abandon the use of crutch straps on his safety harness during 1977. During the winter, surgeons removed a tumour from his groin.

At first it was reported that the operation was of a fairly minor nature, but it soon became clear that Nilsson's problems were serious. It was eventually revealed that he was suffering from cancer. He fought bravely, and even spectated – thinner and hairless – at a couple of Grands Prix during 1978, but he was losing his fight. By autumn he was desperately ill and on 20 October he died, peacefully, in London's Charing Cross Hospital.

In the days before his death, in full knowledge of his plight, Nilsson refused pain killing drugs in order that he might use his influence to set up a fund to help finance the hospital's fight against his disease. The response reflected the way in which Nilsson's bravery had been seen. The Gunnar Nilsson Cancer Treatment Campaign raised money from people throughout the world and stands as a testimony to a driver who might well have joined the sport's all time greats had fate not intervened.   BL

TAZIO NUVOLARI (1892-1953)
Italy

Tazio Nuvolari was supreme in an era when all manner of risks were the order of the day; Nuvolari lived for his sport. A man of small stature, he had uncanny car control, appeared to take enormous risks and yet none of his accidents kept him from the cockpit of a car for long.

Tazio Giorgio Nuvolari was born on 16 November 1892, at Casteldero near Mantua. Of humble background, he quickly found a taste for speed. A bicycle gave way to a horse and then, at the age of twelve, he saw his first car. His uncle Giuseppe, an international cycling ace, became a distributor for Bianchi cars and, at the age of sixteen, Nuvolari found a job as a mechanic. Not only did Tazio have a thirst for speed, but he also appeared to enjoy flirting with death. As a boy, he attempted to jump off a roof with a home-made parachute, somehow without breaking any bones, and later he acquired a dismantled Blériot aeroplane. Attempting to take off, he found his machine careering into a haystack. It burst into flames, but Nuvolari had only an injured shoulder.

After World War I – he was considered 'too dangerous' to drive ambulances for the Italian Army – Nuvolari married his childhood sweetheart, Carolina, and sold motor cars. In 1920, he began to race motor cycles, proving extremely successful for a span of 10 years, but he yearned to race cars. In 1921, driving an Ansaldo (a touring car), he finished fourth overall and second in class in the Circuit of Garda. Later, he raced Chiribiri and Bianchi cars and then, at the end of 1925, he had a trial with Alfa Romeo at Monza. Driving a P2 model, he quickly acclimatised himself to such a fast car, but after eight laps the car's gearbox seized at a corner and Nuvolari crashed into a tree. He was rushed to hospital where a month's recovery was ordered; seven days later, heavily bandaged, he was lifted on to his motor cycle, went racing again . . . and won.

For two seasons – 1925 and 1926 – Nuvolari could but dream of racing cars: financial considerations dictated that he should remain on motor cycles. Then Tazio sold some land

(originally given to him by his father) and in 1927 formed a team with friends, including another motor-cycle ace, 23-year-old Achille Varzi, to race Bugatti T35s bought from the firm's Milan agency. Nuvolari won at Rome and Garda, but on most occasions had to give best to the better organised and better equipped Alfa Romeo team. The 1928 season started better with wins at Tripoli, Pozzo, Alessandria and Messina, although later he had to accept place results to the superior Alfas. Even Varzi had quit and bought an Alfa Romeo. Eventually, Nuvolari, too, acquired one and he entered for the Coppa Montenero at Leghorn in July, a week after a motor-cycle race. He crashed his bike and broke two ribs, yet within a few days he was racing the new Alfa Romeo 1750 in a plaster corset. He was second to Varzi's faster P2 model.

In 1930 – which was his last year on two wheels – Nuvolari won the Mille Miglia in classic style. Varzi appeared set for victory as he neared the end of the marathon drive, but he had a huge surprise in store. Nuvolari had driven like a demon to close the gap and, espying what were obviously the lights of Varzi's car ahead in the early-morning gloom, he switched his own lights off and crept up behind. With less than two miles to go, Nuvolari stole ahead of his shocked rival.

Nuvolari's other major victory in 1930 was the RAC Tourist Trophy at Ards, near Belfast, where he led an Alfa Romeo 1750 1-2-3 victory. In 1931, Nuvolari beat Varzi in the Targa Florio after another of their titanic duels and, co-driving with Giuseppe Campari, he won the Italian Grand Prix at Monza in a 2.3-litre Alfa Romeo Monza 8C. Later victories included the Ciano Cup and the Circuit of Tre Provincie, the latter with his riding mechanic Decimo Compagnoni operating the throttle via his leather belt to Nuvolari's instructions, following an early accident at a level crossing.

Into 1932, Nuvolari mantained winning form. He won the Monaco Grand Prix, the Targa Florio, the Italian Grand Prix, the French Grand Prix, the Prince of Piedmont Race, the Ciano Cup and the Acerbo Cub and was second in the German Grand Prix, crowning these glories with the title 'Champion of Italy'. By 1933, Nuvolari was into his 40s but retirement from his beloved sport could not have been further from his thoughts. He won the Tunis Grand Prix, his second Mille Miglia, the Circuit of Alessandria, the Eifelrennen, the

Nîmes Grand Prix and the Le Mans 24-hours, all driving for Alfa. Romeo. He lost at Monaco, but his vivid duel there with Achille Varzi's Bugatti is legendary. The pair changed places lap after lap and on the last circuit they strained their engines to beyond reasonable limits. Nuvolari's car blew up and caught fire, yet Tazio jumped out and attempted to push his car to the finish, chased by irate marshals carrying extinguishers. He finally collapsed, exhausted, 200 yards from the finish, only to be disqualified.

Although, on paper, Nuvolari's season appeared to be his most successful yet, in the major Grands Prix his Alfa Romeos were letting him down, breaking their transmissions under the strain. So for the Belgian Grand Prix in July he appeared in a new Maserati 8CM – and won. Victories followed in the Italian Grand Prix while he was second in the Acerbo Cup and the Italian Grand Prix (which he lost owing to a burst tyre). Driving an MG K3 Magnette, Tazio won the RAC Tourist Trophy for the second time, completely confounding the experts who thought his handicap too great.

The 1934 Grand Prix season witnessed the debut of the Nazi-backed Mercedes-Benz and Auto Union cars. The year started off badly for Tazio when he was beaten into second place by Varzi in the Mille Miglia, following the wrong choice of tyres. Then came Alessandria when Nuvolari crashed avoiding Count Carlo Felice Trossi's broken-down car. Rather than risk injury to Trossi, in a split-second Nuvolari headed for a large tree opposite. The car threw out its occupant and Nuvolari was lucky to survive with nothing worse than concussion and a broken right leg. At first, he was content to convalesce at home with his leg encased in plaster but, after hearing of yet another Varzi win (at Tripoli), he vowed to make his come-back at Avus in Berlin. Decimo Compagnoni, his mechanic, rigged up the pedals so that they could all be operated by Nuvolari's left foot (no riding mechanics were allowed by now) and, in great pain, Tazio finished a remarkable fourth. It was only in October that he won his first race of the year, at Modena where he overtook Varzi after another of their famous duels, and he followed this with victory at Naples the following weekend.

For 1933, Nuvolari rejoined the Ferrari-managed Alfa Romeo team in an attempt to beat Mercedes-Benz and Auto Union. He won the Pau Grand Prix, the Bergamo Cup, the Ciano Cup and the races at Biella, Turin and Modena. His greatest feat of all, however, was a superhuman drive in the German Grand Prix at Nürburgring in what many people considered his greatest-ever race. He cornered his underpowered Alfa Romeo P3 at death-defying speeds to split the Mercedes-Benz and Auto Unions. He made up lost time after a pit-stop for fuel when churns had to be used after the pressure hose broke down. Into the last lap he caught sight of the leader, Manfred von Brauchitsch's Mercedes. Nuvolari calculated he could catch and beat the German, but his job was made easier when a tyre burst on the Mercedes.

In 1936, Nuvolari suffered another accident. In trying to beat Varzi (now an Auto Union driver) during practice at Tripoli, Nuvolari had a tyre burst at a most difficult corner. He was thrown out and suffered the 'usual' broken ribs, fitted with the 'usual' plaster corset and told not to race for a month. The next morning he was on the grid and raced to seventh place in a spare car. Victories against the German teams followed at Penya Rhin, Budapest, Milan, Leghorn, Modena and at Long Island, New York, where he won the Vanderbilt Cup. Perhaps Leghorn was his greatest win of the year for, after breaking his own Alfa Romeo 12C, he took over the older, less powerful 8C model of team-mate Carlo Pintacuda, caught his rivals and snatched victory. There was tragedy at the end of the year, however. His eldest son Giorgio died of typhoid. Tazio himself survived another terrifying accident practising for the Piedmonte Grand Prix, leaving hospital after only three days.

In 1937, Nuvolari's only win was in the Milan Grand Prix. It was also another year tinged with sadness: his father died. A hint of the future came when he accepted a 'guest' race with Auto Union in the Swiss Grand Prix. He finally accepted an invitation to lead the German team midway through 1938, swearing he would not drive for Alfa Romeo again following a fire at Pau. He won the Italian Grand Prix and the Donington Grand Prix – his third win from three starts in Britain – but at Donington he was corseted in tight bandages following a collision with a deer in practice in which he fractured a rib.

In 1939, Nuvolari won the Belgrade Grand Prix for Auto Union, then World War II intervened. Nuvolari spent most of his time with his wife and son, Alberto, in their luxurious villa at Mantua. In 1946, at the age of 53, he was ready to race again. He entered the Nice Grand Prix, but withdrew as 18-year-old Alberto died of nephritis. A much-saddened man, he later appeared in the Marseilles Grand Prix where he showed his old sparkle before the engine broke. Later in the year, however, he was hit in the face by a jet of fuel, inhaled the fumes and fell ill. The gases caused severe asthma and Tazio's doctors forbade him to race again.

Still he was not finished. He raced small sports or closed cars, came back with a Grand Prix Maserati 4CL to win at Albi, but was forced to quit at Geneva when fumes from alcohol-based fuel made him vomit blood. When, in 1947, Nuvolari announced his intention of competing in the Mille Miglia, a 16-hour non-stop event, people gasped in amazement. It was even suggested he was attempting suicide, for he had often said he wanted to die in a racing car and not a bed. Driving a 1000 cc Cisitalia against cars of two or three times the capacity, Nuvolari drove like a madman to lead the field until, in the closing stages, the tiny car coughed to a halt after hitting a big puddle. A quarter of an hour was lost tracing and curing a soaked distributor and Nuvolari had to be content with second place behind Clemente Biondetti's 2.9-litre Alfa Romeo. When he stopped he had to be lifted from the car. The two following weekends saw Nuvolari winning sports-car races at Forli and Parma, driving a new 2-litre Ferrari 125 Sport built by his ex-team manager at Alfa Romeo, Enzo Ferrari.

Illness prevented Nuvolari racing for most of the year, but in 1948 he persuaded Ferrari to give him a car for the Mille Miglia. Again, the *Mantovano Volante* – or Flying Mantuan as he was known – showed his much younger rivals the way. Then, with a lead of half an hour, first his car's bonnet flew off and next the seat broke; he threw it away, using a bag of oranges and lemons as a cushion. A spring shackle broke and the car became almost a bare chassis. Almost within sight of the finish the brakes failed and Nuvolari was forced to abandon it after a series of skids.

Nuvolari's last race was on 15 April 1950, when he won a short race at Monte Pellegrino in a 1500 cc Cisitalia. Subsequently, his health deteriorated so that it became absolutely impossible for him to race, and presently he developed a paralysis on his left side. After a spell in hospital, in November 1952, he asked

to be taken to his villa so he could die at home. Visits were only allowed by two or three very close friends, to whom he would often say: 'I, who could dominate any car, am incapable of controlling my own body.' On 11 August 1953, he died in the arms of his wife. His last wish was to be buried in his 'uniform', his once-familiar yellow jersey, and blue helmet and trousers.   MK

BARNEY OLDFIELD (1878-1946)
USA
Berna Eli 'Barney' Oldfield was a showman, a rich showman. He specialised in short match races, chiefly on dirt-tracks, shortly after the turn of the century, but he was also an accomplished road racer. Perhaps because of his showmanship on the dirt-tracks, his circuit achievements did not receive the recognition due. In the 1914 Indianapolis 500, for instance, he fought valiantly against tough French opposition in his Stutz and finished fifth, the only American driver of an American car in the first eight.

From a poor family in Wauseon, Ohio, Barney Oldfield was born on 3 June 1878, and left school when he was twelve. He later joked that his first 'driving' job was as a lift boy in a hotel. Bicycle racing became his profession and he won countless events, but in 1902 he had a major break. A fellow cycle-racing friend, Tom Cooper, lent him a petrol-engined vehicle, a tandem racing bike, to race in Salt Lake City, Oldfield's new home town. Several months later, Oldfield heard from Cooper. He and a chap called Henry Ford were building two racing cars – and would Barney like to drive one? He did, and quickly moved east where the cars were under construction.

Oldfield became famous for his driving of the Ford-built *999* and later the *Winton Bullet,* the *Peerless Dragon* and the front-wheel-drive *Christie.* On Memorial Day 1903, he became the first American to cover a mile in a minute during a match race at the Empire City horse-track in New York, an achievement which gave him nationwide acclaim. He toured the country giving exhibition runs match races, although exactly how many of these were genuine is not known as he paid his 'opposition', and Bill Pickens, his manager, was in charge of the stop-watches. Showmanship was his theme and he became famous as an extrovert, cigar-chewing entertainer who used to shout to his fans, 'You know me, I'm Barney Oldfield!' He even played briefly in a theatre in a presentation titled *Vanderbilt Cup,* when he would rev up his racing car on stage on a treadmill and shower his audience with dirt to give a dusty road effect.

By 1908, Oldfield had tired of the fairgrounds and announced his retirement, but the following year saw his return with a German Benz, a 120 hp model. In 1910, another Benz – the 200 hp Blitzen model – was used by Oldfield to establish new one-mile, two-mile and kilometre records at Ormond Beach. Even Kaiser Wilhelm sent his congratulations from Germany.

Because of his participation in unsanctioned match-races, Oldfield was often under suspension by the American Automobile Association and therefore was ineligible for major road races such as the Indianapolis 500 which was inaugurated in 1911. Late in 1912, however, his suspension was lifted and he was invited to take the late David Bruce-Brown's seat in the Fiat team for the annual Grand Prize at Milwaukee; Oldfield accepted and finished fourth.

The Mercer team signed Barney to drive for them in 1913 (although Mercer's team captain, Ralph de Palma, was angry and walked out) and he finished second in a 445-mile road race at Santa Monica. Oldfield's love for stunt and exhibition races (including one against an aircraft) meant he rarely remained in a team for long, and in quick succession he moved from Mercer to Maxwell and then to Stutz. With a Stutz he was fifth in the Indianapolis 500, a seemingly poor position but a great performance against the might of the all-conquering French teams. In the 1915 500, he withdrew his Bugatti as it was not quick enough, and the following year he was fifth in a Delage.

Other successes included second place in the 1914 Vanderbilt Cup driving a Mercer, second with a Maxwell in the 1914 Corona road race, victory in a Stutz in the 1914 Cactus Derby (a 670-mile road race) and victory in the Venice road race of 1915 driving a Maxwell.

In 1917, too old for military service, Oldfield campaigned his final exhibition car, the *Green Dragon*. This was a Miller-engined device with an enclosed cockpit, and to add to the showmanship Oldfield used to drive it clad in a green leather outfit. He retired from racing in 1918 and formed the Oldfield Tire & Rubber Co which he sold to Firestone four years later; it became Firestone's racing division.

Barney Oldfield had become a very rich businessman, but he lost heavily in the 1929 Wall Street crash – reportedly in excess of $1,000,000 – and became virtually penniless. He appeared in a film about himself and also had ideas of breaking the land-speed record in a special 3000 bhp car to be built by Harry Miller, but this remained a dream. Oldfield ended his days as an automotive consultant and died in Beverly Hills in 1946.   MK

CARLOS PACE (1944-1977)
Brazil

The Brazilians take their sport very seriously, and when Carlos Pace (pronounced Par-chay) drove his Brabham to victory in the 1975 Brazilian Grand Prix, they gave their fellow countryman a rapturous welcome. It was a moving moment for the young man from São Paolo. Not only was it a GP win in front of his home crowd, but it was his first World Championship Grand Prix win ever. Sadly, it was also to be his last; on 18 March 1977 Pace died in a flying accident in his native Brazil, just as it seemed that his unstinting efforts for the Brabham team were about to bear fruit.

Born on 6 October 1944, Pace was the son of a fairly wealthy man. At the age of sixteen, he bought a 125 cc go-kart. He then proceeded to win six races, to finish second in the Brazilian championship. He continued to race karts for a further two years and in 1963 began his car-racing career by entering a 1-litre DKW in the inaugural Interlagos race. He proved so impressive in practice that he was offered a Team Willys Renault Dauphine Gordini for the race proper. He finished in second place and this persuaded Team Willys to continue to support him. Their faith paid off because by 1965 Carlos had become Brazilian Saloon Car champion. Two years later, Pace became the Brazilian national champion and this time the runner-up position went to a young driver named Emerson Fittipaldi. Pace then consolidated his position as Brazil's number one driver by taking the national title again in 1968, driving a prototype Bino, and once more in 1969, this time behind the wheel of an Alfa Romeo T33.

By this time, however, Emerson Fittipaldi had arrived in Britain and was causing a sensation with his incredibly fast and tidy driving style. It was Fittipaldi, in fact, who helped Pace arrange a Jim Russell Lotus 59 Formula Three drive when he too arrived in Britain at the end of 1969. From this moment onwards,

Pace, in spite of his more successful record in Brazil, was forced to live under the shadow of Fittipaldi. Nevertheless, it did not affect their friendship or Pace's driving, and he went on to become the Forward Trust Formula Three champion for 1970. In 1971 he was signed by Frank Williams to drive his March 712 Formula Two cars. It proved a troublesome period for Carlos, and he managed only one win, at Imola.

In 1972, Frank Williams invited Pace to join his Formula One team, driving the rather outdated March 721. Try as they might, neither Williams nor Pace could get the cars to work effectively, although Carlos did manage a sixth at the Spanish GP and a fifth at the Belgium GP. He was asked to drive a works F2 Surtees during the second half of the season, which in turn led to an offer from the works Ferrari team to join their sports-car effort. Driving a Ferrari 312P, and sharing with Austrian Helmut Marko, he finished second in the Österreichring 1000 km, and proved that given competitive machinery, he was a force to be reckoned with.

The following season, 1973, saw Pace sign for the Surtees team. At last, Pace was an accepted member of the top class of motor racing and it seemed as though it would not be too long before the talented Brazilian won his first Grand Prix. Alas, it was not to be. Time and time again mechanical failure put him out of races and his best results were a fourth at the German Grand Prix and a third at the Austrian GP. One consolation, however, was setting the fastest lap during the German GP at Nürburgring, traditionally the most demanding and difficult circuit of them all. During this season, he also continued his association with the Ferrari sports-car team and enjoyed some good results. Sharing the car with Arturo Merzario, he finished second at the Nürburgring 1000 km and at Le Mans.

Despite the setbacks of his previous F1 season, Pace signed with Surtees for the 1974 season. A fourth in Brazil augured well for the season but once again it was not to be. 1974 was a troubled time for the Surtees team. During the season they lost their sponsorship and the consequent lack of finance severely hampered the team. By the time seven Grands Prix had been run, Pace left in disgust.

Shortly after leaving Surtees he was signed by the Brabham team. In the Italian GP, he finished fifth and ended the season with a second at Watkins Glen.

For 1975, Brabham designer Gordon Murray updated the Brabham BT44 and gave works drivers Carlos Reutemann and Carlos Pace a thoroughly competitive motor car. In the first race of the season, the Argentine GP, Pace put his car on the front row of the grid but was forced to retire in the race. His second race was the Brazilian GP and it was here that Pace won his GP, and wrote his name into the history books of Brazil. Thereafter the Brabhams were plagued with problems, particularly with tyres, and Pace's best results were second place at the British Grand Prix, third in Monaco, fourth in South Africa and fifth in Holland. His 24 points gave him sixth place in the championship.

For 1976 the Brabham team abandoned Cosworth power in favour of the Alfa Romeo flat-12 and although the car had obvious potential too often it proved embarrassingly slow and fragile. Pace's only points of the season came from fourth places in France and Germany and sixth in Spain.

His intensive testing in the closed season helped transform the BT45 for the beginning of the 1977 season and he made no secret of his confidence in it. It was, it seemed, confidence well-founded; Pace, joined now at Brabham by John Watson, led both of the South American Grands Prix which opened the season. In Argentina (where Watson also led) Carlos surrendered the lead to intense pressure from Jody Scheckter but still clung to second place; in Brazil he led from the start but his home crowd's rapture was short lived as Pace was eliminated on lap 33 in a minor coming-together with James Hunt. His last race was not a happy one; in the South African Grand Prix, which claimed the life of Tom Pryce, Pace suffered repeated tyre problems and finished a lowly thirteenth. A few days later, while John Watson was confirming the team's new-found form by taking pole position at the Race of Champions at Brands Hatch, came the news of Pace's fatal accident. It was the more bitter because Carlos had come so close to real success and finally looked to be within reach of the very top.   MW/BL

MIKE PARKES (1931-1977)
Great Britain
On 28 August 1977 Mike Parkes was killed in a road accident in Italy, where he had lived for over a decade. He was involved with various motor-sporting projects, but do not imagine

that 'Parkesi' – as he was known – was almost an Italian. Nothing could be further from the truth. He remained a polite and charming Englishman – one might almost say a 'typical' Englishman. Photographers crowded around him in the Monza paddock during a practice session for the 1966 Italian Grand Prix, and here was the cool, calm Parkes perched on a wheel of his Ferrari savouring a cup of tea!

Michael Johnson Parkes was born in Richmond, Surrey, on 24 September 1931. His father, John Joseph Parkes, once a test pilot, moved to the midlands in the mid 1940s and was to become chairman and managing director of Alvis. Educated at Haileybury (where Stirling Moss was a fellow pupil), Mike joined the Rootes Group as an apprentice in 1949. He worked for 18 months as a fitter and a further 18 months in the administration department before joining the experimental section, where he was closely concerned with the development of the Hillman Imp between 1956 and 1963.

Mike's first car was a 1933 model MG PB, but it was notoriously unreliable and his father replaced it with a new MG TD on one condition: it was not to be raced. However, Mike did race it – twice – and later went into partnership with fellow Rootes apprentice John Munn to race a 1930 chain-drive Frazer-Nash in vintage meetings. The 'Nash was raced with some success for three years, and in 1956 Mike and another Rootes colleague, Geoff Williamson, jointly purchased a Lotus 11 Club complete with rigid rear axle and 1172cc side-valve Ford engine. The pair designed and built their own light-alloy overhead-inlet-valve cylinder head (a unit which was commercially produced by Willment), and later the car was raced with the engine supercharged and running on alcohol fuel.

Next, Parkes become involved in the Formula Two Fry-Climax project. This was an advanced, rubber-suspended, semi-monocoque car built by David Fry in collaboration with Alec Issigonis. At that time, Issigonis (designer of the Mini) was working at Alvis and Parkes' father suggested that Mike would make a useful test and development driver. It was a somewhat heavy machine, Parkes having little real success bar a second at Brands Hatch on Boxing Day 1959. Mike was also asked to advise Sir Gawaine Baillie with the preparation of his Lotus 15-Climax sports car, and it transpired that Parkes drove the baronet's Lotus Elite in long-distance sports-car races in 1960. Parkes was impressive, but

unlucky, an instance being at Goodwood in the Tourist Trophy where Mike was leading his class when a tyre blew in the closing minutes. In 1960, Parkes also had a couple of races for Rootes in the works Sunbeam Rapiers and drove a works Gemini Mk3 in the Boxing Day Brands Hatch Formula Junior race.

In 1961, it all happened for Parkes. He raced for Gemini in Formula Junior and was invited to join Tommy Sopwith's Equipe Endeavour team and race a Jaguar 3.8, a Jaguar E-type and a Ferrari 250 GT. He won race after race and, following his defeat of Stirling Moss at Goodwood on Easter Monday, Parkes was invited to test a works Ferrari 250 GT at Le Mans during the April test weekend (Parkes was present to oversee the Rootes team's cars). He lapped quicker than the works drivers and was immediately offered a place in the Ferrari team in the 24-hour race itself in June. Driving a 3-litre Ferrari 250 TR61 he finished a strong second to team leaders Phil Hill/Olivier Gendebien. Parkes's total of successes comprised fourteen victories and eight seconds that year, including six wins and six fastest laps in one weekend.

In 1962, Parkes, now 30, was ripe for Formula One. He had offers, but his commitment to Rootes – whose Imp was in its crucial final development stages – led to these being declined. He had a one-off Formula One outing at Mallory Park in a Bowmaker Cooper T53-Climax on Whit Monday, finishing a highly creditable fourth behind John Surtees, Jack Brabham and Graham Hill. His main programme once more comprised saloon and GT racing, while he also enjoyed the occasional works drive for Ferrari in sports cars. He was second in the Nürburgring 1000 km, but at Le Mans a team-mate pushed him off into the sandbank on the first lap. Highlight of the year was the Guards Trophy meeting at Brands Hatch on August Bank Holiday Monday. Parkes won the feature sports-car race in a works Ferrari 246 SP, the GT race in a·Ferrari 250 GTO and the saloon event in a Jaguar 3.8 – all in atrocious weather conditions against top-line rivals.

Parkes finally left Rootes at the end of 1962, accepting Enzo Ferrari's invitation to go to Italy and become a development engineer/test driver/works racing driver. Much of his 8 am–7 pm working day was spent either behind the drawing board or testing production-line cars. In 1963, he was third in the Le Mans 24-hours and second in the Tourist Trophy and Coppa

Inter-Europa. The following year he won the Sebring 12-hours and the Spa Grand Prix, but later was out of action owing to a testing accident, and in 1965 he won the Monza 1000 km and was second in the Nürburgring 1000 km and Reims 12-hours. The 1966 season opened well with victory in the Monza 1000 km and more sports-car successes were gained in the Spa 1000 km and Paris 1000 km. At last he was asked to race a Formula One Ferrari, and in it he took second place in both the French and the Italian Grand Prix.

The 1967 season began with seconds in the Daytona 24-hours, Monza 1000 km and Le Mans 24-hours, but in the Belgian Grand Prix Parkes was involved in a serious first-lap accident. His special Ferrari 312/67 with which he had won the Daily Express Trophy at Silverstone (it had an extended wheelbase so Mike could insert his 6 ft 4 in frame) spun on oil and rolled, throwing out its occupant. Mike's legs were badly broken and if it had not been for immediate attention in the new Grand Prix Medical Unit, amputation would have been likely. Recovery was a long, slow and painful process, but eventually Parkes was back at Ferrari to resume his duties as development engineer. He was determined to continue motor racing as well, and in October 1969 co-drove a Lola T70-Chevrolet in the Paris 1000 km with Dickie Attwood; they were 10th after various problems. Driving an old Ferrari 312P for the North American Racing Team, Mike was fourth in the Daytona 24-hours and sixth in the Sebring 12-hours in 1970. Parnell later raced for the Italian-based Scuderia Filipinetti team for the remainder of 1970 and 1971 in 5-litre Ferrari 512s, and his best re-sult was a fourth in the 1970 Nürburgring 1000 km.

In 1971, Parkes quit Ferrari to work for Scuderia Filipinetti, becoming involved with the preparation of a team of racing Fiat 128 coupés. Later he worked on racing versions of the De Tomaso Pantera, taking time off to race one – and win – at Imola in 1973. In January 1974, the Scuderia Filipinetti having been disbanded owing to the death of its patron Georges Filipinetti, a wealthy Swiss, Parkes moved to Lancia as development engineer in charge of the Lancia Stratos rally-car project and was working for the company at the time of his death. Perhaps it was the Stratos's 2.4-litre Ferrari engine which had made Mike feel so at home.   MK

REG PARNELL (1911-1964)
Great Britain

Reg Parnell was Britain's top Grand Prix driver in the immediate post-war years. He began as a wild, seemingly reckless driver in the mid 1930s, but after World War II his style had matured. Parnell raced successfully into the mid 1950s and then became a team manager. His vast experience and knack of spotting up-and-coming drivers paid dividends and 'Uncle Reg', as he was affectionately known, was sorely missed when he died in January 1964.

Born in Derby in 1911, Parnell was intro-duced to motoring at the age of 15. Although two years under age, he drove his family's lorries and private buses, and in his spare time he performed odd jobs around the garage. In 1934, Reg spectated at Donington Park in Derbyshire and immediately decided to try racing for himself. For £25 he bought an old 2-litre Bugatti single-seater, but it broke its back axle in the paddock at its first meeting. Owing to the expense of purchasing spares for the 'Bug', it was sold and an MG Magnette K3 purchased. The MG was intensively modified – it had a centralised single-seater body, Lancia independent front suspension, a twin-cam McEvoy cylinder head, a two-stage Zoller supercharger and two-leading-shoe Lockheed hydraulic brakes. Wins were secured at Brooklands and Donington Park until an inci-dent on the Brooklands banking during prac-tice for the 500-mile race in 1937. Parnell slid into Kay Petre's Austin and Petre was serious-ly injured. Although she put the incident down to 'bad luck', the RAC revoked Parnell's racing licence for two years (he was not popular with everyone owing to his press-on-regardless driv-ing style and his admission that, although he loved its thrills, he went motor racing primarily to win money).

His licence was restored in 1939 and Parnell was back with a 4.9-litre Bugatti-engined single-seater known as the BHW, with which he was particularly successful at Donington Park. He also began the construction of his own car for *voiturette* racing (the pre-war version of Formula Two). Known as the Challenger, it was to feature a specially constructed, twin-stage supercharged, six-cylinder, 1½-litre engine, double-wishbone front suspension, and torsion bars coupled with a de Dion axle at the rear; however, World War II intervened. Parnell spent the war years completing the Challenger (but using

15 Left: Alan Jones waited in the wings for a long time for his starring role but, teamed with Frank Williams, he set the stage in 1979 for a dominant World Championship year in 1980 and then started 1981 as he had left off, as a winner.

16 Right: Motor sport has seen few more determined drivers than Niki Lauda. Lauda founded his career on borrowing from a bank, won the World Championships for Ferrari in 1975, just lost out to James Hunt after surviving a horrific accident in 1976 and then recaptured the title for the Maranello team the following year. In 1979, decisive to the end, he walked out of the Brabham team into the new challenge of building his own air line.

17 Above Left: Stirling Moss, seen here with Denis Jenkinson before winning the 1955 Mille Miglia for Mercedes, was, unquestionably, one of the greats, yet he never won the World Championship.
18 Above: Cigar-chewing Barney Oldfield, the archetypal American showman-racer.
19 Left: 'The Flying Mantuan', Tazio Nuvolari (right), perhaps the greatest ever, with his Alfa Romeo team-mate Giuseppe Campari at Brescia during the 1931 Mille Miglia.
20 Right: 'King' Richard Petty carried on a family tradition of NASCAR domination started by his father, Lee.

21 *Above:* In his first full Grand Prix season Nelson Piquet marked himself as a potential future champion, winning three Grands Prix and pushing Alan Jones hard in the battle for the 1980 title.

22 *Left:* Clay Regazzoni raced for sheer love of the sport until a terrible accident at Long Beach in 1980 forced him into a retirement.

23 Left: For almost a
decade, Carlos Reutemann
has been a Grand Prix
front runner. On his day
Reutemann can be un-
touchable but a strange
lack of consistency has
kept a World Champion-
ship tantalisingly out of
reach.

24 Right: Jochen Rindt
was one of the fastest and
most spectacular of all
Grand Prix drivers. When
he was killed in practice
for the Italian Grand Prix
at Monza in 1970 he had
already won five of the
season's Grands Prix and
amassed enough points to
make him the sport's first
posthumous Champion.

25 Right: Jody Scheckter made a spectacular rise to fame when he joined the Grand Prix scene and a dignified exit when he left, with a hard fought World Championship in between. *26 Below:* When German nationalism was forcing technical barriers in motor sport the inclusion of young Briton Dick Seaman in the Mercedes team was eloquent testimony to an outstanding talent. Seaman is third from the left in this group photograph taken at the 1938 German Grand Prix, flanked by Manfred von Brauchitsch, team manager Neubauer, Hermann Lang and Rudolf Caracciola. Seaman won this race, much to the chagrin of the German high command.

27 Right: Jackie Stewart won three World Championships and more Grands Prix than any other driver in a spectacurlarly successful and occasionally highly controversial career. Stewart's outstanding combination of speed and consistency is virtually unrivalled but much envied.

28 Below: Many drivers have competed on both two wheels and four, but alone among them in winning World Championships in both disciplines is John Surtees. As well as being an extremely good driver, Surtees was also an outstanding technician but Grand Prix success somehow always eluded Surtees the constructor.

29 Right: Gilles Villeneuve began in snowmobile racing and North American Formula Atlantic before making his Grand Prix debut. He was soon being tipped as a future World Champion.

30 Below: Rodger Ward in the traditional winner's pose after driving the Leader Card Roadster to victory at Indy in 1962, three years after his first win at the Brickyard.

a straight-eight Delage engine in place of the partially completed, home-brewed six) and building up a comprehensive collection of racing machinery. This included Alfa Romeo, Riley, ERA, Delage, MG and Maserati models.

In 1946, with motor racing resuming, Parnell owned and raced a Maserati 4CL, an ERA A-type and several Rileys and Delages. The Challenger was, however, sold. It was a year of poor mechanical reliability, although his Maserati was second to B. Bira's ERA in the Ulster Trophy at Dundrod by a mere second. In 1947, as Britain's most successful driver, Parnell won the BRDC's Gold Star. He began that year by winning two ice races in Sweden with his ERA A-type and later won the Jersey Road Race in the Maserati. He acquired one of the ERA E-types and, but for a broken de Dion tube, would have won at Ulster. The following year Parnell again won the BRDC Gold Star. He was third with the Maserati in the inaugural Zandvoort meeting in Holland and with a new Maserati 4CLT/48 (which replaced the luckless ERA E-type) he finished fifth in the Italian Grand Prix. He won the Goodwood Trophy at the first-ever race meeting at the Sussex track and was second at Penya Rhin in Spain.

In 1949, Parnell maintained his winning ways with the Maserati, gaining many successes at Goodwood (he became known as Emperor of Goodwood) and raced at almost every circuit in Europe; he also drove in the early-season South American races. The following season Reg received a tremendous accolade. He was invited to drive the fourth works Alfa Romeo 158 in the European Grand Prix at Silverstone and finished third. Later in the year, he was signed to drive for the Aston Martin sports-car team, taking a DB2 to first place (fourth overall) in the 3-litre class of the Tourist Trophy at Dundrod. He also gave the BRM P15 V16 Grand Prix car its best ever initial results, winning two short races at Goodwood at the end of 1950 and placing fifth in the 1951 British Grand Prix, despite being almost roasted alive in the cockpit.

Perhaps one of Reg's greatest drives was in the 1951 Daily Express Trophy race at Silverstone. Driving Tony Vandervell's modified Formula One Ferrari 375 (known as the *Thinwall Special*) he left the star-studded field standing in conditions so bad the race had to be stopped after 11 laps due to flooding. He was second to Farina's Alfa Romeo at Dun-

drod and Goodwood and won at Winfield in Scotland. In 1952, he enjoyed class wins at Silverstone and Boreham driving for Aston Martin; at Goodwood he unhesitatingly took over duties as team manager for Aston Martin when a pit fire seriously injured John Wyer. For Parnell, it was a foretaste of things to come. The 1953 season was a particularly successful one: Parnell was fifth in the Mille Miglia (driving on the ignition switch after a broken throttle had to be wired up in the fully-open position), second in the Sebring 12-hours, first in the Goodwood 9-hours and second in the Tourist Trophy, each time driving for Aston Martin.

In 1954, in addition to his Aston Martin commitments, Parnell drove his own Ferrari 625 in Formula One events, winning at Goodwood, Snetterton and Crystal Palace. Next season he secured more victories for Aston Martin (at Silverstone, Oulton Park and Charterhall), but in 1956, following an unsuccessful sortie to New Zealand with an experimental single-seater Aston Martin, Parnell crashed Rob Walker's Formula One Connaught B-type at Crystal Palace on Whit Monday, suffering a broken collar-bone and a badly cut knee. He recovered and took his Ferrari to New Zealand, winning the New Zealand Grand Prix and the Dunedin Trophy, early in 1957.

Then came the news: Reg Parnell, at the age of 45, was to retire from active motor racing. He was appointed team manager to Aston Martin and performed his new duties well. After seven years as a team driver, it was no 'sympathy' job. Parnell was able to use his enormous experience to the full and had the knack of picking out future top drivers. In addition to overseeing Aston Martin's World Sports Car Championship season of 1969 – the year the marque also won the Le Mans 24-hour race, after many seasons of trying – he encouraged such newcomers as John Surtees (the motor-cycle World Champion) and Jim Clark.

When Aston Martin withdrew from racing at the end of 1960, Parnell moved to Yeoman Credit (later Bowmaker) who sponsored a Formula One team. His drivers were John Surtees and ex-Aston man Roy Salvadori. When Bowmaker withdrew at the end of 1962, Parnell opted to continue as a privateer, purchasing the ex-Bowmaker cars and the premises at Hounslow, Middlesex. After a visit to the early-season New Zealand and Australian races in 1963, Parnell signed

19-year-old New Zealander Chris Amon to lead the team and also gave encouragement to motor cyclist Mike Hailwood.

For 1964, Parnell commissioned Les Redmond to design a new car to supplement and eventually replace the ex-works, BRM-engined Formula One Lotus 25s he had purchased for the season. However, following an operation, Parnell died on 7 January. Only 53, the seemingly indestructible, ever-smiling Parnell was gone. R. H. H. 'Tim' Parnell, his son, took over control. Tim Parnell finally disbanded the team in 1970 when he was given the job as team manager to BRM; at the end of 1974, he left BRM to devote his full time to farming in Derbyshire.

HENRI PESCAROLO (b.1942)

France ·

Henri Pescarolo, the son of a top French surgeon, was born in Montfermeil on 25 September 1942. The serious-looking, bearded medical student was, however, not destined to follow his father's footsteps. Motor sport appealed to him and, after navigating for his father in a doctors' rally in 1964, the following year found him at a racing drivers' school and competing in a Ford-backed series of races for novices in Lotus 7 sports cars. Pescarolo dominated the scene and as a result was invited to partner Jean-Pierre Beltoise and Jean-Pierre Jaussaud in the Formula Three Matra team in 1966.

It was not a successful season for Pescarolo: his car was not ready until the tail-end of the season and then it was beset with small, niggling problems. In 1967, however, Pescarolo proved himself. He won the season's most important Formula Three race at Monaco, gained more wins at Barcelona, La Châtre, Bugatti au Mans, Rouen, Magny-Cours, Nogaro, Zandvoort and Albi and became French Formula Three champion. Many experts considered he was the best Formula Three driver in Europe. Towards the end of the year, he was twice invited to race a Formula Two Matra and also won a sports-car race at Montlhéry with the 4.7-litre Ford engined Matra 620.

In 1968, Pescarolo, then 25, was promoted to the Formula Two team full-time, backing up his team-mate Jean-Pierre Beltoise so well that the pair were first and second in the European Formula Two Trophy. Pescarolo won the Albi Grand Prix and finished second five times. In the Le Mans 24-hours, he shared a Matra 630 coupé with Johnny Servoz-Gavin and became the idol of the crowd as he brought the car up to second place. Then, within reach of the lead, the car was put out in the closing stages owing to two punctures and an accident. In September, Pescarolo made his Grand Prix debut in the Matra team in the Canadian Grand Prix. Driving one of the raucous V12 Matra MS11s, he retired after half distance owing to fading oil pressure. He was unable to take part in the United States Grand Prix owing to the lack of an engine, while in Mexico he ran slowly to finish ninth, racing without the Matra's rear wing, owing to a practice accident.

In 1969, Matra gave up Formula One racing, but Pescarolo remained in their Formula Two and sports-car teams. The year began badly with a serious accident during the April Le Mans test weekend when his experimental Matra 640 coupé literally took off at approximately 125 mph down the Mulsanne Straight and crashed heavily. He was thrown from the car and suffered leg and back injuries plus burns. By August, he was back in the cockpit, and on form, winning the Formula Two section of the German Grand Prix in a Matra MS7-Ford. At the end of the year, he shared a Matra 650 with fellow Frenchman Jean-Pierre Beltoise to win the Paris 1000 km.

Matra returned to Formula One in 1970, Pescarolo joining Beltoise to drive the new Matra Simca MS120s. The V12 engines seemed to lack the power of their rivals, but Pescarolo was an excellent third in the Monaco Grand Prix, fifth in France and sixth in Belgium and Germany. Apart from an early-season victory in the non-championship Buenos Aires 1000 km, the sports car scene was not so bright, as the Matra Simca 650s were unreliable and underpowered compared with the 5-litre Porsches and Ferraris. At the end of the year, however, Pescarolo drove for Alfa Romeo in the Österreichring 1000 km and finished second, partnered by Andrea de Adamich. In Formula Two, he raced a Brabham BT30-Ford owned by Bob Gerard, finishing second at Barcelona and Pau.

After Matra dropped Pescarolo for 1971, the Frenchman signed to race for Frank Williams in both Formula One and Formula Two, finding support from the French Motul oil company, and for Alfa Romeo in sports-car racing. Apart from a second in the non-championship Argentine Grand Prix and a fourth in the British Grand Prix, Pescarolo's season with Williams's Formula One Marches was dismal. In Formula Two, the year began with victory at Mallory Park in March, only to be followed by a string of retirements. In sports-car racing, Pescarolo found the Alfa Romeo T33/3 fast and reliable, winning the BOAC 1000 km at Brands Hatch and finishing third in the Sebring 12-hours, Monza 1000 km and Spa 1000 km races. So far as Formula One was concerned, 1972 was a complete disaster. Driving a March for Frank Williams, Pescarolo was third in the non-championship Rothmans 50,000 at Brands Hatch, but in other races he was either poorly placed or retired. He crashed the March at Monaco, Clermont Ferrand, Nürburgring, Österreichring and Monza and wrote off Williams's new Politoys FX-3 Ford at Brands Hatch. However, as compensation, he won the Le Mans 24-hours in a Matra 670 shared with Graham Hill and the Formula Two Mediterranean Grand Prix at Enna in Sicily in a Rondel Racing Brabham BT38-Ford.

Sports-car racing took priority in 1973, a year when Matra returned to this class full-time and clinched the World Championship of Makes. Pescarolo won the Vallelunga 6-hours, the Dijon 1000 km, the Le Mans 24-hours, the Österreichring 1000 km and the Watkins Glen 6-hours, each time partnered by Gérard Larrousse. In Formula Two, driving for the Motul-sponsored Rondel team, he won at Thruxton, while from his three Formula One appearances, the best he could muster was eighth with the ill-handling works March 721G/731-Ford in the Spanish Grand Prix.

With Motul sponsoring the works BRM team, it was back to Formula One full-time in 1974. However, it was yet another unsuccessful Grand Prix year for Pescarolo, the V12-engined British cars not proving competitive. His best placing was a fourth in the non-championship Daily Express Trophy at Silverstone and by the end of the year Pescarolo had quit the team. In sports car racing there was another clean sweep for Pescarolo and Larrousse: the pair won the Imola 1000 km, the Le Mans 24-hours, the Österreichring 1000 km and the Kyalami 6 hours. It marked Pescarolo's third successive victory at Le Mans, a feat only achieved twice before, by Woolf Barnato (1928-9-30) and Olivier Gendebien (1960-1-2).

He continued his sports car form in 1975, partnering Derek Bell to wins at Spa, Österreichring and Watkins Glen, now driving

the Alfa Romeo 33TT12. In 1976 he ran a privately entered Surtees in Grands Prix with little success.

It was back to sports cars in 1977 but Henri's Le Mans luck was out and he blew up the engine of the Porsche which he was sharing with Jackie Ickx while well placed. Ickx took over the team's second car and went on to score his fourth Le Mans win; Henri could only sit on the sidelines and look forward to equalling Ickx's score.

In 1978, he again shared with Ickx until the car broke; Mass then took over as the car was repaired but eventually crashed. He finished tenth in 1979 sharing a Rondeau with Beltoise and in 1980 he did not finish, although he scored a popular win in a Porsche at Dijon in the World Championship of Makes.　MK

RONNIE PETERSON (1944-1978)
Sweden
There have been three basic styles of GP driver: the ones who have looked slow and trailed behind the rest; the ones who have looked steady . but have been fast, like Fittipaldi, Clark and Stewart, and the ones that have looked and gone quickly. In the last-named group, the outstanding examples have been Jochen Rindt and a Swede named Bengt Ronald Peterson.

Ronnie, the son of an Orebro baker and engineer, was born on 14 February 1944 and, due to his father's exploits with 500 cc racers, soon got the taste for motor racing; in fact, he first went to see his father race when he was but four years old. The remaining time in between then and his first kart race was spent with moto-cross and speedway-racing motor bikes. The first step into proper competition came when Ronnie's father built him a German motor-cycle-engined kart with which Ronnie gained much success in three seasons of racing in the 200 cc class. After an even more successful time with a 100 cc kart, the graduation to Formula Three was made in 1966 with a home-built car called the SWVBB, a copy of the 1965 F3 Brabham.

Unfortunately, however, this enterprising venture was not very successful as the '66 Brabhams were one year more advanced. The only thing to do was to buy a proper Brabham, a BT18; this he did, and with the car he finished the season. In his first race with the BT18, he was involved in a shunt which damaged the car's chassis. The car had to be used the following season and, although it was straightened out as much as possible, it still was not quite right; that year, Ronnie had to be content with thirds and fourths.

It was late 1967 when Peterson took the step that would ensure that his next mount would at least be up to the driver's not inconsiderable abilities. With friend, and soon-to-become racing sparring partner, Reine Wisell, he went off to Bologna to see the Pederzani brothers. The Pederzanis had been building karts since 1962 and were, by this time, building the cars to beat in F3, the Tecnos. Reine and Ronnie went home with expensive F3 cars in hand and, while Reine went around Europe racing, Ronnie concentrated on Swedish races for the '68 season, winning twelve out of 26 events and taking the Swedish championship.

For 1969, a new Tecno with a Novamotor engine was purchased, and the car was raced under sponsorship from Vick, the coughdrop makers (who were, incidentally, to carry on sponsoring Ronnie for many seasons). There were numerous victories for Ronnie in 1969, and he went to the prestigious Formula Three event of the year, Monaco, with seven successive wins under his belt. A victory in the Principality always attracted plenty of notice in the right quarters, and Ronnie scored a magnificent win against Reine's Chevron.

Late that same year, Peterson was contracted to drive a completely new car in F3; this was for March, who were taking their first tentative steps which were to lead to a quick jump to Formula One. The first race with the March 693 was at Cadwell Park in England where Ronnie finished third. The next race at Montlhéry was not quite as successful: he ended up in a Paris hospital. The March directors went to see the dazed Peterson at his bedside and took him (along with customary flowers and grapes) a contract for Formula One in 1970.

Although Peterson was the first man to be signed for F1 with March, the experienced Amon and Siffert were to take the works drives. However, the Bicester company lined up a drive for Peterson in a private March 701, with Colin Crabbe's Antique Automobiles team.

The 701 chassis was relatively unproven and uncompetitive, with Stewart picking up the only Grand Prix win for March in Ken Tyrrell's team car in Spain. Peterson plodded through Formula One that year with seventh in Monaco as his highest placing. Driving the

Malcolm Guthrie Racing Team March in Formula Two, he had a more encouraging time, although still far from brilliantly successful, finishing third in the European Trophy series.

It was 1971 when the star from Sweden started to shine brightly. This was when March gave Ronnie a works drive in their STP-backed 711 as team leader. This car was a much lighter, more nimble and generally more competitive machine than its predecessor. The first race in which he showed the expected promise in F1 was the Monaco GP, where he finished second to Stewart, only 25.6 seconds behind. This was despite racing with suspected cracked ribs sustained during a nasty Silverstone shunt. After that, the season turned out well for Ronnie, overshadowed only by Stewart who was in great form. He came very close to winning his first GP in Italy, but he had to be content with second place behind Peter Gethin's BRM which was all of one-hundredth of a second ahead. There was to be a fairly lean season in between that second place and his first GP win, although in Formula Two racing he quickly asserted himself as 'King' in the '71 season, taking the European Championship with the March 712.

1972 was the year of the ill-fated March 721X, the car that promised so much with its low polar moment of inertia. Despite the amazing handling this car promised, trouble with the gearbox and other minor faults meant that it was virtually impossible to develop. So, the year was ended with Ronnie driving the 721G Formula Two chassis, specially converted. In fact, this car was quite successful: Ronnie started from the front row of the grid in Canada and led for a time, and in America he finished the race in fourth place.

However, the damage had been done and he had already made his mind up to leave. Colin Chapman was quickly on the scene and snapped up what was by now the hottest property on the motor-racing scene.

The position offered by John Player Team Lotus was 'joint number one' along with reigning World Champion Emerson Fittipaldi. This venture was quite successful considering the reputation Lotus had with many drivers. In his first seven GP starts in '73, he secured four pole positions, and in that seventh race, the Swedish GP at Anderstorp, Peterson beavered away through the field to lead his home GP, only to have a tyre deflate near the end so he had to watch Denny Hulme's McLaren

Ford win.

The next race saw Ronnie win his first GP, in France, and surely the first GP win must be the most elusive for any driver. This was so in Peterson's case for more victories came in Austria and Italy, where Fittipaldi was upset that Ronnie had not let him win. That year in Formula Two, Ronnie and Emerson raced Texaco Stars with Novamotor Jensen-Healey engines, but they were totally uncompetitive. Fittipaldi left the team at the end of the season and Jacky Ickx came in.

1974 was started with the ageing Lotus 72, but the 76 with electric clutch and double brake-pedals was on the way. This car needed a great deal of development, however, and time could not always be found for this. 'One problem was that the 72 kept winning', said Ronnie, so obviously the team could not wholeheartedly keep testing the new machine. F1 wins at Monaco, one of Peterson's lucky circuits, France and Italy helped the season on, but by the end of the year it was Ronnie's driving that stopped the old 72 from being hopelessly outclassed.

It was then that talks were said to have started with one-time March and then Shadow team manager Alan Rees. During the 74-75 close season there was much negotiating between these two teams for Ronnie's services in one of the new quick cars of GP racing. When the storm cleared, though, it seemed as if it was more of a bluff by Lotus to get its sponsors to give the team more money than a wish to move by the driver himself.

Early 1975 saw the 72 get probably its last breath when a new, lighter chassis was built. The car ran third in South Africa and finished third in the non-championship Race of Champions at Brands Hatch, but it was on the new Lotus model that Peterson's hopes for the World Championship were pinned. The new car did not appear until October, however, and was not raced until the following year. Ronnie had a dismal season, scoring only six points, from fourth place in Monaco and fifths in the shortened Austrian Grand Prix and at Watkins Glen.

Nor was 1976 much better – although it did include one win. The new Lotus appeared in Brazil, where Peterson was joined in the team by Mario Andretti; the two collided while running near the back of the field early in the race. For Ronnie it was the last straw and he headed back to March, in exchange for fellow Swede Gunnar Nilsson.

Although Ronnie had demonstrably lost none of his flair, neither had March found much reliability and by the time Peterson's pure driving skill won the Italian Grand Prix, at Monza in September, he had already signed for Tyrrell for 1977. His only other score with the March had been for sixth place in Austria.

Perhaps he had thought that the six-wheeled Tyrrell would suit his tail-out driving style, but what had looked quite a promising car a year earlier was suddenly hopelessly uncompetitive. In spite of spectacular efforts with the Tyrrell, Ronnie was often slower than team-mate Patrick Depailler and he suffered a whole catalogue of retirements and minor accidents. He did manage third place in Belgium (where, perhaps ironically, Nilsson won), fifth in Austria and sixth at Monza, but a meagre seven points again left him at the wrong end of the championship table.

So, for 1978 it was back to Lotus – this time to back Andretti, who was determined to defend his status as team leader. At last it seemed that perhaps 'Superswede' had put himself into the right place at the right time and when the season began, in South America, he was brimming with a confidence and enthusiasm not seen for many a year. While Andretti scored an effortless victory in Argentina Ronnie scored his first points of the season with a fine fifth place. All that remained to be seen was whether two superstars could exist in the same team without defeating each other's aims.

Officially, Ronnie was number two in the Lotus team, but his performance in South Africa underlined his true mastery. After Andretti was delayed by fuel vaporisation problems, Peterson stormed through the closing laps to catch Patrick Depailler just half a lap from home, achieving a memorable victory.

He scored his last Grand Prix win in Austria, again after Andretti had been sidelined. Throughout the year he was a faithful team-mate to the American, finishing second to him on no less than four occasions – in Belgium, Spain, France and Holland. Having scored third place in Sweden, fourth at Long Beach and fifth in Argentina, Peterson went to the Italian Grand Prix at Monza as the only driver with a chance of beating Andretti for the title. Having run to team orders throughout the season it was unlikely that he would attempt to do so, even though he had decided to leave Lotus, and in fact had already signed for

McLaren for 1979.

As the cars came onto the grid, the starter gave the green light while the back rows were still moving. Peterson made a slow start and was engulfed as the field bunched up before the first chicane. In a dreadful chain reaction he was hit by another car and catapulted head on into the barriers. He was pulled, with multiple leg injuries, from the wreckage by James Hunt. First reports from the hospital were that, although he was very badly injured, he would survive. During the night, he was operated upon; complications arose, Peterson slipped into deep coma and he died on the morning of 11 September.

Ronnie Peterson was widely acknowledged as the fastest driver of his era and his death gave chilling emphasis to the mortality of every member of his profession.   LJC

KAY PETRE
Britain

Ever since the Edwardian heyday of Mme Camille Du Gast, lady drivers have added a touch of feminine glamour to motor sport. One of the most glamorous of all was Mrs Kay Petre, whose petite appearance concealed a steely determination to win, and which made her one of the outstanding racing drivers on the British scene in the 1930s and one of the outstanding lady drivers of any era.

Kay Petre started racing with sports cars, and during 1935 was one of an all-girl team at Brooklands, along with Aileen Ellison and Mrs Tolhurst. At the time, Sammy Davis commented: 'A distinctly decorative appearance and turnout disguised a toughness, and tenacity, that was as unexpected as it was magnificent. If she had orders to hold a certain speed, or drive so many hours, all creation could not have stopped her doing it, whether a large car at 130 mph or a small one at 90 mph was involved. This had been most noticeable in two Monte Carlo Rallies where she had been one of the crew, for on each occasion she lasted through the three days and four nights of driving without turning a hair.'

Quite apart from her track performance, you could not help noticing Kay Petre: in July 1936, she arrived for her first Donington meeting in the 'luxurious magnificence' of a huge Morris in concours condition painted in the same livery as her supercharged Riley. The press recorded: 'Mrs Petre made a fine start, but was outmatched for the nonce.' The

following week, the elegant Kay was on her way to take part in the Ramsgate Concours d'Elegance.

She had already earned a place in Brooklands history, lapping in the big 10½-litre V12 Delage at almost 135 mph, the second-fastest speed at Brooklands achieved by a lady driver (the fastest was Gwenda Hawkes, whose time in the Derby-Maserati equalled virtually 136 mph).

The 1937 season saw Mrs Petre as one of the official Austin works team, driving a side-valve Austin racer, while Dodson and Hadley handled the new ohc cars. The team's first official outing was the 1937 British Empire Trophy meeting at Brooklands, but all three were forced to retire, Kay Petre's car developing accelerator trouble.

However, the cars appeared again a few weeks later at Shelsley Walsh, where the Austin team carried off all the honours in the 750 cc class, making the first, second, third, fourth and fifth fastest times. Kay Petre's time of 46.9 seconds, fourth fastest in the class, was especially noteworthy compared with Bert Hadley's new class record, as Hadley was piloting the new ohc model, and Kay Petre's car was the side-valve.

Later the same month (June), the Austin team lineup was Hadley (ohc), Goodacre (ohc) and Kay Petre (sv). The supercharged Austins were scratch cars, giving 40½ minutes to limit man H.B. Shaw (Samson), who completed 25 laps before Hadley was allowed to start.

Hadley's stint included a new 750 cc class record lap of 121.68 mph, and by the time Goodacre took over, the team had come from the back of the field to fifth place. Goodacre turned in consistent lap speeds of 118 mph, so that when Kay Petre set off, after 70 laps, the team was lying second. On the 80th lap, though, the oil gauge on her car's dashboard suddenly began to leak scalding hot oil into the cockpit of the Austin racer just as she was in the lead.

Regardless of the discomfort, Kay Petre held on to the lead with lap speeds of 100 mph-plus, expecting all the while that the engine would seize from lack of oil pressure. However, her luck held, and the Austin team won the relay with an overall average of 105.63 mph, 15 mph faster than the record held by Morgan since 1934, and well ahead of the second team, MG, who averaged 85.8 mph.

On 13 June 1937, Kay Petre was one of the works team which gave the Austin Nippies their Le Mans debut, but the unblown Jamieson modified cars suffered from teething troubles, and failed to figure in the results (although, rebodied, they subsequently enjoyed considerable acclaim when they were raced in trials and rallies under the new name of Grasshopper).

It was as the Grasshopper that these cars were entered for the 12-hour race at Donington that year, taking second, third and fifth places, the latter position falling to Kay Petre and her co-driver P. Stevenson.

In the Crystal Palace Cup on 15 August, plug trouble spoiled Kay Petre's chance of coming second in the 15-lap race but, at Shelsley Walsh a month later, she climbed the course in 43.78 seconds to earn the Ladies Challenge Trophy.

While practising for the Brooklands BRDC 500 miles event that month, Kay Petre was travelling at 90 mph when her car was struck by Reg Parnell's MG, which had been travelling too high up the banking. The little Austin rolled, and Mrs Petre was taken to hospital with severe concussion, having been fortunate to escape with her life.

Thereafter, she devoted herself to writing about motoring for the *Daily Sketch,* but here, too, tragedy struck, for in the 1939 Monte Carlo Rally, she and Major Reggie Empson were following the competitors through France when their car was hit by a lorry at a crossroad; Empson was killed and Mrs Petre was injured. However, she continued her career after the war, becoming one of the first members of the Guild of Motoring Writers.   DBW

LEE PETTY (b.1941)
RICHARD PETTY (b.1937)
USA

The history of NASCAR racing is both action packed and colourful, and it is a great shame that it has never been seen on European tracks. It is a sport peculiar to America, though, using as it does large-engined saloon cars with, what would appear at first sight to be, fairly standard bodies, albeit with no side windows. There is a great deal more to it than that: NASCAR constructors are probably the most successful rule-benders in the world, and in fact the sport has evolved to a situation where the cars are really as close to standard production cars as they are to steam rollers. Although it might share the same basic engine, the NASCAR stocker will be capable of reaching

speeds of up to 200 mph, and its engine will have been developed to produce close to 600 horsepower.

Naturally it was not always thus and, in the early days, they were a lot closer to living up to their names – stock cars.

The National Association for Stock Car Auto Racing, to give its full title, officially came into being in February 1948. Its founder and leading light until a few years ago was one Bill France, who later handed over full control of the NASCAR operation to his son, William Junior.

It was at one of NASCAR's early races, at Charlotte Raceway on 19 June 1949, that the name of Lee Petty first went onto a results sheet. He came second that day, and went on to win the NASCAR Grand National championship three times. By 1980, only one man had beaten that record, and his name was Petty, too.

As the influence of NASCAR spread, so those first stock-car drivers – many of whom were reported to have gained their skill while trying to outrun 'Revenooers' in pursuit of their illicit whisky trade – had to travel further and further afield in the search for prize money. Lee Petty, along with other famous drivers like Fireball Roberts, Curtis Turner, Joe Weatherly and so on, would drive overnight from one meeting to the next, trailing their race cars behind their trucks and having only their wives for company. The sport was strongest by far in the Southern states, and this is where the majority of top drivers have come from over the years. The track that has come to be regarded as the home of NASCAR is at Daytona Beach in Florida – first on the beach itself and, from 1959, on a new banked track conveniently located just a little further from the sea. It was Lee Petty who won the very first Daytona 500 race on this new track – it was also here that he had his biggest and most spectacular accident, which led to his retirement.

Lee was not a particularly flamboyant driver, not when compared with the likes of Curtis Turner and Fireball Roberts, anyway. He usually won races with skilful and steady driving, although if other drivers ever mistook this for timidity, they usually discovered their mistake the hard way. His accidents, though, were spectacular. History records that during one race on the old beach circuit at Daytona, his windscreen became so caked with sand that he lost sight of the track completely and drove straight out to sea! Realising his error, he rejoined the race to the astonishment of several other drivers on that part of the track, who were not mentally prepared for the sight of his big blue Dodge returning from the waves at full blast. There was rather a fine accident as a result, involving Ralph Moody, who recovered to come third!

Lee's car was always blue, and carried the number 42 which was allocated to him for his entire career. Up until 1957, he always drove a Dodge, but in that year he made the switch to Oldsmobile. 1957 was also the year of what was possibly his most controversial victory. While tussling for the lead with Curtis Turner, it seems he somehow helped Turner's car into the wall. He did not win, as it happens, but the incident caused a certain amount of acrimony in the Ford camp, as Turner had been driving the only surviving Ford in the race!

1958 was a good year for Lee, though. He won the Grand National championship for the second time, his race record including nine outright wins for Oldsmobile. He also won the NASCAR short-track championship. In 1958, too, he competed against his son Richard for the very first time. Junior blew his engine, but Pa won the race.

1959 saw Lee take that Grand National title for the third and final time. He had fourteen victories that year, four with his Oldsmobile and ten with a new Plymouth. 1960, though, started badly, when he got beaten by his son, who took third place at Daytona to Lee's fourth! All in all, it was not a particularly successful year for Lee. 1961, though, was worse. In a qualifying race for the Daytona 500, he tangled with another competitor on one of the high-speed banked turns, and they both went clean over the banking to crash forty feet onto the ground below. Those NASCAR cars were pretty tough even in those days, and Lee got away with injuries restricted to his legs, while the other driver was virtually unhurt. Lee's career was virtually ended by this incident – he did race a few more times but professed that he did not care for it anymore.

So, it was left to Richard to keep the Petty name at the forefront. He had obviously had a good grounding, having attended meetings with his father for many years before getting to race himself. Unlike most fathers, Lee had actively encouraged his son to race, and kept that encouragement up even when his son started off his career with a series of impressive crashes. Richard's first recognition came in 1958, and at that time he was dubbed

NASCAR 'Rookie of the Year'.

1963 was his first year of real success, though. He did not win the Grand National championship – Joe Weatherly just snatched it from him at the last race of the season. However, out of nineteen Plymouth victories that year, he won fourteen, and his revenge was to come the following year, when he became champion for the first time and earned almost $100,000 in prize money. 1965 and '66 were not so good, although he did win Daytona again the latter year. 1967, however, was probably his best year ever. He won the championship together with over $130,000 in prize money, and took ten straight victories in a row. He raced forty-eight times, finished forty-one, and won twenty-seven. In 1971 and '72, he won the championship again, much to the delight of the STP Corporation who were his new sponsors after the Chrysler factory had withdrawn their support in 1970. Apparently, the Petty team was a little reluctant to change the colour of their car from blue to STP red, but at least they were allowed to continue to use the famous 43 racing number allocated to Richard.

The Petty team had long been based at Randleman in North Carolina, and it was here that the Petty workshops were also based. It was a family business with Lee still involved, and so were Richard's brother Maurice and cousin Dale. Richard himself placed a great deal of importance on the family aspect of the team, and said that it was that which made it all worthwhile for him.

It was also interesting to note that Richard just did not want to know about any other forms of motor racing. He was offered Grand Prix drives and Indianapolis cars to race, but he always turned them down with little hesitation. Petty took the championship again in both '74 and '75 but the following year, despite earning over $300,000 in a season for the third time, he scored only three wins, taking the runner-up spot to Cale Yarborough's Chevrolet. It was his worst ever season in terms of hard results and 1977 was little better, five wins again netting second place to Yarborough.

As the famous Dodge was based on a 1974 model Charger and Grand National rules ban cars more than four years older than the current model, the team had open options for 1978 and a Chevvy was on the list of possibles.

He actually started the 1978 season with a Dodge Magnum, which soon proved to have serious aerodynamic shortcomings. Only dogged driving kept him in the hunt. Having gone more than twelve months without a win, he changed, in late August, from Chrysler to Chevrolet. Although he gradually made the Chevvy competitive, he finished a lowly sixth in the championship and failed to score a single win. After more wind-tunnel tests deciding which General Motors product to use, Petty switched cars again before the big Daytona race. This time he chose an Oldsmobile and, lo and behold, after a last lap fracas between the two leaders Cale Yarborough and Donnie Allison which resulted in both of them spinning out, King Richard found himself taking the chequered flag. It was his 186th Grand National victory and his sixth Daytona 500. With it, Petty reaffirmed his position as the 'winningest' NASCAR driver in history.

By the end of 1979 he was NASCAR champion for the seventh time, and his own son, Kyle, was beginning to give him a run for his money. 1980 was not so good for King Richard and as the season drew to a close he was only third in the title race, but no one imagined the Petty name would be off the top for very long.

He did not race until he was 21 – that was his father's only stipulation about his involvement with the sport. In the next twenty years he won over two million dollars all told – probably as much as any other racing driver in the world. He also won almost 200 races – a fantastic record.

Richard and Lee Petty are the only father and son team to have so dominated any form of motor sport, writing their names in the racing history books so many times that they are unlikely ever to be surpassed.   AA

NELSON PIQUET (b.1952)
Brazil

It is usual for the road to the top in Grand Prix racing to be a fairly long haul but for Nelson Piquet it was not so; in only his second full season at the top he was runner-up to Alan Jones in the World Championship and, but for mechanical misfortunes in crucial races at the end of the season, he might well have taken the title himself.

Piquet was born in Rio de Janeiro on 17 August 1952, the son of a Brazilian politician. His early sporting aspirations were as a tennis player, following in his father's footsteps, and when he was sixteen he moved to a high school in California to pursue the sport. While in the

States he 'discovered' cars and motor sports and on his return to Brazil he teamed up with another young, aspiring Brazilian racer, Alex Ribeiro, and made the classic entry into motor sport – driving a kart. In his second season of kart racing he won a national championship and began to think about making the progression to cars. One thing that was for sure, though, was that there would be no financial help for young Nelson from his parents, who definitely did not approve of his new hobby. Even Piquet is not Nelson's real name; that replaced Soutomaior as a rather unsuccessful subterfuge to fool his parents.

In the early 1970s, Nelson was racing Volkswagen-based sports cars and SuperVee and in 1972 won the Brasilia Sports Car championship. He did all the work on his cars himself and learned a great deal from the man who built his Polar SuperVee cars. His mechanical knowledge and sympathy would become a great asset as his career progressed.

He missed out on racing throughout 1973, concentrating, if only a little, on his education, but he was back on the circuits in 1974 to win just one SuperVee race out of a meagre three which he entered. Largely due to mechanical problems he did not score at all the following year, although his practice and race performances underlined to anyone willing to look beyond the results that here was a special talent in the making.

In 1976 better machinery and a little more money enabled him to rack up a few more hard results and with six race wins he became national SuperVee champion. It was in 1977 that Piquet arrived, with his wife, Maria-Clara, in Britain, looking at a future in Formula 3. He bought a March and a Novamotor and set off to contest the European F3 series. His early outings did not augur well and he soon decided that to be a winner he needed a Ralt chassis. By virtue of cutting his living expenses to a minimum he bought his new car and with a late run of success, including two wins, he hauled himself up to third place in the championship, albeit without a great deal of recognition or enthusiasm for his progress back home.

For 1978, Piquet forsook the European F3 series for the British championship, where his main rival would be his fellow countryman Chico Serra – already well known in England thanks to his success in Formula Ford. By virtue of beating Serra hands down in the important F3 races, with a remarkable run at one stage of seven wins in a row, Piquet began to be noticed. He was offered a test drive in a Formula One McLaren at Silverstone and made his Grand Prix debut in Mo Nunn's Ensign at Hockenheim where he impressed mightily, before retiring with engine trouble. Thereafter, Piquet had three races for the B&S McLaren team, finishing ninth in Italy, before being snapped up by Bernie Ecclestone to drive alongside Niki Lauda in the Brabham-Alfa team. Piquet fitted in well with his first major team and the opportunity to learn from Lauda was obviously not wasted on him.

1979 saw him mature remarkably quickly, frequently proving quicker than his illustrious team-mate who was having a season in the depths. He scored points only once during the year, for fourth place in Holland, but that belied the actual level of his achievement and when Lauda unceremoniously walked out of the team and into retirement at the Canadian Grand Prix there was never any question that Piquet would not assume the role of team leader.

His 1980 season was outstanding and very nearly ended with a World Championship. With the new Cosworth-powered Brabham BT49 he took a strong second place in the season opener in Argentina, crashed in Brazil and took fourth at Kyalami. At the round-the-houses Long Beach Grand Prix Piquet was in a class of his own, storming away to his first-ever Grand Prix win and a lead in the championship. He crashed again in Belgium, finished third in Monaco, retired from the outlawed Spanish race, was fourth in Spain, second to Jones in Britain and failed by less than a second to take third place from Jones in Germany. He was fifth in Austria and took full advantage of an uncharacteristic indiscretion by Jones in Holland to storm away to his second win of the year. He added another in Italy and went to Canada with the championship well within reach, but he needed to win. The race was stopped after the first corner when Piquet and Jones, starting from the front of the grid, touched and sparked off a multiple accident. Piquet restarted in his spare car and was driving away in a seemingly unassailable lead when his engine expired and with it his championship hopes. Jones won the race and the title, and Nelson finished his season on a low note by spinning off while under intense pressure from eventual winner Jones in the Watkins Glen race.

Putting aside thoughts of what might have been, Piquet began testing of the turbocharged BMW-powered Brabham which would carry his hopes for 1981. He knew now that his own first World Championship should only be a matter of time.   BL

DIDIER PIRONI (b.1952)
France
In 1978 a very serious looking young Frenchman joined the Tyrrell team and began to make an immediate impression on the Grand Prix establishment. By 1980 he had become a race winner and, in many eyes, a potential World Champion. Didier Pironi had every confidence that his many admirers were quite right.

Didier Joseph-Louis Pironi was born on 26 March 1952 in Villecresnes, Paris, and, around the age of twelve, he was introduced to motor racing by his cousin, José Dolhem, himself a racing driver who twice drove in Formula One for John Surtees. Didier's first outings in a racing car came in 1972, when he impressed his teachers at the well-known Winfield racing drivers' school. During that same year he won the Pilote Elf competition – a useful stepping stone for the ambitious novice in France. Pironi made the most of this good start and in 1973 he made his debut in Formule Renault, rapidly becoming the proving ground for the new generation of French Grand Prix drivers much as Formula Ford had once been in Britain. After a season learning the ropes, he won the Formule Renault championship in 1974 and moved on to the even more prestigious Super Renault championship, finishing third in 1975 and then winning that title as well in 1976, for Tico Martini. He scored a remarkable twelve wins from the seventeen rounds he contested and, not surprisingly, he suddenly became a much sought-after young man.

In 1977 he made the next step in the classic progression to the top, moving into Formula Two, alongside fellow countryman and future Grand Prix rival René Arnoux in the Martini team. Having won the important Monaco Formula Three race, he concentrated on the senior formula. He scored his first win at Estoril, was in the points several times and finished the season with third place in the European Championship – behind Arnoux and Eddie Cheever.

In 1978 he arrived at the top, joining Tyrrell for a full Grand Prix season and taking a famous victory for Renault at Le Mans, shared with the veteran Jean-Pierre Jaussaud.

In Formula One his ability was immediately apparent and, in spite of Tyrrell no longer being right at the top, Didier finished fifteenth in the World Championship, thanks to fifth places in Monaco and Germany and sixth in Brazil, South Africa and Belgium. He also had a number of accidents, in Sweden, Austria, Holland and Italy, but he stayed with Tyrrell for 1979.

To some extent it was a frustrating season; the blue cars were never quite able to challenge for the lead but Pironi scored two second places, in Belgium and at Watkins Glen, fourth in Brazil, fifth in Canada and sixth in Spain, to improve to tenth place in the championship. Again he suffered a run of accidents, some caused by mechanical failure, and he had a miraculous escape from a very big accident at Dijon. He was also seen by television viewers around the world, his Tyrrell climbing over Niki Lauda's Brabham at Monaco, narrowly avoiding decapitating Lauda and crashing into retirement after a headstrong, and frankly impossible, overtaking manoeuvre. Throughout it all Pironi remained absolutely impassive, although, surprisingly enough, his seemingly dour exterior actually belies a very keen sense of humour.

For 1980, Pironi joined Jacques Laffite in the Ligier team and he was immediately among the front runners with a competitive car. His debut for Ligier lasted only one lap before retirement in Argentina but he finished fourth in Brazil, third at Kyalami and sixth at Long Beach before scoring a commanding, flag-to-flag win in the opening European round, in Belgium.

Thereafter he was always among the leaders, if not always around at the end. He crashed out of a runaway lead at Monaco, lost a wheel while leading in Spain and then finished second in France, to eventual champion, Alan Jones. A puncture cost him the lead at Brands Hatch but he stormed back into the points following a pit stop, though only for another puncture to end an inspired performance. He had mechanical failures in Germany and Austria, fell foul of someone else's accident at Zandvoort and took sixth place in Italy. In Canada he actually won, on the road, but a penalty for a jumped start dropped him officially to third place. He was third again at Watkins Glen, his last race before he joined Gilles Villeneuve at Ferrari – and an uncertain future in 1981 as a split between the organisers and the constructors threatened the championship for which Pironi seemed an ever more serious contender.   BL

BRIAN REDMAN (b.1937)
Great Britain

One of the world's top racing drivers, Lancastrian Brian Redman has always raced for sport and enjoyment rather than sheer hard cash. In later years he turned down offers of places in top Grand Prix teams – Lotus, BRM, Tyrrell, Ferrari and others – as he prefers sports car and Formula 5000 racing. He has raced since 1959 and suffered two bad crashes, while at the end of 1970 he also temporarily 'retired' from racing.

Brian Herman Thomas Redman was born in Colne, Lancashire, on 9 March 1937. His family ran a chain of grocery stores and following a three-year course in hotel catering he joined the business. Later he took over his late grandfather's mop manufacturing business, but at the same time his interest in motor cars was developing. He competed in auto-tests with a Ford V8-engined Grenfell Special and in 1959 competed in races, hill-climbs and sprints in his road car which was a Shorrocks-supercharged Morris Minor Traveller estate car.

Brian's early years in motor sport were very much at the club level. Races wore out tyres so Brian concentrated on sprints and hill climbs, while in the winters of 1962-63 and 1963-64 he competed in motor cycle scrambles. His cars included Minis, a Jaguar XK120 and a Morgan Plus 4. By now he had sold the mop business and after a spell managing a garage joined his family's business as a bakery manager.

Redman's big break came in 1965. Local garage owner Gordon Brown asked Brian to drive his Jaguar XK120 in a sprint at Woodvale, near Southport, on Easter Sunday. Brown arranged for Redman to have a test drive at Oulton Park in Charles Bridges's lightweight Jaguar E-type. Bridges, too, was impressed with Redman's ability and entered him for the following Saturday's race meeting at the circuit. Redman won convincingly. Subsequently Brian and the E-type proved almost unbeatable, scoring 16 wins from 17 starts.

Bridges wanted to break into international racing in 1966 and asked Redman to choose a car. He selected a Lola T70 sports car powered by a 450 bhp 6-litre Chevrolet engine. Racing against drivers of the calibre of John Surtees, Bruce McLaren, Chris Amon and Denny Hulme, Redman mastered the powerful Lola and gained much success. He was also invited to drive other people's cars, sharing Peter Sutcliffe's Ford GT40 in the Spa 1000-km. They were fourth. At the end of the year Redman received a coveted Grovewood Award.

Charles Bridges's brother David backed Redman in 1967, providing Formula Two machinery. He was sixth at Jarama and fifth at Vallelunga. At the end of the year he co-drove a Ferrari 250LM with Dickie Attwood in the Paris 1000-km and took sixth place. He also impressed John Wyer, boss of the JW team of Gulf Mirages, and was invited to share a Ford GT40-based Mirage M1/570 with Jacky Ickx in the Kyalami 9-hours in November. They won and Redman gained a contract to drive for the JW team in 1968. Cooper also asked Redman to drive for them in Formula One.

The BRM-engined Cooper T86B was not a strong contender, but it was reliable and Brian finished third in the Spanish Grand Prix. The JW-entered Ford GT40s were successful, however, in World Championship sports car races, Redman co-driving with Ickx to win the BOAC 500 at Brands Hatch and the Spa 1000-km. He was offered a trial race in the Ferrari Formula Two team at Nürburgring, coming away with a new lap record and the offer of a permanent contract. Redman declined.

In June, Brian suffered a major setback. During the Belgian Grand Prix his Cooper broke its front suspension at high speed, was launched over a concrete barrier and overturned, crashing into a parked car. Brian's life was saved by his safety harness, but his right forearm was broken. Redman was out of racing for months and receiving no income, but Chevron came to his rescue and at the end of the year he raced in some sports car events.

For 1969, Brian was offered a works drive for Porsche. As supporting driver to Jo Siffert in one of the very successful Porsche 908/02s he won the BOAC 500, the Monza 1000-km, the Spa 1000-km, the Nürburgring 1000-km and the Watkins Glen 6-hours. He also raced Sid Taylor's Lola Mk 3B in some non-championship sports car events and gave the prototype Chevron B16-Ford a winning debut in the Nürburgring 500-km. In 1970, when the works Porsche team was run by JW Automotive Engineering, Redman partnered Siffert to win the Spa 1000-km and Österreichring 1000-km in one of the powerful 5-litre Porsche 917Ks. Driving a lightweight 3-litre Porsche 908/03 Spyder they also won the Targa Florio, while Brian won the Euro-

pean 2-litre Sports Car Championship for Chevron after a wheel-to-wheel battle with Jo Bonnier's Lola in the final round at Francorchamps. Following Johnny Servoz-Gavin's retirement from racing, Brian was offered the number two drive to Jackie Stewart in the Tyrrell team in June. He declined.

At the end of the 1970 season, Redman decided to retire from racing for family reasons. He emigrated to South Africa with his wife Marion and two children, James and Charlotte. He had been offered· a job at the main Volkswagen agency in Johannesburg, and took a Formula Two-type Chevron B17-Ford with him to compete in local races 'for fun'. But he disliked the work and decided to return to Europe again in 1971, having first finished a creditable seventh in the South African Grand Prix in a works Surtees TS7-Ford. Redman planned a season in Formula 5000, plumping for Sid Taylor's McLaren M18A-Chevrolet. It was a difficult car to handle, however, and apart from two hard-fought wins at Brand Hatch gave disappointing results. The season was also punctuated by a nasty accident when, driving for Porsche in the Targa Florio, his car inexplicably crashed and caught fire. Redman suffered burns on his neck, face and legs.

At the end of the year he raced Sid Taylor's BRM P164-Chevrolet sports car at Imola in Italy and won very convincingly in the wet. This performance earned Redman a place in the Ferrari sports car team in 1972. He won the Spa 1000-km for the fourth time in his career, sharing a·Ferrari 312P-72 with Arturo Merzario, and, driving with Jacky Ickx, he won the Österreichring 1000-km. It was a very busy season for Redman. He raced a McLaren M10B and a Chevron B24 for Sid Taylor in both European and American Formula 5000 races, while he had occasional Formula One outings with McLaren and BRM. Driving a McLaren M19A-Ford, he was second to Emerson Fittipaldi in the Rothmans 50,000 at Brands Hatch.

In 1973, Redman decided to limit his programme. He continued to drive Ferrari sports cars, winning the Monza 1000-km and Nürburgring 1000-km, and raced a works-backed Lola T330 for Jim Hall and Carl Haas in the United States Formula 5000 series, finishing a close second to Jody Scheckter. For 1974, it was almost the same recipe. After 'warming-up' in Europe with two Formula 5000 victories at Oulton Park and Silverstone, he went to

America and this time won the US Formula 5000 championship after a fierce duel with Mario Andretti. He almost came back into Formula One full-time, signing a lucrative contract with Shadow, but after three races he decided to leave. Formula One racing, he said, was 'too professional' and 'too serious'. Instead, Redman carried on in the less hectic atmosphere of US Formula 5000 where he continued to be unbeatable. He took the championship again in both 1975 and 1976, with the Carl Haas/Jim Hall Lola, to complete a popular hat-trick. He also raced saloon cars, for BMW, in America, and shared the winning car at Sebring in 1975. His 1976 F5000 championship was gained with three wins from seven starts in the Haas/Hall Lola T332C. Brian also raced a 2-litre Chevron in the New Zealand rounds of the Tasman championship.

In 1977, US Formula 5000 cars sprouted sports car bodywork to re-emerge in the reborn Can-Am series. Redman was to campaign a new Lola T333CS for Haas/Hall but practising for the first event, at St Jovite in June, the big car took off over a hump, flipped over backwards at very high speed and was destroyed. Redman was lucky to survive at all; critical injuries, including a broken neck, put him out of racing for the foreseeable future and while convalescing in Britain he announced his retirement.

At Sebring in March 1978, Redman did the seemingly impossible – coming out of retirement after his St Jovite accident to win the 12-hour sports car classic in a Porsche. In 1979 Brian had some success in sports cars and in the 2-litre division of the Can-Am championship for Tony Cicale. In 1980, returning to California as a 'non-driving' employee of Carl Haas, he professed himself ready to limit his activities to long-distance racing. Retirement was proving a slow process for Redman.

CLAY REGAZZONI (b.1939)
Switzerland

Clay Regazzoni had a reputation of being a 'charger' and a 'crasher', yet his consistency in 1974 almost won him the World Championship.

The son of a coachbuilder, Gianclaudio Giuseppe 'Clay' Regazzoni was born in Lugano – in the Italian-speaking canton of Ticino – in Switzerland on 5 September 1939. He left school at 18 to join his father's business and became a follower of motor racing. In

1963, he bought an Austin-Healey Sprite and competed in Swiss hill-climbs (racing, as such, had been banned in Switzerland since 1955) and the following year contested assorted events with a 1-litre Mini.

Encouraged by his friend, Swiss racing driver Silvio Moser, Regazzoni decided to go racing in 1965. He qualified for a licence at a Swiss-run racing drivers' course at Montlhéry, France, and purchased a Formula Three de Tomaso-Ford, a most unreliable machine. This was later changed for one of Moser's Brabhams, but the car was destroyed at Monza in September 1966 after a collision with another competitor. Regazzoni escaped with six stitches.

In 1967 Regazzoni received an invitation to join the Tecno Formula Three team, proving a forceful exponent. He was instrumental in giving the Swiss team victory in the European Formula Two Team Trophy at Hockenheim, knocking two rivals off the track in the closing minutes! Early in 1968 he gave up Formula Three following an alarming accident at Monaco. His Tecno spun and crashed into the guard-rail which, not being secured properly, was forced up over the car. It sliced down again between Clay's helmet and the roll-over bar. The Formula Two Tecno was beset with handling and braking problems, Regazzoni's best placing during the year being a third at Crystal Palace. He was, however, involved in a controversial accident with Chris Lambert at Zandvoort: the two collided and Lambert was killed as his car hurtled off course. Regazzoni spun to a halt, uninjured.

For 1969, Regazzoni secured a contract to drive in the Ferrari Formula Two team but, sadly, the Dino 166s were outclassed that season and when they were withdrawn in mid-season Clay returned to Tecno. In early 1970, it was announced that Regazzoni had been offered a Formula One contract by Ferrari. In June he was asked to compete in the Dutch Grand Prix and drove well to finish fourth. He was fourth again in the British Grand Prix, was a contender for the lead in Germany until his engine seized and then was a close second to team leader Jacky Ickx in Austria. The Italian Grand Prix at Monza was overshadowed by Jochen Rindt's fatal accident in practice, but Regazzoni drove one of his greatest races ever to fight clear of a five-car group fighting for the lead to win by nearly six seconds. The crowd was almost delirious with delight as Regazzoni collected his winner's laurels, Clay always being considered an Italian by them! A third in Canada and a second in Mexico followed, giving Regazzoni third place in the World Championship table despite the fact he missed five of the thirteen rounds. Added to this, he won the European Formula Two Trophy. At Hockenheim he was involved in another controversial incident, colliding with Dieter Quester's BMW in a Formula Two event.

The 1971 season began with a testing accident at Kyalami in South Africa when Regazzoni demolished Ferrari's new Formula One 312B-2/71 model, but he more than made amends for this with a runaway victory in the non-championship Race of Champions at Brands Hatch in March. The World Championship series brought disappointment, however, third places in South Africa, Holland and Germany giving a final seventh place in the points table. The Ferrari was beset with handling problems and four times the engine failed. On the sports car front, the new Ferrari 312P-71 showed tremendous promise but never enjoyed a trouble-free race. Regazzoni also crashed in the Spa and Österreichring races.

The next season was almost as bad. In another accident-punctuated season he was seventh in the World Championship table, his best result being second in the German Grand Prix at Nürburgring. Here he was involved in more controversy, tangling with Jackie Stewart's Tyrrell-Ford on the last lap. In the sports car team, sharing a Ferrari 312P-72 with Jacky Ickx, he won the Monza 1000-km. Ironically, Regazzoni's most damaging accident occurred in the paddock at Österreichring when he fell playing football and broke his wrist. As a result he missed the French and British Grands Prix.

In August, Enzo Ferrari announced his retirement from motor racing and released his drivers from their contracts at the end of the year. As often before, it was a false alarm, but Regazzoni accepted an offer to lead the Marlboro-backed BRM team for 1973. Lack of finance and development, however, rendered the BRMs uncompetitive as the season progressed. In the South African Grand Prix Regazzoni was involved in an accident, his car catching fire after colliding with Mike Hailwood's Surtees. Hailwood, in fact, rescued the unconscious Regazzoni from his blazing BRM.

For 1974, it was back to Ferrari and a return to form. Regazzoni proved his season with BRM had not demoralised him by always being in contention with the new Ferrari 312B-3/74. He won the German Grand Prix, leading from start to finish, and was second in the Brazilian, Spanish, Dutch and Canadian Grands Prix, performances which brought him to the grid of the final round equal on points with Emerson Fittipaldi. Shock absorber problems defeated him, however, giving the title to Fittipaldi.

Regazzoni stayed with Ferrari in 1975 and did a fine job in backing up Lauda, who won the championship. Clay finished fifth, having won the Italian Grand Prix and scored several places. He also won the non-championship 'Swiss GP' – held at Dijon – but slipped a little in Spain, where he and Lauda collected each other in the first corner, and at Long Beach, where he was involved in an unseemly baulking match with Emerson Fittipaldi.

At Long Beach in 1976 he scored a brilliant, runaway win. He again gave superb back-up to Lauda – particularly after his accident – and helped Ferrari to another constructor's title.

All was not happy at Ferrari, however, and for 1977 Regazzoni joined Ensign. Although the team showed promise it was a very different proposition to the might of Maranello and Clay scored only five points to finish the season in seventeenth place. Perhaps the highlight of his season was racing at Indianapolis, where he survived a very large practice accident only to retire from the race.

For 1978, he moved to Shadow, starting the season with fifth place in Brazil, failure to qualify in South Africa and a blame-free shunt which eliminated Villeneuve's leading Ferrari at Long Beach. It was not a happy year, with the Shadow team struggling to find form and never succeeding. Four more times during the season Regazzoni failed to qualify. His only points scoring outing after Brazil was in Sweden where he again finished fifth. Try as he might he simply could not get things right.

For 1979, Regazzoni joined Alan Jones in the Williams team, in which his unquenchable enthusiasm for the sport and undeniable ability might be better rewarded, and so it was. With the now ageing FW06 he ran steadily, if unspectacularly, to tenth place in Argentina, fifth in Brazil and ninth in South Africa. His last race with FW06, at Long Beach, ended with engine problems after 48 laps and engine failure also cut short a promising first outing in Spain with FW07 when Regga looked to be heading for his first points of the season.

Another good weekend came to nought after a minor fracas with Ferrari team-mates Scheckter and Villeneuve on the second lap.

In Monte Carlo he was nothing less than inspired, doggedly taking advantage of others' problems and the Williams's obvious speed to claw up from sixteenth on the grid to second place – just 0.44 seconds behind Jody Scheckter in spite of gearbox problems. Another lap and perhaps the smile on Regga's face could have been even broader.

He scored another point for sixth place in France before the great day when he scored a memorable first Grand Prix win for the Williams team in the British Grand Prix at Silverstone. It was his own first win for over three years and the fact that it was inherited as team leader Alan Jones's engine failed detracted nothing from its popularity with the public.

Throughout the season Regazzoni was an ideal number two to Jones. At the next race, Hockenheim, he shadowed Jones's ailing car to a one-two finish. He was fifth in Austria and third in Italy and Canada, to take fifth place in the championship.

The announcement that for 1980 Clay would move from Williams to the struggling Unipart Ensign team came as a surprise to many. It was to be a tragic season. The Ensign proved troublesome in the first three races but was beginning to show promise. At Long Beach Regazzoni was into fourth place (from the back of the grid) when, approaching the hairpin from the fastest part of the circuit, the Ensign's brake pedal snapped. Regazzoni hurtled down the escape road at undiminished speed, glanced off Zunino's already abandoned Brabham and slammed head on into the tyre protected concrete barriers. He was eventually released from the completely destroyed car with badly broken legs and a crushed vertebra. In spite of lengthy surgery he did not regain the use of his legs although there remained a possibility that he eventually might. Ever the true enthusiast and cheerful as always, Regazzoni watched from his wheelchair while he waited.   MK

DARIO RESTA (1882-1924)
Italy

One of the most skilled and versatile racing drivers of his age, Italian-born Dario 'Dolly' Resta was brought to London at the age of two in 1884. Resta went into the motor trade and eventually opened his own business in the West End of London as a naturalised citizen.

He took part in the opening meeting at Brooklands on 6 July 1907, driving a 1906 Grand Prix Mercédès entered by the wealthy F.R. Fry. He was leading the Montagu Cup, the main race of the day, and all set to win when he missed the semaphore signal indicating the final turn into the finishing straight. He went round for another lap, letting Jack Hutton, driving a similar 120 hp Mercédès, through to victory – and a purse of 1400 gold sovereigns.

But at the August Bank Holiday meeting, Resta made no mistake. Driving the same car, he beat Hutton in the prestigious Prix de la France event. In 1908 Resta was back at Brooklands with a Mercédès, and at the second meeting of the season he was involved in a spectacular collision with Frank Newton. Trying to overtake Resta, Newton drove his 90 hp Napier too high on the banked track and the wheels of the two touched at around 110 mph, ripping spokes from the Napier and a hubcap from the Mercédès. Resta was sufficiently distracted for Newton to take the lead and win. His subsequent protest was overruled.

He was still driving well enough to attract the attention of the Austin Motor Company, who invited him to join their team for that year's Grand Prix. Resta's performance in this event is chiefly remembered for the fact that the French threw him in jail for crashing twice in practice, for the Austins were little more than stripped touring cars, and were hopelessly outclassed in the event. Resta was only able to place 19th.

Resta didn't reappear on the racing scene until 1912, when he joined the Sunbeam team for the Coupe de l'Auto, which he led for several laps before being passed by his teammate, Victor Riga, shortly before the finish. Even so, he was second in the Coupe de l'Auto and fourth in the concurrent Grand Prix.

He also appeared at Brooklands that year, both with the Sunbeam and with a 9½-litre Mercédès. But it was as a record-breaker that he made his mark on track history that year, taking world records from 50 to 1000 miles in a 3-litre Sunbeam, and later he used one of the Coupe de l'Auto cars to add further records to his already impressive collection.

In 1913, Resta was in the Sunbeam team for the Grand Prix (in which he finished sixth), drove a 41.9 hp Mercédès at Brooklands, and was one of the team which averaged 90 mph for 1000 miles in a six-cylinder Sunbeam at that track.

Again driving in the Sunbeam team, Resta came fifth in the 1914 French Grand Prix, though in the Isle of Man Tourist Trophy that year, his car failed to last a lap. At Brooklands he drove the fearsome V-12 Sunbeam, which had a 9-litre aero-engine and was capable of lapping the track at speeds approaching 115 mph, with a top speed of over 120 mph.

When war was declared, Resta's lap speed of 113.97 mph at the August Bank Holiday meeting had been the fastest of the season. He left for America in the autumn of 1914 on a protracted business trip, during which the American branch of Peugeot signed him to drive one of the 1913 Grand Prix cars in the principal races of 1915. He won the Grand Prize and the Vanderbilt Cup against stiff opposition from the leading American drivers, then took over a 1914 GP Peugeot which was even faster. With this car he came second in the 1916 Indianapolis 500, as well as taking first places at Chicago and Sheepshead Bay, which took him into second place in the US national championship, earning $37,700 in prize money.

There were greater successes in 1916: first place at Indianapolis and in the Vanderbilt Cup crowned a string of victories which earned him $44,400 in prizes and made him the only foreign driver to become the national champion of the United States of America.

But the racing calendar was greatly curtailed in 1917, when the Americans entered World War I, and Resta gradually became preoccupied with commercial considerations, trying to set up an import business dealing in Sunbeam cars.

He reappeared in racing in America in 1923, in the autumn of which year he returned to Britain and rejoined the Sunbeam team. He won the *voiturette* race at Penya Rhin in Spain driving a Talbot-Darracq, in which he also took third place in the Grand Prix at the same meeting.

He helped with development of a new Sunbeam Grand Prix car for the 1924 season, though in that event the cars were plagued by misfiring and could not display their full performance. However, Louis Coatalen decided to go for records with one of the cars, and it was while Resta was in the middle of a successful record session on 3 September, which included a flying half-mile at 122.7 mph and 5 miles at 114.23 mph, that a tyre burst and the car smashed through a fence and burst into flames, killing Resta instantly.   DBW

CARLOS REUTEMANN (b.1942)
Argentina

Carlos Reutemann is the first major world-class racing driver from Argentina since the days of the legendary five-times World Champion Juan Manuel Fangio. He first made his mark at the top by winning Grands Prix in 1974, taking his works Brabham BT44-Ford to victory in South Africa, Austria, and the United States.

Reutemann learned to drive at the age of seven, in 1949, piloting his father's 1928 Model A Ford round the family farm. Soon he laid out a 'circuit' and taught himself the art of fast driving with any machine he could borrow. He spectated at race meetings and in 1965 met a wealthy local Fiat dealer and talked his way into a test drive at Cordoba. Immediately Reutemann's natural ability was obvious and, although he retired in his first race owing to lack of oil pressure, a month later he won a three-lap, 180-mile road-race.

There was no looking back. 'El Lole', as he is known, won 15 races that season and the following year was invited to drive a single-seater de Tomaso (a car built by an Argentinian in Italy) powered by a 1½-litre Fiat engine for local Formula One events. He also raced a Fiat saloon in the 1600 cc class. Reutemann's performances earned him respect and he won the touring class championship in 1966 and 1967. The latter years also saw him in the Turismo Carretera racing, a strange category comprising very quick, much modified V8 saloons.

At the end of 1968 the Argentinians decided to run a four-race Formula Two championship series and invited a large contingent of European drivers to participate. They also wanted to provide the Europeans with local opposition and invited the Argentinian motoring press to nominate six drivers to take part in a contest to determine the drivers of two Tecno TF68-Fords. Reutemann emerged as one of the – seemingly – lucky men. The Tecnos were not competitive but in the fourth race Carlos arranged to borrow a Brabham BT23C and duly impressed everyone with his performance.

Originally Reutemann was to have ventured to Europe for a full Formula Two season in 1969, but he could not agree terms with his proposed backer and instead ran a BWA-Fiat in Argentinian Formula Two races. He won the championship, with ten wins from twelve starts, and also found success in touring, Turismo Carretera and sports car races.

For 1970 Reutemann came to Europe to drive a new Brabham BT30-Ford Formula Two car, sponsored by YPF (the state petrol company), the Argentine Automobile Club, the Argentine Tourist Office and the Ministry of Sport. The whole deal, which included a second car for ex-motor cyclist Benedicto Caldarella, a lavish transporter, plus workshops in London, was arranged by Hector Staffa of the Argentine Automobile Club who was intent on putting another Argentinian on the international motor racing map.

The season began controversially as Reutemann collided with Jochen Rindt's Lotus 69-Ford at Hockenheim, which caused ill feeling between Reutemann and Rindt. Many good practice performances but few results came the unlucky Reutemann's way that season and he returned to Argentina at the end of the year.

The outlook appeared even bleaker when Reutemann was criticised for racing a 4½-litre Porsche 917K 'too slowly' in the Buenos Aires 1000-km in January 1971. However, Carlos made amends in the non-championship Formula One Argentine Grand Prix when YPF hired an old McLaren M7C-Ford for him to drive. He covered himself with glory by finishing third and as a result sponsorship was secured for another Formula Two season in Europe. This time the team was better prepared and more organised. He won a non-championship race at Hockenheim and, following several good results, was second to Ronnie Peterson in the European Formula Two Trophy. In October he had another Formula One race, driving a Brabham BT33 in the non-championship Brands Hatch race. As a result he was signed to drive for the Brabham Formula One team full-time in 1972.

Reutemann began 1972 on top form. He set pole position time for the Argentine Grand Prix in the 'lobster-claw' Brabham BT34-Ford, sending the local crowd into raptures of delight. In the race, tyre problems dropped him to seventh, but a few weeks later he won the non-championship Brazilian Grand Prix. Then a Formula Two practice accident at Thruxton resulted in a broken ankle and Reutemann, early-season favourite for the European Formula Two Championship, was out of action for several weeks. He wound up fourth in the table, while in Formula One he suffered much bad luck in the Brabham BT37-Ford and only had a fourth place in the Canadian Grand Prix to show for his efforts.

In 1973, with the new Brabham BT42, Reutemann showed he could be a leading contender in Formula One. He was poised to win the Spanish Grand Prix when the engine failed, but finished third in the French and United States Grands Prix and fourth in the Swedish and Austrian to be placed seventh in the World Championship. Driving for Ferrari, he was second in the Vallelunga 6-hours and Monza 1000-km sports car races. For 1974 Reutemann showed tremendous form in Brabham's improved BT44. It was a bitter disappointment when he ran out of fuel within minutes of victory in the Argentine Grand Prix, but he made amends by winning the South African Grand Prix in March. Then, following some disappointing mid-season races, he rounded off a good year with wins in the Austrian and United States Grands Prix and sixth place in the World Championship. He was second in the Imola and Nürburgring 1000-km sports car races for Alfa Romeo.

With his end of season dominance, generous sponsorship from Martini and the Brabham BT44B, Reutemann was widely tipped for the 1975 title. In fact, he finished third, scoring only one win – in Germany. He almost won in Sweden but eventually finished second – as he did in South Africa. Although he finished twelve races from fourteen starts his results were regularly spoiled by tyre troubles.

In 1976 Brabham introduced the Alfa Romeo-engined BT45 and Reutemann simply never liked the car; his best result of a disastrous season was fourth in Spain; he finished only three times from twelve attempts. For the Italian GP he left Brabham, to support the convalescent Niki Lauda at Ferrari. As Lauda recovered from his Nürburgring accident, Carlos sat out the rest of 1976 before replacing Regazzoni as Ferrari's number two driver.

Pre-season testing had suggested that Reutemann might threaten Lauda's supremacy but it was Niki who took the 1977 championship. Carlos won only once – in Brazil. His results lacked consistency and he ended the championship in fourth place. Relationships between himself and Lauda were very strained and Niki left Ferrari for 1978 – ironically, to drive the Brabham-Alfa.

Reutemann started 1978 well; with the latest

Ferrari, on Michelin radial tyres, he comprehensively trounced the opposition in the Brazilian Grand Prix. Yet, at the next race, in South Africa, he was never in contention and ended his drive in the catch fences. Four weeks later, at the US Grand Prix West, he was back in the winner's circle.

At the next street circuit on the calendar, Monaco, Reutemann, after dominating practice, was involved in a first corner barging match and was forced into the pits to change a wheel. He stormed out just ahead of the leaders, almost a lap down. For a while he pulled away but then he was held up in traffic and decided he was not going to regain a full lap, slowing marginally to finish in a safe eighth place.

He finished third in Belgium, behind the Lotuses, and crashed heavily in Spain when a drive shaft broke. The Ferrari and its Michelin tyres proved extraordinarily fickle in Sweden where Carlos could manage no better than tenth, and in France where he was a lowly eighteenth.

He was back on form in Britain, however, pressing hard throughout and taking advantage of an uncharacteristic moment of indecision by Niki Lauda, when lapping Bruno Giacomelli, to inherit the lead a few laps from home. He retired from the German Grand Prix, was black flagged from the Austrian race (for being push-started after a spin) and just conceded sixth place to team-mate Villeneuve after a troubled race in Holland. He was back in the points with third place at Monza and then scored a faultless victory in the United States Grand Prix (East) at Watkins Glen. Third place in Canada took him to third place overall in the championship.

Even though he had demonstrated admirably during 1978 that he was one of the few capable of beating the Lotuses, his relationship with Ferrari had deteriorated dramatically and he went to join Andretti. In front of 80,000 wildly patriotic fans in his native Argentina he was spurred to second place in the season opener, behind Jacques Laffite's Ligier. He scored third and fifth places in the next two races, Brazil and South Africa, retired at Long Beach, then took second in Spain, fourth in Belgium and third at Monaco. They were his last points of the season. Lotus were struggling and Reutemann's relationship with Andretti was increasingly strained.

For 1980, Reutemann again settled for a number two seat, this time to Alan Jones in the

then dominant Williams team. Surprisingly, perhaps, the partnership worked perfectly. While Jones won the world title, Reutemann won the Monaco Grand Prix and demonstrated that he was still an outstanding driver by a remarkable series of point-scoring finishes – second (ahead of Jones) in Germany, Canada and at Watkins Glen (behind Jones), third in Belgium, Great Britain, Austria and Italy, fourth in Holland, fifth in South Africa and sixth in France – contributing to a convincing steamrollering of the constructors' championship for Frank Williams and third place in the drivers' series for himself. He also showed a quite remarkable adaptability, not only enjoying his regular outings in BMW's Procar series but also finishing an amazing third in a Fiat in the South American Codasur round of the World Rally Championship! No doubt Williams was very pleased to sign Carlos again for the 1981 season!   MK

PETER REVSON (1939-1974)
USA
Peter Jeffrey Revson's success in European style racing, set him apart from his fellow Americans before his death in 1974. His family wealth (the Revlon cosmetics empire) and exceptionally handsome appearance made him more than popular journalists could resist. In daily papers all over the world, he was Peter Revson, handsome millionaire racing driver. They made him sound like a playboy from the fifties or a thrill-seeking movie star. Nothing could have been further from the truth. He was a dedicated man who worked hard for his racing experience and who wanted more than anything else to be World Champion Grand Prix driver and to win the famous Indianapolis 500 mile race.

Revson was born on 27 February 1939, in New York. In 1960, after studying mechanical engineering at Cornell University and liberal arts at Columbia, he moved towards a career in market research. He had already started motor racing as a hobby, with Austin-Healey and Morgan sports cars and occasionally with a Formula Junior single-seater. He was second in his first race and won his second. In 1962 he formed the Revson-Mayer Formula Junior team with Teddy Mayer, a friend from Cornell and later Team Manager at McLaren. Encouraged by some reasonable results with his Cooper, Revson gave up his job to become a full-time racing driver.

Like many others whose families are known to be wealthy, Revson was handicapped by people presuming that he had unlimited funds to promote his racing career. In fact he had virtually only what he had saved. His first serious step in racing was on the well trodden path to Europe. He arrived in 1963, armed himself with a Formula Junior Cooper and a very secondhand van, then set off to the Continent for the gipsy-like travel–race, travel–race existence, that was just financially possible in those days. He won one event and returned again in 1964 to race a Lotus 24 in Formula One for the Parnell team. Naturally he was often refused entries, so he tried lower formulae again in 1965. This time he won the prestigious Formula Three race at Monaco and drove several Formula Two races in the Ron Harris team when Jim Clark was unavailable. He drove a Ford GT40 in World Championship sports car races the following year then returned to America to race sedans and various Can-Am cars. Not even the death of his brother Doug in a race in Denmark sapped Revson's determination to succeed, though the tragedy did nothing to improve the strained relationship he had with his family who bitterly opposed his racing career. Certainly they made no financial contribution to something they so strongly disapproved of.

As a saloon driver Revson had at least become a paid professional, his big break coming in 1969. Goodyear arranged for him to drive the second Brabham at Indianapolis where he finished fifth. Carl Haas invited him to drive his Can-Am Lola and Revson became the new American road-race hero. In 1970 he drove for McLaren in their first Indianapolis car though it failed to finish. Undoubtedly his long-standing friendship with McLaren director Teddy Mayer helped him get the job. But Mayer is a businessman and equally logically Revson would not have been offered the opportunity unless he had been equal to the task. Then McLaren himself was killed and Revson took over his Can-Am car a year later. Now with a competitive mount, he proved his ability, beating Denny Hulme for the 1971 title. It became almost a formality then, that he should be invited to partner Hulme in the Yardley McLaren Grand Prix team in 1972 and '73.

Revson returned to Europe and he came back at the top. He had talent but it took years of dedication and practice to prove it. And as one man will have a reputation as the best rain driver, another as a Nürburgring specialist, un-

questionably Revson could have claimed to have been the driver who achieved most success on European road circuits *and* American super-speedways. It was during this period that he became famous for his relationship with Marjie Wallace, the 1973 Miss World.

In 1972, as well as filling in for ulcer-stricken Jackie Stewart in the Can-Am McLaren, Peter scored third places in the South African, British and Austrian Grands Prix, fourth in Italy and fifth in Spain before crowning his season with second place in the Canadian Grand Prix. He was fifth in the World Championship. 1973 was even better and he won two Grands Prix, in Britain and Canada; the British Grand Prix was restarted after Revson's McLaren team-mate Jody Scheckter triggered the infamous first lap accident, and the Canadian Grand Prix was soured by controversial use of the pace-car after an accident, but Revson had proved that he was a winner. He also scored second in South Africa, third in Italy, fourth in Spain and Holland and fifth in Monaco and Watkins Glen, to finish fifth in the championship once again.

His surprise move to the UOP Shadow team for 1974 heralded a tragically short association. From the second row of the grid he was eliminated in a first lap collision with new team-mate Jean-Pierre Jarier in the Argentine Grand Prix. He was out after just eleven laps of the Brazilian Grand Prix, and then, in unofficial practice for the South African Grand Prix, at Kyalami, his Shadow inexplicably turned sharply into the barriers at high speed. Revson was killed instantly and the sport mourned the loss of a highly respected, much loved and enormously talented friend. As Teddy Mayer once reflected, 'It's stupid really. The man gained more publicity over his romance with Marjie Wallace, the reigning Miss World, than he ever did for all his racing achievements.' And that perhaps is a comment on what a handicap Peter Revson's name and family background were to him.   PGH

JOCHEN RINDT (1942-1970)
Austria

Jochen Rindt was the 1970 World Champion racing driver, but he never lived to receive the acclaim. With an overall 20-point lead in the series, he was killed practising for the Italian Grand Prix at Monza. No one subsequently beat his score and Rindt became the first and only driver to be awarded the championship posthumously. Although acknowledged as one of the very best drivers in the world he was always unlucky. It took him five seasons in Grand Prix racing to win a World Championship race. That was at the end of 1969. The very next year he won five Grands Prix – and was killed. Rindt had more success in Formula Two than in Formula One, winning countless races from 1964 onwards and beating drivers of the calibre of Jack Brabham, Jim Clark, Graham Hill and Jackie Stewart.

Karl Jochen Rindt was born in Mainz-am-Rhein, Germany, on 18 April 1942. His father was a wealthy spice-mill owner and his mother, from Austria, once studied law. Both were killed during a bombing raid on Hamburg in 1943, so Jochen was raised by his maternal grandparents in Graz, Austria. He considered himself to be Austrian, not German. Rindt was a rebellious schoolboy and after rows with his teachers he was banished to England in the summer of 1959 to learn the language. In fact, he spent most of his time sailing at Chichester; he also witnessed his first motor race meeting at nearby Goodwood.

Rindt learned to drive while under age – he drove a Volkswagen to school – and for his 18th birthday his grandfather bought him a modified Simca Montlhéry. The car was entered in rallies and hill-climbs, giving Jochen the taste for something faster. Rindt's grandfather had died, but his grandmother was talked into buying a race-prepared Alfa Romeo Giulietta TI from the local dealer in Graz, who also agreed to race-prepare it for Jochen if he did well. He did, winning his first major race at Aspern, near Vienna, in 1962, ahead of Jaguar 3.8s. It was the first of eight major race and hill-climb wins that season.

In 1963 Rindt, aged 21, inherited some money and bought a year-old Formula Junior Cooper T59-Ford from top Austrian driver Kurt Bardi-Barry. First time out at Vallelunga in Italy, Rindt set best practice time but the starter jammed on the grid. At Cesenatico he won, beating Italy's top drivers and Bardi-Barry, who raced a new Cooper. With Bardi-Barry's mechanics also looking after Jochen's car, the standard of preparation declined as the season wore on, but Rindt won major placings in events all over Europe, including two behind the Iron Curtain. His reputation spread: his exuberant 'sideways' style became his trade mark.

For 1964 Rindt sacrificed everything to get into Formula Two and compete against the world's top drivers. He sold the spice mill he had inherited, his Cooper and his road car and purchased a new Brabham BT10 with a Cosworth SCA engine. Support was found from Ford of Austria (who planned to back Bardi-Barry until his death in a road accident) and later from BP, who supported all of Rindt's own team efforts in seasons to come. Following a good fourth at Nürburgring, Rindt arrived in Britain for the Whitsun weekend races at Mallory Park and Crystal Palace. At Mallory Park he raised eyebrows by setting pole position, but he stalled on the grid and was away last. Driving superbly, he carved his way back to third place behind works Lotus drivers Jim Clark and Peter Arundell. At Crystal Palace the following day he won after a race-long duel with Graham Hill. Jochen Rindt had arrived.

Subsequent results were not as encouraging, but Rindt was invited to drive Rob Walker's Formula One Brabham BT11-BRM in his home Austrian Grand Prix (he retired with steering problems) and also had an offer from Ferrari to race sports cars, but he had to refuse owing to fuel contract difficulties. Rindt signed to drive for Cooper in 1965 Formula One races, but apart from a fourth in the German Grand Prix and a sixth in the United States Grand Prix he had nothing to show in the way of results.

In Formula Two, however, as a member of the Winkelmann Brabham BT16-Cosworth team Rindt scooped a win at Reims and thirds at Pau and Vallelunga, while teamed with Masten Gregory in a Ferrari 250LM entered by the North American Racing Team he also won at Le Mans.

Rindt remained with Cooper in Formula One for two more seasons, but the 3-litre Maserati-engined Cooper T81 of 1966 was both underpowered and overweight. Apart from providing a spirited challenge to John Surtees's Ferrari 312/66 in the soaking wet 1966 Belgian Grand Prix at Francorchamps (including a 180 mph spin!) Rindt was not the serious challenger for the World Championship he should have been. He was third in the 1966 table thanks to a second in Belgium, a third in Germany, fourth in France and Italy and a fifth in Britain. The following year, however, with the advent of the Ford-engined Lotus 49s, the Cooper-Maseratis were even more outclassed, despite the lighter T86 chassis introduced at the time of the British Grand Prix. Rindt was not on very good terms with

Cooper by the end of a dismal season which netted but two fourths in the Belgian and Italian Grands Prix. In Formula Two, however, Rindt again showed he was among the world's top drivers. In 1966 his Winkelmann Brabham BT18-Cosworth netted him wins at Nürburgring and Brands Hatch when the Honda-powered works Brabhams were obviously superior, but with the coming of the 1600 cc Formula Two in 1967 Rindt was on equal terms with his rivals.

Repco-engined Brabhams won the World Championship in 1966 and 1967 so when Jack Brabham invited Rindt to join the team in 1968 to drive the more powerful Brabham BT26 he accepted. He was third in the season-opener, the South African Grand Prix, with a '67 model Brabham BT24-Repco, but the new car lacked reliability and despite much speed shown in practice his only other result of the year was a third in the foggy German Grand Prix. Again he excelled in Formula Two with Winkelmann's Brabham BT23C-Ford, winning at Thruxton, Zolder, Crystal Palace, Hockenheim, Tulln-Langenlebarn and Enna.

Behind the scenes Rindt became involved in a new Formula One project for 1969. He had raced successfully in Formula Two for Roy Winkelmann's team since 1965 and it was planned to construct a Formula One car designed by Robin Herd and sponsored by Firestone and BP. However, BP dropped out, effectively killing the idea, and Rindt accepted an offer to join Graham Hill, the 1968 World Champion, in the Lotus team instead. With a Ford engine behind him and a competitive chassis Rindt *should* have been a contender for the World Championship. In South Africa his fuel pump failed when he was well-placed; in Spain he led from pole position until the outsize rear wing broke and he crashed heavily, suffering injuries which put him out of the Monaco race; in Holland Rindt refused to drive the new four-wheel-drive Lotus 63-Ford, preferring the conventional 49B with which he led until a drive-shaft broke; in France he was ill; in Britain he battled with Stewart for the lead until a rear wing end-plate fouled a tyre and later, when he was second, the car ran out of fuel; in Germany ignition trouble intervened; in Italy Rindt was second, narrowly beaten to the line by Stewart; in Canada tyre problems dropped him to third; in America – Rindt finally won. But it seemed too late to resolve the open feuding between the Austrian and Colin Chapman of Lotus.

Rindt once more drove in Formula Two for Winkelmann, this time with semi-works Lotus 59B-Fords, and had won at Thruxton, Pau, Zolder and Tulln-Langenlebarn. Alan Rees, the team manager, became a founder of March Engineering who planned to run a Formula One team in 1970. March wanted Rindt, but Jochen declined their offer, hoping instead to lure March's designer, Robin Herd away to build a car which Rindt would run himself. Herd refused and Rindt instead agreed to re-join the Brabham team, which was once more competitive with the adoption of Ford engines.

Money provided the salve for Rindt's relationship with Chapman in the end. Lotus, with the promise of an exciting new car on the stocks, topped Brabham's offer and Rindt agreed to remain with the team which had given him so many frustrations the previous year. Rindt was now a big businessman. He had forsaken Austria to live in Switzerland with his wife Nina, daughter of Finnish racing driver Curt Lincoln, and their baby daughter Natasha. Their house, formerly owned by Swedish boxing star Ingemar Johansson, was near that of Jackie Stewart, Rindt's great friend as well as rival. A new £80,000 house was also being built for the Rindts. Among Rindt's business ventures was the organisation of successful racing-car shows in five countries, an Austrian television show and financial involvement in the Austrian Grand Prix.

For once it seemed Rindt had made the right decision. At first the old problems remained as the new Lotus 72 was uncompetitive on its first outings. Rindt reverted to an old Lotus 49C-Ford for the Monaco Grand Prix, but driving brilliantly (and thanks to a last corner indiscretion by Jack Brabham) he came through to win. The Lotus 72, re-engineered, was back in time for the Dutch Grand Prix and Jochen led almost from the start to the finish. He won in France, then in Britain and Germany to go to his 'home' Austrian Grand Prix on the crest of a wave. Fans wearing 'Jochen Rindt Fan Club' tee-shirts mobbed him. This time his engine failed. In Formula Two, running his own team of Lotus 69-Fords, managed by Bernie Ecclestone, Rindt was also successful. He won four races and finished second in two others. Many people considered 28-year-old Rindt to be the world's best driver.

Jochen Rindt went to Monza for the Italian Grand Prix determined to clinch the World Championship there and then. He had a theory that stripped of its aerodynamic appendages his Lotus 72 would offer less wind resistance and attain a higher top speed for the ultra-fast track. He went out to practise with the car geared to achieve over 200 mph, but it went out of control at the Parabolica, a fast right-hand corner at the end of the long back straight. The Lotus veered left and struck the guard-rail at well in excess of 100 mph. The front of the car was torn off in the impact and Rindt, who did not wear crutch straps, was thrown forward in what remained of the car and suffered severe injuries from which he died shortly afterwards. The cause of the accident was never explained. Theories suggested either a front brake-shaft or that the Lotus was simply unstable without its aerodynamic aids. MK

PEDRO RODRIGUEZ (1940-1971)
RICARDO RODRIGUEZ
(1942-1962)
Mexico

The handsome Rodriguez brothers, Ricardo and Pedro, were the 'boy wonders' of motor racing. Encouraged by their rich father, they were winning motor races when their contemporaries were still worrying about school examinations. Both became national heroes in Mexico. Both were killed in horrific racing accidents, the hot-headed Ricardo at the age of 20 and Pedro, who had matured into a top-flight Formula One and sports-car driver, when he was 31.

Pedro Rodriguez was born on 18 January 1940, in Mexico City. Ricardo Valentine Rodriguez was two years younger, born on 14 February 1942. Pedro began racing bicycles at the age of eight. By 1950 he was class-winner in the Mexican championships and had already begun motor-cycle racing with a 125 cc Adler, becoming national champion in 1953 and 1954. In 1952 he had a sortie on four wheels, driving a Ford in a rally with no success, but in 1955, aged 15, he started racing full-time. In local events he raced a Jaguar XK 120 and a Porsche 1600 Super. Later in the year, however, he was sent to a military academy in the United States as his father considered he needed 'building up' after a bout of malaria. This move was not popular with Pedro as it put Ricardo back into the limelight.

Ricardo Rodriguez seemed to receive more enthusiastic backing from his father than his elder brother. At the time he was also considered to be the better of the two, but subsequent events were to suggest otherwise. Like Pedro, he had started on bicycles and motor-cycles. He was a national bicycle champion at 10 and motor-cycle champion at 13. His motor racing debut came in an old Fiat Topolino which in standard form gained several successes in the 750 cc class. Later he graduated via an Opel saloon and a 1-litre OSCA sports car to a 1½-litre Porsche RS Spyder. Ricardo made his American debut at the inaugural Riverside meeting in October 1957. Driving coolly and neatly, he won, beating top American Porsche drivers. Both Pedro (who had been racing a Chevrolet Corvette in Mexico) and Ricardo appeared in the Nassau Speed Week at the end of the year. Pedro's performance in a 2-litre Ferrari 500 TR drew adverse comment: he was wild and caused a pile-up. Ricardo was as smooth as ever in the Porsche, once more trouncing America's best.

Don Pedro Rodriguez spent a fortune on his boys' motor-racing exploits, but it paid off. They entered their 2-litre Ferrari in the Le Mans 24-hours, but Ricardo was not permitted to participate as, at 16, he was considered too young. Pedro, now 18, sought José Behra as substitute co-driver but a burst water hose put them out. Later in the Reims 12-hours for GT cars Pedro was second in class and eighth overall driving a Porsche Carrera with Behra. Pedro was second in the end-of-season Nassau Trophy driving a 3-litre Ferrari 250TR, while Ricardo retired his Porsche after having led the 1½-litre class. Both brothers also excelled in supporting races during the traditional Speed Week in the Bahamas.

It was decided to explore Europe further in 1959. Pedro, at the Nürburgring 1000-km to spectate, was co-opted into an experimental Porsche 1600 Super with American Leo Levine and finished 13th overall and second in class. Next, Ricardo and Pedro teamed-up for Le Mans in a 750 cc OSCA but retired early. The 1960 season saw them more in contention. Pedro opened the season well by taking his Ferrari 250TR to second place behind Stirling Moss's Maserati T61 in Cuba's Liberty Grand Prix. Later, driving a 2-litre Ferrari Dino 196S, the pair were sidelined in the Sebring 12-hours owing to clutch trouble, but survived to finish seventh in the Targa Florio despite several off-road excursions. They retired once more at Nürburgring, but in the Le Mans 24-hours they were split. Pedro was an early retirement, but Ricardo finished a strong second in the North American Racing Team-entered Ferrari 250 TR shared with Belgian André Pilette. Successes followed for both in the Bahamas.

Successes also followed into 1961, when both added single-seater racing to their repertoire by competing in Formula Junior. They led the Sebring 12-hours for a while, but had to be satisfied with a third after electrical problems afflicted their 3-litre Ferrari 250TR. They failed to survive the Targa Florio and Nürburgring 1000-km, but in the Le Mans 24-hours they battled impressively with the works Ferraris until their engine failed with only two hours to go. Enzo Ferrari invited them to race works cars in 1962, including Formula One.

This was the opening Ricardo had been looking for and he accepted, fully expecting to be World Champion in 1962. Pedro, with a motor business in Mexico City to run, declined.

The Ferrari Dino 156 which was the World Championship-winning car of 1961, was outclassed in 1962. Ricardo crashed in Holland (a race in which he made himself unpopular by colliding with Jack Brabham), did not race in Monaco, was fourth in Belgium after a hectic dice with team-mate Phil Hill, missed France and Britain owing to an Italian metalworkers' strike, was a good sixth in Germany despite the handicap of an old engine and retired in Italy. Ferrari then announced no cars would go to the season-closing United States and Mexican Grands Prix. In sports-car racing Ricardo was a member of the trio who shared the Targa Florio-winning Ferrari 246SP and he was second in the Daytona Continental, co-driving with Phil Hill. Pedro retired at Sebring, Nürburgring and Le Mans, but won a race at Bridgehampton in the United States with a 4-litre Ferrari 330TR/LM. In October the brothers co-drove a Ferrari 250 GTO to win the Paris 1000-km for the second successive year.

Both brothers entered the Mexican Grand Prix, the first Formula One race in that country. Ricardo, in the absence of Ferrari, agreed to drive Rob Walker's Lotus 24-Climax. He was very quick in practice, but then lost control on the banked corner before the pits and crashed heavily. He was thrown out of the car and died of multiple injuries. Reports varied as to the cause of the accident. Some blamed Rodriguez's excessive speed, saying that after his bad season with Ferrari he wanted to prove himself in his home country. Others said the car's rear suspension broke. Pedro immediately withdrew from the race and is reported to

have stated he would retire from racing.

Ricardo was only 20 when he died, an age at which most drivers are beginning their careers. Mexico mourned him, and before the race the President of Mexico read a eulogy for Ricardo.

Pedro returned to the tracks early in 1963, winning the Daytona Continental in February in a Ferrari 250 GTO of the North American Racing Team. He was third in the Sebring 12-hours in a 4-litre Ferrari 330TR/LM, co-driving with Graham Hill, did not qualify the Aston Martin-engined Cooper T54 in the Indianapolis 500 and had his first taste of Formula One at the end of the season. Lotus offered him a works car for the United States and Mexican Grands Prix, but he retired in each race. The following year he won the Daytona Continental for the second year running, also the sports-car Canadian Grand Prix, while he was second in the Paris 1000-km and third in the Bahamas Tourist Trophy. In a Ferrari 156 he finished sixth in the Mexican Grand Prix.

Three more Formula One drives came Rodriguez's way in 1965. He was fourth in a Lotus 33-Climax in the Daily Express Silvertone Trophy, and with a Ferrari 1512 was fifth and seventh respectively in the United States and Mexican Grands Prix. He won the Reims 12-hours, co-driving a Ferrari 375P with Frenchman Jean Guichet, and was also third in the Canadian Grand Prix for sports cars. Results were poor in 1966, but Pedro's performance had been impressive. Deputising for the injured Jim Clark in the French Grand Prix he ran fourth until an oil pipe broke on his Lotus 33-Climax, while in the Mexican Grand Prix the transmission failed when he was in third position. Again standing-in for Clark, he finished third in the Rouen Formula Two race.

This led him to an invitation to join the Cooper Formula One team for the South African Grand Prix in January 1967. Pedro drove sensibly and came through to win in the heavy, underpowered, Maserati-engined Cooper T81. He signed a contract to drive for Cooper for the remainder of the year, finishing fifth at Monaco (a circuit he disliked), sixth in France, fifth in Britain, eighth in Germany and sixth in Mexico. He crashed his Protos-Ford in the Enna Formula Two race, sustaining leg injuries which caused him to miss three Grands Prix.

For 1968 Rodriguez switched to BRM, a move which upset Cooper as he had a contract to drive with them. Pedro 'warmed-up' in the Tasman Cup series and returned to Europe to take a superb second place in the Brands Hatch Race of Champions after having been delayed at the start. He crashed in Spain when he hit oil and at Monaco when the brakes failed. He almost won the Belgian Grand Prix, but his BRM P133 spluttered short of fuel on the last lap and he had to be content with second. He was third in Holland, sixth in Germany, third in Canada and fourth in Mexico, but highlight of the season was undoubtedly his victory in the Le Mans 24-hours. Driving a JW-entered Ford GT40 with Belgium's Lucien Bianchi, Pedro won the race at his eleventh attempt.

Complicated team politics caused Rodriguez to be dropped from the 1968 works BRM team, although he raced a privately entered BRM P133 for Tim Parnell. Hopelessly underpowered, it was eventually withdrawn, but he subsequently raced in four Grands Prix for Ferrari.

It was back to BRM in 1970. More powerful V12 engines and the new P153 chassis combined to make Pedro Rodriguez a truly competitive contender in Formula One for the first time. Highlight of the year was certainly his victory in the Belgian Grand Prix at Francorchamps when he held off a determined attack from Chris Amon (March 701B-Ford). He also briefly led the Italian Grand Prix until his BRM failed. As a member of the JW-Gulf Porsche 917K sports-car team, Pedro enjoyed his most successful season ever in long-distance racing. After driving for 16 of the 24 hours, he won at Daytona with Finn Leo Kinnunen. In pouring rain he won the BOAC 1000-km at Brands Hatch by five laps. He also won at Monza and Watkins Glen, was fourth at Sebring and second in the Targa Florio where he handled a lightweight 3-litre Porsche 908/03. He retired in the Spa 1000-km but had the consolation of a new lap record at an astonishing 160.53 mph.

In 1971 he won the non-championship Rothmans Formula One race at Oulton Park in the new BRM P160, finished fourth in the Spanish Grand Prix and duelled with Jacky Ickx's Ferrari for the lead in the Dutch Grand Prix in treacherous conditions; a slightly offsong engine lost him the battle, but he was a safe second, and only 8 seconds behind Ickx. Once more he excelled in long-distance sports-car races, taking his JW-Gulf Porsche 917K to wins at Daytona, Monza and Francorchamps (with Jackie Oliver), and Österreichring (with

Dickie Attwood). He was also second at Buenos Aires and Nürburgring and fourth at Sebring.

In July 1971 Pedro Rodriguez drove a 5-litre Ferrari 512M in a minor sports-car race at Norisring in West Germany. On the 12th lap, while leading, Rodriguez suddenly lost control. The Ferrari cannoned into the guard-rails and caught fire. Pedro was trapped in the wreckage and died of multiple injuries in hospital. The cause of the crash was not definitely established, although it was suggested a slow backmarker about to be lapped caused him to swerve and lose control.

Pedro Rodriguez was one of motor racing's most colourful characters. He thoroughly enjoyed his motor racing and was extremely spectacular in sports cars. Of small stature (he was 5ft 6in and weighed 10½ stone) he dressed well and he and his wife, Angelina, enjoyed music, parties and good food – he always carried with him hot peppers and a jar of tabasco sauce to enliven his food. He was much missed in the racing world. MK

BERND ROSEMEYER (1909-1938)
Germany

The only car Bernd Rosemeyer ever raced was the tricky, 400 bhp, rear-engined Auto Union, yet in his meteoric three-year career, he established himself as the world's fastest road-racing driver. Born in 1909 in Lingen, Germany, Rosemeyer was already a successful member of the DKW motor cycle racing team – DKW was one of the component companies of Auto Union – when he was selected for trials with the new racing car, whose difficult handling characteristics were proving an obstacle to drivers used to more conventional cars. Rosemeyer's lack of experience proved a positive asset, and he hurled the big car about like a two-wheeler, broadsiding round corners absolutely on the limit.

He retired in his first race, the 1935 Avusrennen, but in the next event, the Eifelrennen on the Nürburgring, he almost beat Caracciola, establishing himself as a driver to watch.

By the end of the season, Rosemeyer had won his first major race, the Masaryk Grand Prix on the Czechoslovak Brno circuit; in 1936 he won the Eifelrennen, the German Grand Prix, the Coppa Acerbo, the Italian and Swiss GPs – and the German championship. 'Young, good-looking, dashing and carefree,' the likeable young Rosemeyer was soon established as a firm favourite with the German motor-racing public. He was married to a popular heroine, Fraulein Elly Beinhorn, the international flyer, who flew her husband to many of his meetings in her Messerschmitt Taifun record-breaking monoplane.

Both Rosemeyer and his wife were confirmed fatalists, believing that risks could be run with impunity...in the majority of cases. Their lucky number was a fate-tempting '13'.

'The risks he takes, sometimes bordering on the reckless, are unbelievable,' wrote George Monkhouse in 1937, 'until one has seen him trying to get or increase his lead, with the Auto Union on the verge of leaving the road the whole time. So far his self-confidence is unshaken, due I think to the fact that, although he crashed many times, to date I'm glad to say he has not hurt himself.'

However, Doctor Porsche, designer of the Auto Union (and several other cars with reputations for tricky handling), declared: 'Rosemeyer never took any foolish risks. It was just that he drove faster than other people could.'

For the 1937 Avusrennen, at the rebuilt Berlin Avus track, Rosemeyer's streamlined Auto Union proved capable of around 200 mph, but was held back by mechanical defects. In the Eifelrennen a few weeks later, Rosemeyer was more successful, leading for most of the race and winning at an average speed of 82.95 mph.

Then came the Vanderbilt Cup, on the Roosevelt Raceway on Long Island, a track on which the performance of the Auto Union was totally superfluous. Commented Rosemeyer: 'From corner to corner on the circuit my soul was more and more afflicted. I tell you frankly that my hope to win dwindled away....Imagine a simple track, rather narrow, with very many curves, really something for a stunt driver. At both sides a wooden fence, about 30cm high, making it impossible to see a curve in advance and act accordingly, as on our European tracks. So the whole technique of braking to which we are accustomed on our European tracks was of no use. I needed a couple of cognacs to recover from this surprise.'

Nevertheless, Rosemeyer started the race as favourite, even though his practice lap times had been beaten by Caracciola and the American dirt-track racer Rex Mays. For once, the pundits were not disappointed, for Rosemeyer did win the race, though he had to fight hard to keep ahead of Dick Seaman's

Mercedes, setting a new lap record in the process.

He later recalled: 'The race was, perhaps, the hardest I ever ran. For each lap I had to brake firmly seven times and eight corners had to be dealt with. This makes a total of 560 brake operations and 720 corners. I really pushed my car through corners in order to gain time, and this was very tiring. I do not remember any other race which tired me so much. (Incidentally, when I weighed myself in the evening that day I had lost 5lb!)'

In the German Grand Prix, trying to regain ground lost when a hub began to break up, Rosemeyer left the track and collected a haystack, despite which he still managed to finish third!

Though Rosemeyer lost the German championship to Caracciola, he still managed to beat Mercedes in the Coppa Acerbo (despite blowing his engine up in practice and losing a wheel in the race) and the Donington GP – the thirteenth event in which he had driven in 1937.

On 28 January 1938, trying to regain the flying kilometre record just taken from him, at 268.3 mph by Caracciola on the Frankfurt-Darmstadt autobahn, Rosemeyer's car was caught by a sudden gust of wind as it emerged from a cutting, swerved, lost a tyre, hit a concrete bridge and somersaulted several times. Rosemeyer was hurled out and killed instantly. He had tempted fate once too often...   DBW

LOUIS ROSIER (1905-1956)
France

Born in 1905, Louis Rosier, a *garagiste* from Clermont-Ferrand in the Auvergne, had driven a blown SCAP 1100 sports car in local hill-climbs since 1928, graduating to one of the new Talbots of the Lago regime in 1938, which he campaigned further afield, including Le Mans – though without success.

His first major victory came in 1947, in the Albi Grand Prix, with his old 4-litre 'streamlined, pseudo-racing' Talbot, with which he had taken seventh place at Spa a fortnight before and sixth place at Reims a week after that. Such a rapid succession of major races had, inevitably, reduced the number of front-line racers competing at Albi; and the ranks were still further thinned by the Albigensian weather, which was overpoweringly hot, with as he was later to remark feelingly 'few movements of air noticeable...typical of the hottest part of the Midi in being like blasts from a furnace door'.

The Albi race was held over 40 laps of the fast, triangular Les Planques circuit, 5.5 miles round, with a lap record of 100 mph; the 100 degrees-in-the-shade weather played havoc with more sensitive carburations, and several of the ace Continental drivers blew their cars up driving too hard. But while others retired, Rosier kept on driving his old Talbot with steady consistency, with the result that five laps from the end he was in the lead – and kept there, although harried from behind by Raymond Sommer's 1100 cc Simca.

That year, the steady old Talbot also netted third place at Chimay in the Grand Prix des Frontières, fourth in the French GP at Lyon, and third in the GP de Strasbourg.

Then in 1948, Rosier acquired the first of the new 280 bhp Lago-Talbot racers, and promptly won the Coupe du Salon at 90.56 mph, though he could do no better than third at Albi.

Tropical weather was against Rosier in the 1949 Le Mans, where, in company with his son Jean-Claude, he was driving a re-bodied GP Talbot; the car overheated after 21 laps when lying fourth, and under the rules was unable to refill the radiator without being disqualified.

In more conventional racing, Rosier's Talbot was consistently highly placed – third in the British Grand Prix, first in the Belgian Grand Prix, third at Albi, gaining sufficient points during the season to establish him as champion of France, a position which he was to hold for the next four years.

The 1950 Le Mans was a more auspicious event for the father/son Rosier team, with Louis driving for 20 hours out of 24 to win. That year, with his single-seat Lago-Talbot, Rosier also won the Dutch and Albi Grands Prix, and ventured to South America for the Argentine 500 Miles' Race, in which he was rewarded with second place; in 1951 he took first place in the Dutch GP and also won the Bordeaux Grand Prix.

Two Ferraris, a 4.5-litre Formula One car and a 2-litre Formula Two car, were bought in 1952; with the F1 car Rosier won his 'favourite' race at Albi in 1952 and 1953, while with the smaller Ferrari he took firsts at Cadours in 1952 and Sables d'Olonne in 1953, but a change of major formula in 1954 compelled another change of allegiance, this time to a 250F Maserati, backed by a Ferrari.

In 1956 Rosier, now famed as a builder of

open sports conversions of the 4CV Renault, won his last major victory, co-driving with Jean Behra in the Paris 1000 km race at Montlhéry, in a sporting Maserati. That October, on a wet track at Montlhéry, Rosier's Ferrari spun off during the Coupe du Salon, and overturned. Three weeks later, Rosier succumbed to the head injuries he received in the crash. He was 51. DBW

ROY SALVADORI (b.1922)
Great Britain

Roy Salvadori was an exceptionally accomplished racing driver whose career spanned twenty seasons. An all-rounder, he won countless races in Formula One, Formula Two, sports, GT and saloon machinery and competed professionally for leading works and private teams.

Although he had the good looks of an Italian, Roy Francesco Salvadori was British. He was born to Italian parents at Brentwood, Essex, on 12 May 1922, and lived most of his early life in or around London. After leaving school, he worked in his father's refrigeration plant business before going into the motor trade in 1946, at the age of 24. He began as a kerbside trader in London's infamous Warren Street and later ran a garage at Tolworth, Surrey.

Salvadori had yearned to be a racing driver in the late 1930s, but World War II delayed the fulfilment of his dreams.

Some success in a supercharged R-type MG and an ex-Dobbs Riley in 1946 led to the acquisition of an allegedly ex-Nuvolari Alfa Romeo P3 the following year and it was with this machine that Salvadori competed in his first Continental race, the Grand Prix des Frontieres at Chimay, Belgium, where he came fifth though locked in top gear. An old Maserati of 1934 vintage replaced the Alfa, but this was a disappointing car and soon made way for an ex-Prince 'Bira' Maserati 4CL. This was reduced to ashes at the Curragh races in Ireland at the end of 1949.

Sports car racing became Roy's forte. In 1951 he raced a Frazer-Nash for Tony Crook, but his season was curtailed after a serious accident at the Daily Express Silverstone meeting. He also raced for Connaught in Formula Two and in 1952, sharing a 2.7-litre Ferrari 225 Sports with Bobby Baird in the Goodwood 9-hours he was third. In 1953 he co-drove an Ecurie Ecosse-entered Jaguar C-type with Ian Stewart to be placed second in the Nürburgring 1000-km and that year Salvadori began an association with the works Aston Martin team that lasted until 1960.

Syd Greene, the one-armed private entrant, provided Maseratis for Salvadori to race in the mid 1950s, a 2-litre A6GCS sports car plus the last word in Formula One machinery, a 2½-litre 250F. Wins and good places in innumerable British Formula One and *formule libre* races made Salvadori one of Britain's most successful racing drivers. In 1955, the 250F brought Roy second place in the Daily Express Trophy at Silverstone and victory in both the Glover Trophy at Goodwood and the Daily Telegraph Trophy at Aintree. In 1956 Salvadori starred at Silverstone. At the May Daily Express Trophy Meeting he won the 1500 cc sports car race in a works Cooper T39-Climax and the over 1500 cc event in a works Aston Martin DB3. In the Formula One Trophy race itself he was battling for second place when he crashed badly, suffering concussion and leg injuries. In July's Grand Prix meeting he won the Formula Two race in the prototype Cooper T41-Climax and then came close to winning the Grand Prix itself. He lay second behind Stirling Moss's Maserati 250F and ahead of Juan Manuel Fangio's winning Lancia-Ferrari D50 when, with 51 of the 101 laps completed, he was forced to stop with a fuel tank fixing strap loose.

In 1957 Salvadori signed to drive for BRM in Formula One, but he was far from happy with the ill-handling car. At Goodwood's Easter Monday meeting his BRM spun very early with a seized brake and then Roy failed to qualify for the Monaco Grand Prix. Salvadori quit the team, concentrating instead on racing for Aston Martin in sports car races and for Cooper in Formula Two. He was not finished with Grand Prix racing, however, being invited to drive a Vanwall in place of the injured Tony Brooks in the French and Reims Grands Prix. Then Cooper began to run 'oversize' 2-litre-engined Formula Two cars in Formula One. Salvadori ran fourth in the British Grand Prix at Aintree before stopping near the end with a split gearbox casing, but was able to salvage fifth by pushing his car over the line. He was later second in the Caen Grand Prix.

Remaining with Cooper for 1958, Salvadori was second in the German Grand Prix, third in Great Britain and fourth in both Holland and Italy with the diminutive cars. He also won the sports car Gold Cup at Oulton Park driving a

2-litre Lotus 15-Climax. Roy's greatest win came in 1959 when he shared the winning Aston Martin DBR1/300 with Carroll Shelby in the Le Mans 24-hours. The Formula One Aston Martin DBR4/250 was a disappointment; an initially promising second place in the Daily Express Trophy at Silverstone was followed only by poorer performances.

Apart from Formula One, Roy's 1960 season was a good one. He won eight out of ten sports and GT races (and was second to Stirling Moss in the other two). He was third at Le Mans, sharing a privately-entered Aston Martin DBR1/300 with Jim Clark. For 1961 Roy partnered John Surtees in the Yeoman Credit Racing Team, beginning the season well in New Zealand and Australia with second places at Levin and Teretonga Park and victory at Longford. Highlight of the year was Whit Monday when Salvadori won all four major races at Crystal Palace: the Formula One race in a Cooper T55-Climax, the GT race in a Jaguar E-type, the sports car race in a Cooper T55-Climax, and the touring event in a Jaguar 3.8-litre.

The 1962 season was Salvadori's last in Formula One. It was a disappointing one with the Bowmaker-sponsored Lola Mk 4-Climax cars, best positions being second in small races at Crystal Palace and Karlskoga. Earlier in the year he was involved in a bad crash at Warwick Farm, Australia, when his Cooper T55-Climax crashed at 130 mph. He was flown to Britain for medical treatment and suffered partial paralysis to the left side of his face. In another crash at the end of August a front tyre burst on his 3.8 Jaguar at Oulton Park and the car somersaulted at 90 mph into the lake. Roy struggled from his safety harness and escaped from the submerged Jaguar out of the back door.

In 1963 Salvadori concentrated on sports, GT and saloon car racing. With patron Tommy Atkins's Cooper T61 Monaco-Climax he won at Snetterton, Goodwood, Aintree and Silverstone and in July he co-drove a Jaguar 3.8 with Denny Hulme to win the *Motor* 6-hours at Brands Hatch. In June he was involved in another accident at Le Mans. Salvadori was rescued from his wrecked E-Type Jaguar by a fellow driver, fortunately not too seriously hurt.

The last full season for Salvadori was in 1964 when he drove Tommy Atkins's 5-litre Maserati-engined Cooper T61M and AC Cobra in British sports and GT races and assisted John Wyer with the race-development of the Ford GT40s. In fact, he left the Ford team after a disagreement at the April Le Mans test days. After a race at Silverstone in a Ford V8-engined Cooper T78 early in 1965 Salvadori retired from motor racing at the age of 41. Subsequently he became team manager of the Cooper Grand Prix Team, eventually quitting early in 1968 to concentrate on his motor business interests. MK

JODY SCHECKTER (b.1950)
South Africa

How was it possible, many have asked, that a virtually unknown, inexperienced and very young South African could rise from anonymity to a Formula One debut in a mere twenty months? That was the remarkable record of Jody Scheckter's progress – club racer to Grand Prix professional in quicker time than most of his contemporaries.

For Jody Scheckter, the real beginning of his career came in early 1971. Until that time motor racing had been a hobby for him, passionately pursued, but nevertheless a secondary pursuit to an apprenticeship in his father's East London, South Africa garage. Jody's springboard to fame was the Sunshine Series of Formula Ford races held on five South African circuits during January/February 1971. For three years, Formula Ford had been growing in popularity, and through the efforts of local racer Dave Clapham, BOAC, the Ford Motor Company and a Johannesburg newspaper provided the finance to bring several overseas competitors to race against the increasing number of South African Formula Ford adherents. The big prize was a fully paid racing trip to England.

The author competed in this series, which gave him a unique opportunity to watch Scheckter's talent developing race by race. Jody competed with an early model Lola T200 provided by Ford at the end of 1970. He used it first for two club events, allegedly spinning fourteen times in his first race and finding that a single-seater needed more precise handling than the modified Renault saloon in which he had previously gained a certain local reputation and the name 'sideways Scheckter'.

With this smattering of experience, Jody pitted himself against the better equipped and more experienced visiting racers. The author recalls Scheckter shyly introducing himself in a Bloemfontein garage, seeking tips about his car and general advice on race tactics! The advice was quickly forgotten, for at the first event the local Lola disappeared into the scenery with rapidity and a fair degree of inevitability, it was judged. With enthusiasm dampened at finishing in seventh place, the 'boy from the bush' as he sometimes titled himself, finished the day off in typical beer-drinking, hot-climate, post-race fashion! A far cry from the abstemious, champagne-spraying days to come. To everyone's amazement, the youngster calmed down, finished second at Pietermaritzburg and Kyalami, taking pole position for the latter race as well. He finished third in the championship, easily winning the trip to England. It was a considerably more confident Scheckter seen uninhibitedly celebrating after the series final at Capetown! The author returned to England proclaiming the discovery of a future World Champion, an opinion which was received with the usual scepticism. Needless to say, subsequent performances silenced the doubters.

From Formula Ford to Formula Three in a few months, Jody progressed in a series of victories, lap records and equally unavoidable crashes in British club racing. A McLaren Formula Two contract and a Grand Prix debut in a McLaren M19 at the United States Grand Prix came in 1972. Do acclamation, fame, recognition and money affect the personality of a young man from an unsophisticated, conservative South African city? Yes, just as it would affect anybody else of the same age put in a similar position. Jody initially exhibited the same wonderment at the sights of London as do most of his fellow countrymen, and developed an almost permanent attachment to TV for the first few days. Perhaps over-confident at the end of his first year in England he became much more subdued after an uninspiring 1972 season with the McLaren Formula Two car. He was infinitely more thoughtful after the infamous 1973 Silverstone Grand Prix débâcle, where he wiped out almost half a GP field, although still believing firmly that he had all the necessary ability to make it to the top.

After his time at McLaren, Scheckter was signed by Ken Tyrrell to replace Jackie Stewart in the Elf Tyrrell team. Under the firm hand of Tyrrell, Scheckter matured into one of the most formidable drivers in F1. In 1974, his first full season of F1, he won the Swedish and British Grands Prix, and finally finished third in the World Championship with 45 points. In

1975 came the highlight of his career when he won the South African Grand Prix in front of 100,000 cheering fellow countrymen. Thereafter, Jody struggled against mechanical bothers and his best results came in Belgium, where he was second, Great Britain, where he was third and at Watkins Glen where he finished sixth. He came a disappointing seventh in the championship.

1976 was his last year with Tyrrell. The team dropped a bombshell with the announcement of their six-wheeler for the coming season and Jody simply never liked the car. Nevertheless, he persevered and made history by winning the Swedish Grand Prix on six wheels. He also showed remarkable consistency, scoring points in eleven other races – including second places in Monte Carlo, Great Britain, Germany and at Watkins Glen. He finished third in the championship.

At season's end Scheckter caused a minor sensation by signing for Walter Wolf's all-new team quickly followed by a *major* sensation when he won the team's debut Grand Prix in Argentina. He scored two more wins in 1977, in Monaco – his own adopted home – and in Canada – Walter's adopted country. Jody was competitive for most of the year but a troubled period in mid-season cost him any chance of the world title and he finished as runner up to Niki Lauda.

Towards the end of 1977 Scheckter was approached by Ferrari as replacement for Lauda but he opted to stay with Wolf who could give him the exclusive attention he demanded. The team's 1978 season started badly and it was not until the Monaco Grand Prix that Jody scored his first points – for a dogged third place. In that race he showed that he had lost none of his will to win and with a new car already in the wings his fortunes looked set for an upward turn.

The new WR5 'wing car' which now made its debut, did little to improve matters, however, and Jody had a miserable season for the most part. He managed fourth place in Spain but it gave him little encouragement. He gained another point for sixth place in France and four more for a sensational drive to second place in Germany. Having already signed, as he had threatened to do a year earlier, for Ferrari, he finished the season with third place at Watkins Glen and second place in the Canadian Grand Prix behind future Ferrari teammate Gilles Villeneuve.

Strangely, considering his insistence on one hundred per cent personal attention, Jody settled in well with his new team and even had few qualms when Villeneuve not only won at Long Beach but beat Scheckter on his 'home' circuit, Kyalami. This only made Jody more determined to show his class and, in Belgium and his newly adopted home of Monaco, he romped home to win and make a break for the lead in the World Drivers' Championship.

Jody subscribes to the Lauda school of thought: he who is around at the end picks up the spoils. To Jody the championship was everything, the races secondary. Throughout the year he worked assiduously at building his points' tally rather than taking risks just for the sake of race wins. From Belgium onwards he never lost the lead of the championship. He was out of the points in France and finished a struggling fifth at Silverstone where the Ferrari's prodigious power was not such an advantage. He fought hard for fourth place in Germany and then lost third place to Laffite on the last lap in Austria. He was a hard charging second at Zandvoort and then clinched his title in fairytale fashion by leading a Ferrari 1-2 in front of a hundred thousand screaming *tifosi* at Monza. With his burning ambition fulfilled Jody said that now he could relax and go out for the last two races of the year simply to win! It was not to be however; in Canada he finished fourth after a pit stop for fresh tyres and at Watkins Glen a puncture brought Scheckter's first retirement in a remarkably consistent year.

Jody's year as World Champion was to be his last in the sport and, sadly, it was a year spent struggling, frequently well down the grids and even including the ignominy of failing to qualify in Canada. Scheckter, however, did not complain and when he announced his retirement he did so formally and with the utmost consideration for the needs of his team. Nor did his announcement mark a lessening of his commitment to trying his hardest. Although the Ferrari lacked both pace and reliability Scheckter soldiered on, but his only points of the year came from fifth place at Long Beach and he was very lucky indeed to survive a truly monumental accident in Italy with nothing worse than a strained neck.

Scheckter was not always the most popular of drivers and in the last couple of years of his career, as a leading light in the Grand Prix Drivers' Association, he was much criticised for some of his actions as drivers' spokesman, but nothing could detract from the rare talent he brought to the sport and the dignity with which he left it.   PGH

DICK SEAMAN (1913-1939)
Great Britain

During a short, but meteoric, career as a professional racing driver in the 1930s, Dick Seaman, born in 1913, was acknowledged by the *aficionados* as Britain's best. Indeed, during the two-and-a-half seasons before a tragic accident which claimed his life when he was only 26, he was Britain's sole representative in Grand Prix racing.

Motor racing began in earnest for Dick in 1933 when his parents were talked into buying a 2-litre Bugatti. It was raced at Brooklands and Donington without success.

In early 1934, after another term at Cambridge, Seaman told his parents he was leaving university to take up a new appointment: a professional driver for Whitney Straight's racing team.

His first major race with their MG was at Brooklands, where the British Empire Trophy was run on 23 June. A 300-mile race, it was the first long-distance event in which Seaman participated, but he was to retire with mechanical problems. Next race was his first foreign event, the Grand Prix de l'Albigeois at Albi, France. He stalled at the start and once more retired. The Coppa Acerbo at Pescara, Italy, followed, and Seaman finished third. In the Prix de Berne in Switzerland, at the end of August, he scored his first major victory. In the Grand Prix de Masaryk at Brno, Czechoslovakia, he was fifth, and at Donington, on home ground, he was second to Raymond Mays's ERA in the Nuffield Trophy. In December, Seaman raced in South Africa.

Seaman next raced an ERA and, like the MG, it was painted black and had silver wheels. The arrangement was that Seaman purchased the car but ERA would maintain and transport it to each meeting at Dick's expense. It was, however, an unsatisfactory arrangement, as the car let him down on many occasions.

For 1936, Seaman wished to continue in the 1500 cc *voiturette* category (the pre-war equivalent of Formula Two). Realising that either an ERA or a Maserati would be delivered late, he sought advice from Giulio Ramponi and Tony Birch who suggested he ought to buy the old 1927-model Delage of Lord Howe. After a win at Donington in

Harry Rose's ex-Whitney Straight Maserati, Seaman presented the Delage at the same circuit five weeks later where he won two minor events.

At the Eifelrennen, Seaman crashed, then at Péronne for the Grand Prix de Picardie he crashed again. A brief interlude of sports-car racing followed. Co-driving F. E. Clifford's Lagonda, Seaman won his class and was fourth overall in the Spa 24-hours. Then he had his first taste of Grand Prix racing, but in an uncompetitive 3-litre Maserati. He retired after three laps in the German Grand Prix and later took over Carlo Felice Trossi's car, finishing a lowly twelfth. The Delage was repaired by August and after a misfiring sixth in the Coppa Ciano at Livorno, Dick won the Coppa Acerbo, the Prix de Berne and the JCC 200 at Donington. His Aston Martin failed in the Tourist Trophy, but he won the Donington Grand Prix sharing a 3.8-litre Alfa Romeo with the Swiss driver Hans Ruesch. Seasman was close to winning the BRDC's Gold Star award, one point separating him from Siam's Prince B. Bira.

Before Donington, Seaman had written to the Mercedes-Benz team asking if he could borrow a car. Not surprisingly, they refused, but after the race Dick had a telegram summoning him to Nürburgring to test their cars. These trials, plus others at Monza, resulted in Seaman being invited to join Mercedes-Benz's Grand Prix team in 1937 alongside Rudi Caracciola, Manfred von Brauchitsch and Hermann Lang.

Despite a lean season in 1937, Seaman remained with Mercedes for 1938, but as the team had a large complement of drivers he did not compete in all events the team entered. In fact, he had a thin season. He was not entered for Pau and was reserve at Tripoli and Reims, so his first race was in July's German Grand Prix at Nürburgring. Driving a restrained race, he shadowed von Brauchitsch's car, but this caught fire during a pit-stop and Dick found himself leading; he went on to win. It was the greatest victory of his career, and the first Grand Prix win by a British driver since 1923.

Despite international tension, Seaman remained with Mercedes-Benz for 1939. The 1939 season started with Pau, but despite being fastest in practice Seaman did not start as he was reserve driver. His first race, therefore, was on 21 May, the date of the Eifelrennen. He retired after one lap due to clutch problems. Next outing was the Belgian Grand Prix at Spa

Francorchamps, the often-sinister circuit in the Ardennes. Here Seaman appeared to be on top form. Despite rain, which caused even wet-weather expert Rudi Caracciola to crash, Seaman lapped at high speed to lead the race. Victory seemed well within his grasp when, with thirteen laps to go, his car skidded and crashed into a tree. The Mercedes wrapped itself around the tree and caught alight, Seaman being trapped in the cockpit. He was rescued by a brave policeman and rushed to hospital but, despite briefly regaining consciousness and talking to his friends, he died that night of terrible burns.   MK

SIR HENRY SEGRAVE
(1896-1929)
Great Britain

'Sir Henry Segrave', recalled his biographer and friend James Wentworth Day when the author interviewed him, 'was in every sense of the word a gentleman.'

Although Segrave indeed epitomised all that is best in the British character, he was in fact born in Baltimore, Maryland, of an Irish father and an American mother, in 1896, and only educated in England. 'The name "Segrave" is of very great antiquity,' commented Mr Wentworth Day. 'It dates back to the Vikings, and means "Lord of the Sea".'

Segrave's interest in motor racing apparently dated from a wartime visit to the Sheepshead Bay track on Long Island; his first experience with fast motor cars was gained in America with Marmon, Packard and Stutz cars.

Returning to England, he did war service with the Royal Flying Corps, using a 120 hp Itala racer converted for road use for military duties in London in 1916-17.

When Henry O'Neal DeHane Segrave – he was always 'DeHane', never 'Henry', to his friends – left the Service after the war, with the rank of Major, he decided to go in for motor racing professionally. But the only British motor company which took racing at all seriously was Sunbeam, which was headed by the Breton engineer, Louis Coatalen.

Segrave was determined to become a member of the Sunbeam works team, but not unexpectedly Coatalen told him that he must prove himself before he was even considered for the team.

'I therefore purchased an old Opel racing car,' recalled Segrave in his autobiography *The Lure of Speed*. 'This had been designed for the 1914 Grand Prix, in which, driven by Karl Joerns, it had finished eighth. It was equipped with a four-cylinder engine, having four valves per cylinder, and taking it by and large was a very decent motor car. It was one of the two white Opels which had appeared at Brooklands on the August Bank Holiday immediately before the outbreak of the War, during the whole of which it had remained stored away in England. This Opel was raced fairly consistently at Brooklands in 1920, and succeeded in winning several races. I also ran it in the Southend and Southport speed trials and at the Kop Hill-Climb.'

Every time Segrave met Coatalen that season, he lost no opportunity to plead his ambition to become one of the Sunbeam works team: Coatalen agreed that Segrave appeared to be quite a competent track racer, but lacked any sort of experience in road racing. However, he was prepared to give him a chance.

Coatalen had entered seven cars for the 1921 French Grand Prix – three Talbot-Darracqs, two Talbots and two Sunbeams, all mechanically identical – and gave Segrave the opportunity to drive one of the Talbots, on the condition that if he finished the race inside the time limit, he might be taken into the team on probation. Because of insufficient preparation, the S-T-D cars were almost withdrawn from the race, but the Talbots and Talbot-Darracqs eventually made the start. Flying stones were the main hazard in the race, which was won by Jimmy Murphy's Duesenberg. Segrave's car's oil tank was holed by a stone early in the race, and repaired by his mechanic Moriceau, who blocked the aperture with a plug of cotton waste; Moriceau was later knocked unconscious by a flint hurled by the rear wheels of the Duesenberg. More time was lost through punctures: Segrave changed wheels fourteen times, and Coatalen had to borrow tyres from other teams to keep the Talbots and Talbot-Darracqs in the race.

Segrave was determined to finish, however: 'If, during this first road race of mine, the engine had fallen into two pieces or one of the axles had cracked in the middle, I would somehow have succeeded in finishing the full distance. To get there meant more than anything else in the world at that time.' Get there he did, finishing ninth.

Having qualified as an official member of the team, he next took part in the Coupe des Voiturettes, run two months after the Grand

Prix, over the same course at Le Mans. The Talbot team drove an impeccable race to Coatalen's orders, and finished one-two-three. The order was René Thomas, Kenelm Lee Guinness and Segrave, and only ninety seconds separated Thomas from Segrave. Driving the same car, Segrave then won the Junior Car Club 200-mile race at Brooklands, driving the last lap on a flat tyre.

In 1922, contact-breaker trouble cost Segrave the Isle of Man TT when he was leading by a comfortable margin; already it was being noted that 'his breezy nature and his plucky attitude immediately made him a favourite with racing enthusiasts'.

The Sunbeams entered for the Grand Prix at Strasbourg proved very fast – they were driven to the race, and could reach over 100 mph on the open road – but all three were eliminated by broken valves. 'Segrave, whose car was rather faster than that of his companions, drove a very fine race,' reported *Autocar,* 'and raised British hopes when on the seventh and eighth laps he got into third place behind two Fiats'. By the halfway mark, however, Segrave was forced to retire.

To compensate for these failures, Segrave won the 2-litre and 5-litre championships at the Essex Motor Club meeting at Brooklands, came third in the 200-mile race at Brooklands and the Coupe des Voiturettes at Le Mans, fourth in the Penya Rhin race in Spain (despite a broken inlet valve, which set the car on fire) and second in the Coppa Florio in Sicily.

In the 1923 Grand Prix, Segrave was initially slowed by worsening clutch slip, but just as he was considering retiring altogether, a clutch stop fitted to his car broke off, allowing the clutch to grip properly. With only seventy miles to go to the end of the race, Segrave, with a car in perfect condition, which had not been overstressed because of the clutch slip, frightened the two leading Fiats into making stupid errors of judgment, and won the race – the first-ever British victory in the premier event of the motor-sport calendar. In September that year, Segrave triumphed again in the Coupe des Voiturettes in a 1500 cc Talbot.

The 1924 season was not so successful: magneto trouble cost him the Grand Prix, while his third place in the 200-mile race, behind the sister Darracqs of Guinness and Duller, was pre-arranged. However, he won at San Sebastian and came second at Montlhéry.

Segrave's first race in 1925 was the GP de Provence, on the Miramas circuit near Marseilles, which he won at an average speed of 78.5 mph; he was third in the 1500 cc Grand Prix at Montlhéry (in which the second place was taken *upside down* by Conelli in another Darracq, following a violent skid). He won the Brooklands 200-mile race, again in a Darracq, and repeated the victory the following year, in which he also won the GP de Provence.

The noteworthy feature of the 1926 season, though, was the appearance of the new and versatile Sunbeam V12 racer, with which Segrave set up a new land-speed record of 152.33 mph on Southport sands, and was going well in the lead of the Spanish GP at San Sebastian when his front axle sheared in two.

Subsequently, Segrave drove this car to victory in the Boulogne Speed Trials, at a hair-raising 140.6 mph, but his interest in motor racing was now waning; 1927 saw him concentrating on record breaking, and he became the first driver to exceed 200 mph, setting a new land-speed record of 203.79 mph in the '1000 hp' Sunbeam, which had two 22.4-litre Sunbeam aero engines. Convinced that it would be unsafe to exceed 200 mph in England, Segrave had the car shipped to Daytona, Florida, at his own expense for the successful attempt. Incidentally, the car had maximum speeds of 90 mph in bottom gear, 135 mph in second and 212 mph in top. Segrave's track-racing career ended in anti-climax with disqualification in the Essex Six hour race at Brooklands in 1927.

It was around this time that Segrave propounded his unique theory of safety at cross-roads: 'Supposing you take the crossing at 60 mph, you are in the "zone of danger" for something less than a second, whereas if you cross at 20 mph you are in the dangerous area for three times as long, and consequently the risk of meeting cross-traffic is three times as great...such a manoeuvre is only to be undertaken by people with experience.'

His last great motoring achievement was the raising of the land-speed record to 231.44 mph in March 1929, driving the Irving-Napier *Golden Arrow*; but his enthusiasm for speed on land had already been supplanted by a new interest – speed on water. While in America with *Golden Arrow* he also won the International Championship for motor-boats at Miami. On Segrave's return to England, he was knighted for his motoring achievements.

He was also developing a fast aeroplane, the Segrave Meteor, but on 13 June, having unofficially broken the speed-boat record on Lake Windermere with his *Miss England II*, Segrave struck a floating log at speed, tore the bottom out of the boat and received injuries from which he died a few hours later.

He left an indelible memory of generosity and kindness: Mr Wentworth Day recalled an occasion when Segrave, knowing of his friend's enthusiasm for ancient things, sent him a taxi-load of armour and old weapons. 'That', he recalled, 'was the measure of the true gentleman that Segrave was.'   DBW

WILBUR SHAW (1903-1954)
USA

Warren Wilbur Shaw, who was born in 1903 in Shelbyville, Indiana, was one of the more successful American competition drivers of the 1920s and 1930s; and after the war, he became one of motor sport's most ardent promoters.

Wilbur Shaw was working in Detroit for a company supplying electric vehicle batteries when he met Bill Hunt, who ran the Speedway Engineering Company, building racing cars and supplying ohv conversions for Model T Fords. Shaw, who wanted to become a racing driver, persuaded Hunt to take him on at a nominal salary and during his spare time built a racing car called the Imperial Special. All this hard work went for nothing when he wrote the Imperial Special off in its second race, at Lafayette in 1921.

But he had attracted the attention of Roscoe E. Dunning, starter at the Hoosier Motor Speedway at Indianapolis, who gave Shaw the opportunity to tune and race his Fronty-Ford RED Special, with which Shaw managed to win an $18 purse on his first outing. He went on to take the national Light Car championship with this vehicle; during the next few seasons he enjoyed an increasing amount of success in 'unsanctioned' events on dirt-tracks before joining the AAA late in 1926.

He qualified for the Indianapolis 500 in 1927, driving the Jynx Special, which was basically the Miller in which Jimmy Murphy had been killed in 1924, with the engine capacity reduced to make it eligible for the '500'. Driving a consistent race in an outclassed car, Shaw contrived to last the distance and collected the $3500 fourth-place prize money.

His career seemed to be going well when his wife of less than 12 months died in childbirth. It was a year before he regained his old form. His remarriage in 1929 marked a turning point

and he was readmitted to the AAA – but refused permission to compete in that year's Indianapolis 500; though he won three 100-mile events in a row in the same week as the '500', and accumulated enough points to rate third in the AAA national championship table.

The 1930 season, which Shaw started at the helm of a Miller-powered racing speedboat and ended with a crash in a Fronty-Ford at Los Angeles, was none too successful, and the spring of 1931 was spent in helping August Duesenberg build a supercharged Indianapolis racer which blew up spectacularly on test, shedding its engine on to the track in two separate halves the day before the race. Fred Duesenberg offered Shaw a place in one of the 'official' Duesenberg cars, which went 'over the wall' in a spectacular pile-up when running with the leaders. After hospital treatment, Shaw rejoined the race as relief driver to Jimmy Gleason in the other Duesenberg team car, which finished sixth.

Back-axle trouble put Shaw out of the 1932 '500' when he was leading after 152 laps but the 1933 season marked the beginning of a more successful period, with Shaw coming second at Indianapolis in Leon Duray's Mallory Special, and taking third place in the AAA championship ratings. His car shed all its oil in the 1934 '500'; however, a session with a Chrysler Airflow on the Utah salt flats proved more successful, with Shaw and his co-driver, Harry Hartz, covering 2205.64 miles in 24 hours for a new class record.

In 1935 Shaw came second at Indianapolis with a front-wheel-drive car he had designed and built with financial help from Gil Pirrung, a young Yale graduate. Shaw then financed his own Offenhauser-powered racing car, the Gilmore Special, which was leading the '500' field when it began to shed its bonnet panels; repairs cost Shaw the race.

Rebuilt after a crash on the Roosevelt Raceway in the autumn of 1936, the Gilmore Special won the Indianapolis 500 at a record speed of 113.58 mph the following summer; it was even faster the following year, averaging 115.58 mph, but nevertheless was beaten into second place by Floyd Roberts.

In 1939 Shaw drove an 8CTF Maserati under the name 'Boyle Special'; and won, at 115.04 mph. He repeated this success – still with the Maserati – in 1940, at 114.03 mph, and was all set to become the first four-time winner at the Brickyard in 1941 when a rear wheel collapsed on the 152nd lap, putting Shaw into hospital suffering from a back injury.

During the war, Shaw persuaded an Indianapolis businessman named Anton Hulman, Jr, to put up the money needed to buy the decaying '500' track from its owner, Eddie Rickenbacker, and put it back into racing condition. Shaw was appointed President and General Manager of the new corporation, and turned the resuscitated race into a sell-out success.

On 30 October 1954 a hired aircraft in which he was flying crashed in unexplained circumstances in a cornfield near Decatur, Indiana, killing all three occupants.   DBW

CARROLL SHELBY (b.1923)
USA

Carroll Shelby helped to forge the motor-racing link between the United States and Europe. He began as an accomplished racing driver who showed Europeans that Americans were not limited to the confines of banked ovals such as Indianapolis, graduated to become a driver for a European Formula One team and won the 1959 Le Mans 24-hour race. Although not an engineer, he 'married' a British AC chassis and a powerful Ford V8 engine to produce the Cobra, a very popular sports car. This led to close ties with Ford, Shelby being involved in the Ford GT40 project which culminated in the Americans winning the Le Mans 24-hour race in the mid 1960s.

The son of a Texas mail clerk, Carroll Shelby was born at Leesburg on 11 January 1923. Later the Shelby family moved to Dallas and at the age of ten Carroll developed a heart murmur, but overcame it. He married after enlisting in the Army Air Force and was a pilot during World War II. After the war he returned to Dallas and worked in various jobs, most of them unsuccessful. Shelby was a motor-car enthusiast, having owned several old machines from the days of his youth. He had also been a keen racegoer.

In 1952, aged 29, Shelby helped a friend prepare several MGs and made his competition debut in an MG Special at a Texas drag race meeting. In May that year he raced his friend's MG TC on a road racing circuit for the first time and won his class. He also borrowed a Jaguar XK 120 and won with this, too.

Shelby rocketed to fame in SCCA amateur racing. In 1953 he raced Cadillac-engined Allards for Charlie Brown and Roy Cherryhomes and in January 1954 he competed with Cherryhomes's Allard in the Buenos Aires

1000-km, his first foreign race, with Dale Duncan as co-driver. They did well, finishing tenth and winning the Kimberly Cup for being the first SCCA amateur crew home. But the race was not without its drama: there was a carburettor fire during a pit-stop and it was only Duncan's quick thinking in the absence of any fire-fighting apparatus that saved the intrepid pair – he urinated on it!

The trip to Argentina resulted in a meeting with John Wyer, Aston Martin's race director, who offered Shelby a ride in the Sebring 12-hours (where the rear-axle broke) plus a drive in Europe if he could pay his own way. Shelby made an arrangement with Guy Mabee, a Texan oil millionaire who dreamed of building an American sports car, to finance the European exercise. He tentatively agreed and Carroll arrived in Europe. Driving a 2.9-litre Aston Martin DB3S, he was second at Aintree, retired at Le Mans when a front stub axle broke in the 24-hour race, was fifth in the Supercortemaggiore Grand Prix at Monza co-driving with Graham Whitehead and followed this up with third in an Aston Martin 1-2-3 clean-sweep at Silverstone. But then Mabee decided not to go ahead with the purchase of the Aston and Shelby returned to the United States.

Back home Roy Cherryhomes offered Shelby his Jaguar C-type for two races and then he teamed up with George Eyston, Donald Healey and Roy Jackson-Moore to tackle Class D speed records in a pair of Austin-Healeys. They set more than 70 records at the Bonneville Salt Flats in Utah. The season ended badly with a testing accident in the Carrera Panamericana; Shelby's Austin-Healey crashed into a road marker and Carroll suffered a badly broken arm.

Shelby was back in action in the 1955 Sebring 12-hours, where he drove Alan Guiberson's 3-litre Ferrari 750 Monza into second place with Phil Hill. They were under the impression they had won, but an eight-day check of official and unofficial lap-charts revealed they finished 25.4 seconds behind the winning Jaguar. They did, however, win the Index of Performance. It was a grim, determined drive by Shelby: he had removed his plaster cast, replaced it with a glass-fibre one and taped his hand to the steering wheel for support. Later in 1955 a new-found sponsor, West Coast construction man Tony Parravano, went with Shelby to Europe to purchase some Ferraris. With a 4.4-litre Ferrari 121

LM he retired at Oulton Park and his co-driver Gino Munaron crashed their 3-litre Ferrari 750 Monza in the Targa Florio. While in Europe Shelby also finished ninth overall and won the 1500 cc class in the Tourist Trophy at Dundrod in a Porsche 550 shared with fellow-American Masten Gregory and at the wheel of a Formula One Maserati 250F he was sixth in October's Syracuse Grand Prix.

Nineteen-fifty-six was a year of mixed fortunes. Shelby was divorced as his wife disliked the strain of racing and constant travelling; he set up a sports-car garage business, financed by Dick Hall, brother of Jim Hall of Chaparral fame, but this was not a success as Shelby was unable to devote sufficient time to it owing to his racing activities; and Parravano withdrew from racing. The season began with an invitation to share a works Aston Martin DB3S in the Sebring 12-hours with Roy Salvadori, the pair finishing fourth. Then Shelby was invited to race Ferraris for a new sponsor, John Edgar, much success being scored in Edgar's 4.9-litre Ferrari 375 Plus. He also successfully raced a 2-litre Ferrari 500 Testa Rossa, a 4.4-litre Ferrari 121 LM and Edgar's ex-Formula One 4½-litre Ferrari 375, with which he won the Mount Washington and Grants Despair hill-climbs in record time.

The 1957 season began with Shelby's Ferrari 375 Plus taking second place in the Cuban Grand Prix behind Fangio's Maserati 300S, but at Sebring where he was invited to race a works-entered Maserati 300S with Roy Salvadori the pair were disqualified for refuelling too early (they were to have their glory...). There was talk of racing for Maserati in European Grand Prix, but this came to nil. Instead Shelby had yet another successful sports-car season in the United States, driving both John Edgar's new machines, a 3-litre Maserati 300S and a 4½-litre Maserati 450S. He won nineteen races and gained his second SCCA championship. In the inaugural meeting at Riverside International Raceway in September, however, Shelby crashed the bigger Maserati on the first lap of practice and suffered severe back and facial injuries. In November, though, he was back, at the same circuit (John Edgar, Shelby's sponsor, was a major Riverside shareholder) in the repaired car. He spun on the first lap, but fought back like a hero to conquer Dan Gurney's Ferrari and the rest of the field. It was a superb victory.

In 1958 Shelby attempted to run in the Indianapolis 500-mile race, the world's richest motor race, but was prevented by officialdom. The owner of the car, an ex-Pat O'Connor machine, had already taken his 'rookie' test at the famed oval, but USAC rules said that two 'rookies' could not use the same car and Shelby was barred from his attempt. Shelby joined the Aston Martin sports-car team. He retired at Sebring when the gear-linkage broke, was third in the Spa Grand Prix, retired in the Nurburgring 1000-km with transmission failure, withdrew from Le Mans owing to illness and was third in the Tourist Trophy at Goodwood, co-driving with Stuart Lewis-Evans. On the Formula One front, Shelby drove Maserati 250Fs for both Scuderia Centro-Sud and American Temple Buell, best result being a shared fourth place with Masten Gregory in the Italian Grand Prix. Driving Alan Brown's Cooper T45-Climax, Shelby also raced in the Formula Two Kentish 100 at Brands Hatch.

For 1959 Shelby remained with Aston Martin, joining Salvadori to drive one of the new DBR4/250 Formula One machines in addition to the sports cars. The season started 'Down Under' in the New Zealand Grand Prix where he handled a Buell-entered Maserati 250F. Harry Schell took it over in mid-race to claim fourth place. So far as the sports-car programme was concerned the highlight of the year – indeed, the highlight of Shelby's career – was victory in the Le Mans 24-hour race in an Aston Martin DBR1/300 co-driven with Roy Salvadori, despite an attack of dysentery. He was also a member of the winning crew in the Tourist Trophy at Goodwood, thereby greatly assisting Aston Martin in the World Sports Car Championship-winning season. He had no luck at Sebring, however, retiring when the gear-lever came off! The Formula One Aston Martin lacked speed, best result in an abbreviated season being eighth in the Portuguese Grand Prix.

The 1960 motor-racing season was Shelby's last. The 37-year-old driver had heart problems, a reminder of his childhood troubles. The cause was overwork and the strain of racing. Nevertheless, dosed with pills, he began the racing season with a 2.9-litre Maserati T61. He won at Riverside in May and Castle Rock in June, but following the Riverside Grand Prix in October, when he was fifth, he quit racing.

A new chapter in the life of Carroll Shelby opened, one that was to bring him even more fame. In 1961 he moved to California and opened a racing tyre distributorship and a racing drivers' school at Riverside. He was also able to give thought to a project he had dreamed of since the late 1950s – the AC Cobra. In 1970, after many successful years as a constructor, Shelby, now a millionaire, retired from motor sport to attend to his other extensive business interests.   MK

JO SIFFERT (1936-1971)
Switzerland

Fate sometimes plays strange tricks on racing drivers. While few would dispute that Jo Siffert was one of the fastest Formula One drivers of his time, it was in the exacting and exhausting field of endurance sports-car racing that he excelled. Siffert was born in Fribourg, Switzerland, on 7 July 1936. He started racing motor cycles in 1957 and by 1959 was the Swiss 350cc champion. Shortly afterwards he switched to four wheels using a Formula Junior Stanguellini. In 1961, he exchanged this machine for a Lotus 22 and soon began to make his mark on the European circuits. At the end of the year he was declared joint European Formula Junior Champion with Trevor Taylor and Tony Maggs.

For 1962, Siffert bought a Formula One Lotus 24 and his World Championship F1 debut was made at the Belgian GP but with little success. The following season he joined the Swiss Ecurie Filipinetti team, driving their F1 Lotus-BRM. Apart from a win in the non-championship Syracuse GP and a second in the Imola GP, he again had a frustrating season. Having broken with the Filipinetti team during the 1963 season, he bought a Brabham-BRM for the following year. Although not ultra-competitive, the car enabled him to take a fourth place in the German GP. By this time his talent had been spotted by entrant Rob Walker who drafted the slim, mustachioed Swiss into his team alongside Swede Jo Bonnier. He immediately repaid Walker's confidence in him with a third in the United States Grand Prix behind Granham Hill and John Surtees.

For the following year, 1965, Rob Walker retained both Siffert and Bonnier. Siffert began the season well by winning the Mediterranean GP at Enna, beating Jim Clark in the process. He also finished fourth in the Mexican GP but the rest of his season was punctuated by mechanical failures and retirements.

In 1966 Siffert repeated the pattern. Driving Rob Walker's heavy and uncompetitive Cooper-Maserati he could manage no better than fourth in the United States GP; 1966, however, was the year that Siffert began his sports-car racing career. It was the start of a very successful period that would establish Siffert as one of the greats.

Driving Ferraris and Porsches in 1967 he finished fourth at Sebring and Daytona, fifth at Monza, second at Spa, sixth at the Targa Florio and fifth at Le Mans while in World Championship Formula One events he finished fourth in both the French and US Grands Prix.

It was obvious by now that sports-car racing was Siffert's forte yet his 1968 season is best remembered for a spectacular win in the British Grand Prix driving the privately-entered Rob Walker Lotus 49 Cosworth. Apart from being perhaps the highlight of Siffert's career, it was also one of Rob Walker's proudest moments. Siffert followed this success with a fifth in the US Grand Prix and a sixth in the Mexican Grand Prix. In the field of sports-car racing he was now a member of the works Porsche team and provided them with some remarkable successes. He won the Daytona 24-hour event, the Sebring 12-hour race and the Nürburgring 1000 kms and, single-handed, the Austrian 1000 race. In addition to these successes, he had also set fastest lap times in the British, Canadian and Mexican Grands Prix.

In F1 in 1969 he took fourth in South Africa, third at Monaco, second in Holland and fifth in Germany. In sports cars, Siffert proved unbeatable. Sharing a works Porsche with British sports-car ace Brian Redman, Siffert won the BOAC 1000 kms, the Monza, Spa, and Nürburgring events and the Watkins Glen 6-hour race. Co-driving a Porsche 917 with Kurt Ahrens, he also won the Austrian 1000 kms. Apart from being his most successful season, 1969 was also his most varied. Driving a Formula Two BMW he finished second at the Eifelrennen and fourth overall in the Can-Am sports car series.

For 1970, Siffert signed to drive for the much-publicised new March Formula One team. Alas, Siffert's year proved to be a disaster with retirement after retirement. In sports cars, however, he continued to excel. Sharing with Brian Redman, he drove a Porsche 908/3 to victory in the demanding Targa Florio. He followed this with a win in the Spa 1000 kms, seconds in the Daytona 24-hour and Watkins Glen 6-hour events and victory in the Austrian 1000 kms race.

Unhappy with his year at March, Siffert signed for the BRM F1 team in 1971. He finished sixth in Holland, fourth in France and then led the Austrian GP from start to finish to take his second World Championship Grand Prix victory. Later in the year he finished second in the US GP thus gaining enough points to finish joint fourth with Jacky Ickx in the World Championship table. In sports-car events he was also successful, gaining a win in the Buenos Aires 1000 kms, seconds at Monza, Spa, Nürburgring and Watkins Glen and a third in the BOAC.

At the end of 1971, the Mexican GP was cancelled. To replace it, a non-championship F1 race was organised at Brands Hatch to celebrate Jackie Stewart's World Championship title victory. The event was held on 24 October 1971 and it proved to be Jo Siffert's last race. At over 130 mph, the BRM left the track, cannoned into an embankment, overturned and exploded into flames, killing its driver. The race was halted and slowly the stunned spectators made their way home, mourning the loss of one of motor racing's most fearless and popular drivers.   MW

RAYMOND SOMMER (1906-1950)
France

The racing driver Raymond Sommer was the son of Roger Sommer, a wealthy manufacturer of felt, who from 1909 to 1912 had been one of France's best-known pioneer aviators and manufacturers of aircraft, but had sold his aviation business to MM Bathiat and Sanchez-Besa in 1913 and 'returned from aviation to the less exciting but more remunerative business of making felt slippers and such things'.

Thus, young Raymond, born in 1906, was brought up in an atmosphere of 'mechanical sport and progress'; he first started motor racing with a 4.6-litre Chrysler straight-eight, which had a carburettor for each cylinder, and, though he retired at Le Mans in 1931, he and his co-driver Delemer won the sports car class in the Belgian 24-hour race at Spa.

In March 1932, still driving the Chrysler, he was first in the general classification of the Paris - Nice Trial, and also set a new class record in the La Turbie hill-climb. Soon afterwards, he bought an 8C2300 Alfa Romeo and, by way of a try-out, won the Torvilliers race at Troyes. With Luigi Chinetti as co-driver, he entered the Alfa for the Le Mans 24 hours, and drove for 18 hours out of the 24 as his partner

was unwell; the result was a victory for the team, with the Alfa covering 2954 km. A month later, Sommer came second in the Nice Grand Prix, while in September he won the Marseilles Grand Prix with his 2.6 litre P3 Alfa, defeating Nuvolari with spectacular ease and style.

Nuvolari shared the Monza with Sommer in that year's Le Mans 24 hours, and despite frequent halts for fuel caused by a leaking petrol tank, the Alfa notched up Sommer's second victory in this event.

Sommer's verve and courage at the wheel earned him the nickname of *Raymond Coeur de Lion*; he drove like a devil, it was said, and would never retire from a race while there was still hope, even when a breakdown had lost him all chance of winning.

Driving a Maserati, he was third in the 1935 Belgian Grand Prix; with a new 3.2-litre Alfa P3 he won the Comminges Grand Prix and was third in the Marne GP, while 1936 saw him take fourth place in the Vanderbilt Cup on the Roosevelt Raceway.

Just before World War II, in 1937 and 1939, Sommer earned himself the title of champion of France. When war broke out, he refused a commission in the French Army, preferring to fight as an ordinary *poilu*: even so, he still managed to shoot down a low-flying German aeroplane with his rifle.

After the war, backed by veteran motoring journalist Charles Faroux, Sommer was at the head of the unpopular - but eventually successful - campaign to free Doctor Porsche from Dijon prison, and was soon back in motor racing, coming second in the very first post-war event, organised in the Bois de Boulogne in 1945. The following season saw victories in the Marseilles Grand Prix, the Circuit de Trois Villes and the St Cloud GP, a second in the Turin Grand Prix and at the Brussels meeting, a list of successes which were enough to earn him his third French championship.

In 1947, Sommer crashed at Pau, nearly biting off his tongue in the impact, and was eliminated from both the Grand Prix d'Europe at Spa and the Prix de la Marne at Reims after his Maserati chassis frame broke on both occasions. He then tried the CTA-Arsenal at Lyon - it broke its back axle on the starting line.

His luck seemed to have changed at Turin, at the wheel of one of the new V12 2-litre Ferraris, and he led all the way from the start, running away from the rest of the field with consummate ease and making the fastest lap of 69.88 mph and recording an average of 67.5 mph over the 312.5 mile distance.

He raced a Talbot in 1948 and 1949, and drove the unlucky 16-cylinder BRM in its debut at Silverstone but, recalling the CTA-Arsenal, its transmission broke on the starting line.

Then, while taking part in the unimportant Haute Garonne Grand Prix on the Gardours circuit on 10 September 1950, Sommer crashed fatally in his 1100 cc Cooper, apparently the victim of a seized wheel bearing.

'Drive your hardest, take the lead early and frighten off the opposition – if possible,' had been Raymond Sommer's credo. Not long before his death, France had awarded him the Cross of the Legion of Honour as 'the greatest driver in the country'.•   DBW

JACKIE STEWART (b.1939)
Great Britain

If Jackie Stewart was not the world's greatest Grand Prix driver, he will certainly go down in history as one of the shrewdest. It was Stirling Moss who pioneered professionalism and commercialisation in motor sport, but Jackie Stewart took every opportunity in his nine seasons of Formula One racing to accrue as much money and publicity for himself as possible. A financial expert estimated he earned over £300,000 per annum during his last years as an active driver.

Stewart was also a pioneer in the controversial cause of motor racing safety. Following his serious accident in the 1966 Belgian Grand Prix at Francorchamps, he adopted a stance which made him extremely unpopular with motor racing's purists. But his actions certainly saved life and injury in a dangerous sport. As if to underline the fact that he was a true professional, even if he had declared a circuit to be unsafe, he would still put all his effort into race driving. No one could say Stewart's race performances were halfhearted.

When he retired from motor racing in October 1973, Jackie Stewart OBE ended a brilliant career. He had scored more World Championship Grand Prix wins than any other driver – 27 from 99 starts. He scored a record total of 360 points and was World Champion three times, in 1969, 1971 and 1973. Stewart retired at the relatively early age of 34. At a farewell press conference, he said, 'I made the decision as I had had mixed emotions about

motor racing for some time.' The decision of Jackie and his young wife Helen to move to Switzerland and, five years later, retire, followed the fatal accidents of several of their close friends.

Born on 11 June 1939, John Young Stewart – always known as Jackie – was the son of a garage proprietor, Robert Stewart, who once raced motor cycles as an amateur. The boy was introduced to motor racing by his brother Jimmy, eight years his senior, who was an accomplished sports car driver. Jimmy raced for the Ecurie Ecosse Jaguar team and the works Aston Martin team until a serious crash at Le Mans in 1954 ended a promising career. That same year 15-year-old Jackie left Dumbarton Academy, where he excelled at sports, and joined the family Dumbuck Garage as a petrol attendant. Later he switched to the mechanical side of the business and joined his father and brother as a partner.

Jackie wished to follow his brother into motor racing, but following Jimmy's fearful accident family permission was not forthcoming. Instead he turned his attention to clay pigeon shooting, becoming a member of the British team in 1959. The following year he narrowly missed selection for the Olympic team and in 1964 would have been included but for his motor racing.

In 1960 Glasgow enthusiast Barry Filer, for whom the Stewarts' garage prepared a stable of racing machinery for him and his friends to drive, offered Jackie the chance to race at a club meeting at Charterhall, Scotland's only circuit at that time. He declined, worried about his mother's reaction, but instead, with the approval of his father and brother, went down to Oulton Park in Cheshire to test Filer's Porsche Super 90. The bug had bitten! Stewart competed in a sprint and looked forward to a season of racing in 1961.

Filer bought a Ford-engined Marcos GT, an ugly, wooden-chassis car, but effective in Stewart's hands in four local races. He once raced Filer's Aston Martin DB4GT. Early in 1962 he wanted to decide whether or not to go racing seriously and with a party of friends – including well-known motor cycle racer Bob McIntyre – went to Oulton Park to test Filer's Aston and AC Ace-Bristol plus the Jaguar E-type demonstrator from the family garage. Stewart's times in the E-type were comparable to Roy Salvadori's in a similar car the previous year and he decided there and then to pursue his new interest further. In August he married

Helen McGregor, his sweetheart for five years, and the write-up in the local newspaper gave his racing game away. His mother now knew, but received the news more calmly than anticipated.

In 1963 Stewart raced in England for the first time, venturing to Yorkshire's Rufforth airfield circuit on Easter Saturday where he won two races in the Jaguar. His excellent performances won him further drives in friends' Jaguars and ultimately David Murray of Ecurie Ecosse allowed Stewart to drive one of the difficult Buick-engined Tojeiro EE Mk 2s at Charterhall. Stewart won and was later offered the wheel of the team's Cooper T49 Monaco-Climax, winning impressively at Goodwood in Sussex. Stewart was also a member of the winning team in the Five-Hour Relay Race at Oulton Park, driving a Jaguar 3.8, and at the end of the year his score was 14 wins, one second, two thirds and six retirements from 23 starts. *Autosport* hailed him as the leading club driver of the year, while he also won the Chris Bristow and Ron Flockhart Memorial Trophies.

The 1964 season saw Stewart's career snowball. He signed with Ecurie Ecosse to drive their old Cooper and a Ford-engined Tojeiro EE Mk 3 in sports car races and with Charles Bridges to race a Lotus Ford Cortina in saloon car events. But these drives were to pale into insignificance as the months went by. Goodwood's track manager Robin McKay, in conversation with Ken Tyrrell, suggested Stewart's name as a driver for Tyrrell's team of Formula Three Cooper T72-BMCs. McKay had watched Stewart at Goodwood the previous year and had been very impressed. The outcome was that Tyrrell invited Stewart to test the new car at Goodwood and quickly signed him up when Jackie lapped quicker than Formula One driver Bruce McLaren. His first race was at Norfolk's Snetterton circuit on 15 March in torrential rain. After one lap Stewart led by 11 secs; next time round it was 25 secs; by the time the 10 laps were over Stewart had eased up to get home with a 44 sec advantage over the second finisher. Stewart had arrived and within days was offered a Formula One drive by Cooper. He declined, preferring to gain more experience.

Stewart went on to win the Express & Star Formula Three championship, failing to win only two races with the Tyrrell Cooper. Once his clutch failed and once he spun. He was invited to race Ian Walker's Lotus Elan, proving quicker than the works drivers, handled John Coombs's lightweight Jaguar E-type and by June was reserve driver for the Maranello Concessionaires' Ferrari team at Le Mans; he practised but did not race. During unofficial practice for the European Grand Prix at Brands Hatch (where Stewart was competing in all three supporting races) he was suddenly offered a trial in a Formula One Lotus 33-Climax. He duly accepted and quietly impressed Colin Chapman of Lotus and fellow-Scot Jim Clark, the reigning World Champion, with his cool but quick driving. But he considered himself still not ready for Formula One and turned down an offer from Lotus. He did, however, race for the Lotus Formula Two and saloon car teams before the season was over. First time out in Formula Two, he was second at the difficult Clermont-Ferrand circuit in a Lotus 32-Cosworth, and in a Lotus-Ford/Cortina he won the US Marlboro 12-hours.

Turning down offers from Lotus and Cooper, Stewart signed to race alongside Graham Hill in the works BRM Formula One team in 1965. But in December 1964 he had his first official Formula One race in Jim Clark's Lotus. Clark had injured his back in a non-racing incident and was unable to take part in the non-championship Rand Grand Prix in South Africa. Stewart deputised. He broke both drive-shafts starting the first heat, but won the second. In his first World Championship race, the South African Grand Prix of 1965, Stewart drove sensibly into sixth place. He impressed the Formula One 'circus' with his ability. As the season progressed he very quickly learned the art of Grand Prix racing and adapted to tough circuits such as Francorchamps and Nürburgring with apparent ease. He won the non-championship Daily Express Trophy race at Silverstone in May and the Italian Grand Prix at Monza in September after a wheel-to-wheel battle with Graham Hill's similar 1½-litre BRM P261. With three seconds, a third, a fifth and a sixth to add to these wins Stewart was third in the World Championship. Next was a quieter year for Stewart: whereas he had started 53 races in 1964 the total was much lower in 1965. He concentrated on Formula One but also handled Ken Tyrrell's unsuccessful Formula Two Cooper T75-BRM, was 10th in the Le Mans 24-hours in the gas turbine Rover-BRM, and in a Team Surtees Lola T70 Mk1-Chevrolet sports car he finished third in the Guards Trophy at Brands Hatch.

For 1966 BRM built the H16-engined P83 for the new 3-litre Formula One, but the machine proved a disaster. Stewart preferred to use a 2.1-litre V8 engine in an older P261 chassis and began the season well with victory in the Tasman Cup series and the Monaco Grand Prix. He almost won the Indianapolis 500 at his first attempt, the engine of his John Mecom-entered Lola T90-Ford expiring with only 20 miles to run. A few days later Stewart's career almost ended in the Belgian Grand Prix. On the opening lap his BRM P261 spun wildly in pouring rain at the Francorchamps circuit and plunged off the road. Stewart was trapped in the overturned car and was rescued, soaked in petrol, by fellow drivers Graham Hill and Bob Bondurant, who had also crashed nearby.

Stewart suffered a broken shoulder, a cracked rib and internal bruising, but was back in racing two months later. The BRMs, were, however, outclassed and no further wins came his way. He remained with the Tyrrell team in Formula Two, beginning an association with the French marque Matra, but no wins came his way. During a visit to Australia in August, however, Stewart co-drove a Ferrari 250LM to victory in the Rothmans 12-hour sports car race at Surfers Paradise.

So far as Formula One was concerned, 1967 was a disastrous season for Stewart, best result being second in the Belgian Grand Prix in an H16 BRM P83. Driving Matra MS5s and MS7s for Tyrrell, however, Stewart enjoyed some success in Formula Two, winning at Karlskoga, Enna, Oulton Park and Albi. Driving his one and only race for Ferrari, he was second in the BOAC 500 sports car race at Brands Hatch in a 4-litre 330P shared with Chris Amon.

It came as no surprise when it was learned Stewart was to quit BRM. He almost joined Ferrari for 1968 but didn't care for Italian politics. Jackie gambled instead on a newcomer to Formula One, none other than Ken Tyrrell, who arranged to instal the Ford DFV engine in a chassis built by Matra, the MS10. It was not a brilliant car, but a combination of Stewart's exceptional driving and ever-improving tyres from Dunlop enabled Jackie to win the Dutch Grand Prix (in torrential rain), the German Grand Prix (in fog) and the United States Grand Prix. This put Stewart in contention for the World Championship, even though, in April, he cracked his wrist in a Formula Two practice accident at Jarama in Spain. This prevented participation in the Spanish and Monaco Grands Prix plus the Indianapolis 500 and meant that Stewart had to race with a plastic 'sleeve'. In the final round of the championship in Mexico his engine let him down and the title went to his mentor, Graham Hill.

By now the Stewart family was installed in Switzerland, a move precipitated by Stewart's busy schedule as much as financial reasons.

Jackie made amends in 1969. He won his first World Championship following wins in the South African, Spanish, Dutch, French, British and Italian Grands Prix, also the Daily Mail Race of Champions at Brands Hatch, all but the first victory being achieved in Matra's new Ford-engined MS80. In Formula Two Stewart won at Nürburgring and Jarama to crown his best year to date. For 1970, however, Chrysler's takeover of Matra dictated the end of Ford engines for the French cars. Stewart tested a car with Matra's own V12 engine but insisted on Ford power for 1970. Tyrrell gambled on a design from a completely new manufacturer, March. It transpired that the conventionally-designed March 701-Ford was sufficient to give Stewart victory in the Daily Mail Race of Champions and the Spanish Grand Prix, but thereafter it was outclassed by the Lotus 72. In August, however, Tyrrell unveiled one of motor racing's best-kept secrets, his own Tyrrell 001-Ford Formula One car. It was plagued by niggling problems which kept it from finishing but showed sufficient promise for Stewart to look forward to the 1971 season.

Sure enough, the Tyrrell Formula One car lived up to its promise. In 1971 Stewart won the Spanish, Monaco, French, British, German and Canadian Grands Prix to be acclaimed as World Champion for the second time. All his victories were in the same car, Tyrrell 003-Ford, a car presented to him on his retirement. Lured by the large prize funds, Stewart attempted a full season in Can-Am with a Lola T260-Chevrolet following an outing in the Chaparral 2J 'vacuum cleaner' the previous season. Although the car was uncompetitive compared with the all-conquering McLarens, Stewart won two rounds: St Jovite and Mid-Ohio.

In 1972, Stewart was handicapped by illness, a gastric ulcer preventing his participation in the Belgian Grand Prix and handicapping his performances in earlier events. Nevertheless, he fought back strongly to win the French,

Canadian and United States Grands Prix which, added to his win in Argentina in January, placed him second to Emerson Fittipaldi in the World Championship. His illness also meant the cancellation of plans to drive a works McLaren in the Can-Am series, but he raced a Ford Capri RS2600 in the Paul Ricard 6-hour touring car race and finished second. Stewart was awarded the Order of the British Empire in 1972.

On 5 April 1973, Jackie Stewart came to a decision. He was to retire from motor racing at the end of the year. He confided in three close friends, but kept the news from journalists and his family until he had competed in his last race. Fittingly, Stewart gained his third World Championship that year after wins in South Africa, Belgium, Monaco, Holland, Germany and Austria. His last race was to have been the United States Grand Prix, coincidentally his 100th Grand Prix, but he withdrew following the fatal accident to his team-mate and good friend François Cevert in practice. It was a sad note upon which to retire.

Since his retirement Stewart has been active on the promotional front, commentated on TV and radio, and coached his successors in the Tyrrell team. Despite his avowal to make a clean break from racing, Stewart did carry out a series of test drives on the Formula One cars of 1978 for *Autocar* at the Paul Ricard circuit in France. He appeared to be as fast as ever, and was prompted to say that little, save the Lotus, had changed since his day. He has also been seen at the wheel of a camera-equipped Formula One car at various circuits, giving viewers a driver's-eye view of Grand Prix racing; although retired, Stewart still figures strongly on the motor racing scene.   MK

HANS STUCK (1900-1978)
Germany

Hans Stuck was known as the 'King of the Mountains'. His forte was hill-climbing – or mountain races, as they were known abroad. Stuck was also an accomplished Grand Prix driver and record breaker. He competed until his early 60s, collecting trophies and championships before finally retiring from motor sport to coach his son Hans-Joachim, who by the 1970s was one of Germany's leading racing drivers.

Born in Warsaw (his parents were in business in Poland) on 7 December 1900, Hans Stuck enlisted in the artillery during World War I. Afterwards he studied agriculture and engineering before settling down to help manage his parents' estates.

His first car was a Dürkopp, little known outside Germany but it was both fast and well-constructed. Hans soon set his engineering knowledge to good use modifying it for competition. A quick road driver, his friends suggested he should compete in the Baden-Baden hill-climb in 1925, and bet him a crate of champagne he could not survive the distance! He did, and won his class. The following winter, Stuck tried his hand at ice racing while on holiday at Garmisch and won again. Then, he decided to try some more famous events in 1926, entering his 2-litre Dürkopp P8B in the Salzburg and Latisbon hill-climbs and the Solitude races for fun. Again, he won his class each time.

In 1927, Stuck was approached by Austro-Daimler to race one of their sports cars. Later, he graduated to a special, short-wheelbase 3-litre racing version. He won seven events in 1927, fourteen in 1928, nine in 1929 and twelve in 1930. In 1928, he was Swiss Mountain Champion, in 1929 and 1930 he was acclaimed as Austrian Mountain Champion and in 1930 he was European Mountain Champion. He was known as the 'King of the Mountains', the crowds loving the spectacular driving style of the 6ft 2in blond extrovert. In 1930, he visited Britain, and set a new course record at Shelsley Walsh.

In 1931, Stuck was approached by Mercedes-Benz to drive their 7-litre SSK cars, and he won the Lemberg Grand Prix. The following year when Mercedes withdrew, he bought his own SSK and took it to South America where he won the Brazilian Mountain Grand Prix. Upon his return to Europe, he repeated his win in the European Mountain Championship once more.

In 1934, Stuck was chosen to lead the new Auto Union Grand Prix team, and soon learned how to handle the difficult, sixteen cylinder, rear-engined machines. After establishing new records for one hour, 100 miles and 200 km on the banked Avus track in Berlin, Stuck won the German, Swiss and Czechoslovakian Grands Prix, was second in Italy and fourth in Spain. With four hill-climb victories to add to this list of achievements, he was undisputed German champion (had there been a World Championship in pre-war times, Stuck would almost certainly have won this too). He concluded his most successful season by taking a streamlined Auto Union to a 201 mph flying-mile record.

The remaining pre-World War II years were less successful. In 1935, Stuck won the Italian Grand Prix, while his best achievements on the race tracks the following season were seconds in the Tripoli and German Grands Prix. In 1939, he won the Bucharest Grand Prix. However, he was still the 'King of the Mountains' and snatched many hill-climb victories. In 1939, he also broke the one-hour water-speed record with a 5.6-litre Auto Union-engined boat and he was chosen by Mercedes-Benz to pilot their six-wheeled, aero-engined car designed by Dr Ferdinand Porsche to attack the land-speed record. The war prevented this project getting underway.

Following the war, the now ageing Stuck remained in the sport. Having gained Austrian citizenship, he was able to obtain an international licence (Germans were not allowed to compete internationally until 1950). At first, he campaigned an 1100 cc Cisitalia in small-capacity single-seater races and later he was a strong contender in the 2-litre Formula Two with an AFM designed and built by Alex von Falkenhausen. He enjoyed a heat win in the 1950 Monza Grand Prix, heading the Ferraris, while in 1951 he won at the extremely fast Grenzlandring circuit. For the 1951 Italian Grand Prix, he attended as a spectator, but the night before the race was asked to drive a works BRM P15, one of the infamous V16 machines. But after trying the car on race morning, it had to be withdrawn due to gearbox-lubrication problems.

In 1957, Stuck joined BMW as a demonstration and racing driver. Driving a 3-litre BMW 507, he won the GT class in many hill-climbs. Later, he switched to the 700 cc BMW saloon – in 1960, he won a twelve-hour race at Hockenheim with the little BMW, co-driving with Sepp Greger – and later he piloted a specially-built BMW sports car powered by the 700 cc engine. In 1963, Stuck finally retired at the age of 62. He had participated behind the wheel in over 700 events during the 38 years, and won 427 times.

More recently, Stuck coached his son, Hans-Joachim. Young 'Hanschen' was driving karts at the age of nine and lapped Nürburgring in competitive times at thirteen. He began racing saloon cars, being a member of the Ford Germany and BMW works teams, and also began a notable career in single-seaters, driving for March in both Formula One and Formula Two in 1974 and later for Shadow in Formula One. Hans senior died in February 1978.　　MK

JOHN SURTEES (b.1934)
Great Britain

Italian motor-sport enthusiasts are proudly partisan. The only thing that matters to them is that it should be an Italian car (preferably a Ferrari), that wins an international motor race and an Italian driver at the wheel. They have adopted a certain patronising acceptance of Ferrari drivers who come from just over the borders in Austria or Switzerland, especially if the man concerned has (like Clay Regazzoni) an Italian name. Should the leading Ferrari driver come from further afield – should he be an Englishman, a New Zealander, an American or a German – then the Italian crowds can be unreasonably critical and unforgiving. There was one Englishman, however, who stood out as a distinguished exception during the two-and-a-half seasons in which he led the Ferrari team, and that was John Surtees. Whatever the outcome of the event, it was the man they called 'Big John' whom the Monza crowds cheered to the echo as drivers paraded on the starting grid before the Italian Grand Prix or the 1000-kilometre sports-car race. He had earned their respect in the previous decade by bringing honour to Italy as he won honours for himself, leading the works team of MV Agusta motor cycles: the famous four-cylinder 'fire engines' (they were red, and no siren ever howled to such good purpose) from Gallarate.

John Surtees was first, and remains foremost, a racing motor cyclist; he was virtually born one. While still under regulation minimum age, he was riding as passenger in the racing sidecar piloted by his father, Jack. Things were not made easy for him: he was taught to work hard, and he never stopped. After leaving school (he was born in 1934 in Kent), he was apprenticed to the Vincent motor-cycle company, and he built for himself what must have been one of their most successful bikes, a 500 cc short-circuit racer which became known as the *Grey Shadow*. On it, he gained his first victory, in a race at Brands Hatch in 1951, his first year as a solo racer. On the track and off it, John Surtees continued to work hard, scratching successfully around all the British short circuits where courage and track craft are bred, and rapidly developing both qualities to an exceptional degree.

Before long, it was clear that his abilities exceeded the potential of the Vincent, and he acquired a Norton. This hyper-developed machine, the apotheosis of the vintage motor cycle, but still the *ne plus ultra* for the British racer, had a far higher performance and inherently better handling than the Vincent, but its ground clearance was less and Surtees at first found himself in difficulties. Using his brain – and no racer's suffered more cudgelling than his – Surtees invented a new riding technique: unable to bank his Norton as far as he wished in corners, he leaned over on the inside of the bend, shifting the combined centre of gravity of bike and rider further than the bike itself could be tilted. It worked, and has been cultivated to extremes by other riders since; but it was something to offend the purists because it was untidy. In those days, the greatest rider, the only one to elevate motor-cycle racing to an art form, was Geoffrey Duke, who was the epitome of smooth and stylish riding, seeming not to move on his mount except to raise his head a little on the way into a corner. After a couple of seasons, by which time Duke had moved on from leading the works Nortons to winning more World Championships for Gilera, Surtees took him on and beat him, not only at John's home circuit of Brands Hatch, but also at other British short circuits. His fans, overlooking the unsuitability of the four-cylinder Gilera for these tracks, went wild with enthusiasm, and Big John was on his way. In 1955, he joined the Norton team, and at the end of that year he signed to ride for MV Agusta, winning the Senior World Championship in 1956 and following through with a hat-trick of double championships.

There seemed little left for him to do. With his combination of riding skill, courage and engineering ability (he had assisted significantly in its mechanical development), he had made the fire-engine the fastest road-racing motor cycle in the world; and with seven World Championships to his credit, he announced his retirement from motor-cycle racing. He had already tried his hand in racing cars, first at the invitation of Reg Parnell, who invited him to join the Aston Martin team. Surtees tried the car at Goodwood, did well, but declined the offer, saying that he did not want to start so near the top. He also tried the rear-engined Grand Prix Vanwall, and in 1960 drove a Formula Junior Cooper for Tyrrell. Then he bought a Formula 2 Cooper, and was given a couple of drives in a Formula 1 Lotus by Colin Chapman. At Silverstone for the British GP, Surtees finished second, just four months after his first motor race; still, though, he would not sign for a works team. For two years, he drove Coopers and Lolas for Yeoman Credit and Bowmakers, under the tutelage of Parnell, even refusing the invitation to drive for Ferrari.

When he knew himself to be ready for the big time, he accepted Ferrari's repeated offer, and joined the Italian team for the 1963 season. Again, he toiled as development engineer as well as a driver, working doggedly on the new V6-engined car, the Grand Prix Dino 156, to such good purpose that he won the German, Mediterranean and Rand Grands Prix, as well as sharing two long-distance sports-car victories, finishing the season in fourth place in the World Championship.

The following year, after particularly fine victories at the Nürburgring and at Monza, Surtees won the championship. He had proved his point, and had made himself the first and only World Champion on two wheels and four. Other racing motor cyclists had tried car racing; some like Duke had failed, others – mostly of an earlier generation such as Caracciola, Nuvolari and Rosemeyer, but also more recently such as Siffert, and Surtees's own protégé Hailwood who had followed him into the MV Agusta team – had been very successful. Nevertheless, it was only Surtees who reached the top in both.

During all this time, Surtees had not allowed his association with Eric Broadley, the designer of Lola cars, to lapse. With his commitments to Ferrari limited to single-seaters and the long-distance sports-car races for the manufacturers' championship, he was free to race and help in the development of the Group Seven sports car, which became known as the T70 Lola. At this time, 'big-banger' sports cars in this category were attracting considerable attention, especially in the Can-Am series of races in North America; and it was there (at Mosport) that Surtees suffered the only really serious racing accident of his career. A suspension upright broke, and the Lola crashed violently, causing Surtees extensive injuries so serious that his career – and his life – was in great danger for some time.

Throughout the winter and the spring, Surtees devoted all his furious concentration, his indomitable willpower and his dogged courage to the impossible task of recovering his health and fitness. It was his greatest and hardest earned victory, and he confirmed it by resuming his seat in a racing car again at no less taxing an event than the 1000-kilometre sports-car race at Monza – an event that he won, with co-driver Michael Parkes, in torrential rain with a faulty screenwiper on the big 330 P3 Ferrari.

He won in the wet for Ferrari again at Spa in the Belgian Grand Prix, in the new V12 car with which he had started the new three-litre formula by winning at Syracuse and being fastest in practice at Monaco. The Spa race was to be Surtees's last for Enzo Ferrari: the two men were very fond of each other, but the Surtees personality clashed violently with that of team manager Dragoni. Things came to a head during practice for the Le Mans race of 1966, when Dragoni professed doubts about Surtees's fitness – despite the compelling evidence to the contrary – and entered a third reserve driver for the car Surtees had been scheduled to drive. In retrospect, this must be seen as the occasion rather than the cause of Surtees's resignation from the Ferrari team, but there was no doubt of that resignation being complete and final as Surtees called a press conference in the paddock to announce what he had done.

Had he stayed with Ferrari, he would probably have won himself another World Championship. As it was, in mid-season he had to hunt around for a drive, and finally came to roost with the Cooper team who were campaigning their new, heavy, and evidently very ungainly Maserati-engined car. At the Nürburgring for the German GP, Ferrari saw Big John put it on the front row of the grid, and bring it home in a damp second place behind a flying Brabham who that year was having perhaps his best and certainly his luckiest season. Surtees was having to work much harder for his success but, dogged and persevering as ever, he transformed the Cooper from a car with severe handling deficiencies to one that was capable of using more power than it had. One of the things that contributed to this change was his choice of the new low-profile Firestone tyres, in place of the older-fashioned Dunlops on which, or despite which, the Cooper had been designed. Surtees was very tyre-conscious (what good motor cyclist is not?), and his experience with the Can-Am cars undoubtedly taught him a lot in this respect.

He formed a very friendly relationship with Firestone at about this time; it was their racing manager who once made a remark in private that deserves to be made public, saying that Surtees was 'one of the only two honest men in motor racing'. It may be this quality rather than any other that made Surtees so unpopular in many quarters. He was fearlessly honest and uncompromising with himself. Perhaps hard work was an obsession, or perhaps he was just one of nature's worriers; at any rate, he always insisted on doing what he thought right without regard for his results or his reputation. If that meant that he worked everybody else to a standstill, it could only mean in turn that he had worked himself at least as hard. If some could find him pleasantly mild-mannered and an intelligent conversationalist, others could complain the same day of his being an intolerant despot.

In this lies the clue to the Surtees character that has been the object of so much critical, but rather less than objective, assessment. He is not an intense person but a serious one, who gives different impressions to different people because he is less concerned with that than with being consistent with himself. In this, he prompts recollection of a dictum of George Bernard Shaw: 'The reasonable man adapts himself to the world; the unreasonable man persists in trying to adapt the world to himself. Therefore, all progress depends upon the unreasonable man.'

We certainly saw progress made with the Cooper as the 1966 season drew to its close. At the end, Surtees won the Mexican GP with it, something that nobody would have thought possible earlier in the year. It was his second impossible achievement in twelve months, and he gave us a reminder of his first by taking a Mk II Lola T70 through the Can-Am to emerge as the overall winner.

Few victories came his way after this. In 1967, he undertook the burden of making the grotesquely overweight Honda V12 into an effective and successful Grand Prix car. Its engine, as one might expect, was quite magnificent; the rest of it, as was no more surprising, was pretty dreadful. Including the conditions under which Surtees worked; admittedly, he was supplied with Japanese mechanics, and they in turn were supplied with acceptable food and plenty of clean white gloves air-freighted from Tokyo, but he had no effective liaison with the factory design staff, and the difficulties of designing and developing a complex machine at such a long distance from the factory were daunting in the extreme. Surtees simply worked hard and made everybody else associated with him do likewise – and then justified it all with a superb ·victory at Monza in 1967. It was one of the greatest races in the history of the sport, one in which the late Jim Clark put up one of the most incredible performances of his career, only to run out of petrol on the last lap. Close behind him (so close that they nearly ran down Colin Chapman, who was looking for Clark to take the chequered flag) came Surtees and Brabham, the old master of tactics and proprietor of the year's most successful racing car. With one crucial corner left, Surtees sold Brabham the most exquisite dummy imaginable, leaving him all crossed up and nowhere to go, while Big John slipped across behind him to take the lead.

One thing Surtees seems never to learn is not to back a loser. After another year persevering fruitlessly with Honda, he joined the BRM team, hoping to make the P153 car raceworthy. The best he managed was third place in the United States GP, but neither the organisation nor the vehicle seemed to match the standards to which he had once been accustomed, and he felt increasingly tempted to be his own master. Already he had developed substantial business interests, and now he established Team Surtees as car manufacturers as well as entrants. Having severed his connection with Lola, Surtees went to the designer Leonard Terry to ask for a Formula 5000 design. Terry had one already, developed for Roger Nathan but not taken up; and with slight modifications to satisfy Surtees's critical eye, this car, the Terrier Mk 15, became the Mk 17, and thenceforward the Surtees TS5.

The TS5 was almost immediately successful in competition, Trevor Taylor and David Hobbs winning most of their races on both sides of the Atlantic by the end of the 1969 season. It was followed by the TS7 Formula One car, which Surtees often drove himself, having kept his hand in meanwhile with a McLaren he had bought.

In the 1970s John Surtees concentrated on designing his own Formula One cars and running Team Surtees, but he was never anywhere near as successful in this field as he had been as a driver. In fact the best result from a Surtees car in a Grand Prix was the fourth place Vittorio Brambilla managed in the 1977 Belgian GP, behind Nilsson, Lauda and Peterson.

The 1978 season was a disaster for Surtees. His last car, the TS20, proved to be little better than the TS19, British driver Rupert Keegan ended a dismal season with a broken wrist at Zandvoort in practice for the Dutch GP, and Vittorio Brambilla was badly injured at Monza. Possibly taking this run of bad luck as an omen, John Surtees retired from the Formula One scene at the end of that season, but nothing can take away the fact that Surtees's great skill and determination had made him the only man to master racing on both two wheels and four.   LJKS

PIERO TARUFFI (b.1906)
Italy
An engineer, a racing driver, a motor-cycle racer, a record-breaker and a team manager, Piero Taruffi enjoyed a long and involved career participating in motor-sport, stopping only when he had satisfied his greatest ambition: to win the Mille Miglia. This was in 1957, when he was fifty, 27 years after his first attempt at this classic Italian road race. He was known as the Silver Fox because of his grey hair.

Born on 12 October 1906, Taruffi was presented with a 350 cc AJS racing motor cycle and entered for his first race in January 1925. At the Monte Mario hill-climb near Rome the enthusiastic eighteen-year-old was second overall and winner of the 350 cc class. More successes followed with a variety of machines: P&M, Guzzi, Norton and OPRA. It was inevitable that Taruffi would move on to four wheels and he was invited to co-drive his friend Lelio Pellegrini's 2.3-litre Bugatti on the 1930 Mille Miglia. After some problems with loose wiring, overheating and misfiring, they were fortieth.

Next they entered the Tunis-Tripoli regularity trial and won in Pellegrini's Alfa Romeo 1750. In 1931 Pellegrini acquired a 2-litre Itala Model 65 sports car and it was entered for several hill-climbs and races. At Montenero Taruffi was eighth behind topline drivers and, following some minor race wins plus a 112 mph lap on his Norton motor cycle at Monza, Taruffi was invited to drive for Scuderia Ferrari.

Taruffi won his two events for Ferrari at the end of 1931, driving a 2.3-litre Alfa Romeo to victory in the Lake of Bolsena regularity trial and the Coppa Frigo hill-climb. In 1932 he led the Mille Miglia, but was sidelined with electrical and engine faults. He was second in Rome's Royal Grand Prix and the Francorchamps 24-hours and won the Coppa Grand Sasso race and the Coppa Frigo hill-climb. In 1933, Enzo Ferrari took over the responsibility of running the works Alfa Romeo team; he had more drivers than cars, which meant missing some races.

Piero thought of returning to motor cycles, but with the aid of two friends purchased a 3-litre Maserati 8C for 1934. He also joined an aeronautical and motor cycle firm, assisting on development. After a fifth place in the Mille Miglia in an 1100 cc Maserati, he was invited to drive Maserati's most fearsome car in the Tripoli Grand Prix. The V5 model, it featured a 4½ litre V16 engine which developed 350 bhp. However, Taruffi locked his brakes at the end of a very fast straight and crashed heavily, putting himself in hospital for several weeks. He emerged to be offered a Scuderia Ferrarii Alfa Romeo.

Following World War II, Taruffi was invited to join Piero Dusio's Cisitalia set-up in Turin; the single-seater Cisitalias were small, using 1100 cc Fiat engines. As well as overseeing these machines he raced them, winning his class in the 1947 Italian championship. Driving an 1100cc Cisitalia sports car he was second overall and class winner in the 1948 Giro di Sicilia. That year Piero also gained four world speed records in Tarf I, a Guzzi motor-cycle-engined 'twin-boom' record-breaking car. With Guzzi, Gilera and Maserati-engined Tarfs Taruffi continued to break records until his retirement in 1957.

Taruffi raced for many teams in the immediate post-war years, but he rejoined the Ferrari team in 1951. The highlight of the year was victory in the Carrera Panamericana in a 2.6-litre Ferrari 212 Export shared with Luigi Chinetti. During the following year, in which he married Isabella, he won his only World Championship Grand Prix, the Swiss at Berne, in a 2-litre Ferrari 500. He was ultimately third in the championship. He also raced in Britain, driving Tony Vandervell's *Thinwall Special* (a modified 4½-litre Ferrari 375) to victory at Dundrod and Silverstone, while he sampled a 500 cc Cooper at Brands Hatch.

In 1953, Piero was invited to join the Lancia sports-car team, but the car broke down in the Mille Miglia, the Targa Florio (when he crashed while leading, having mistaken a pit signal) and Le Mans. In the following year, the Mille Miglia slipped out of his grasp yet again when a slower car moved over and caused Taruffi to crash his leading Lancia. He did,

however, win the Targa Florio and the Giro di Sicilia. Lancia withdrew from sports-car races at the end of 1954, so Taruffi went back to Ferrari for next season. He won the Giro di Sicilia in a 3.7-litre Ferrari 118LM, but quit the team at the end of the year after a row with Enzo Ferrari about a suitable car for the Targa Florio.

The 1956 season was disappointing. He raced for Maserati in sports-car events and accepted the offer of a British Vanwall for the Italian Grand Prix, being sidelined with transmission failure. In 1957, fifty-year-old Taruffi was still racing. He was a member of the works Chevrolet team in the Sebring 12 hours and also drove a Formula One Maserati 250F to fourth place in the Syracuse Grand Prix. For the Mille Miglia he was offered a works Ferrari, a 4-litre 335 Sport. Despite almost giving up when rain made conditions frightening, Taruffi crossed the finish line to be told by Isabella he had won. He did not know rival Peter Collins had retired within 125 miles of the finish! Taruffi had won the Mille Miglia at last!   MK

MAURICE TRINTIGNANT
(b.1917)
France

Son of a farmer, Maurice Trintignant was born on 30 October 1917, youngest of five brothers, Raoul, René, Louis and Henri. René and Louis raced Bugattis and other machinery and, as an 11-year-old schoolboy, Maurice sometimes acted as a riding mechanic.

In 1938, after his brother Louis was killed, Maurice purchased the very Bugatti T51 in which his brother had been killed and entered his first race, the round-the-houses Pau Grand Prix. Racing against tough opposition he was fifth. He won his second race, the Grand Prix des Frontières at Chimay, and repeated this victory in 1939. But for the outbreak of war he would have joined the famous Ecurie Bleue to race Delahayes and Maseratis.

Returning home from the war in the summer of 1945, he rebuilt his beloved Bugatti (which had been dismantled and stored in a barn) and entered the first post-war motor race, the Coupe de la Libération in the Bois de Boulogne. He retired when the engine cut out and upon opening the bonnet discovered the fuel filter was clogged – with rat droppings. Evidently, a nest of rats had enjoyed the hospitality of the Bugatti's fuel tank while the car had been dismantled. Race winner Jean-Pierre Wimille enquired of his friend Trintignant the reason for retirement and Maurice said the filter was clogged with *petoule*, a word in the local dialect which meant rat-droppings. Wimille collapsed with laughter and Trintignant was immediately landed with the nickname *Le Petoulet*.

In 1946 the faithful Bugatti – known as *Le Grandmère* – brought Trintignant second place in the French championship, and later he turned to various other machinery: Amilcar, Delage, Simca-Gordini. In 1948 he became a member of the Simca-Gordini works team, a team for whom he raced until the end of 1953. However, his first season with Amédée Gordini's cars was almost his last. At Berne, the difficult Swiss road circuit, he was running second in the Formula Two race when his 1500 cc Simca-Gordini spun and crashed. Maurice was hurled from the cockpit and was narrowly missed by four other drivers. He was taken to hospital and was unconscious for eight days. A newspaper carried a story about his 'death' the next day. But he underwent an operation and fifteen days later Maurice Trintignant's name was removed from the critical list. He returned to racing again in 1949.

In 1954 French privateer Louis Rosier bought two Ferraris for Formula One racing and entrusted Trintignant with one; he won the Buenos Aires Grand Prix against Ferrari and Maserati works opposition. By the time the European season got underway he was a member of the official Ferrari team. He won the Hyères 12-hours and the Le Mans 24-hours, the Caen and Rouen Grands Prix and the Tourist Trophy (on scratch with Mike Hawthorn), was second in the Belgian Supercortemaggiore, Pau and Syracuse Grands Prix and at Dakar. Not surprisingly he was champion of France, a title which he regained in 1955. This was the year his cool, calculated driving won him the Monaco Grand Prix in a Ferrari 625, his first World Championship Grand Prix victory.

For 1956 Trintignant signed with Bugatti, the French firm intending to make a post-war comeback to Grand Prix racing. The Bugatti T251 was a disaster, only running in the French Grand Prix where Trintignant retired with a seized throttle linkage.

It was back to Ferrari for 1957, but his only success was a win in the Reims Formula Two race. At the end of the year he was invited to drive a BRM P25 in the Moroccan Grand Prix and finished third, silencing critics who thought that at 39, Trintignant was on the decline. Far from it. In 1958 he agreed to race for private entrant Rob Walker in both Formula One and Formula Two. He won the F2 Pau Grand Prix and then the Monaco Grand Prix, beating the Ferrari team. He later won the F1 Caen Grand Prix, the Clermont-Ferrand Formula Two race, was third in the German Grand Prix and was crowned champion of France once more.

In 1959 Trintignant remained with Walker, finishing second in the United States and third in the Monaco Grands Prix, and piloted a works Aston Martin DBR/300 to second place in the Le Mans 24-hours. For 1960 he agreed to race Aston Martin's new DBR5/250 Formula One car, but it was a disaster. Nevertheless, he won the Buenos Aires Grand Prix in Rob Walker's Cooper T45-Climax and, driving for Porsche, was fourth in the Nürburgring 1000-km. His own Formula Two Cooper T45-Maserati entered by Scuderia Serenissima results.

In 1961 an underpowered Cooper T45-Maserati entered by Scuderia Serenissima provided little success for Trintignant in the new 1½-litre Formula One. Next season he was back with Rob Walker, but apart from a victory in the Pau Grand Prix with an old Lotus 18/21-Climax, he had no luck. His last success in Formula One was in 1964 when, at 46, he was a rousing fifth in the German Grand Prix in his own privately-entered BRM P57. His last competitive racing appearance was in the 1965 Le Mans 24-hours where he retired his Ford GT40 after having some difficulties with his gearbox.

But Maurice Trintignant was more than a racing driver. He took control of his family's vineyard (naming the wine *Le Petoulet*) and developed it into a thriving concern. In 1959 he was also elected mayor of Vergèze, and a year later he gained further distinction when he was created a Chevalier of the Legion of Honour for his services to France.   MK

BOBBY UNSER (b.1934)
AL UNSER (b.1939)
USA

Al and Bobby Unser are both multiple Indianapolis winners. Both have been winners at Pike's Peak hill-climb, a venue which was almost considered the property of two generations of the Unser family. Both have tried road-racing in addition to their forte, the USAC national championship trail. And both are deadly rivals.

The Unser family, with origins in Switzerland, is legendary in American motor racing circles. Their father, Jerry, raced from time to time before retiring in 1934. So did their two uncles. One, Louis – nicknamed 'Old Man Mountain' – competed at Pike's Peak and won nine times. He last raced there in 1967 at the age of 71. The other uncle, Joe, was killed there in 1929. There were four Unser brothers. The eldest were twins, Jerry and Louis. Jerry's Kuzma-Offenhauser hit the wall in the 1959 Indianapolis 500 and caught fire, the 26-year-old driver succumbed to serious burns two weeks later. As a result of the accident drivers were made to wear fire-resistant clothing. Louis won the stock car category at Pike's Peak in 1960 and 1961, but subsequently fell victim to multiple sclerosis and became involved with building competition boat engines.

Bobby was born on 10 February 1934, and Al on 29 May 1939. Both were affected by Jerry's accident. Bobby's trademark since has been his flat-out driving style, one that has resulted in engine blow-ups and crashes as well as victories. Al, taught to race by Bobby, developed a more analytical approach.

Bobby Unser began racing modified stock cars in 1949 at the age of 15. He won the New Mexico modified stock car championship in both 1950 and 1951 and then graduated to midgets and sprint cars. In 1956 he won the championship car division of the demanding 12½-mile Pike's Peak hill-climb, a demanding dirt road in the Rocky Mountains of Colorado. In 1957 he was fifth and from 1958 won it six times in succession. Brother Al broke his string of victories in 1964. Bobby won again in 1966, 1968 and 1974. In all he had twelve wins at Pike's Peak, nine times in championship cars, once in a sports car and twice in stock cars.

In 1963 Bobby had his first taste of the Indianapolis 500, driving one of Andy Granatelli's fabulous 837 bhp supercharged Novis, extremely quick but unlucky machines. He qualified sixteenth fastest and had rocketed to tenth before crashing into the wall on lap 3. For 1964 Unser handled a specially-commissioned four-wheel-drive Novi with a Ferguson P104 chassis, but retired early again after suffering minor burns running through a wall of blazing fuel on the track. The next year, Unser was handily-placed until an oil line broke on the 69th of the 200 laps.

A move was made to a turbocharged Offenhauser-engined Huffaker for the 1966 race, but Bobby only managed eighth. For 1967 he raced an Offy-engined Eagle for Bob Wilke, finishing ninth at Indianapolis following a six-minute pit-stop.

The 1968 season was Bobby Unser's greatest, highlighted with victory in the Indianapolis 500 in the Wilke-entered Eagle-Offenhauser. It was a surprise win, Joe Leonard's leading Lotus 56-Pratt & Witney turbine failing with a mere nine of the 200 laps to run. In practice, however, Unser had become the first person to lap the 2½-mile Indianapolis Motor Speedway at over 170 mph, registering 170.778 mph. Earlier in the year he had placed fifth at Hanford, first at Las Vegas, Phoenix and Trenton; after Indy he suffered occasional sour luck and the outcome of the USAC national championship depended on the final round at Riverside. Bobby was a safe second to Dan Gurney and won the title by the narrow margin of 6.8 points – 4326 to Mario Andretti's 4319.2.

In 1969 Unser raced the four-wheel-drive Lola T152-Offenhauser at Indianapolis, finishing third in the difficult-to-handle car. Back in an Eagle, he won the Langhorne 150, but in the latter part of the season he had to give best to his brother Al…it was the same story in 1970, except for Langhorne where Bobby beat Al by a second after charging to the front in the closing minutes. Al won at Phoenix and in the Trenton 300 and Ted Horn 100. Eleventh was his Indianapolis placing in an Eagle-Ford. The following season, racing a works Olsonite Eagle-Offenhauser, Bobby led almost every USAC national championship race only for mechanical failure to intervene. His only bright spot was victory in the Trenton 200 where he beat Mario Andretti by no less than two laps at a record average of 140.771 mph.

It was the same story in 1972. Unser had the fastest car in his works Eagle-Offenhauser. He had seven pole positions in succession to prove it. But again his car flattered only to deceive. He registered only four wins, two at Phoenix, one at Trenton and one at Wisconsin. In 1973 Unser's luck was again down, with only a repeat win in the Rex Mays 150 at Wisconsin to show for Bobby's efforts. But next season his luck turned. He appeared to play more of a waiting game, coming into the competition in the closing stages of a race. He won the Californian 500 at Ontario Motor Speedway and continued with victories in the Trentonian 200, the Michigan 200 and the Trenton Times 300 to clinch the USAC national championship for the second time in his career.

Bobby Unser won the Indianapolis 500 for the second time in 1975 and pushed his USAC earnings over the £1 million mark. He also ran in some Formula 5000 races in the turbo-charged Eagle-Offenhauser and underlined the fact he could be competitive on road courses as well as oval tracks.

After Bobby's 1975 Indianapolis win, in the Jorgensen Eagle at a 149.2 mph average, he was somewhat overshadowed by brother Al. This was due in part to Bobby Unser's choice of car; his Lightning Offenhauser of 1977, for example, failed to finish a single USAC round. An outing in the final round in a Lightning with the Offenhauser engine replaced by a Cosworth prompted him to switch his allegiance to Dan Gurney's Eagle team which used the increasingly popular Cosworth DFX. 1978's Indianapolis, won by Al Unser, featured a very creditable fifth place for Bobby in a new Eagle hampered by a broken rear anti-roll bar.

After an eighth place at Silverstone and a failure to finish at Brands Hatch in the two British USAC rounds which were introduced in 1978, Bobby Unser's season finished on a low note.

1979 was the year of the big split between CART and USAC and both Bobby and Al stuck with the former. Bobby very nearly won the CART championship, by virtue of six wins, including the prestigious California 500, in his Norton-sponsored Penske. In the end he gave best to his team-mate, Rick Mears, who not only finished every race but also took the all important win at Indy, where Bobby fell from a commanding lead to an eventual fifth place with gearbox problems.

With the Penske team's total domination of the 1979 CART trail, it was not surprising that 1980 saw Bobby campaigning the team's new PC9. He finished runner-up again, having won the California and Pocono 500s, this time to Johnny Rutherford's all-conquering Chaparral. He ended the season as a spectator, having injured his foot in a big practice accident at the final round of the series, at Phoenix.

Al Unser began racing at the age of 18, racing Supermodified cars from 1957 to 1963. His business, however, was the running of a scrap yard which his father had purchased for him. In 1960 he ran at Pike's Peak for the first time, finishing second to Bobby. He was runner-up to his elder brother again in 1962, but in 1964 he broke the hill record *and* Bobby's run of six successive victories. In 1964 he entered the world of USAC racing, competing in both the sprint and national championship divisions, and the following season saw him tackle that pinnacle of American motor racing, the Indianapolis 500. Al passed his rookie's driving test in a machine entered by the Arciero brothers and powered by a Maserati engine, but the Italian unit blew up and as there was no spare it seemed Al would not make the official qualification runs. At the last minute he was offered a ride in A.J. Foyt's back-up Lola T80-Ford, qualified 32nd on the 33-car grid and soldiered through to finish ninth. His only win that year was at Pike's Peak.

In 1966 Unser offered his services to Lotus, who had a vacancy alongside '65 winner Jim Clark in the STP-backed works team of Lotus 38-Ford. Al climbed as far as third place before crashing. In other USAC national championship events he was second in the Hoosier Grand Prix, the Trenton 200 and the Phoenix 200, finishing fifth in the points table. In 1967, as number two to Jackie Stewart in the John Mecom Lola T90-Ford team, Al finished second in the Indianapolis 500. In this team he began to work with George Bignotti, the famed preparer of USAC cars.

First USAC win for Al Unser came in 1968 – the year brother Bobby won the Indianapolis 500 – when he won at Nazareth on a mile dirt-track. He later won two races at Indianapolis Raceway Park (a separate track to the Indianapolis Motor Speedway) and two at Langhorne. At Indianapolis he escaped injury when his four-wheel-drive Lola T150-Ford lost a wheel and was destroyed when it slammed into the wall.

For 1969 the Al Unser/George Bignotti partnership joined with Vel Miletich and Parnelli Jones, who fielded a new Lola T152-Ford for Unser to drive at Indianapolis. After setting rapid practice times he fell off a motor cycle fooling with Jones and broke his leg. Angry with himself, he put his all into his racing when he returned to the tracks later in the year. He won five of the final six races in the USAC national championship – at Milwaukee, Sacramento (with broken suspension), Seattle, Phoenix and DuQuoin – and was a close second in the sixth at Riverside to Mario

Andretti. Despite his curtailed season, Unser was second in the championship trail.

There was no stopping Al Unser in 1970. Racing the Bignotti-developed Colt, based on a Lola, Unser won at Phoenix, was second at Sears Point, third at Trenton and then won the Indianapolis 500. It was the highlight of his career, at a time when brother Bobby's fortunes were in the doldrums. And like Bobby in '68, Unser went on to take the USAC national championship, winning ten of the eighteen rounds. He won at Indianapolis Raceway Park, won on the Springfield, DuQuoin, Sedalia and Sacramento dirt tracks, won at Milwaukee by a margin of three laps and conquered brother Bobby in the Trenton 300. In the inaugural California 500 at the Ontario Motor Speedway, Unser would have won again if his turbocharged car had not failed fourteen laps from the finish.

Once again racing Vel's Parnelli Colt-Ford, Unser began the 1971 season on top form. He won the opening USAC national championship round at Rafaela in Argentina and hammered brother Bobby at Phoenix. Then he won the Indianapolis 500 for the second year in succession, driving a confident race and never dropping lower than fourth throughout the 200 laps.

In 1972 the Vel's Parnelli team fielded new Maurice Phillippe-designed VPJ-001 cars for a formidable array of three former USAC champions, Mario Andretti, Joe Leonard and Al Unser. It was a disappointing year for Al. He failed to win a single championship race, best place being second in the Indianapolis 500, while his brother won four races.

The 1973 season began well with victory in the Texas 200 in April, but the new Offy-engined Vel's Parnelli VPJ-002s suffered from understeering problems as well as gearbox and engine failures and Al failed to win another USAC national championship round. Most galling was his luck in the California 500 at Ontario. He was a contender for the lead until the closing minutes when the gearbox broke. Some consolation was his clinching of the three-race USAC national Dirt Track championship from team-mate Andretti. A change to the ubiquitous Eagle chassis brought better fortune in 1974, Al winning the Norton 250 at Michigan and taking sufficient place results – including second to brother Bobby in the California 500 – to be fourth in the end-of-season points table. Unser also added another string to his bow, racing in Formula 5000 in

late 1974 and 1975 and proving to be a strong contender.

In the last rounds of the 1975 USAC championship Al drove the Cosworth DFX V8-engined Parnelli, a car which he used throughout 1976 when he won three championship rounds, including the Schaefer 500 at Pocono to give the turbocharged Cosworth engine its first USAC victory. 1977 saw Al Unser and the Parnelli VPJ6B gain only one USAC victory, in the California 500 at Ontario Motor Speedway at an average speed of 154.7 mph, although he did manage third place at Indianapolis, and came second in the championship behind Tom Sneva.

A move to Jim Hall's Chaparral Cars' Lola for 1978 gave Al a much better season, and he became the first man in USAC history to win the 'big three' races – the California 500 (for the second year running), the Schaefer 500 at Pocono, and Indianapolis. The speed of the Cosworth-powered Lola enabled Al Unser to round off the season by coming second in the USAC Citicorp Cup national championship.

Like Bobby, Al went with the CART championship in 1979. From Indy onwards, with John Barnard's new Pennzoil-backed Chaparral 2K, he looked to be the man to beat. In the end, however, unreliability kept him from the winner's circle until the race of the season – the Phoenix 150. He had led Indy as he pleased until an oil leak brought him to a halt. In the end he took fifth place in the CART series.

Surprisingly, 1980 saw Al leave Chaparral for the fledgling Longhorn team and their Williams-based cars. In spite of promising testing results and the Williams domination of Grand Prix racing, Unser had a disappointing year, dogged by straightforward lack of pace, but the association continued for 1981.

A favourite American parlour game in recent years has been to argue which of the Unser brothers is the better. Some go for Bobby's speed and guts; others for Al's impassive, calculated approach. On the track there's nothing between them, and although good friends, they are deadly rivals until the chequered flag drops.   MK

ACHILLE VARZI (1904-1948)
Italy

Dour, unsmiling and worldly, Achille Varzi was one of the greatest drivers of his day, but fate had singled him out to play a kind of *Fidus Achates* to Tazio Nuvolari, and so it was inevitable that he should be overshadowed by the extrovert personality of his contemporary.

Born in 1904, the son of a comfortably off textile manufacturer in Galliate, near Milan, Varzi first came to public notice as a motor cyclist (as indeed was his brother Angelo), riding Sunbeam and Garelli machines. Varzi's cold, calculating, precise style contrasted vividly with the ebullience of Nuvolari, and both were given top billing during 1924, although, oddly enough, they rarely appeared together.

In 1924, Varzi was the first Italian to enter for the Isle of Man TT, riding a Dot-Bradshaw, and was well up with the leaders when he was forced to run off the road to avoid a rider who had fallen off ahead of him. For this 'brave and sporting action' he was awarded the Nisbet Trophy.

In 1927, Nuvolari and Varzi entered into partnership to form a racing stable of Type 35 Bugattis, which made its debut at the 1928 Tripoli Grand Prix. Varzi took Guido Bignami as mechanic, an association which was to last throughout Varzi's racing career (Bignami subsequently became Fangio's mechanic). Varzi took the lead at an early stage, but Nuvolari fought back, and eventually Varzi was slowed by ignition trouble, and finished third. After only a few races, Varzi felt that his style was being cramped by Nuvolari, so he took advantage of the family finances to buy himself a P2 Alfa Romeo, and set up on his own late in 1928. In the Italian GP, marred by Materassi's tragic crash, Varzi came second, ahead of his erstwhile partner, and during 1929 won so many victories that Nuvolari was stung into buying a P2 so that he could compete on the same terms. In the Coppa Montenero at Leghorn, Varzi finished no less than two minutes ahead of Nuvolari, who was driving encased in plaster as the result of a crash in the Coppa del Mare motor-cycle race that occurred only a week earlier.

The 1930 Mille Miglia saw Varzi, driving an Alfa 1750 sports car, outsmarted by Nuvolari's driving tactics, to be beaten by a matter of seconds; but he took his revenge in the Targa Florio. By now, Varzi had become a member of the Alfa works team, and had sold his P2 racer to the company; but he drove this racing car in the Targa (which was really a sports-car event) and won at record speed.

Nuvolari joined Alfa Romeo in 1930 and, predictably, Varzi left, to join the rising star of Maserati, winning the Coppa Acerbo on his first time out with his new car. He was also victorious in the Spanish and Italian Grands Prix, as well as coming third in an Alfa 1750 in the Ulster TT. These achievements earned him the title of champion of Italy for the season.

For 1931, there was yet another change of mount, this time to a 2.3-litre Bugatti Type 51, with which he won at Tunis, Alessandria and the French GP; 1932 was not such a good season, with only one victory, at Tunis, combined with retirement in the Mille Miglia and in the Monaco Grand Prix.

Varzi was back on form in 1933, with the 4.9-litre Bugatti Type 54, and the Monaco Grand Prix saw a most exciting duel between the Bugatti and Nuvolari's Scuderia Ferrari Alfa, with the two men fighting for supremacy for 99 out of the hundred laps. On the final circuit, Varzi jabbed the gear lever into third, and held it there, gunning his engine at well over the safety limit to take the lead. Nuvolari responded with similar tactics, but his engine burst into flames and he had to abandon it fifty yards from the finishing line. The Tripoli GP was another close fought battle between the two rivals, again ending in a win for Varzi; but the event was not as competitive as it might have been, for several of the other drivers had agreed to hold back and give Varzi a clear run through the field in exchange for a percentage of the prize money from the winning lottery ticket.

It was back to Alfa for 1934, and in a Scuderia Ferrari car, Varzi won the Mille Miglia, having wisely equipped his machine with wet-weather tyres to compensate for the appalling conditions. With a 2.9-litre Alfa racer, Varzi took nine firsts and several other good places during the season, although at Modena, on the Ferrari team's home ground, Nuvolari's Maserati overtook Varzi with sufficient ease for the 'Flying Mantuan' to cock a snook at his rival as he passed.

Nuvolari rejoined the Scuderia Ferrari in 1935, but Varzi moved on, to drive one of the new and treacherous rear-engined Auto Unions. He won his first race with this model, the Tunis GP in May, but the cars seemed dogged by minor development troubles during the rest of the season.

In 1936, Varzi took second place in the Monaco GP, despite torrential rain, then won at Tripoli with a record lap of nearly 142 mph. The following week, though, at Tunis, Varzi had his first-ever racing crash. There were no more outright victories that season; however, there was a third in the Hungarian GP at Budapest and a narrow defeat by Nuvolari in the Italian GP in Monza Park, in which Varzi had entered his Auto Union as a privateer.

Indeed, it seemed as though Varzi's career had passed its peak: he was out of racing for much of 1937 (it was rumoured there was a woman in the case), although he won the San Remo Voiturette GP in a Maserati 6CM. His health was said to be bad, there was talk of drug addiction, and Varzi did not make a comeback to his old form until 1946, with an Alfa Romeo 158. But, after two successful seasons, Varzi skidded on a rain-soaked track while practising for the Swiss GP on the Bremgarten circuit, and was killed instantly.

DBW

GILLES VILLENEUVE (b.1952)
Canada

Gilles Villeneuve's rise to fame in Grand Prix racing was quick, controversial and unorthodox. It was also almost inevitable, because a talent like Villeneuve's is a rare commodity, even in the highly competitive world of Formula One. Indeed, it was his talent that saved the day when, in the early stages of his Grand Prix contract with Ferrari, his career nearly ended almost before it had begun.

Villeneuve was born in Canada on 18 January 1952 and it was his father who introduced him to the world of speed. By the time he was thirteen, Gilles had already begun to race snowmobiles. His progress was impressive and by 1973 the French-speaking youngster had won the Canadian snowmobile championship and with it some $13,000. The money was quickly spent in acquiring a locally built Formula Ford machine and Villeneuve's four-wheeled racing career officially began.

Villeneuve's first season in Formula Ford was highly successful and he won seventy per cent of the races in which he competed. Fired up by the enthusiasm of success, he set his sights on the Canadian Formula Atlantic championship and after scraping together all his finances, plus some sponsorship money from Schweppes, Villeneuve signed for the Ecurie Canada team. It was not, however, a very happy time for either him or the team, both of whom were busy learning the ropes of Formula Atlantic racing. In fact, the season ended in disaster with Villeneuve breaking a leg in an accident during practice for an event at Mosport.

Luckily, help was not far away. During the previous winter Villeneuve had scooped the world snowmobile championship and, encouraged by his success, the Canadian Skiroule company signed him to a contract which included a deal for Gilles to continue racing in Formula Atlantic. For the 1975 season Gilles also acquired the services of Ray Wardell as team manager and it was largely Wardell's influence that enabled the diminutive French-Canadian to develop into a regular race-winning driver. By the beginning of 1976 the Villeneuve/Wardell combination had become the team to beat in Formula Atlantic in Canada and that year saw Villeneuve drive his white March 76B to achieve nine wins in ten races.

The turning point in Villeneuve's career came at the end of the 1976 season with a spectacular win at the Trois Rivières circuit over drivers of the calibre of James Hunt, Patrick Depailler and Vittorio Brambilla, specially imported to add colour and competition to the occasion. Villeneuve's victory was hard-fought and his achievement brought him instant international recognition.

Shortly afterwards Villeneuve was invited to Europe by Teddy Mayer, head of the McLaren Formula One racing team, and offered a contract whereby McLaren would run a third car for Gilles at selected Grands Prix during the 1977 season. From relative obscurity, Villeneuve was now on the verge of the big time in Grand Prix racing.

As events subsequently proved, however, the McLaren contract was not as promising as it first appeared. The pressures of running three cars were soon felt by the highly-competitive team from Colnbrook and the only event in which Villeneuve competed was the British Grand Prix at Silverstone. Villeneuve nevertheless seized the opportunity and his performance was most impressive. He qualified on the fourth row of the grid and during the race maintained seventh place, eventually dropping back to eleventh position when a faulty temperature gauge cost him a couple of laps in the pits.

After his superlative performance at Silverstone it was expected that Villeneuve would be drafted into the McLaren team for 1978 but this was not to be. Towards the end of the season he was advised that Patrick Tambay of France was to be taken on as McLaren number two and that he should look elsewhere for a drive.

By this time, however, it was obvious that here was a talent that could not be overlooked and Gilles was quickly snapped up by the Ferrari team. Shortly before the premature departure from Ferrari of team leader Niki Lauda, towards the end of the 1977 season, Villeneuve suddenly found himself a works Ferrari driver alongside Carlos Reutemann. Gilles's Ferrari debut was at Mosport in his native Canada where he was eventually classified twelfth, in spite of crashing heavily during the race due to oil on the circuit.

Villeneuve's next Grand Prix race proved even more disastrous. During the Japanese Grand Prix at Fuji, his car collided with that of Ronnie Peterson and cartwheeled off the circuit, killing two onlookers standing in a prohibited area. It was a bleak start to his career with Ferrari but fortunately the Italian team refused to lose faith in their new recruit, a faith which was eventually to be rewarded during the forthcoming season.

For the 1978 season Villeneuve again teamed up with Carlos Reutemann and the Ferrari camp was a much happier place than it had been for some time. Villeneuve started his season with eighth place in Argentina, but there then followed a string of retirements (which included a spectacular accident while he was leading the US Grand Prix West) before he scored his first championship points with fourth place in Belgium. As the season progressed, so too did the young Canadian's confidence. He took an eighth place in Germany and followed this up with a fine third place in Austria. Then came Monza and a stirring performance on a most unhappy day; Villeneuve led for most of the race, only to be penalised one minute for a jumped start. This dropped him to seventh place but it was by now obvious that Villeneuve had established himself as a front runner. To prove the point, Gilles returned to Canada and, in front of 80,000 ecstatic fellow countrymen, proceeded to drive the race of his life to win the Labatt-sponsored Grand Prix of Canada.

The start of the 1979 season only emphasised the enormous potential of the quietly spoken French Canadian for, after a couple of disappointing results in South America, he won the next two races in the series, the South African and the US Grand Prix West with the new T4 Ferrari. In the end it was Villeneuve's teammate Jody Scheckter who won the championship but Gilles was a worthy runner-up, adding to his early season successes with second places

in France, Italy and Canada and a superb victory in the United States Grand Prix East, at Watkins Glen. While Villeneuve was obviously maturing as a Grand Prix driver he still had not yet shaken off some of the image that being such a hard charger creates. In France his last lap wheel-to-wheel dice with René Arnoux brought reactions varying from acclaim to outright condemnation and his three-wheeled drive to the pits after a tyre exploded in the Dutch Grand Prix was severely criticised by many, but the simple fact is that Villeneuve does not know how to give up – while there is any hope he will drive on.

With a little more luck Villeneuve might even have been champion in 1979 but in the event he was a superb team-mate for Scheckter and no-one was surprised to see the partnership continue in 1980. Sadly, however, the Ferrari team was well out of the running with mechanical and tyre problems and it was only sheer guts that hauled Villeneuve into any sort of competitive position during the year. He scored only four times, with fifth place in Monaco and Canada and sixth in Belgium and Germany – all earned the hard way. He had several accidents during the year, including one miraculous escape when a rear tyre disintegrated at near maximum speed in Italy.

During practice for that race Villeneuve had tried the new Ferrari 126C turbocharged car with which he would lead the team in 1981. Most people in motor racing would consider it only a matter of time before the young Canadian becomes World Champion, as he is one of the all time great natural talents.   MW/BL

LUIGI VILLORESI (b.1909)
Italy

Luigi Villoresi was born in Milan on 16 May 1909, and began racing in 1931 at the same time as his elder brother Emilio. In the 1935 Coppa Ciano *voiturette* event at Montenero his modified Fiat sports car was third, and the following year he was third again in the same event driving a Maserati. He showed his versatility in 1936 as a class winner in the Monte Carlo Rally.

In 1937, driving a Maserati 6CM (he remained faithful to the Maserati marque for many years), Villoresi won the *voiturette* event at Masaryk, his first major victory. The following year saw him winning the Albi Grand Prix, the Pescara *voiturette* race and the Circuit of Lucca. In a works 3-litre Grand Prix Maserati

8CTF he was second at Naples and made fastest lap in the Coppa Acerbo at Pescara. The 1939 season was bitter: his brother Emilio was killed in an Alfa Romeo 158 at Monza. Nevertheless, Luigi decided to carry on his racing activities and his tally for the year was highlighted with victory in the South African Grand Prix, the Circuit of Abazzia and the Targa Florio (at a record-breaking average speed of almost 85 mph), before war intervened and brought an enforced halt to racing in Europe for six years.

Villoresi was quick to resume motor racing in 1946, now white-haired after a long period as a prisoner of war. He was one of the most accomplished drivers of the immediate postwar era, taking his works Maserati 4CL to victory in the Nice Grand Prix and Circuit of Voghera and placing second at Modena. He participated in the Indianapolis 500-mile race in a 3-litre Maserati 8CL, being the only European entry to qualify, and finished seventh. Together with Jean-Pierre Wimille of France, Villoresi was considered the best European racing driver. He was Italian champion in 1947 and 1948.

In 1947 Villoresi's Maserati 4CL took him to victory at Lausanne, Nice, Strasbourg and Nîmes and the Buenos Aires and Mar del Plata Grands Prix in Argentina. His South American success was repeated the following year when he won the two Buenos Aires Grands Prix; he also won at Silverstone (the first post-war British Grand Prix), at Comminges, Albi and Penya Rhin and was second in the Italian Grand Prix and at San Remo with his 1½-litre Maserati 4CLT/48. Driving an 1100cc OSCA he won the Naples Grand Prix. Now 39, in 1949 Villoresi and his 'pupil' Alberto Ascari, the 30-year-old son of famous pre-war exponent Antonio Ascari, joined the new Ferrari team. Villoresi had tremendous success with both Formula One and Formula Two models from the stable of the Prancing Horse, winning at Rome, Luxembourg, Brussels, Garda and Zandvoort. He was second in the Belgian and Swiss Grands Prix and third in the Daily Express Trophy at Silverstone. Earlier in the year he had finished second twice in Argentina and won the Interlagos Grand Prix in Brazil.

In 1950 Villoresi won the Buenos Aires, Rosario, Marseilles and Monza Autodrome Grands Prix plus the Circuit of Erlen; he was also second at Rome, San Remo, Mons, Zandvoort, Pau and Luxembourg. But then he had a serious accident at Geneva, crashing badly and being deposited in the middle of the track where fellow-Italian and arch-rival Giuseppe Farina had to crash to avoid him. There was talk that Villoresi would never race again, but his reply to the gossip was victory in the 1951 Mille Miglia driving a new 4.1-litre Ferrari 340 America. He also won the Marseilles, Syracuse and Pau Grands Prix, the Circuit of Genoa, Circuit of Senigalia and Coppa Inter-Europa at Monza.

A touring car accident caused him to miss several races in 1952, but he bounced back to win Formula One races at Turin and Boreham and was second in a *formule libre* event at Silverstone. In a Formula Two Ferrari 500 he won at Sables d'Olonne, was second at La Baule and third in the Dutch and Italian Grands Prix.

Now well over 40, Villoresi gave no signs of giving up race driving. He showed the old skill was still there by winning the 1953 Tour of Sicily and Monza sports car races, was second at Bordeaux, Casablanca and Buenos Aires and third in the Italian Grand Prix. In 1954 he was invited to join the new Lancia team alongside Alberto Ascari, but the new D50 Grand Prix car project was delayed until the very end of the year so from time to time Villoresi was 'borrowed' by Maserati. In the Italian Grand Prix at Monza he drove one of his best-ever races, urging his Maserati 250F into the lead only for it to blow up shortly after half-distance. His season was punctuated by another serious accident during practice for the Mille Miglia; Villoresi overturned his Lancia while trying to avoid a private car on the route of the famous 1000-mile race. His family begged him to retire. He refused.

In 1955 Villoresi remained with the Lancia Formula One team, finishing third at Turin and Syracuse before the team pulled out of racing early in the year following Ascari's fatal accident. But still Villoresi carried on, driving a Formula One Maserati for Scuderia Centro-Sud plus an OSCA sports car. It was with one of the latter machines that he crashed badly in the October 1956 Rome Grand Prix, suffering multiple fractures of his right leg. Early in 1957 he reluctantly announced his retirement from racing after a 25-year career which included over 50 major victories. He was not *quite* finished, however. In 1958, at the age of 48, he drove a Lancia in the Acropolis Rally – and won. Thereafter he moved into a more permanent retirement, though punctuated by occasional appearances.   MK

WOLFGANG VON TRIPS
(1928-1961)
Germany

Wolfgang Graf Berghe von Trips was an aristocrat, a tall blond German Count who was a lover of fast cars and of life itself. Familiarly known as 'Taffy', von Trips survived a succession of high-speed accidents until he crashed to his death at Monza in 1961.

After having dabbled in racing for a number of years, von Trips entered an old Porsche in some rallies. His success persuaded him to contact Porsche's racing director, Huschke von Hanstein, to ask for free parts to modify his machine. Von Hanstein offered von Trips a drive in the 1954 Mille Miglia as co-driver to Hampel. Against all odds, the pair were second in the 1500 cc GT class and the first 1300cc car to finish. He later acquired a 1500 cc engine for his Porsche Super and entered his first race at Nürburgring with the bill for the engine still unpaid. He won then settled the account. Soon he had won the German GT championship.

In 1955 both Porsche and Mercedes-Benz smiled on von Trips. He was reserve driver for Porsche at Le Mans and after some impressive performances in his 1300 cc Porsche he was offered a works Mercedes-Benz 300SL for the GT race at the Swedish Grand Prix meeting. He led for 16 of the 20 laps before the brakes failed, thereby earning a place in the sports-racing car team of 300SLRs in the Tourist Trophy at Dundrod. Co-driving with Kling and André Simon he was third.

With Mercedes' withdrawal from motor racing at the end of 1955 it was back to Porsche for 1956. In a works Porsche 550RS he won the 1500 cc class in the Sebring 12-hours, Nürburgring 1000-km and Le Mans 24-hours. This led to an invitation to race for Ferrari. He was second with Peter Collins in the Swedish Grand Prix sports-car race and was invited to pilot a Formula One Lancia-Ferrari D50 in the Italian Grand Prix at Monza. In practice the steering broke at high speed, von Trips being thrown clear of the rolling wreckage and emerging almost unhurt.

In 1957 von Trips remained with Ferrari in both Formula One and sports cars. He was sixth in the Argentine Grand Prix, and second in the Mille Miglia only 3 mins 1sec behind Taruffi. At Monaco he was very disappointed when his engine blew up with only 11 laps to go. After being absent due to a spinal injury, at the Nürburgring 1000-km, he was back in

late August and went on to finish third in the Italian Grand Prix and third in the sports-car Venezuelan Grand Prix. Driving for Porsche, he participated in three end-of-season European Hill-climb Championships events, winning the Swiss Mountain Grand Prix and at Mont Parnes, and taking a second at Aosta-Gran San Bernardo.

The format was similar in 1958. Best placing in Grand Prix racing was third in the French Grand Prix, while in sports cars he was second in the Buenos Aires 1000-km and third in the Targa Florio and Nürburgring 1000-km. He won the European Hill-climb Championship, his works Porsche winning at Mount Parnassus, Monte Bendone and Gaisberg. In the Reims 12-hours for GT cars he shared a Ferrari Berlinetta with fellow-German Wolfgang Seidel into third place. However, in September another accident temporarily put him out of racing: his Ferrari Dino 246 collided with Harry Schell's BRM P25 on the opening lap, crashed and von Trips broke a leg.

Enzo Ferrari dropped von Trips from his team the next year, leaving the German free to race for Porsche in sports-car and Formula Two racing. Best result was a second in the Tourist Trophy at Goodwood, although it was galling when he broke down on the last lap of the Targa Florio when leading. 'Taffy' von Trips blotted his copybook at Monaco, where he gave the new Formula Two Porsche its debut and spun on the second lap, causing a pile-up involving the other two Formula Two cars in the race! In December he was back with Ferrari for the United States Grand Prix. After colliding with team-mate Tony Brooks on the first lap he recovered to finish seventh. Continuing to drive for Ferrari in 1960, von Trips found the front-engined Formula One machines inferior to the latest Coopers and Lotuses and had to be satisfied with minor placings, best being a fourth in Portugal. In Formula Two, he won the Solitude Grand Prix and, making a 'guest appearance' for Porsche was second in the F2 German Grand Prix at Nürburgring. He was also second for Ferrari in the Buenos Aires 1000-km and Targa Florio sports cars races, but ran out of fuel at Le Mans.

For 1961 Ferrari were ahead of their British rivals, providing Phil Hill, Wolfgang von Trips and Richie Ginther with cars capable of winning the World Championship. Von Trips won the Dutch Grand Prix at Zandvoort, becoming the first German to win a Grande Epreuve since

1939, and later won the British Grand Prix after a brilliant performance on the sodden Aintree track. Into the Italian Grand Prix at Monza, von Trips had a one-point lead in the championship. Entering the Parabolica on lap 2 Jim Clark moved to overtake von Trips's Ferrari Dino 156 under braking. The two cars touched at 140 mph and spun. Clark's car halted safely, almost undamaged. Von Trips's hurtled up the banking into the spectator area, killing fourteen people before plunging back on to the track, overturning and killing its occupant.   MK

LOUIS WAGNER (1882-1960)
France

Louis Wagner, who was born in Paris in 1882, was one of the most famous drivers of the 'heroic age' of motor racing. Wagner joined the racing department of Darracq at Suresnes in 1901, and became a team driver in 1903.

Alexandre Darracq believed in entering his racing cars in as many speed events as possible, and throughout the 1903 season, Wagner was fully occupied with races, hill-climbs and sprints. He won the Circuit of Bastogne, and was lying third in the *voiturette* class of the Paris-Madrid race when it was halted at Bordeaux.

Wagner crossed the Atlantic in 1906 to compete in the Vanderbilt Cup: he won, after a hard-fought race, and it was reported that he could have gone even faster had it not been for the crowds swarming onto the track. He did indulge his taste for speed during his visit, however, with a quick burst down Broadway, which so scandalised the local constabulary that they clapped him into New York's Tombs prison for 48 hours!

Mechanical failure spoiled the Darracq chances in the 1907 Targa Florio, when Wagner and Hanriot were forced to retire with broken half-shafts: Alexandre Darracq blandly announced that he was going to attribute the breakages to the carelessness of the drivers, who must surely have run off the road. Angered by this slander, Wagner stormed off to offer his services to Fiat, who agreed to repay the bond linking him to the Darracq company, and to take him on at double the appearance money, as well as guaranteeing him starts in more major races. Alexandre Darracq, who does not appear to have been a particularly likeable character, protested, and threatened to take the case before the French

government; he wasn't going to have one of his leading drivers walking out to join a foreign rival company! However, his threats proved impotent, and by the next major race, the Kaiserpreis, Wagner was a member of the Fiat team, along with Nazzaro and Lancia.

But Nazzaro won the Kaiserpreis; and he won the 1907 French Grand Prix, too, though Wagner led for the first two laps until a broken camshaft caused his retirement.

The 1908 Grand Prix saw *all* the Fiats eliminated by the end of the fourth lap, but to compensate for this Wagner carried off the American Grand Prize at Savannah.

In 1909, with Grand Prix racing temporarily in abeyance, Wagner switched his attention to flying, and joined the aircraft manufacturing company formed by his erstwhile team-mate Hanriot; he was a participant at many of the early flying meetings, and was actually airborne at the 1910 Bournemouth event when C.S.Rolls crashed with fatal results in his Wright Flyer.

The 1912 French Grand Prix saw the swansong of the monster racing cars, with Wagner, de Palma and Bruce Brown driving Fiats with engines displacing over 14 litres: at the end of the first day's racing, Wagner was lying third, despite recurrent tyre trouble: he finished in second place, behind George Boillot's Peugeot. Wagner elected to drive for Mercédès in the 1914 French Grand Prix – Fiat, it is said, realising that their new GP cars were insufficiently developed to stand a chance, sportingly offered to let Wagner transfer his allegiance to the German marque. In the race he finished second behind the sister car of Christian Lautenschlager.

Back with Fiat after the war, Wagner competed in the 1921 Brescia Grand Prix, but was slowed to third by tyre trouble.

He joined Ballot that season, finishing seventh in the 1921 French Grand Prix on a straight-eight of that marque; the following year he took part in the Grand Prix in a Rolland-Pilain, but failed to last the race out. In 1924 he was driving for Alfa Romeo; in 1925 he was with Delage, Peugeot and Ariès as a freelance.

The 1926 season saw a sixth place in the Targa Florio and a second place in the Coppa Florio, on a sleeve-valve Peugeot, while 1927 found Wagner at the wheel of a Talbot, in which he made a record lap in the French Grand Prix, despite mechanical troubles. Then, after almost a quarter of a century in motor racing, Wagner retired.

After World War II, tuberculosis of the bone compelled the amputation of a leg, and Wagner was given the post of instructor and supervisor at the Montlhéry circuit: but the disease worsened, and by the late 1950s he was housebound. Wagner died in 1960, and was buried at Montlhéry.   DBW

RODGER WARD (b.1921)
USA

Rodger Ward was born in Beloit, Kansas, on 10 January 1921, but the family soon moved to Los Angeles. Ward briefly worked for the aircraft industry and joined the Air Force during World War II where he qualified as a pilot on multi-engined aircraft and became an instructor on instrument flying.

In 1946 Ward had his first attempt at motor racing. For some time he had been allowed to act as mechanic during leave from the Air Force, looking after a Willys-engined midget. He yearned to race one and, at last, one day the driver did not arrive for a meeting. Ward jumped into the vacant cockpit. But although the seeds of a racing career were sown that night at Wichita Falls the actual result was dismal: Ward spun and was hit by another competitor.

Later in the year Ward left the USAAF and began to race in midget car events, participating in perhaps a dozen events around the Texas/Kansas border area without luck. When he finally ran out of money Rodger returned to Los Angeles to work for his father and soon became involved with midget racing in California. For five years he remained in this hectic class of racing – there was a race a night for those who could stand the pace – and in 1948 he won the San Diego Grand Prix in his Ford-engined car. The following season he moved up to the faster, Offenhauser-engined midgets and in 1950 he startled the midget racing *aficionados:* his humble Ford-powered midget beat all the Offys to win the feature event at Gilmore Stadium. The feat was considered all the more remarkable as in 1949 Ward had crashed badly at San Diego, an accident which left him with only 20 per cent movement in his right shoulder.

In 1951 Ward won the AAA's stock car championship. He also attempted the Indianapolis 500, passing his 'rookie' test but retiring in the race when an oil pipe broke. In 1952 he failed again at Indianapolis, as he did the following year. In 1954 he ran out of petrol in the Indianapolis 500, while in 1955 he became involved in a multi-car pile-up which claimed the life of a competitor. Ward's car flipped, but Rodger escaped with a cut nose. Some people asserted that he was responsible for the accident and Rodger wondered which way to turn. The previous year at a midget race his car had been knocked off the course, freakishly killing Clay Smith, the mechanical wizard behind many of Ward's successes. And now this driver, Vokovick, had been killed.

The strain was enormous and within weeks Ward was fired from sponsor Lyle Greenman's team. He turned to stunt driving, becoming one of Irish Hogan's 'Original Lucky Hell Drivers'. But driving cars up ramps was only a stop-gap measure, a means of paying off debts accumulated during better days. Ward stopped smoking and drinking altogether and was supported by his wife Jo, a Quaker with strong religious beliefs.

By the end of the year Ward was 'on trial' again, being hired for two end-of-season races and the 1956 Indianapolis 500. He finished for the first time, placing eighth. Although his car failed in the 1957 Indianapolis race, Ward had a good year, winning at Milwaukee, Springfield and Sacramento. In 1958 he again failed in the 500, but won at Milwaukee and Trenton.

In 1959, following the death of his sponsor, Ward teamed up with A.J. Watson, USAC racing's famed car builder/mechanic, and Bob Wilke, the wealthy greeting-card company owner. Driving a Watson-built Leader Card Special, Ward won the Indianapolis 500. With further victories at Milwaukee, DuQuoin and Indiana Fairgrounds he was USAC national champion. Next year late-race tyre problems caused Ward to ease up and be satisfied with second place at Indianapolis.

For 1961, driving for another sponsor, Ward was third at Indianapolis. The following year he returned to Wilke's team and gave the Leader Card team its second Indianapolis victory and, thanks to successes at Milwaukee, Trenton and Syracuse, its second USAC national championship. At that time he was also all-time USAC points leader.

Then the Indianapolis 'revolution' took place. Rear-engined cars replaced the famous, cumbersome 'roadsters'. In 1963 an old-style car was good enough for third place in the Indianapolis 500, while he also won 100-mile races at Milwaukee, Springfield, Indiana Fairgrounds, Sacramento and Phoenix. In 1964, however, second place at Indianapolis in a rear-engined machine was his only moment of glory. Next year he failed to qualify for the race after suspension problems and in 1966 he retired shortly after Indianapolis which had begun with a multi-car pile-up. He survived the drama (which did not result in serious injury to anyone) but following a subsequent race at Trenton he decided to hang up his helmet for good.

In 1969 there were rumours of Ward's return to motor racing. Now 48, he wanted a season in Trans-Am – modified 5-litre saloon cars – plus another try at USAC stock car racing... and perhaps another crack at Indianapolis? His ambitions were not realised and Ward concentrated on his 'retirement' jobs, as a retail tyre distributor in Indianapolis and a motor racing television commentator.   MK

JOHN WATSON (b.1946)
Great Britain

John Watson may be Irish, but the luck traditionally associated with his countrymen has often seemed conspicuously absent from the Ulsterman's frustrating Grand Prix career.

Watson was born in Belfast on 4 May 1946. His father was a motor trader, himself a racing driver and winner of Ireland's first saloon car race. John often watched his father race and by the time he left school, to join the family garage business, the racing bug had bitten. John's father retired from racing but remained ready to encourage his son; with his father's financial support, John's road-going Mini made way for an Austin Healey Sprite, fitted with a BMC Formula Junior engine and used extensively during 1963. After this successful debut season John progressed with a Ford powered Crossle sports racing car.

In 1967 Ireland's racing showcase was a domestic formula using cars similar to the then current Formula 2 but with engine regulations aimed at controlling cost. Watson became the youngest of the regular runners, with a twin-cam engined Brabham BT16, and soon began to dominate the formula, also making occasional forays to England where he might attract the attention that no amount of success in Ireland would bring.

For 1969, Watson attracted a patron in Gerry Kinnane, one time driver turned sponsor. Kinnane bought two ex-works Lotus 48s and entered both for the European Formula 2

Championship round at Thruxton on Easter Monday. At this unfamiliar circuit, against top class opposition he qualified comfortably for the final and climbed from eighteenth to fifth place before destroying the car in an accident.

Thereafter, John was forced to revert to a family financed Lola T100, with little success, until his father financed a Brabham BT30 for the 1970 season.

On a shoestring, he contested the European Formula 2 series; however, his season ended dramatically at Rouen when a puncture precipitated a huge accident from which he emerged with a broken arm and leg.

In 1972 John drove Alan McCall's Tui in Formula 2, until the money ran out. He then drove the ex-Eiffeland Formula 1 March for Tony Brown in an Irish Libre race. After he drove a Chevron to an impressive fifth place in the Rothmans 50,000 at Brands Hatch, Bernie Ecclestone signed John to a three-year contract with Brabham for Formula 2 and occasional Formula 1.

He began 1973 sharing the Gulf Mirage sports car with Mike Hailwood at Daytona but then at the Race of Champions at Brands Hatch, in the prototype Brabham BT42 he had a very large accident after the throttle stuck open. He was released from the wreckage with a broken right leg. He returned with Gulf at Le Mans and drove an elderly BT37 for Hexagon at the British Grand Prix, where he retired. He drove a works BT42 at Watkins Glen but retired with engine failure.

Hexagon financed his 1974 season, with a Brabham BT42 and later, helped by John's Brabham connections, with a new BT44. He was sixth at Monaco in the BT42 and a stirring fourth, despite a pit stop, with the BT44 in Austria. After crashing the Hexagon car (through mechanical failure) in practice at Monza he drove the spare works car and finished seventh. With six points Watson finished fourteenth in the championship.

He surprised many by signing for the struggling Surtees team in 1975. Second place in the Race of Champions and fourth in the International Trophy flattered only to deceive; the Grand Prix season was dogged by mechanical misfortune and his best result was eighth in Spain – earned through sheer hard driving. Surtees did not contest the last two races and, after Mark Donohue was killed in Austria, Penske put Watson into their car at Watkins Glen. Ninth place earned him a contract for 1976.

With the March-based Penske PC3 and then the team's own PC4 Watson was almost always competitive, placing fourth in South Africa and third in both France and Great Britain before taking his, and Penske's first Grand Prix win in a hard fought Austrian Grand Prix. As a result of that win and a wager with Roger Penske Watson lost his famous beard and has been clean shaven ever since! After Austria the Penske was less competitive and at the end of the season the team retired from Grand Prix racing.

Watson was quickly re-signed by Brabham to partner Carlos Pace in the Alfa Romeo powered BT45, a car which had proved unreliable and, often, uncompetitive through 1976 but following development by Pace promised great things for 1977. When Carlos was killed in a flying accident in March John became team leader. He had already led the Argentine Grand Prix until drive shaft failure intervened, the first stroke in an appalling run of bad luck. He scored a point for sixth place in South Africa but, although he always qualified near the front and ran in the first six places he did not finish another race until he claimed fifth place in Sweden, mechanical failures, one accident and disqualification for receiving outside assistance at Long Beach keeping him out of the points. In France he led from lap four onwards, holding off Mario Andretti until the very last lap when fuel starvation slowed him just enough to let Andretti through. It was cruel bad luck. Thereafter the pattern was much the same and he scored no further points, ending the season thirteenth in the championship.

He stayed with Brabham for 1978, alongside World Champion Niki Lauda and, although he proved quite capable of giving Lauda a run for his money his luck remained the same. Nevertheless he gained sixth place in the championship, scoring second place in Italy, thirds in South Africa and Germany, fourth places in Monaco, France and Holland and fifth in Spain.

For 1979 John Watson was snapped up by McLaren after their number one choice of driver, Ronnie Peterson, was killed at Monza. In pre-race testing in South America, John was easily the most impressive performer with the honeycomb-construction M28. The car's promise was not realised in racing, however, as it proved far too heavy and unreliable. Even a complete revamping in mid-season which involved shortening and narrowing the car had little or no effect, and John eagerly awaited the arrival of the new M29 to stem his tide of bad luck and improve on what was for him a disastrous early 1979 season. He finished fourth when the M29 made its debut at the British Grand Prix but although he finished fifth in Germany and sixth in both Canada and America it had to be admitted that it had been a disastrous season, further clouded by blame and a £3000 fine for a multiple first lap accident in Argentina.

1980 served only to plunge Watson's reputation further into the depths, although not entirely with justification. John was joined at McLaren by young Frenchman Alain Prost who made a sensational impression in his early performances, rather overshadowing Watson. Nevertheless he soldiered on, eventually overcoming his detractors and showing with some stirring performances – not always rewarded by hard results – that he still had the ability to mix it with the front runners. He scored fourth in Long Beach and Canada (where he was briefly up to second place) and towards the end of the year he made a real revival which perhaps salvaged his reputation as well as his contract for the following season.   BL

JEAN-PIERRE WIMILLE
(1908 1949)

France

Jean-Pierre Wimille, son of a journalist, was born in Paris on 26 February 1908. He began his career as a racing driver at 22 by entering a Bugatti in the 1930 French Grand Prix at Pau. Early in 1931 he competed with a Lorraine in the Monte Carlo Rally and finished second. Soon he became a regular at the racing tracks. Together with Jean Gaupillat he drove a new 2.3-litre Bugatti T51 in the Italian Grand Prix at Monza, finishing fourth in the gruelling, 10-hour race. However, Wimille was destined not to finish the French Grand Prix at Montlhéry owing to a broken radius rod.

The 1932 season put Wimille on the road to success. He won the Oran Grand Prix in North Africa and led at Casablanca until the Bugatti retired at half-distance. He also campaigned one of the none-too-successful 4.9-litre Bugatti T54s, notably in hill-climbs, and at the end of the year he acquired a 2.3-litre Alfa Romeo Monza and won the Lorraine Grand Prix at Nancy. At Comminges, however, he crashed while in the lead, adding fire to his critics' forebodings about him being wild. Place results were achieved in 1933, a year in which his driving style noticeably improved: he was second at Comminges and in the Marne Grand Prix, third at Brno in Czechoslovakia and fifth at San Sebastian.

In 1934, first year of the new 750 kg Grand Prix formula, Wimille was invited to join the official Bugatti works team. Sadly, however, the new 3.3-litre Bugatti T59 was outclassed and not always reliable. He won the Algiers Grand Prix, a race in which neither of the German works team competed, and at the end-of-season Spanish Grand Prix at Lasarte held a fine second place, splitting the Mercedes team until carburettor problems intervened and dropped him to an eventual sixth. Next year the car was faster and more reliable, giving Wimille a second to Achille Varzi's Auto Union at Tunis, a second to Louis Chiron's Alfa Romeo at Nancy and fourth behind the superior Mercedes-Benzes of Caracciola, Fagioli and von Brauchitsch in the Spanish Grand Prix.

Bugatti withdrew from full-scale Grand Prix racing in 1936, when the French Grand Prix was for sports cars and was won by Wimille in Bugatti's T57S, 'The Tank'. Wimille also won the Comminges and Marne Grands Prix for sports cars and, with the Grand Prix Type 59, won the Deauville Grand Prix but retired in the German and Swiss Grands Prix and was a poor sixth at Monaco. He also raced in South Africa and the United States, taking second place in the Vanderbilt Cup at Roosevelt Raceway in a 4.7-litre Bugatti.

In 1937 Wimille shared the winning Bugatti T57S with Robert Benoist in the Le Mans 24-hours and also took 'The Tank' to victory in the Marne, Pau and Bône Grands Prix, all sports car races. Next year Bugatti attempted a return to full-scale Grand Prix racing with the new 3-litre formula in force. Engine trouble kept Wimille on the sidelines in the Cork Grand Prix and the new car only lasted a lap in the French Grand Prix before an oil pipe failed. Exasperated, Wimille joined the Enzo Ferrari-run Alfa Romeo team for the Coppa Ciano and Swiss Grand Prix, before rejoining Bugatti in 1939. Highlight of the year was victory in the Le Mans 24-hours, sharing a Bugatti T57C with Pierre Veyron, he also managed to win the Coupe de Paris and Luxembourg Grand Prix and was second in the Prescott hill-climb in a 4.7 litre Bugatti.

During World War II Wimille served with the French Air Force and later joined the Resistance, finishing the war as a liaison officer with the Allied troops. In September 1945 the first post-war motor race was run in the Bois de Boulogne in Paris, the Grand Prix de la Libération, and Wimille unearthed the 4.7-litre Bugatti and won.

In 1946 Wimille campaigned a pre-war 3-litre Alfa Romeo 8C-308 in the *formule libre* events that comprised international motor racing in those days. He won the Burgundy and Perpignan Grands Prix plus the Coupe de Paris and was invited to join the works Alfa Romeo Grand Prix team, finishing second at Turin and third at Geneva in the successful 1½-litre Tipo 158 models. Next year Wimille won the Belgian and Swiss Grands Prix, won the Coupe de Paris and the Benoist Cup in his old Alfa Romeo and in a Simca-Gordini was also second at Nice and Lausanne.

Wimille became involved with the development of a road car in 1947 with rather sleek lines but with a Cotal electric gearbox fitted to the front of the engine necessitating stepdown gears to take the drive line to the rear axle.

The 1948 season was Wimille's last. He was on the crest of a wave. Whereas in previous years he often had to let a team-mate take victory – such was Alfa Romeo's superiority they could decide beforehand who should win – this time he was definite team leader. He won the French, Italian. Monza and Valentino (Turin) Grands Prix for the Italian marque as well as winning the early-season Rosario Grand Prix in Argentina in a Simca-Gordini.

Wimille was acknowledged as the best driver in Europe when he went to Argentina in January 1949 for a series of races. Now 40, he showed no inclination towards retirement, nor had his prowess diminished. Yet practising for the Buenos Aires Grand Prix at Palermo his tiny Simca-Gordini left the road and crashed into a tree. Wimille died of severe injuries. Why it happened has remained a complete mystery to this day.   MK

CALE YARBOROUGH (b.1939)
USA

William Caleb 'Cale' Yarborough (not to be confused with Lee Roy Yarbrough, another NASCAR exponent, who has one less 'o' in his name) was born on 27 March 1939, in Timmonsville, North Carolina. At school he became a football fanatic, representing Timmonsville High School as an all-state fullback. Later he played semi-professional football with the Sumter Generals, nearly making the big time.

Yarborough married Betty Jo, whom he had met at his uncle's drug store, and tried to support her, farming turkeys, and racing cars. At neither was he successful, although he just scraped along as a stock car exponent. As an eighteen-year-old he added three years to his age to be eligible for NASCAR racing. In 1957, 1959, 1960 and 1961 he participated in one NASCAR Grand National championship race each season, winning a mere $535.

In 1962 he ran in eight Grand National races, once finishing in the first ten. Next season the total was eighteen and three times he was placed in the top five, his earnings amounting to $5550. Things were looking up. The first big break came in 1964 when Yarborough was chosen by Herman Beam (nicknamed 'The Turtle') to drive a works-prepared Ford. In his first race he crashed and later a replacement machine suffered wheel bearing failure. Cale was not out of a job for long. He was taken on by top racing car preparers Holman & Moody as a $1.25-an-hour carpenter. He kept his foot in the door and in 1965 he was team driver and earned $25,140, winning one race and finishing in the first ten no fewer than 34 times out of 46.

For 1966, Yarborough joined the legendary Wood Brothers' team, an organisation which guaranteed the fastest pit work anywhere in the world – in less than twenty seconds they could change two tyres and add fifteen gallons of fuel. The season brought no victories, although from fourteen starts Yarborough was placed in the top five three times. He also raced in the Indianapolis 500. In 1966, driving a Vollstedt-Ford he was involved in the first-lap pile-up, but the following year Cale drove impressively, reaching fourth place before hitting the wall.

In 1967, driving only in the SuperSpeedway rounds of the NASCAR Grand National series, Yarborough won twice from sixteen starts, including his first 500-miler, the Atlanta 500. Next year he set the NASCAR tracks alight: at the wheel of a Mercury Cyclone he took part in 21 races and won a record four SuperSpeedway victories, amassing $136,786 for his efforts. He won both the Daytona classics (the 500 and the Firecracker 400), the Atlanta 500 and the Southern 500.

Next season was disappointing by comparison: two victories (the Atlanta 500 and the Motor State 400) and 'only' $74,240 in NASCAR earnings. The year ended with a smashed shoulder at Texas International Speedway in December when his Wood Brothers' Mercury Cyclone was wrecked. Doctors said he would never race again, but in February 1970 he took a new Mercury around Daytona International Speedway at a record 194.015 mph to claim pole position for the Daytona 500 classic.

When Ford pulled out of racing at the end of the season Yarborough decided to try his hand at USAC racing. He entered the Indianapolis 500, finishing sixteenth in a Laycock-Ford in 1971 and tenth in an Atlanta-Foyt in 1972. It was a disappointing time in the wilderness for the short, tubby Yarborough and in 1973 he made a return to the NASCAR Grand National circuit. He won the SouthEastern 500, the Music City 420, the Southern 500 and the National 500 to wind up second in the championship. Next season he fought a season-long battle with 'King' Richard Petty, to come second once more.

Cale did not have to wait too long for greater success, however; he won the Winston Cup Grand National championship in 1976 and 1977. Both years he won around one-third of the races; in 1977 Yarborough's Junior Johnson Chevrolet won nine rounds to finish the season with 5000 points ahead of Richard Petty.

In 1978 it was the mixture much as before, except for the fact that Yarborough's mount was now an Oldsmobile. Even before the season had finished he had ensured himself of his third consecutive championship. Johnson added a Chevvy to the Busch-sponsored Oldsmobiles for 1979 but, dogged by unreliability, Yarborough could manage no better than four wins and fourth place in the championship, which was won yet again by Richard Petty.

With NASCAR rules largely unchanged for 1980, Yarborough stayed with Johnson, joining a season-long battle at the top with Dale Earnhardt who was having a spectacularly successful second season. In October, as he and Earnhardt continued to run neck and neck for the title, Cale announced that he was to end his longstanding partnership with Junior Johnson, to contest a 'short' season with M.C. Anderson's Melling Tools Chevrolet team – running only at the SuperSpeedways.

Meanwhile Cale's sixth win of the year, at Altanta in November, forced the title race into the last round, at Ontario. Although

Yarborough took pole position and finished second, Earnhardt's fifth place was enough to wrest the championship from him.   MK

LEE ROY YARBROUGH (b.1938)
USA

Lee Roy Yarbrough decided when he was a small boy in Jacksonville, Florida, that one day he would race cars. At fourteen in 1952 he lied about his age to obtain a licence and left school to race self-built machines on dirt tracks. It was obvious from his successes there that he would graduate to become one of the United States' top motor sportsmen. Such was his fame and total domination that promoters offered $500 to anyone who could beat him and he also ran in challenge events at night.

In 1960 he took part in his first NASCAR Grand National race, finishing a lowly 33rd in the Atlanta 500. Two seasons later he raced exclusively in NASCAR-sanctioned races, running in the Sportsman class as well as the premier Grand National category:in one of his first major victories at Daytona International Speedway he won the Permatex 250.

Successes began in Grand National contests in 1964 when he gained two victories and won $15,155; in thirteen other races he placed in the top ten. But he was lucky to be alive. Earlier in the season he had crashed in the Permatex 250 and was trapped in the fiery wreck of his machine. Quick action by fellow drivers Lorenzen, Frank and Spencer saved his life.

Top entrant Ray Fox invited Yarbrough to drive for him in 1965. He was always in contention, but either his machinery failed or he became involved in rivals' accidents. He did, however, lap Daytona at 181.818 mph in a specially prepared Dodge on a dull day when a 20 mph crosswind affected the car's stability.

Next year Yarbrough attacked the Indianapolis 500. He had passed his 'rookie' test in 1965, and for 1966 was armed with a Gerhardt-Offenhauser. His ambition was shattered when Greg Weld destroyed it during a test run. As some small consolation he won his first SuperSpeedway NASCAR Grand National race, the National 500 at Charlotte.

In 1968 Yarbrough had Ford factory support for a ride in Junior Johnson-prepared Fords and Mercuries. After the enormous promise shown in previous years, victories should have come by the dozen. But it didn't work out quite like that. Somehow misfortune overtook him time and again. In the classic of SuperSpeedway races, the Daytona 500, he led until the closing seconds when Cale Yarborough beat him. In the Atlanta 500 he was black-flagged for allegedly overtaking under a yellow caution flag and in the Rebel 500 he was a poor fifth after tyre problems. The only real bright spot of the season was victory in the Dixie 500 at Atlanta.

And then came 1969 and Yarbrough's record-breaking season. He scored a superb victory in the Daytona 500, overtaking Charlie Glotzbach within seconds of the chequered flag. He won the Rebel 400 and the World 600 and, despite making one more pit stop than his rivals, put the Firecracker 400 under his belt as well. He had equalled NASCAR's all-time record of four SuperSpeedway victories in a season, and there was more to come. Despite wrecking his car during midweek testing, it was back in one piece to win the Dixie 500 and then win a car-length victory over David Pearson in the Southern 500. His car was wrecked again during trials prior to the American 500, but his spare machine was taken hurriedly from an exhibition in time for the second day of qualifying and Yarbrough won again. Seven SuperSpeedway victories plus fourteen other places in the top ten from the thirty starts gave Lee Roy a record prize total of $188,605 for the year. He had also competed in the Indianapolis 500 in an Eagle-Ford, qualified on the third row of the grid and despite an accident still won $12,508.

Ford ended his winning streak by withdrawing from racing at the end of the year, leaving Yarbrough without a sponsor. He found some backing from Jim Robbins, but the budget did not permit a full season of SuperSpeedway racing to be contemplated for 1970. He won the National 400 at Charlotte and in the World 600 at the same track took over Donnie Allison's car after his own broke down.

Yarbrough was now a rich man, living in luxury with his wife Gloria in White Rock, South Carolina, but his successes were becoming fewer. He tried USAC racing once more, qualifying for the fifth row of the grid for the 1970 Indianapolis 500 but retiring in the actual race. Driving a works Brabham BT32-Offy, he also led the inaugural California 500 at the Ontario Motor Speedway until the engine gave out eight laps from the end. The 1971 season was spoilt by illness and in 1972 it was back to NASCAR. He scored nine finishes in the top ten, although no victories were chalked up to his credit; then he retired.   MK